The
LOST
CIVILIZATION
of
LEMURIA

The
LOST
CIVILIZATION
of
LEMURIA

*The Rise and Fall of the
World's Oldest Culture*

FRANK JOSEPH

Bear & Company
Rochester, Vermont

Bear & Company
One Park Street
Rochester, Vermont 05767
www.BearandCompanyBooks.com

Bear & Company is a division of Inner Traditions International

LIBRARY OF CONGRESS CATALOGING-IN-PUBLICATION DATA

Joseph, Frank.
   The lost civilization of Lemuria : the rise and fall of the world's oldest culture / Frank Joseph.
      p. cm.
   Includes bibliographical references.
   ISBN 978-1-59143-060-5 (paper)
   1. Lemuria. I. Title.
   GN751.J693 2006
   001.94--dc22

                                                        2006007631

Printed and bound in the United States

10

Text design and layout by Jonathan Desautels
This book was typeset in Sabon with Calisto used as a display typeface

Extracts on pages 276 and 279 reprinted with permission from *Watermark: The Disaster That Changed the World and Humanity 12,000 Years Ago* by Joseph Christy-Vitale, Paraview Pocket Books.

To send correspondence to the author of this book, mail a first-class letter to the author c/o Inner Traditions • Bear & Company, One Park Street, Rochester, VT 05767, and we will forward the communication.

To Professor Nobuhiro Yoshida, President,
the Japan Petrograph Society

Contents

Scene from the Ramayana, *the Hindu epic depicting the flight of survivors from their Pacific motherland. Mural is located at the Wat Phra Keo temple complex, Bangkok, Thailand.*

Terra Incognita

We are tempted to inquire how far the fact that some of those beliefs and legends have so many features in common is due to chance, and whether the similarity between them may not point to the existence of an ancient, totally unknown and unsuspected civilization of which all other traces have disappeared.

PROFESSOR FREDERICK SODDY,
NOBEL PRIZE WINNER, 1910

The menacing silhouette of a stranger rushed out of the dark. As I raised my fists to defend myself, two accomplices seized me from behind, one on either side. Someone grabbed me forcibly around my neck, and in moments I sank, choking, to the paved street.

It took a long time for consciousness to flow slowly back into my oxygen-starved brain. I was alone in the night. The attack seemed distant, vague, unreal, and dreamlike as I gazed up serenely at the night sky sparkling with that celestial necklace we call the Milky Way. For some moments, I lay there peacefully on my back, as though among the serene prairies of my Illinois boyhood. In fact, I was sprawled in the middle of a cobblestone side street in Cuzco, the ancient capital of Peru. Hardly more than an alleyway, it connected the city's postconquest cathedral with the Coricancha, the Inca's preeminent temple, known as the Enclosure of Gold. I had been assaulted, as it were, between worlds. Cuzco was the Navel of the World, the sacred center of eternal rebirth.

Staggering to my feet, I was grateful to be alive and unscarred by the daggers traditionally carried by muggers in this part of the world, where theft in all its manifestations is a national industry. But my throat was raw, and I could not swallow without pain. Worse, I had been stripped of all money and identification—traveler's checks, credit card, passport. I was without any visible means of support or identity in a very strange land, not a condition to be recommended.

Even in the blurred aftermath of my violent encounter, I could not help but think of the last Inca emperor, Atahualpa, strangled to death by the Spanish five centuries before. I knew now what it was like to be murdered. It wasn't so bad. It was living that was painful. You know you're alive when you're in pain. Still, I felt something of a bond with old Atahualpa.

Despite this misadventure, I pushed on via rickety railways through the Andes to the sky-city of the Inca. At midnight, alone with the surrounding mountaintops, I saw a fog bank slowly part like a ghostly curtain to reveal Machu Picchu shimmering in eerie moonlight. From there, I explored Lake Titicaca, our planet's highest lake, and the nearby ruins of Tiahuanaco, the inexplicable capital of an impossible empire. In a Lima back street, at the Herrera Museum, I had found the blond and red-haired mummies of a pre-Inca people, obviously not Indian, who long ago ruled the Pacific Coast. Days later, from the vantage point of a rented plane high above the driest desert on Earth, the largest art collection in the world spread out 3,000 feet below my camera amid the gargantuan images of plants, animals, geometric figures, and lines running dead straight for dozens of miles over the earthquake-prone Nazca Plain.

Later, back on more solid ground in northern Illinois, I still resonated with the images and emotions built up during almost two months of intensive travel into South America's pre-Spanish past. To celebrate my homecoming (if not my survival), friends took me to a favorite restaurant in Chicago's Chinatown, on the city's South Side. The Saturday night dinner was going to include more than a good meal, however. Evening entertainment featured the revue of a university-sponsored folk-dance troupe visiting from Hong Kong. It was a kind of pageant, in which performers dressed in regional costumes pantomimed highlights of Chinese history.

A disembodied voice announced over the public address system in broken but intelligible English that the first number would be the oldest known dance in China, performed by a young lady wearing an outfit believed to date back in its design to the legendary dynasty of Emperor Shin How Twi, from whom China derived its name, more than 4,000 years ago. With that, the strident live orchestra struck up its anticipated sweet-and-sour music. I was utterly astonished, however, by the sudden appearance of the dancer on stage. My mind faltered for a prolonged moment of disbelief. Here was this little Chinese maid executing her land's most ancient dance, dressed in singular attire almost identical to that of the Aymara Indian girls I had seen performing their country's oldest folk dance in the High Andes of Peru just a few days before.

The resemblance between their dress was as amazing as it was undeniable. There was no doubt in my mind that someone from China had once (at least) very long ago crossed a formidably vast ocean to leave an indelible cultural mark on the natives of South America at the beginning of their history. The Chinese have been skilled seafarers for many centuries, although Peruvian fishermen were not known to venture beyond sight of land. Influences must have come from west to east across the Pacific, I assumed. Even so, Andean civilization was not Chinese. They seemed to have nothing in common, other than a nearly identical costume worn by dancers in both parts of the world.

Some months later, I was freelancing as a reporter for *Asian Pages,* a St. Paul newspaper serving the Asian community in Minnesota. An assignment took me to a local cultural center, where the Cambodian New Year was being celebrated with traditional performing arts. Having already visited Southeast Asia, I was at least aware of the attractive synthesis of musical and dance themes interwoven between Thailand

and India, Vietnam and Laos, Burma and Cambodia, and so on. But one of the numbers, supposedly from a province revered for the living traditions of its cultural antiquity, was like nothing I had encountered in all my travels—at least not in Asia.

It was totally un-Cambodian. Separate lines of male and female dancers performed together, dressed not in typically ornate and glittering costume, but in simple loincloths and sarongs, with large green leaves in their hair, the men bare-chested. They chanted more than sang to the rhythmic *clop-clop* of halved coconut shells while making fluidly graceful gestures with their hands and arms. It was the most Polynesian performance I had ever seen outside Honolulu.

Could Cambodians during ancient times actually have ventured thousands of miles into the Pacific Ocean and taught the islanders their dance? Or did Polynesians bring something of their ceremonial activity to Cambodia? Both possibilities seemed unfounded and preposterous. Yet the "Cambodian" New Year's dance was the mirror image of something more commonly known in Hawaii. Were these resemblances, no matter how many or how close, entirely coincidental? If not, what did they really mean? I remembered Chicago's Chinese lass dancing in Peruvian attire. Rather than South American visitors in ancient China, or Cambodians in Polynesia, perhaps Pacific Islanders, Aymara Indians, Southeast Asians, and third-millennium-B.C. Chinese were themselves culturally influenced by another, separate, outside source common to them all.

Such speculations were far from new. Beginning almost concurrently with my quarter-century-long research into the more controversial civilization of Atlantis, I occasionally encountered references to its alleged Pacific Ocean counterpart, known as Lemuria, or Mu. Urged to consult James Churchward's five-volume investigation as the subject's best resource, I could not help recoiling from his uncomfortably peremptory tone. Worse, the writing was turgid, mostly undocumented, and generally unconvincing. The rest of the Lemurian genre appeared preoccupied with Theosophical or Anthroposophical musings about conjectural "root races," giants endowed with rearward vision, and other flights of imagination better suited to contemporary pulp fantasy magazines than serious inquiries into the ancient past.

I lost all interest in any Pacific (sometimes Indian) "sunken continent" and was therefore ill prepared for its unexpected reappearance in my life. Again for *Asian Pages,* I had just concluded interviewing a well-spoken representative from the government of Malaysia briefly assigned to the Minnesota state capitol in St. Paul. Following our half-hour exchange, we were chatting informally about her country, of which I confessed an almost perfect ignorance, when she mentioned that her own citizens were hardly less in the dark concerning their origins before the Great Flood.

"The what? I assumed your people are not predominantly Christian," I said.

"We're not," she smiled. "We have our own version of the Flood. It's an old folktale familiar all over the archipelago. Every child knows it from his or her parents or learns it in early school."

I asked her to relate the story.

"The legend goes that once, a very long time ago, there was a great kingdom on a large island far to the east, in the Pacific Ocean. It was a most splendid place, sort of a paradise, where God created the first humans. They built magnificent cities with big temples and palaces, the earliest ever made, and were very wealthy, because the seas were as yet unfished and crops grew easily everywhere in the sunny climate. Being wealthy meant they had time for other things, so they invented writing, religion, sailing, astrology, medicine, music—just about everything. And they flourished for thousands of generations. They were very great sorcerers, with magical powers, like floating heavy stones through the air.

"But one day, the waters began to rise over the shore and threatened the interior of their country. The wise men knew their kingdom would eventually be engulfed, so they evacuated most of the people in time. They watched sorrowfully as their island gradually slid under the waves forever. But just as it went down, another territory, to the west, arose from the bottom of the sea. To this new dry land, the survivors happily escaped and eventually they populated it with their descendants. That is how Malaysia came to be," she concluded, with almost childish pride in having so succinctly recited her country's enduring tradition.

"And that is the story they teach at home and in school?" I asked with some surprise.

"It kind of makes sense," she responded. "You know, the tectonic forces of one landmass dislodging another? Something like that could have happened. Who can say for sure? What goes down must come up, geologically, too!"

After a pause to catch my breath, I looked at her seriously and asked, "Have you ever heard of Lemuria or Mu?"

"Who?"

Years later, I learned that the controversial catastrophist Immanuel Velikovsky recounted precisely the same folk tradition used by natives of Samoa to explain the origins of *their* island. But until meeting the Malaysian government official, I was unaware of any native circum-Pacific deluge account that had not been tainted or invented by Christian missionaries. If the Malaysian version was practically a national epic, I wondered how many other similar folk memories of a sunken homeland might still exist. I was struck as well by its marked difference from renditions of the destruction of Atlantis, invariably portrayed as a violent catastrophe of consuming flames and colossal killer waves overwhelming a doomed people during the course of a single day and night. Here, a world away from the Atlantic Ocean, the process of inundation was repeated. Clearly, however, the Malaysian story was a spin-off from neither Genesis nor Plato. What, then, could explain its origin?

Plunging into the rich heritage of Polynesian mythology for the first time, I found several convincing answers. They led to others beyond the Pacific, across Asia, into the Near East, and, unexpectedly, to Italy. There I learned that the term Lemuria was used for the first time in recorded history by the Romans. It was the name of their oldest ceremony, conducted every year on the 9th, 11th, and 13th of May. Somewhat like our Halloween, the Lemuria was intended to propitiate the restless spirits of people who had died violently or prematurely. These troubled souls, the Romans believed, were accompanied by those of an ancestral people who perished tragically when their distant homeland, known by the same name, was overwhelmed by a natural catastrophe in some far-off sea. There is some philological suggestion that the founder of this ceremony, Romulus, and his twin brother, Remus, were Lemurians.

In any case, at the ceremony's conclusion, small effigies representing the untimely deceased were tossed into the Tiber River, signifying their demise in the Great Flood. They were referred to as the *lemures,* from which the ritual derived its name. According to myth, these ghosts were supposed to have had large, glowing eyes, like a peculiar kind of primate late-nineteenth-century zoologists associated with the Roman spooks. Consequently, scientists resurrected the concept of a "lost continent" to explain the monkey-like lemurs' otherwise unaccountable distribution from Madagascar to Borneo.

Roman geographers before these Victorian scholars had made a clear distinction between Lemuria and Atlantis, which was believed to have dominated the Atlantic Ocean before its own subsequent destruction and never figured into any religious activity. The latter once ruled the West; the former was somewhere much farther away, in the East. The famous geographer Strabo referred to Lemuria as Taprobane, the "beginning of another world," located twenty days' sail from the southern tip of India. A number of unspecified islands, probably the Cocos, were supposedly passed en route to the large island with its 500 towns.

It was known even earlier to Euhemerus, a prominent Greek thinker, whose discovery and translation of "sacred writings" in various parts of the Peloponnesus gained him the patronage of Kassander, ruler of Macedonia, in 301 B.C. The texts described the supposedly true origin of the gods, not atop Mount Olympus, but in a great kingdom many months' sail across a remote ocean to the east. Kassander provided a manned expedition in search of the obscure civilization, which Euhemerus and his crew eventually located and visited. It was known as Panachaea, and he reported that its inhabitants "excel in piety and honor the gods with the most magnificent sacrifices and with remarkable votive offerings of silver and gold. There is also on the island, situated on an exceedingly high hill, a sanctuary of Zeus, which was established by him when he was king of all the inhabited world, and was still in the company of men. And in the temple there is a stele of gold on which is inscribed in summary, in the writing of the Panachaeans, the deeds of Uranus and Kronos and Zeus." The inscription went on to recount that Uranus was the first king of the Earth and an outstanding astronomer, hence the title bestowed on him: "Heaven." He was succeeded by Kronos, whose sons, Poseidon and Zeus, traveled the world before they too ruled the sea and land, respectively.

Returning to Macedonia, Euhemerus published his report, *Sacred History*, which partially survived the collapse of the classical world in the works of another Greek writer, Diodorus Siculus. Although most modern scholars dismiss the *Sacred History* as nothing more than a fable, its author might have found a remnant of Lemuria, perhaps like Easter Island, whose inhabitants did, in fact, have writing of their own, just as the Panachaeans were said to have had. Lemuria was allegedly the first global civilization, and Euhemerus referred to Panachaea as an *oikumene*, or ecumenical power that ruled the whole Earth in the depths of prehistory. He related that one of its early kings who dominated the oceans was Poseidon, described in Plato's fourth-century-B.C. dialogue as the divine founder of Atlantis.

Investigators have long puzzled over the role this sea-god played in Plato's *Critias:* Was he a mythic symbol for the natural forces that shaped the Atlantic island or did he represent the culture-bearing people who arrived there in the distant past to found a new society? Plato wrote that a native woman, Kleito, bore Poseidon ten male twins, the first kings of Atlantis. Was the Greek philosopher implying that the Atlanteans were originally Lemurians?

The very name, *Panachaea*, suggests as much. It is Greek for the home of all primeval peoples, from *pan* for "all" and *Achaea*, by which name Greece was known in preclassical times—that is, the Bronze Age, 3000 B.C. to 1200 B.C., an era encompassing the cultural apogee and final destruction of Lemuria. Appropriately, Panachaea was also a title belonging to Athena, the goddess who bequeathed the civilized arts to humankind. As though in wildly incredible confirmation of Euhemerus,

Churchward stated that the Greek alphabet itself was not only introduced into the Peloponnesus by culture bearers from Mu, but had actually been arranged to recount the destruction of their homeland as well. His interpretation, letter by letter, from *alpha* progressively to *omega*, was intriguing enough not to merit immediate dismissal. The twelfth letter of the Greek alphabet is, after all, *mu*.

In the midst of pouring over these revelations, Professor Nobuhiro Yoshida, president of the Japan Petrograph Society, invited me to address his national congress in Ena. I used the opportunity to research Lemurian leads not only in Japan, but also throughout Southeast Asia and Polynesia. I would have been awed into shyness by Professor Yoshida's potent intellect were he not so innately compassionate and fun-loving. We became instant friends at our first meeting in 1996, but I still revere him as my true *sensei*, the greatest living authority on the roots of Japanese civilization. His samurai sword–keen mind exposed them as no book or university class ever could. He brought me to remote, seldom visited archaeological sites, rarely or never seen by Westerners, and introduced me to numerous professional and amateur historical investigators deeply devoted to the appreciation and preservation of their national past.

While in Tokyo, before departing for Thailand, I met with a small group of Japanese publishers and journalists. One of them showed me a recently published series of images that dramatically inflected my Lemurian quest. They showed what appeared to be the massive stone ruins of a ceremonial building rising in tiers from the bottom of the ocean near Yonaguni, Japan's southernmost island. The photographs and newspaper accounts seemed authentic. Had Lemuria been discovered?

On my return to Wisconsin, I used the underwater find as the cover feature for a popular science magazine I edited. *Ancient American* scooped the story, and readers in the United States learned for the first time about the tiny, distant island with its curious sunken monument just offshore.

I returned annually to Japan for the next six years, each time escorted by the learned professor Yoshida to obscure ruins otherwise unknown to foreigners and unsuspected even by most Japanese. Venturing farther afield, I found a Lemurian memorial in Thailand, and I walked among the remains of a temple—not unlike the structure near Iseki Point, attributed by natives to an ancient people they still referred to as the Mu—in the forest-jungles of Oahu.

Following these extensive travels, I was invited to present my accumulated evidence publicly for the first time at a Quest for Knowledge conference featuring leading experts in alternative science—Maurice Cotterell, John Anthony West, and others—meeting in Saint Albans, England. Reactions were mixed to the notion that humans had built the Yonaguni "Monument," although a general consensus urged its further study. Returning to my home in Wisconsin, I published several articles about my Lemurian research in *Atlantis Rising,* a much needed champion of unconventional views in anthropology, geology, astronomy, and spirituality. One of these pieces caught the attention of an independent film producer, who asked me to write a script for a documentary she was preparing about Yonaguni and its implications on behalf of Pacific archaeology. She had already collected a great deal of superb underwater footage. Reediting these visual materials and weaving them together with some of my own research, I came up with a narrative script for *The Temple of Mu.*

First telecast over Australian television in 2000, the documentary was also shown throughout Japan by the Fuji Television Network, then was up for consideration at the following year's International Film Festival. More significantly, *The Temple of Mu* described a benchmark in modern science still unacknowledged by mainstream academics. For more than a century, until the underwater discoveries in Japanese and Taiwanese waters during the last few years, those academics shunned the merest suggestion of Lemuria as a Theosophist's fantasy—"worse than Atlantis," in the words of a college anthropology professor who insists on anonymity like Quasimodo claiming "Sanctuary!" But our hour-long documentary offered physical evidence backed up by some leading expert opinions, and showcased in a reasoned presentation not quite so easily dismissed. Despite official reluctance, the Pacific Ocean civilization was irrepressibly rising from the depths of myth into archaeological reality.

Part of that myth was articulated during the early twentieth century by Edgar Cayce, the so-called Sleeping Prophet. Doubtless, including the trance-state utterances of a psychic will only drive skeptics further and faster away from any consideration of the subject. But no amount of unimpeachable evidence can ever win over such closed minds. The cause of a new history is well served by incorporating Cayce's penetrating descriptions of an otherwise inaccessible past.

I was already acquainted with Cayce's "life readings" concerning Atlantis, but not so familiar with his less numerous statements regarding its geographically opposite counterpart. It was thrilling to observe that his remarks dovetailed remarkably well with everything learned thus far about either lost kingdom while throwing new light on their separate, albeit related, origins and destinies. A book was published by the organization perpetuating his work, the Association for Research and Enlightenment in Virginia Beach, Virginia. *Edgar Cayce's Atlantis and Lemuria* examined his pronouncements regarding these controversial civilizations in the light of the latest scientific findings.

Since publication in 2001, new proofs were brought to my attention that tended to confirm as never before the existence, history, and fate of the Pacific Ocean realm. In preparing for the composition of this book, I assembled a mountain of research materials. During the long process of organizing them, I found it impossible to escape several primary conclusions that repeatedly emerged of their own accord from the combined evidence:

- Lemuria undoubtedly did exist in the ancient past.
- It was the birthplace of civilized humans.
- It was the biblical "Garden of Eden."
- The Lemurians developed and used an incredibly high-level technology, unlike our own and superior to it in some ways.
- They suffered not one but a series of natural catastrophes over many thousands of years before ultimately vanishing.
- Their mystical principles survived to fundamentally influence some of the world's major religions.

*Original painting of Lemuria
by L. T. Richardson.*

These unavoidable determinations form the basis of *The Lost Civilization of Lemuria.* The task of its investigation is to assemble this best and latest proof on behalf of Lemuria as a real place in time, inhabited by a great people whose spiritual achievement is humankind's most priceless legacy. Fresh disclosures suggest that the time is rapidly approaching when the undersea realm will be universally understood for what it really was: namely, the undisputed fountainhead of humanity. In its modern recognition, the Lemurians will live again. The forces they set in motion so long ago are even now building toward an inevitable moment when we will once more come face-to-face with the imperishable essence of that vanished homeland. Then the realization will dawn on us that we are the Children of Mu.

ONE

A Lost Super Science

And all about, strung on their canals, are the bulwarked
islets with their enigmatic walls peering through the dense
growths of mangroves—dead, deserted for incalculable
ages; shunned by those who live near them.

ABRAHAM MERRITT,

THE MOON POOL

One of the world's supreme ancient mysteries is also among its most obscure. In a remote corner of the western Pacific Ocean, nearly 1,000 miles north of New Guinea and 2,300 miles south of Japan, stand the massive ruins of a long dead city. Incongruously built on a coral reef only five feet above sea level between the equator and the eleventh parallel, Nan Madol is a series of rectangular islands and colossal towers choked by draping vegetation. During its prehistoric lifetime, sole access to Nan Madol was via the ocean, from which vessels entered an open-air corridor flanked by artificial islets. At the end of this sea-lane still remains the only entrance to the city, a dramatically impressive flight of broad stone steps rising to a plaza. Ninety-two artificial islands are enclosed within the "downtown" area's 1.6 square miles. All are interconnected by an extensive network of what appear to be canals, each twenty-seven feet across and more than four feet deep at high tide.

An estimated 250 million tons of prismatic basalt spread over

Nan Madol (photograph by Sue Nelson).

170 acres went into the construction of Nan Madol. Its stone girders rise in a Lincoln Log–like cribwork configuration to twenty-five feet. Originally, the walls rose higher still, perhaps by another ten or twenty feet. Better estimates are impossible to ascertain, because the Pacific metropolis is being slowly, inexorably dismantled by relentless jungle growth, which is dislodging the unmortared ramparts and scattering their roughly quarried blocks to the ground. David Hatcher Childress, who conducted several underwater investigations at Nan Madol in the 1980s and early 1990s, concludes that "the whole project is of such huge scale that it easily compares with the building of the Great Wall of China and the Great Pyramid of Egypt in sheer amounts of stone and labor used, and the gigantic scope of the site." In fact, some of the hewn or splintered basalt prisms built into Nan Madol are larger and heavier than the more than two million blocks of Khufu's Pyramid. Between four and five million stone columns went into the construction of the Caroline Islands' prehistoric metropolis.

Outcrops of basalt were quarried by splitting off massive splinters into the quadrangular, pentagonal, or hexagonal "logs" that went into building Nan Madol. They were hewn roughly into shape, then loosely fitted without benefit of mortar or cement, in contrast to the finely lined and joined stonework found in the supposed canals. These prismatic columns usually range in length from three to twelve feet, although many reach twenty-five feet. Their average weight is around five tons each, but the larger examples weigh twenty or twenty-five tons apiece. According to *Science* magazine, "At places in the reef there were natural breaks that served as entrances to the harbors. In these ship-canals there were a number of islands, many of which were surrounded by a wall of stone five or six feet high."

In fact, the entire site was formerly encircled by a sixteen-foot-high wall originally 2,811 feet long. Only a few sections of this massive rampart have not been broken down by unguessed centuries of battering storms, against which still stand two breakwaters. One is 1,500 feet in extent, but the other, nearly three times greater, is almost a mile long. Some of Nan Madol's walls are more than twelve feet thick, to what purpose no one has been able to determine because they are not part of any military fortifications. There is no evidence of keystones or arches, just a simple slab lintel placed over doorways. None of the presumed "houses" have windows; nor are there any streets, only what may be canals. Yet the site did not result from haphazard episodes of construction over several generations. Its overall layout of structures deliberately grouped and positioned into orderly sections attests to an organized plan carried out with single-minded purpose in a relatively short time.

The city's best-preserved building is known as Nan Dowas, a tall, square, hollow, windowless tower composed of fifteen-foot-long hexagonal black basalt pillars laid horizontally between courses of rudely cut boulders and smaller stones. The islet is a double-walled enclosure comprising 13,500 cubic meters of coral, with an additional 4,500 cubic meters of basalt. Although the site comprises numerous other structures, they are dominated by Nan Dowas. Childress points out that "the entire massive structure was built by stacking stones in the manner in which one might construct a log cabin." The southeastern side of Nan Dowas features the city's largest block, a single cornerstone weighing no less than sixty tons. Digging underneath this impressive megalith, archaeologists were surprised to discover that it had been intentionally set on a buried stone platform.

They were in for yet another surprise when they found a large tunnel cut through coral running from the center of Nan Dowas. An entire network of underground corridors connecting all the major man-made islands was subsequently revealed, including an islet known as Darong joined by a long tunnel to the outer reef that surrounds the city. Incredibly, some tunnels appear to run beneath the reef itself, exiting into caves under the sea. Darong is also notable for its stone-lined artificial lake, one of several found throughout the complex. What appears to be its longest tunnel extends from the city center out into the sea for perhaps half a mile. Larger even than Nan Dowas is the artificial islet of Pahnwi, containing 20,000 cubic meters of coral and basalt rock.

Estimates of the 20,000 to 50,000 workers needed to build Nan Madol are in sharp contrast with the native population of Pohnpei. This inhabited island just offshore could never have supported such numbers.

Nan Madol (photograph by Sue Nelson).

But not a single carving, relief, petroglyph, or decoration of any kind has been found at Nan Madol, nor any idols or ritual objects—in fact, few artifacts at all to identify its builders. No statues or sculpture ever adorned its watery boulevards. Not even one of the small, portable stone images commonly found throughout the rest of Micronesia and across central and western Polynesia was discovered at the site. Nor has a single tool or weapon so far been recovered.

Although a ruin, the city is not difficult to envision during its heyday. Remove all concealing vegetation, and visitors would behold crudely worked masses of basalt contrasting with orderly courses of stone rising in massive towers and overpowering walls amid a complex of smaller rectangular buildings and artificial lakes interconnected by dozens of canals, spread out over eleven square miles. No wonder Nan Madol has been referred to as the Venice of the Pacific. But it had no marketplace, temples, or storage areas, not even a cemetery to bury its dead.

The name Nan Madol means "spaces between," referring to the spaces created by the network of canals, while Pohnpei (Ponape, until its incorporation in the Federated States of Micronesia, in 1991), means "on an altar." Its ruins are not confined to the coral reef facing Madolenihmw Harbor, but may be found across Pohnpei itself and on several offshore islands. A rectangular enclosure forty-six feet long by thirty-three feet wide, with a bisecting three-foot-high interior wall, was discovered in a remote, swampy meadow high in the mountains, near Salapwuk. Although the twin courtyards enclose a 1,520-square-foot area, a pair of inner platforms are only one foot high. As at Nan Madol, roughly cut basalt boulders and basalt logs were stacked to form the enclosure. Several others stand on Pohnpei's southwest coast, with the largest example atop a 720-foot mountain. The summit is surrounded by walls five and seven feet high connected by paved walkways to several terraced platforms.

About a quarter of a mile away, to the southwest, several so-called crypts were found at Pohnpei, but no trace of human remains have ever been recovered from the 12.5- to 14.8-foot-long containers, whose real function has not been identified. Nearer the coast, Diadi features a finely made basalt enclosure with a platform 1,060 feet square. Alauso's two-tiered, 340-foot-square pyramid with a central fire pit stands not far from the sea, near Kiti Rock's 24-foot-square platform, with four upright basalt columns at each of the inner corners. Sokehs Island, separated from Pohnpei by a mangrove swamp, is crossed by numerous stone pathways connecting platforms.

Significantly contributing to the mystery of these structures, it would be difficult to imagine a more out-of-the-way place than Pohnpei, a mere speck amid the 4.5 million square miles of western Pacific Ocean surrounding Micronesia. Sea-lanes and trading routes are thousands of miles away. As the encyclopedist of ancient anomalies William R. Corliss observes, "Only one hundred twenty nine square miles in area, it is almost lost in the immensity of the Pacific."

Totolom, Tolocome, or Nahnalaud, the "Big Mountain," rises 2,595 feet from the middle of the squarish, twelve-by-fourteen-and-a-half-mile island, overgrown with mangrove swamps but devoid of beaches. Pohnpei is just thirteen miles across and is surrounded by a coral reef, together with twenty-three smaller islands. Abundant rainfall—195 to 200 inches annually—conjures a profusion of ferns, orchids, creepers, bougainvillea, and hibiscus throughout thickly wooded valleys and across steep mountainsides. Humidity is excessive, and mildew, rot, and decay permeate the island. Additionally, its remote location hardly seems to qualify Pohnpei as an ideal spot to build a civilization. Indeed, the island has nothing to offer for such a gargantuan undertaking as Nan Madol.

Yet its very existence implies city planning, a system of weights and measures, division of labor, and a hierarchy of authority, plus advanced surveying and construction techniques on the part of its builders. All this was needed to raise the only premodern urban center in the entire Pacific. But what kind of a place was it, this city without streets, windows, or art? Bill S. Ballinger, whose *Lost City of Stone* was an early popular book on the subject, observed, "Nothing quite like Nan Madol exists anywhere else on Earth. The ancient city's construction, architecture and location are unique."

At Pohnpei's northern end, Kolonia, its capital and the only town on the island, stands in stark contrast to the magnificent achievement just across the bay. Unlike the orderly precision evident at Nan Madol, Kolonia grew haphazardly, with no regard to planning of any kind, and is today inhabited by perhaps 2,000 residents who live in mostly one-story, cinder-block buildings with corrugated tin roofs. In contrast to the prehistoric stone pathways that still crisscross the island, some fifteen miles of dirt roads are often impassable, especially during the frequent downpours. Many islanders dwell in small shacks of dried grass, cane, and bamboo, not monumental stone. "Kolonia is anything but beautiful," writes Georgia Hesse of *the San Francisco Examiner,* "a cluster of weathering wood and rusting corrugated buildings strung anyhow along a wide street." Employment opportunities are virtually nonexistent, so the natives lead subsistence lives from the richly fertile, volcanic soil, their diet supplemented by fish and chickens.

The Carolines have never supported a population growth commensurate with the labor needed to build the Venice of the Pacific. As Ballinger put it, "The point is that large reserves of manpower were never readily available in and around Ponape. This is a factor that must always be considered when trying to solve the mystery of the construction of Nan Madol." Pohnpei's 183 square miles are mostly mountainous and uninhabitable, barely able to support its 30,000 inhabitants. Only a far greater number would have justified, let alone been able to build, a public works project on the huge scale of Nan Madol. A leading New Zealand scholar of the early twentieth century, John Macmillan Brown, noted, "The rafting over the reef at high tide and the hauling up of these immense blocks, most of them from five to twenty five tons weight, to such a height as sixty feet must have meant tens of thousands of organized labor; and it had to be housed and clothed and fed. Yet, within a radius of fifteen hundred miles of its centre there are not more than fifty thousand people today." Just about that many workers would have been needed to assemble Nan Madol's four or five million basalt logs in approximately twenty years.

Today, Pohnpeians lay little claim to the archaeological site outsiders find so awe-inspiring. *Science* magazine reports, "The natives have no tradition touching the quarry, who hewed the stone, when it was done, or why the work ceased." They mostly avoid the place as evil and dangerous, where visitors after dark were known to have been killed by some mysterious power. Indeed, the islanders appear to have always considered it taboo, at least into the late nineteenth century. More than 100 years later, a few local guides are willing to escort outsiders to the site, but never after dark. According to Ballinger, "Present Ponapeans and their preceding generations have demonstrated no skill, or even interest, in any kind of stone construction. The building of the city demanded considerable engineering knowledge," which the indigenous residents have never demonstrated. "I had to use all my powers of persuasion even to find two boys to take me over to Nan Madol every day," complained the famous "ancient astronaut" theorist Erich von Daniken, when he visited Pohnpei in the early 1970s. Citing the thousands of work hours, complex organization, and well-directed labor required to quarry, transport, and erect 250 million tons of basalt, a U.S. Department of the Interior report stated, "The unwritten history of Ponape indicates that Nan Madol was constructed by or under the direction of people not native to the island of Ponape." Von Daniken dismissed the modern natives as "poor and incurably lazy and [with] no interest in business." William Churchill, an early-twentieth-century American ethnologist at Pohnpei, concluded that the prehistoric city was "utterly beyond the present capacity of the islanders." He echoed the sentiments of the ship's surgeon of the *Lambton*, a British cutter that anchored at the island in 1836. Dr. Campbell concluded that Nan Madol was "the work of a race of men far surpassing the present generation, over whose memory many ages have rolled, and whose history oblivion has shaded forever, whose greatness and whose power can only now be traced from the scattered remains of the structures they have reared, which now wave with evergreens over the ashes of their departed glory, leaving to posterity the pleasure of speculation and conjecture."

To be sure, the islanders' own traditions suggest as much. They recount that seventeen men and women who arrived from a land far to the south created Pohnpei by piling rocks upon the local coral reef. This work accomplished, the inhabitants—mixed offspring of natives and newcomers—descended from these first inhabitants. Over time, their numbers multiplied, but they lived in perpetual anarchy. Much later, riding in a "large canoe," the twin brothers Olisihpa and Olsohpa arrived from a different homeland in the west, remembered as Katau Peidi. When this Motherland, known by many different names to various Pacific Islanders, was referred to as Kanamwayso, its myth depicted a splendid kingdom from which a people of great power very long ago sailed throughout the Pacific. Falling stars and earthquakes were responsible for setting Kanamwayso aflame and dropping it to the bottom of the ocean, where it is still inhabited by the spirits of those who perished in the cataclysm, who preside over the ghosts of all those who die at sea.

Olisihpa and Olsohpa were sorcerers, wise and holy men, and very tall. They first landed on the northern end of Pohnpei but found the geography there somehow unsuited to their purposes. Three times more they tried to establish themselves along the east coast—at the summit of Net Mountain, Nankopworemen, and U, where the supposed remains of these failed attempts are still pointed out by local guides.

But each location failed some predetermined requirement. At last, after a careful search, the perfect site was found at Sounahleng, a reef at Temwen Island, upon which Olisihpa and Olsohpa built Nan Madol with the aid of a "flying dragon." After it cut through the coral, dredging the canals, the twin sorcerers levitated the ponderous basalt logs through the air, piling them to a great height, and fitted them neatly into place. The work took only a single day to complete. Thereafter, Nan Madol became a sacred city and administrative center, from which the brothers brought government and social order to Pohnpei. They ruled together for many years, until Olisihpa died of old age, and Olsohpa assumed sole power as the first Saudeleur, or lord of Deleur, an early name for the island. He married a local woman, from whom he sired twelve generations of Saudeleurs, who continued to rule wisely and peacefully until the arrival of the ancestors of the modern Pohnpeians.

They were led by a warrior chief from the south, Isokelekel, who killed Saudemwohl, the last of the Saudeleurs. His was an easy victory, because the lords of Deleur never concerned themselves with military affairs. Isokelekel's line endured through the centuries into the modern era, despite years of occupation by foreign powers, until shortly before Pohnpei became first part and then capital of the independent Federated States of Micronesia, in 1984. Samuel Hadley was the last Nahnmwarki to assume the title, in 1986.

Something of this mythic version of Nan Madol's origins came to light during 1928, when Japanese archaeologists excavated human skeletal remains near several prehistoric sites on Pohnpei. While the bones numbered only a few dozen pieces and were incomplete and in poor condition, enough survived to show that they belonged to people unlike the indigenous islanders. Their ancient predecessors were far taller and more robust. Discovery of these anomalous skeletal fragments was supported by surviving evidence. The men of Pohnpei still make and use a kind of throwing spear they claim as an inheritance from the Saudeleurs of long ago. While Polynesians and other Micronesians traditionally employ spears five to seven feet long, the Pohnpei spear is a unique twelve feet, suggesting the tall descendants of Olisihpa and Olsohpa.

They were said to have flown the stones that went into the construction of Nan Madol through the air. Remarkably, this same explanation is found in other parts of the world far removed from the western Pacific to account for the existence of similarly ancient megalithic wonders. The most famous example is Britain's Stonehenge, where legend had Merlin floating its fifty-ton *saracen* stones into position. If these reports of levitation, widely separated in distance and time by radically different peoples on opposite sides of the world, do not represent some universally shared human response to the survival of otherwise inexplicable ruins, then they may be the folk memory of a lost technology.

As unacceptable as conventional investigators may find such a conclusion, they are hard-pressed to explain how twenty-five-ton pieces of basalt were lifted thirty, perhaps fifty feet and placed neatly in the rising walls and towers at Nan Madol, or how a sixty-ton boulder was positioned atop its own platform. Today, the largest crane on Pohnpei can lift thirty-five tons. Duplicating the assembly of 200 million metric tons of stone, not on solid ground but on a coral reef only a few feet above the surrounding ocean, represents a daunting challenge even for modern construction engineers using state-of-the-art machinery.

A physicist from Michigan's Marquette University, Dr. Randall Pfingston, who visited Pohnpei with Childress in the late 1980s, theorized in Childress's book *Lost Cities of Ancient Lemuria and the Pacific* that

> gravity is really a frequency, part of Einstein's Unified Field. Crystallized blocks of basalt need only be resonating at the frequency of gravity, 1012 hertz, or the frequency between short radio waves and infrared radiation, and they will lose their weight. Crystals, even basalt crystals, are ideal for resonating in such a way. If that was the way that the stones "magically" flew through the air, then they might have spun upward and to the east, just as the legend says, because of the spin of the Earth. The centrifugal force of the Earth's spin caused the stones to rise. Then it might be possible for people to ride on the logs of basalt, and then help lower them into the place at Nan Madol as the vibration lessened, and the stones gained weight again.

According to Paul Devereaux, who confirmed an undeniable relationship between ancient megalithic centers and telluric energies, "Above some fault zones, various minerals and rocks have been violently mixed together, causing magnetic and electrical anomalies, and even measurable variations in gravity. Far from being fixed, gravity, magnetism, and the direction of true north may all vary at points on the surface of the Earth. For example, the type of metallic ore in rock determines its magnetic properties, while the thickness of the Earth's crust or the altitude of a certain site can influence the gravitational force measurable there. Under tectonic pressure, fault zones can show changing energy fields, too."

As Arthur C. Clarke postulated in the last of his Three Laws, "Any sufficiently advanced technology is indistinguishable from magic."

It is true that yams and cassava, which originated in South America, are cultivated at Pohnpei, suggesting to some researchers, like the late Thor Heyerdahl, a cultural connection to the civilizations of Peru and

Bolivia. Childress wonders about more than a phonetic resemblance between Pohnpei's Nahnmwarkis and ancient Egyptian nomarchs. Both are terms for a regional governor. Parallels may even be made between the first Saudeleur, or lord of Nan Madol, Olisihpa, and Elasippos, a king from Atlantis mentioned in Plato's fourth-century-B.C. dialogue, *Critias*. Extending the comparison further, Atlantean monarchs, like the statuesque Olisihpa and Olsohpa, were twins described in Greek myth as Titans. But Inca and pre-Inca cities have absolutely nothing in common with anything at Nan Madol, and putting city planners from Egypt or Atlantis at a dot in the western Pacific is a stretch, even for extreme cultural diffusionists. Apparent correspondences between an otherwise insignificant Micronesian island and South America, dynastic Egypt, or Atlantis seem rather to suggest that these places and Pohnpei were themselves influenced by some outside X-civilization the natives recall vaguely as Katau Peidi.

Determining a time frame for the construction and occupation of Nan Madol could go a long way toward discovering the identity of its creators, because some contemporary civilization might be singled out as a likely candidate for its parentage. Various attempts at dating the site have been made, especially since the advent of the carbon-14 process. During the 1960s, archaeologists employed by the Smithsonian Institution tested cooked residue inside what they took for a turtle oven to come up with a habitation period around 1285 A.D. Additional testing of a nearby ash layer showed it was older by two centuries. Broader thermoluminescence testing by Steven Athens during the 1970s for the Pacific Studies Institute (Honolulu) dated pottery shards found below artificial fill at Nan Madol's Dapahu Islet to more than 2,000 years ago. This result was remarkable for more than establishing human habitation at Pohnpei in antiquity, because pottery was not known to have ever been used on the island. As noted by European visitors who met them for the first time during the early nineteenth century, the natives had no knowledge of pottery. Consensus among these first foreigners, such as Dr. Campbell mentioned above, held that the ruins bore "an antiquity as great as that of the pyramids."

But the wide-ranging dates provided by scientific testing are not very helpful. They cannot be associated with the city's construction or florescence, and indicate only that someone ate a turtle at Nan Madol in the late thirteenth century or dropped a jug at the time of Christ. Reliable carbon-datable specimens are impossible to obtain in the jungle humidity, which rots organic materials out of existence in a very short time. As John H. Brandt wrote in *Archaeology* magazine, "The oft-repeated question of the true age of Nan Madol must still go largely unanswered."

A more trustworthy method of ascertaining Nan Madol's date parameters than uncertain radiocarbon testing is sea-level rise. As long ago as 1885, *Science* magazine reported, "The singular feature of these islands is that the walls are a foot or more below the water. When they were built, they were evidently above the water, and connected to the mainland; but they have gradually sunk until the sea has risen a foot or more around them."

During the 1970s, preliminary to Pohnpei's independence, the island was professionally surveyed for the first time by Dr. Arthur Saxe, from the University of Oregon, for the Trust Territory of the Pacific. Surprised to learn of the strange tunnels running out into and under the sea to their submarine caves, he expanded his survey to the surrounding waters. Dr. Saxe and his team of fellow divers found a single line of uniformly sized boulders perpendicular to the dropoff at about eighty-five feet below Madolenihmw Harbor. The line eventually vanished into the sandy bottom after another ten feet. The boulders' artificial arrangement was established when the surveyors confirmed a deliberate orientation between two islands—Pieniot and Nahkapw. It was here, appropriately enough, that local traditions placed a sunken ruin remembered as Kahnihmw Namkhet.

Myth materialized when Dr. Saxe and his divers discovered a number of stone pillars seventeen and twenty-five feet tall standing at depths of ten to sixty feet. The islanders told him of yet a second underwater site said to feature an immense stone gate or arch in a deep channel between Nahkapw and Nanmwoluhei. Sure enough, additional columns were observed standing or fallen across the ocean floor, although the large gateway was never found. Altogether, some twelve or fifteen basalt uprights were documented in the waters surrounding Nan Madol.

A few years later, divers for Japanese television photographed an additional dozen stone pillars standing in double rows on the bottom of Madolenihmw Harbor. Learning of their discovery, executives at Australian Television dispatched their own subsurface camera crew to explore the depths around Nahkapw. There the coral-encrusted columns surveyed by Dr. Saxe were relocated and filmed for a documentary entitled *Ponape: Island of Mystery*. After it was telecast, a copy was obtained by the directors of the Community College of Micronesia, at Kolonia.

Childress made a determined search in the early 1990s for the underwater ruins of Kahnihmw Namkhet and the lost gateway reputed to stand somewhere between Nahkapw and Nanmwoluhei Islands. He and his diving party from the World Explorers Club located neither Kahnihmw Namkhet nor the arch. "We did, however, find a great deal of evidence," he reported, "that there are sunken structures to the south of the island, lending credence to the story of a sunken city beneath Nakapw." Across Madolenihmw Harbor, on Nakapw's south side, directly east of Nan Madol itself, Childress and company observed unnaturally straight lines running across the reef caused by organized stone architecture covered with centuries of concealing coral accretion, and dove on numerous pillars, which they estimated at roughly ten tons each. Low tide actually exposed the tops of some monoliths, transitional evidence for ancient construction from the bottom of the sea to the land.

These underwater discoveries not only reveal that the original extent of Nan Madol was substantially broader and larger than its dry-land portions, but also provide a far more credible time reference than carbon-14's skewed limitations for prehistoric civilization at Pohnpei. Depths at which the sunken pillars and boulder formations were found in the waters around Nan Madol reached more than seventy-five feet. Dr. Saxe and his team saw at least one stony arrangement disappearing under the sands of the ocean floor at ninety-five feet, suggesting a maximum depth to 100 feet for probable archaeological material at Pohnpei. Sea levels have not been that low since the close of the last ice age. The presently submerged boulders could have been oriented as they were between Pieniot and Nahkapw islands only when their position, now covered by 100 feet of water, was dry land, some 12,000 years ago. Even though standing columns are not found on Pohnpei, its subsurface site or sites do not substantially differ enough from Nan Madol itself to suggest that a later city was built upon an earlier, different one, since inundated. Rather, a continuity of construction using basalt and organized groups of boulders flows contiguously from the bottom of the sea to the land as part of a single, unified plan.

Obviously, Nan Madol's canals must have been built long after the present underwater pillars and boulders were positioned and subsequently inundated: 12,000 years ago, the canals stood 100 feet above the surface of the ocean. They could have functioned, therefore, only after sea levels had already reached their present height, about 5,000 years ago. It would seem, then, that Nan Madol originated before 10,000 B.C. at what is now a 100-foot depth. With postglacial rise, the residents kept adding on to their city and building above increasing sea levels, keeping pace with the Pacific's encroachment on the land, until present levels were reached around 3000 B.C. The discovery of archaeological structures at various depths of ninety-five (or one hundred), seventy-five, twenty, and ten feet defines rising water conditions with which the ancient construction engineers kept pace.

These considerations may be thrown into a cocked hat, however, if the structures deemed "canals" by investigators were actually something else. Nothing resembling locks or sluice gates of any kind has been found so far to positively identify them as part of some watercourse. They may have been something entirely different, perhaps large basins or holding tanks for the sacred eels allegedly stocked by the Saudeleurs.

Although none of this can tell us just how long ago Nan Madol was founded, its first and hence oldest strata suggest that it must have originally been built to accommodate sea levels before the end of the last ice age. Underwater archaeology around Pohnpei shows that, despite subsequent millennia of flooding, the site was occupied—to all appearances, continuously—at least until the end of the fourth millennium B.C. When it was abandoned is so far impossible to determine. Carbon dates for occupation going back only to the fifteenth century or a few hundred years earlier say nothing about its builders or inhabitants, and indicate only that people—certainly the ancestors of today's Micronesians—resided among the ruins from time to time long after the site had been vacated by its creators.

Nan Madol shares its depth and age with another ruin more than 1,300 miles across the open Pacific: a sunken stone platform near the Japanese island of Yonaguni. These two widely separated sites are nonetheless connected to each other by more than the common enigma of their underwater contemporaneity. Childress and his team found crosses, squares, and both closed and open rectangles adorning boulders half grown over with coral atop a nine-foot-deep reef near Nan Madol. Their important discovery also helped verify the artifactual context of these petroglyphs, because similar ideograms were already known to exist in the mountainous interior of Pohnpei itself. A direct connection was made, therefore, between the underwater location and the land. Far more significantly, at least one cross and several squares on the sunken structure off Yonaguni have since been photographed by Japanese investigators. The appearance of identical petroglyphs at both the Japanese and Caroline structures establishes vital connections shared by both and provides important clues to their real identity.

During his far-flung travels, David Childress also noticed similarities between the columns under Nan Madol's waters and the so-called *lat'te* pillars he studied firsthand on the island of Guam, some 450 miles north of Pohnpei. But closer resemblances occur 340 miles to the southeast, at the island of Kosrae. Easternmost of the Carolines, this forty-two-square-mile island was a somewhat smaller-scale mirror image of Nan Madol. Nowhere else were such immense basalt boulders and rudely shaped monoliths organized into Lincoln Log–like towers, massive walls, and extensive canals. Even the setting at Kosrae was made to resemble its Pohnpei counterpart, with most structures located on a smaller, artificial island—Lelu—fronting a harbor in the east.

The ruin itself is referred to as Insaru, although Kosrae features other archaeological sites inland on the southeast side of the island at Menka, and in the southwest, at Walung, connected by a five-mile-long canal to Utwe, on the south coast. Most building was concentrated at Insaru, where forty-ton basalt blocks were used to raise identical versions of Nan Madol's originally thirty- or sixty-foot-high ramparts, although there are some interesting differences. In 1999, Dr. Felicia Beardsley led an archaeological survey at a site known as Safonfok, near Walung, for the Kosrae Historical Research Preservation Office (KHRPO). She did not expect to find much in the test dig beyond some telltale evidence for early-nineteenth- or eighteenth-century influences in apparently badly disturbed ground.

"Yet, the wealth and integrity of the buried archaeological record," according to a contemporary KHRPO report, "revealed a technological industry never before seen in the Pacific"—a large factory for the mass production of finely made coral fishhooks and tools. Also recovered was a simple but almost elegant basalt knife, the first of its kind ever found in Kosrae, Pohnpei, or anywhere else, and a peculiar, diamond-shaped bead. Remarkably, it had been beveled, a technique utterly unknown throughout Micronesia. Dr. Beardsley's 5.5-square-meter excavation brought to light less than 10 percent of the subterranean complex, which must have entailed several dozen, perhaps hundreds of workers engaged in organized labor for large-scale manufacture of industrial goods. The Safonfok site is unique in the Pacific, and testifies to a former time when a higher culture dominated the island.

Kosrae's approximately ninety "canals" represent the same number found at Nan Madol, but examples at Insaru are almost dry. The small island of Lelu on which the city was built has been rising in irregular spurts of uplift over time. This geologic instability combines with sea-level fluctuations since the last ice age to render any credible dating for Insaru impossible to ascertain. Nonetheless, even the latest carbon-14 testing of human material from Kosrae conducted around the turn of the twenty-first century showed that the island was at least inhabited 3,000 years ago. But only the close resemblance of its ruins, minus any changes, implies a shared chronology with Pohnpei.

The archaeological remains at Lelu differ from counterparts at Nan Madol solely in their lesser extent and the addition of two piles of basalt boulders stacked into pyramidal mounds, referred to by natives as kingly "tombs," although they never yielded any trace of human remains. Otherwise, the overgrown rock paths, squarish buildings, boat docks, and imposing walls are the same as their larger versions far to the northwest. Childress stated the obvious when he wrote, "Because of the similarities in construction techniques between Nan Madol and the Lelu ruins of Insaru, it can be easily concluded that both were built by the same master stonemasons."

Whatever local traditions might have revealed something about the site were mostly effaced by missionary zeal to Christianize the islanders. Only the faintest echo of an otherwise lost foundation myth recounts that Insaru was built overnight by a pair of sorcerers, although even this fragment appears borrowed from Pohnpei's story of the twin brothers, Olisihpa and Olsohpa. Kosrae's version differs only in the addition of a race of "white giants" referred to as the Kona, who carried and erected the stones under the direction of their magician overlords. The loss from the severe erosion of Lelu's oral accounts was almost surpassed around the turn of the twentieth century, when Insaru was used as a quarry for the construction of a pier. These depredations seriously diminished the ancient city; its best photographs are still among those few taken at Lelu during the late 1890s. Today, this surviving ruin of a ruin is hardly more than a shadow of its former greatness that lingered as recently as little more than a century ago.

One other legend describes a foreign ship, or *Auk Palang*, sailing out of the northwest and carrying a crew of maritime engineers who landed at Kosrae and raised its mighty structures very long ago. In any case, the mythic evidence, paltry as it is, describes these visitors as outsiders, master builders possessing supernatural powers far beyond anything imagined by the natives. Neither they, university-trained archaeologists, or geologists nor professional construction engineers can explain how a preindustrial people could have lifted and accurately positioned forty-ton stones into walls twenty or more feet high.

Attempts have been made to duplicate what conventional scholars presume must have been the only means by which the boulders were moved into place. They tried to put their theory to the test in a 1995 Discovery Channel documentary by lashing a one-ton column with bamboo stays to a coconut raft. Despite repeated attempts, the experiment was an utter failure. At most, the re-created rafts could manage stones of only a few hundred pounds, quite a cry from the twenty-ton logs and sixty-ton boulders handled with apparent skill by the builders of Nan Madol and Insaru. A vessel capable of ferrying high tonnage that went into building these places is far beyond the known limitations of native Micronesians or presumptuous archaeologists, and even today it constitutes a major challenge for materials-handling experts outfitted with all the state-of-the-art, machine-driven lifters and movers available.

Investigators have still not even determined how such prodigious basalt logs were quarried, let alone transported. "Presumably," Brandt speculated, "the miners heated the cliff face with huge fires and then drenched the surface with cold water. The resultant expansion and contraction broke off the splinters desired for construction." But this is all speculation; there is no evidence for such a so-called spalling method ever having been known or used at Pohnpei. In the absence of tool marks there, however, its application is at least a possibility. Or perhaps this enigmatic Venice of the Pacific was raised by a lost technology unlike our own.

What really was Nan Madol? Its uniformly windowless buildings, starkly utilitarian design, and lack of identifiable storage areas resemble nothing of its kind anywhere else on Earth, save at Kosrae. Nan Madol and Kosrae also make for unlikely cities at either island. Neither yielded any real evidence that they had actually been inhabited by large metropolitan populations. No burial grounds, tools (save those buried at Safonfok), or domestic items nor manufactured goods were ever found. And a total absence of adornment seems to disqualify both as a ceremonial center for the enactment of ritual activity. "As a construction," Ballinger wrote of Pohnpei's strange metropolis, "it was stark, strict and raw."

Perhaps Nan Madol was originally meant to be something so altogether different that its true purpose eludes us because it is so utterly unthinkable. Yet dramatic places such as these invariably reveal themselves, if only we are open to their own story undistracted by closedmindedness. Nan Madol is no exception. Surely, a secret must remain forever locked against anyone willing to use only a set number of scientifically acceptable keys. Just because the right one is not at hand does not mean it does not exist. Confronted by a mystery of Pohnpei's magnitude, investigators are justified in trying just about anything, however unorthodox, to understand it, if only because conventional scholars have failed to explain how Nan Madol was made and who built it, when, or for what purpose. They cannot even find the source for its construction stone.

The question of its location could be a first step toward some final answer: Why was such an obscure island, vastly remote from any other population centers, and too small to support a teeming city, chosen for what undoubtedly was a massive, complex construction project involving large numbers of workers and engineers in a concerted effort? Of the more than 500 islands of the Carolines, why were Pohnpei and Kosrae chosen for the construction of such important and expensive public works projects? Neither possesses anything to recommend it as a candidate for the important outpost of some highly organized society. Both, however, are unique in their position roughly halfway between Hawaii and the Philippines. After sweeping some 5,800 miles across the central Pacific from about twenty degrees longitude, the north Equatorial Current suddenly divides north and south between Kosrae and Pohnpei. The split is important because it generates severe storms when cold air is brought into contact with the warm waters of the Carolines.

"It is a meteorological fact that many of the typhoons in the northeast Pacific begin in the vicinity of Pohnpei," Childress points out. "The island itself is not usually hit by cyclones, since it is the place where cyclones begin." Could Pohnpei have been deliberately chosen by the builders of Nan Madol because they somehow appreciated the island's singular location? It is, at the very least, an intriguing coincidence that they elected to establish their unparalleled city at what just happened to be the safest spot in all the Pacific from its worst storms. A people with sufficient genius to loft twenty-five-ton stone logs at least thirty feet above a flinty coral base in the middle of the ocean; manipulate sixty-ton blocks into their walls; or excavate a network of tunnels running from the land down through a coral reef and under the sea to submarine caves might have likewise understood more about their environment than we are willing to give them credit for. If so, did the ancient inhabitants of this out-of-the-way, if favored, isle choose to settle there as a natural refuge from typhoons that otherwise ravaged the eastern Pacific? Or could they have had some other purpose for going to the immense trouble of organizing 250 million tons of quarried stone into a city of towers and canals?

Between them, Pohnpei and Kosrae create a 300-mile-long zone, a kind of nursery, in which typhoons are born and nurture the first stages of their power. They soon grow rapidly into monster tempests that ravage the Philippines each year, leaving widespread death and destruction behind. Until recently, they were thought to be the exclusive result of masses of cold air convectored into conflict with water's warmer surface temperatures. Mainstream meteorologists believe cyclones are produced during a three-step process by the initial intensity of a storm, temperature changes in the air it brings about, and subsequent heat exchange with the ocean. In the late twentieth century, however, an American inventor, Joseph Newman, wrote:

The major effect with respect to hurricanes is electromagnetic. For a hurricane to become or remain a hurricane, it does not depend solely upon the heat of the water over which it travels. Proof: The average temperature of the waters of the Gulf of Mexico, twenty miles off the Louisiana coast, is as follows:

- June, 82 Degrees F.
- August, 87 Degrees F.
- September, 82 Degrees F.
- October, 76 Degrees F.
- November, 66 Degrees F.

If what the weather experts said were true, the greatest number and most destructive hurricanes would always occur in July and August. Not so! Fact: The peak hurricane season is in September—not July or August. Even in 1984, I published a listing of the most destructive hurricanes ever recorded, which indicated this fact. September and October had more than three hundred per cent more hurricanes of greater destruction than did July and August. Even November (with a 66 Degree F. average water temperature) had eighty per cent as many hurricanes as had occurred in August with its 87 Degree F. water.

Newman is convinced that "the major, dominating factor in producing hurricanes is fundamentally electromagnetic in nature; heat is secondary. Understanding this fact can ultimately lead to our ability to control or even mitigate hurricanes."

Or was that "ability" already achieved, not in our time, certainly, but very long ago, on two remote islands in the eastern Pacific? Nan Madol and Insaru bracket the meteorological "nursery" where typhoons are born. Consider, too, that they are unique throughout the world for their millions of tons of magnetized basalt. If molten lava is properly subjected to rapid cooling, it solidifies into the very fine-grained prisms that characterize basalt, among the heaviest, hardest rocks on Earth. During its solidification process, iron filaments trapped in the cooling lava are so affected by the still very high, if declining, temperatures that they become magnetized.

Curious to learn of any magnetic anomalies Nan Madol's basalt logs might possess, a late 1980s explorer of the site slid his pocket compass across one of the massive walls. "The needle spun around and around," Childress recalled. His excitement attracted the attention of a visiting geologist. "It is normal for basalt to become magnetized like this as part of the cooling process," he said, "but it should be magnetized vertically. The needle should not spin like that. These stones are strangely magnetized!"

Nan Madol and Insaru were built almost entirely of magnetized basalt.

Pohnpei was a colonial holding of Kaiser Wilhelm's Germany until his defeat in the First World War, when the island was one of several crumbs that fell from the Western allies' victory table into the outstretched hand of imperial Japan. From 1919 over the next twenty years, archaeologists from Tokyo University conducted several exploratory dives around the island and more excavations at Nan Madol itself. Tragically, virtually all the material the Japanese collected and their extensive field reports were lost during the next world war. Their discovery of human skeletal remains belonging to a people taller than the native islanders has already been mentioned. The oversized bones were found in the complex's main structure, described by local guides as the House of the Dead.

Digging deeper beneath its stone floor, the Japanese made an even more spectacular find: a collection of large coffins made of platinum. On closer inspection, the eight-foot-long metal boxes did not appear like sarcophagi because of their lack of any funerary decoration. Archaeologists were further mystified to learn that the receptacles had been sealed watertight, although to what purpose could not be imagined, since the supposed coffins were empty. As particularly valuable property belonging to the imperial government that administered Pohnpei, they were apparently sent to Japan, where they vanished during the firebombing that almost totally incinerated Tokyo in 1944. But before that hideous catastrophe, additional sources of platinum and even silver bars were found at Nan Madol.

Due to their political isolation from most of the outside world during the 1930s, the Japanese shared their platinum discovery only as late as 1939 with Herbert Rittlinger, because he was visiting Nan Madol from Germany, an allied nation and fellow member of the anti-comintern Axis. Rittlinger was himself one of the most prominent travel writers of his time, with an international reputation for reliable, firsthand depiction, whose works—some of them, at least—are still in print, although the book about his travels through the Carolines, *The Measureless Ocean*, still awaits republication. In his accurate portrayal of the island and its ruins, the author reported that Japan's main exports of copra, mother-of-pearl, sago, and vanilla from Pohnpei during the interwar period were supplemented by shipments of platinum. "The natives' stories, encrusted with centuries-old legends, are probably exaggerated," he wrote skeptically of their Saudeleur myths. "But the finds of platinum on an island, where the rock contains no platinum, were and remain a very real fact."

Michael Sage, one of Childress's colleagues during their exploration of Nan Madol in the late 1980s, "looked into whether platinum had really been exported out of Pohnpei at the University of Indiana Library. It is difficult to get records of these islands in those times. I could not get any specific data on platinum, but I was able to ascertain that there was a big leap in precious metals exported out of the Caroline Islands in the time period just before the war." Sage's research is all the more remarkable because these precious minerals do not exist anywhere else throughout the Pacific. But why they should have been found only at this forsaken island suggests its ultimate mystery.

For an inhabited city, Nan Madol exhibited yet another anomalous feature. An islet known as Darong encloses a small artificial lake, its sides lined with nicely cut and fitted stone. Beneath Darong, a tunnel runs through the underlying coral reef, out into the open sea, for no apparent purpose. Fish presently swim through the tunnel and into its connecting man-made lake from the ocean outside, but this hardly seems to have been its original intention, and is more a consequence of neglect. Childress adds, "The pool was said also to contain a sacred eel with magical powers." Could these "magical powers" have belonged to an electric eel?

Pohnpei is geologically unstable, hardly a unique characteristic given the ubiquity of seismic activity across the whole Pacific. Nonetheless, tremors still occasionally ripple through the gaunt ramparts of Nan Madol, where ghostly lights allegedly encountered by the natives continue to be seen and feared. "The people believed," writes Childress, "that if one spent the entire night in the empty city, one would die, presumably killed by the ancestral spirits (or dying of fright!)." Or perhaps by something else.

What he calls "the strange light phenomenon" associated with the city is a very real, scientifically recognized event known as the Andes Glow. Although most commonly observed in the high peaks of South America, it is observed in many other parts of the world wherever tectonic pressures accumulate beneath heavy masses of crystalline rock, such as mountain granite. Seismicity squeezes the crystal, which transforms the geologic tension into electrical energy, just as old crystal radio receivers used to "jump a spark" when tightened in a vise. The result is known as piezoelectricity, the ability of certain crystals to generate voltage when under pressure. This released voltage physically manifests itself in a "corona discharge" of activated ions, usually appearing as an animated, illuminated cloud or haze of blue light dancing over a mountaintop prior to an earthquake, or at least signaling the onset of local seismic activity.

While the Andes glow is usually harmless, it sometimes takes the form of ball lightning, which has been known to burn and infrequently kill animals or humans in its proximity. Just before its first tremor at 3:42 A.M., when 650,000 people in Tangshan, China, died in the great earthquake of June 5, 1976, the *New York Times* reported that "multi-hued lights, mainly red and white, were seen up to two hundred miles away. Leaves on many trees were burned to a crisp, and glowing vegetables were scorched on one side, as if by a fire-ball." So too the corona discharge's luminous cloud or mist is more often spooky than dangerous, although it also has been known to suddenly coalesce into less nebulous, brighter concentrations of light as a reaction to increased tectonic stress.

In view of their island's geologic instability, capped by Nan Madol's 250 tons of magnetized basalt, the "ghost lights" reported there by generations of Pohnpeians into the twenty-first century are probably truthful eyewitness accounts of the Andes Glow phenomenon. These sightings cannot be written off simply as examples of superstitious hallucination, because they have been made by outsiders unaware of the phenomenon. Childress was told by a 1970s veteran of the Peace Corps that the American volunteer was gazing toward Nan Madol from his porch at nearby Temwen Island after dark when he saw a strange, glowing object about the size of a basketball moving through the ruins. The following day, he challenged his class of elementary school students: "You'll never guess what I saw last night at Nan Madol." They cried out in unison, "You saw the light!"

About sixty years before, the German governor of Pohnpei insisted on spending a night alone amid the ruins, despite native warnings. His lifeless body was found next morning, although the cause of death could not be ascertained. Corpses of people killed by static discharge occasionally exhibit no burns or external indications whatsoever, a case in point being an unusual victim of the 1871 Chicago fire. A man had been caught between two conflagrations that generated so much energy as they approached each other that he was electrocuted before the flames could touch him. In fact, they were blown apart by the force of the blast. While the pocket watch in his vest had melted, there was not a mark on his body. Far more examples—ten-thousandfold—were recorded in the firestorms let loose by Allied bombers on the German city of Hamburg during World War II.

Pulling together all these seemingly diverse, even disparate elements could reveal Nan Madol's true identity. It begins with a leading theme repeating itself through Pohnpei's stark ruins: electricity. At Nan Madol and Insaru, tons of magnetized basalt by the millions were constructed into great enclosures, towers, walls, rooms, and canals. Their artificial lakes were stocked with what appear to have been electric eels. One species, *Electrophorus electricus,* can produce up to 650 volts. Perhaps all of Nan Madol's artificial pools, lakes, and supposed canals were originally meant to be filled with thousands of these creatures. They would have constituted a potent, if irregular, power source that may have somehow interfaced with Pohnpei's geo-piezoelectricity in ways related to the watertight "coffins" found by Japanese archaeologists at the House of the Dead. The platinum from which these receptacles were fashioned has a high melting point, possessing an extreme electrical resistivity that makes it essential for the manufacture of electrodes subjected to intense heat. Platinum is used for electrical contacts and sparking points because it resists both high temperatures and the chemical attack of electric arcs. In other words, the installation of platinum in a powerful electric field tends to dampen the accumulation of more energy than can be contained by a conductive device or instrument and thus prevents it from either melting or exploding.

Finding any platinum—let alone prehistoric artifacts made of this scarce mineral, more valuable than gold—at Nan Madol is all the more remarkable, because it was not even known to exist until the Spanish mathematician Antonio de Ulloa and a British assayer, Charles Wood, collected the first recognizable samples from South America in 1741. Yet someone on an obscure island in the western Pacific was working in sufficient quantities to build a series of coffin-sized receptacles thousands of years ago. Moreover, platinum is not native to Pohnpei, nor anywhere else in the Carolines. Its nearest source lies 2,200 miles southwest, in Borneo, to which the Saudeleurs undoubtedly sailed to obtain the precious metal they apparently valued so highly.

Then there is Nan Madol's ghost light, apparently a variant of the Andes Glow phenomenon generated by seismic pressures still occasionally at work on the great conductive piles of magnetized basalt. As Childress's geologist acquaintance discovered with his pocket compass, the prismatic logs were "strangely magnetized." Their magnetic field should have stood vertical to the plane. Instead, it spun his compass needle, indicating that the stones' magnetic field had been somehow reconfigured into a corkscrew pattern. What or who could have effected such a drastic change, and why? In any case, transforming the basalt's naturally vertical magnetic field into a spiral would amplify the power of any piezoelectric discharge by swinging it around in a narrowing, tightening circuit, then focusing the beam of its concentrated corona discharge skyward.

What, then, is being described here? The mere suggestion of some ancient technology superior to our own boggles the modern mind, but Nan Madol nonetheless appears to represent just that. Let us reconsider its unique location, where eastern Pacific typhoons originate, and its no less coincidental arrangement with a practically identical companion city, Insaru, on the island of Kosrae. Tempests are born within the 300 miles separating these two sites. Meteorologists now recognize an essential electromagnetic component in tropical storms and believe such dangerous weather phenomena can be mitigated or even prevented in the first stages of development by somehow diffusing the electromagnetic core of a hurricane before it gains strength.

Joseph Newman was cited earlier for his convincing evidence on behalf of electromagnetism as the most important element in tropical storms, an observation supported by a growing number of scientists, beginning with the renowned inventor Nikola Tesla. As long ago as the late nineteenth century, Tesla discovered that our planet pulsates with an electrical current in the ELF (extremely low frequency) range. He theorized that 10 Hz of ELF beams bounced off the ionosphere, the atmosphere's highest layer, would initiate electron resonance about seventy miles up, thereby generating a dielectric breakdown over storm clouds, shorting out their electromagnetic core and diffusing their energy. He called for erecting colossal magnifying transmitters acting as global generators that would create the same electromagnetic circuit functions found in severe thunderstorms.

Tesla firmly believed this process could stop hurricanes shortly after they began to form, and he appealed to his financial backers for the construction of an electrical power station. Returning to New York in 1900 from the successful demonstration of the world's first radio-controlled model boat, he undertook construction of his most ambitious project. With a $150,000 advance from financier J. P. Morgan, Tesla began working on a huge tower to ricochet 10 Hz of ELF beams off the ionosphere and down against brewing storm clouds. In the middle of his weather-control project, however, a financial crisis struck the U.S. economy, and Morgan suddenly withdrew his promised support, leaving the great tower half-finished. Its demolition for lack of funding marked the turning point in Tesla's life. On January 7, 1943, Nikola Tesla passed away alone and penniless in a shabby single room in a low-rent hotel in New York City.

But his dream of weather modification lived on long after his death. In the April 1969 issue of *Spectrum,* published by the prestigious Institute of Electrical and Electronics Engineers, aeronautical engineer Seymour Tilson pointed out, "Workers in the fields of atmospheric electricity and cloud physics have accumulated sufficient evidence to suggest that electric fields, forces and changes in the Earth's lower atmosphere play a critical role—perhaps the critical role—in the development and behavior of clouds that produce precipitation. This, in turn, suggests that manipulation of the electrical properties in clouds may someday provide the long-sought key to modification of weather by man."

Eighteen years later, Dr. Bernard J. Eastlund, a physicist with the Atlantic Richfield Oil Company (ARCO), was issued a patent for a weather-control design, which, according to a National Public Radio broadcast of September 6, 1987, "uses an Earth-based power source to create electro-magnetic radio waves and focus them way up into the atmosphere." The March issue of *Omni* magazine the following year told how Dr. Eastlund "calculated that once the radio waves reached the ionosphere, they would interact powerfully with the charged particles trapped there. The result would be a magnetic phenomenon known as the 'mirror force.' Essentially what would happen is that a huge section of the charged atmosphere would be pushed upward and outward from Earth by this electro-magnetic force powerful enough to diffuse a hurricane."

Dr. Eastlund's design was incorporated into an enormous U.S. government project, the High Frequency Active Aural Research Program, better known as HAARP. Set up in Alaska, it consists of a thirty-acre field of antenna towers beaming powerful radio signals at the ionosphere, ostensibly for weather research. Some observers suspect more nefarious intentions, however—namely, manipulation of the weather for military purposes and/or mass psychological warfare. They are even more alarmed by a similar federal government project, the Ground Wave Emergency Network, or GWEN, whose official purpose during its construction in the 1980s was to maintain defense communications in the event of a nuclear attack on North America. Like HAARP, GWEN operates a tower array for beaming very low ELF transmissions against our planet's upper atmosphere.

These efforts aimed at controlling the weather generally and hurricanes specifically—from Tesla's half-finished attempt to HAARP and GWEN—all employed towers served by electromagnetic power plants. They seem like modern versions of ancient Nan Madol's own massive towers with their spiral-magnetized basalt connected to artificial pools of electric eels and energized by tectonic pressures beneath Pohnpei. If, like them, the entire complex was actually an enormous conduit attracting dangerously potent energies from the earth and sky, it would have needed something to damp down both geological and meteorological forces to prevent them from destroying the whole establishment in a flash of electrical violence. Hence, the anomalous appearance of platinum "coffins" buried at the center of the site.

Nan Madol was never a city, certainly not in any ordinary sense of the word, but a power station undoubtedly constructed by the Pohnpeians' ancestors, who supplied the labor but under the direction of the foreign Saudeleurs. Indeed, it looks nothing like any other inhabitable metropolis in the world. Instead, its starkly unadorned features and complete lack of social facilities suggest an energy plant created for something vastly different from ritual activities performed at a ceremonial center.

This is how it may have worked: As a tropical storm entered its early stages of formation in the 300-mile-long zone from Pohnpei to Kosrae, it initiated an intensifying resonance with many millions of tons of complementary magnetized basalt on the islands below. When the would-be typhoon grew to a certain magnitude, its own inflated electromagnetic energies were attracted to and interfaced with those over which it passed. The receptor stations at Nan Madol and Insaru formed a polarity not unlike the positive and negative ends of a dry-cell storage battery. At some point of maximum energy concentration within the borders of this polarity, a mutual exchange of electromagnetic discharges occurred, in effect "shorting out" the storm by causing Tesla's dielectric breakdown in its electromagnetic core. The clouds would suddenly rain themselves out in a downpour, then dissipate.

In short, Nan Madol, in tandem with Insaru, was a weather-modification project purposely built to prevent tropical storms from becoming typhoons. No other characterization can account for its fortuitous location where cyclones are born; its many million tons of unnaturally magnetized basalt; platinum "coffins" acting as electrical dampeners; or seismically induced ghost lights.

But why should anyone have been interested in controlling the weather so long ago? The answer lies 1,750 miles east of Pohnpei, at Luzon, in the Philippines. One hundred fifty-five miles north of Manila, at 4,000 feet above sea level, is found what many visitors describe as the Eighth Wonder of the World, in scope still the grandest engineering feat ever undertaken by humankind, although scarcely recognized and little appreciated by outsiders. A growing, living stairway rises continuously and unbroken to 3,000 feet from the valley floor of Ifugao Province in a genuinely stupendous series of artificial plateaus, their vertical distance from bottom to top exceeding the height of the world's tallest skyscraper. The Banaue rice terraces span 49,400 acres along the Cordillera mountain range. If laid end to end, the paddies would form a line halfway around the Earth. Yet little more than 50 percent of the original agricultural network still exists.

During its heyday, when intact and complete, the rice terraces yielded phenomenal food production, not only because of their vast scale, but due to ingeniously efficient irrigation as well. Widespread neglect, inferior replacement watering techniques, pollution, and growing numbers of shantytowns squatting on the paddies, however, have forced UNESCO officials to shift Banaue from their list of World Heritage sites to the List of World Heritage in Danger. At the currently accelerating rate of abuse, they do not expect the Philippines' Eighth Wonder of the World to survive the twenty-first century.

Who built it eludes archaeologists, because agriculture of such a huge, organized magnitude cannot be associated with any contemporary culture. While ancestors of Luzon's indigenous population are assumed, minus any real evidence, to have painstakingly carved them out of the harsh terrain using primitive hand tools, today's Ifugao natives demonstrate a declining proficiency and even interest in the terraces. Moreover, local oral traditions recount that their ancestors did not conceive or initiate the world's foremost agricultural project, although they did build it at the behest of "powerful sorcerers" who arrived from over the sea in the dim past, a story similar to foundation accounts of alien magicians responsible for the creation of Nan Madol. But the two archaeological sites have more in common than myth. They share the same carbon-14 time frame of 200 B.C., although this period was more likely some cultural surge that took place simultaneously in the Philippines and the Carolines, and does not necessarily, or even probably, represent a foundation date for civilization in Luzon and Pohnpei.

A closer link between the two sites, as different as they are from each other—one industrial, the other agricultural—is the colossal scope of their execution. Nan Madol's 250 million tons of magnetized basalt and Banaue's original 100,000 acres of farm seem like expressions of the same sorcerer culture that preferred building on such an immense scale. If both sites did indeed belong to a common society, their complementary relationship becomes clearer. Five thousand or more years ago, the demands of local nutrition could have required only a fraction of the crops yielded by the Philippine rice terraces, which appear to have been the main source of food production for a very much larger population. Although Luzon's mountainous slopes represented an ideal location for the establishment of such an important agrarian enterprise, it was vulnerable to the frequent ravages of typhoons. Thus, to protect the national breadbasket of some greater civilization, the engineering genius responsible for Banaue likewise built a weather-control station in the Caroline Islands.

Clearly, it is no longer functioning, because typhoons continue to plague the western Pacific, including the Philippines, with devastating effect. As recently as November 2004, a typhoon slammed into Luzon, killing 4,000 people, many of them victims of catastrophic landslides. Today, only an occasional ghost light flitting amid the toppled stones indicates that long unused tectonic energies are still active at Pohnpei. Nan Madol is, after all, a ruin, its original forty- or fifty-foot towers reduced to perhaps half their intended height, while much of Insaru was dismantled more than 100 years ago. Although their purpose seems clear enough, we do not know precisely how it was achieved. Lacking any equivalent of our modern energy sources, their builders may have used thousands of electric eels to "jump the spark," as it were, to initiate the larger electromagnetic process. Old fragments of burned eel occasionally scraped off the stones of Nan Madol might not be, as archaeologists suppose, remnants of a feast cooked in some Saudeleur's oven, but instead pieces of seared flesh from eels that exploded during power surges or energy overloads, as undoubtedly happened from time to time, particularly when exceptionally powerful tropical storms were involved. It is no wonder that native Pohnpeians still regard Nan Madol as a House of Death!

"The first and most obvious question to be asked about Nan Madol is: Why ninety two artificial islets?" asks that encyclopedist of anomalous archaeology, William Corliss. "Ample terra firma was available to the Pohnpeians. We cannot answer this question, so a minor anomaly can be declared here." But perhaps it is not so minor, after all, if the man-made islets were component parts of a prehistoric electromagnetic complex that has not been duplicated since. An ancient technology more advanced than our own on an obscure island in the remote western Pacific, of all places, far removed from the traditional centers of civilization, is probably too much even for unconventional scholars to accept. They might argue that any society that achieved such a high level of material sophistication would have required many centuries of previous development, for which there is no physical evidence. Yet Nan Madol and Insaru stand relative to Banaue through their strategic location in the zone where tropical storms are formed. In truth, these three colossal sites offer abundant physical proof for the existence of a lost civilization whose leaders deeply understood and applied the laws of nature to feed millions of their people and protect their food supply from natural disasters. W. S. Cerve, author of the classic *Lemuria: The Lost Continent of the Pacific,* might have been referring to Luzon's great rice terraces when he wrote, "In botany [the Lemurians] were so expert that agriculture with them became like the expert work that is shown in a botanical garden."

All of this is far beyond parallel with any ancient culture known anywhere on Earth, but is indicative of everything known or suspected about the Pacific Motherland. If the origins of this legendary place did indeed go back to some preglacial epoch, its inhabitants would have been afforded the centuries or millennia necessary for long-term developments of all kinds. According to James Churchward, the foremost investigator of his kind in the early twentieth century, "At the time of the destruction of Mu, the Motherland, which occurred about 10,000 B.C., the sciences which were then known and practiced, were the development of over one hundred thousand years of study and experience, if we date their commencement from a stated time." One hundred thousand years may be far too long a preliminary history, even for the Lemurians, who alone appear capable of having achieved such large-scale public works projects. Even so, people were no more intelligent or ignorant in the past than they are today. Doubtless every generation, then as now, produced its own share of geniuses. Given the proper stimulus and more time than our civilization has known, what was to prevent them from advancing farther than ourselves along the path of technology?

As Cerve credibly surmised, the Lemurians

> had outgrown any earlier beliefs that their primitive forebears might have had that storms and strifes, cataclysms and destructive forces, were sent by the gods of evil or by a loving god expressing his wrath. They looked upon all of the processes of Nature as constructive, even when temporarily destructive, and considered these as established laws of evolution having been created by a loving god at the beginning of time. I have already intimated that scientific knowledge constituted the religion of the Lemurians, inasmuch as a fundamental principle of their understanding was that God, or the creator of all things, revealed to man all knowledge as a process of evolving man to the same degree of understanding as possessed by God. Therefore, the acquirement of knowledge was considered the acquirement of spiritual attunement, and growth of knowledge was looked upon reverentially, instead of as a commercial asset.

Hence the Lemurians' observation and subsequent application of natural laws in their creation of a weather-control project.

The "flying dragon" summoned by Olisihpa and Olsohpa, as depicted in native myth, was how a preliterate people remembered an otherwise unfathomable construction technology the Lemurian builders used to raise Nan Madol. So too Pohnpei's ancestral natives may have been witnesses to the ancient application of Einstein's unified field theory, when the great basalt stones were floated through the air into place by getting them to resonate at the frequency of gravity, something twenty-first-century scientists regard as at least theoretically possible.

After completion, the power stations of Nan Madol and Insaru awaited the meteorological drama high above. When the first tropical storm began to coalesce in the atmosphere between Pohnpei and Kosrae, its electromagnetic field interfaced with perhaps an original half-billion tons of prismatic basalt assembled on both islands. Great, blinding arcs of energy flashed from sea to sky, causing a short in the tempest's electromagnetic core. Deprived of this natural generator, its clouds yielded their accumulated precipitation in a downpour, then dissipated harmlessly into the west. Farmers at work among the rice terraces of faraway Banaue would be allowed to tend their crops unthreatened by typhoons. Agriculture had been saved by science.

This high-technology interpretation of archaeological evidence in the Carolines is not without support from native tradition. Twenty-two hundred miles away to the southeast, on the small, remote New Hebrides island of Vao, are a number of standing stones erected in the ancient past by an ancestral people possessing abundant *mana*, or spiritual power. The prehistoric monoliths have been hewn from andesite, a form of granite infused with quartz and capable of generating the same piezoelectric effect produced by Nan Madol's magnetized basalt. Childress cites archaeologists at New York City's American Museum of Natural History to the effect that Vao's standing stones, "linked to ancestor rituals and used in weather magic, are thought to represent the spirits that control the weather." Clearly, the indigenous residents preserve something of the fundamental meteorological purpose originally associated with the andesite pillars.

If the physical means by which the energy complexes at Pohnpei and Kosrae came into being are controversial, no less so is the source for their stone. "The Lelu ruins of Insaru," Childress points out, "must contain several million tons, at least." And certainly much more before the site was partially demolished around 1900. Local guides describe an outcrop at the southern end of Kosrae, at Utwe, as the location from which the stones were removed for construction. "However, no evidence of extensive quarrying has been found at Utwe," Childress writes, "and the amount of material used is so enormous that the entire basalt outcrop would have had to have been dismantled."

The same problem occurs at Nan Madol. Its builders supposedly got their construction material from Sokehs Rock, near Kolonia, and from the western side of the island. But neither location was much quarried, certainly not nearly enough to supply the 250 million tons that went into the making of Nan Madol, which consumed an entire mountain of basalt. Moreover, Pohnpei's steeply mountainous, thickly forested jungle interior prevented removal of any quarried materials overland to the opposite side of the island, where the power station was built. As mentioned earlier, rafting twenty-five-ton basalt monoliths around the coast to the construction site would have been utterly impossible, unless the Saudeleurs operated some super-freighting vessel commensurate with the rest of their apparent high technology.

Gene Ashby, a spokesman for the Community College of Micronesia, was cited by Childress as having stated that no one knows from whence came all the stone that went into building Nan Madol. In truth, the quarry or quarries have never been found, at either Kosrae or Pohnpei, or anywhere else throughout the vast Pacific. The source for their many millions of tons of prismatic basalt has vanished, most probably during one of the several geological convulsions that sank the lost Motherland or one of her associated islands. Given no other conceivable alternative, we may not be wrong in concluding that the great stones erected at Pohnpei and Kosrae were brought from Mu, where they were quarried and removed by the same sorcerers commissioned to build a weather-control center in the Carolines.

As described earlier, the ghost light associated with these stones appears in many other parts of the world where massive quantities of crystalline rock respond to tectonic forces. It should come as no surprise, then, that the same luminous effect occurs throughout the Pacific, with its seismically active Ring of Fire. But Chinese tradition specifically identifies a sunken realm, referred to as P'eng-lai, the Dragon Palace, under a remote island in the Eastern Sea. Dragons were mythic personifications of telluric power, all the subterranean energies that course beneath the surface of the Earth. Hence, mountains were regarded as the spiky backs or spines of the terrestrial dragon. The Dragon Palace, therefore, was a place of extraordinary Earth-power. A bright red light was said to some-times rise burning just above P'eng-lai, illuminating both sea and sky for great distances in all directions.

The Chinese tradition appears to identify P'eng-lai with Pohnpei as still standing above a sunken city otherwise known as Mu or Lemuria. This characterization calls to mind the underwater pillars and delib-erately oriented boulders discovered around the base of Nan Madol, which Churchward likewise associated with the sunken civilization. Quoting from the *Ramayana,* he told how the Caroline Islands lie "one moon's journey towards the rising sun [from Burma]," where, accord-ing to the Naacal tablets and the great Indian epic's fourth-century-B.C. author, Valmiki, "the Motherland of Man once stood, the spot whence came the first settlers in Burma and India." Churchward claimed to have translated the story of Mu from some Hindu monastery records known as the Naacal tablets while he was a British Army officer serving in India during the 1870s.

References to seismically active Mu, with its resultant Andes glow, found their Japanese rendition in a shining "red mass resembling the rising sun" that occasionally hovered over a great kingdom known as Horaizan in the Eastern Sea. A related story told how a priest living beside a "dragon hole" saw a goddess of fire rise in the air over Mount Mu-robu, thereby connecting the piezoelectric phenomenon with the sunken Motherland itself. To be sure, the Chinese P'eng-lai, Japan's Horaizan, or the Carolines' Katau Peidi or Kanamwayso, described in native tradition as the Saude-leurs' sunken homeland from which they brought civilization to Pohnpei, could only have been Mu. Their first voyage to the island was described in native tradition as a *uaii ala,* from which the modern *wawaila* derives. It means to go secretly or stealthily, strongly indicating, according to Nan Madol historian David Hanlon, "escape or flight from some oppressive circumstance," perhaps from the natural catastrophe overwhelming their Lemurian homeland. More likely, the oppressive circumstance was the threat posed by recurring typhoons, which the installation at Nan Madol was meant to prevent. In any case, its antediluvian credentials are more than inferential. Although it has no correspondence outside Kosrae, related sites and structures found elsewhere across Pohnpei were built in a stark, rectilinear form associated with monumental building styles at Mu. The ceremonial platforms of Alauso, Diadi, and Kiti Rock, together with Nan Dawas itself, are examples of Lemurian public architecture.

Numerous local place-names are themselves remnants of a pre-flood civilization that left its faded if indelible imprint at both Pohnpei and Luzon. Fronting the Banaue rice terraces stands Mount A-mu-yao. Its revealing name is made yet more significant by the Ifugao natives, who revere Mount A-mu-yao as the place where their ancestors landed in a canoe after escaping the Great Deluge. Wigan and his sister, Bugan, were the only survivors from an unusual period of extreme drought imme-diately prior to the catastrophe, which was accompanied by a sudden darkness (caused by volcanic eruptions). The association of this founda-tion myth with a mountain incorporating the name of the lost Mother-land is remarkable confirmation of primal Lemurian influences long ago at work in the Philippines.

Just forty miles northeast of Mount A-mu-yao is the town of Ga-mu, while A-mu-lung is another fifty miles north. All of them are near the agricultural center Nan Madol was evidently engineered to protect. Interestingly, incorporation of *mu* in the identification of either a moun-tain or a town is found nowhere else throughout the Philippines. In fact, the lost relationship between Banaue and Nan Madol is wonderfully preserved through common place-names they shared in ancient times. For example, Patapat is a sacred hill near the southeastern coast of Pohnpei, where it was associated with ritual practices instituted by the Saudeleurs. Not only does Patapat reappear in the Philippines, but it is likewise the name of a holy hill not far from northern Luzon's Tolnagan River, in the vicinity of the colossal rice terraces.

On Pohnpei's southeastern coast and virtually adjacent to Patapat is a town named after one of the Saudeleurs. Known as Kalongavar, it is an obvious variation of Kalongalong, a town in Mindanao. While these lingering place-names define an undeniable relationship between the Philippines and distant Nan Madol, the Caroline island appears to have exerted its influence even more. Tanataman is both another sacred hill at Pohnpei and what has been described by the Hungarian scholar Dr. Vamos-Toth Bator as the oldest jungle in the world, in Malaysia.

Several features of Pohnpei's ruins are themselves traditionally identified with discernibly Lemurian toponyms, such as Mupt, a rectangular structure near the southwest side of the site. The next building over, to its west, is abutted by a sea entrance known as Mupteniulli. The east side is fronted by Muptalap, a sea wall, and a land partition, Pon-mu-asanap. A curving paved road in the northeast forms a precinct called Pon mu-itak. Nanlong, an islet lying off Pohnpei's southern coast, features an archaeological site referred to as Nanparad Mu-tok. These are certainly hybrid denominations, Pohnpeian inflections of original Lemurian versions modified by native influences, which further mutated the original Mu into a *mw* sound—as in Madolenihmw, Nan Madol's harbor bay, and Kitamw, another important landing point—to accommodate the language considerations of an indigenous Carolines population. The outermost wall protecting the entire complex from battering ocean waves and undermining currents is Nan Mwoluhsei, "where the voyage stops," a reference to Nan Madol's only entrance from the sea. Its Lemurian implications are further underscored by native accounts, which relate that Nan Mwoluhsei is likewise a gate that leads to the sunken city of Kahnimweiso.

Perhaps the most apparent linguistic reference to Lemuria at Nan Madol was found at the artificial islet of Pahn Kadira. Native lore describes it as the spiritual hub of the entire complex, where the most important decisions were made by the Saudeleurs. Even today, locals refer to Pahn Kadira as "the city of proclamation" or "the forbidden city." It is the site for a temple known as Nan Kieil Mwahu, where the Earth Mother in the form of Nan Sapwe, "dear land," was worshipped. *Ahu,* in the language of far distant Easter Island, means altar or altar platform, and seems here to reference the same concept—an altar for Mu.

An identical dialectical shift is apparent in a dynasty instituted by the foreign king who, according to Pohnpei tradition, invaded the island and deposed the last lord of Deleur. In replacing the old regime with his own dynasty, known as the Nahnmwarkis, Isokelekel showed his

respect for the superior culture of the overthrown Saudeleurs by deliber-
ately intermarrying his own family with them, as evidenced in the mixed
Saudeleur names of many Nahnmwarkis, such as Luhk en Mwei Maur,
Luhk en Mwer, and Luhk en Mwei—all apparent variations on Mu.

In a clear derivation from the name Lemuria, Limwetu is remembered in native traditions of the *keilahn aio,* "the other side of yester-
day," as a woman who reluctantly settled with her children on Pohnpei
after leaving her distant homeland. Indeed, the very epoch describing
the construction of Nan Madol is referred to in local oral accounts as
the Mwehin Kawa, or building time, a period of deep antiquity. Most
significant of all, the islet on which Nan Madol is itself located was
originally known as Te-Mu-en, and the very center of the complex is still
referred to as Usenamw.

Linguistic parallels persist in the Carolines 430 miles northwest of
Pohnpei, in the Hall Islands, at a dot on the map known evocatively as
Mu-riio. Nor does Nan Madol's counterpart at Kosrae lack Lemurian
names. Rising 1,951 feet from the center of Lelu Province is Mount
Mu-tunte. Just north along the coast from the archaeological zone at
Insaru is Mu-tuneneah, an artificial channel overgrown with mangroves.
Opposite Insaru, on the northwest side of Kosrae, lies the small island of
Mu-taniel, off Okat Harbor. Like the ruins they identify, these designa-
tions still whisper the name of that ingenious people who so very long
ago recognized and worked with the elementary forces of nature. In so
doing, the Lemurians created a world of social abundance and scientific
greatness throughout the vast Pacific.

While physical evidence for their technological eminence survives
only in the spectacular public works project at Nan Madol, lingering
Pohnpei traditions still speak of other, not unrelated accomplishments
that our own industrialized civilization has either recently achieved or
seems about to achieve. Levitation of the twenty-ton basalt stones to
thirty or more feet with the assistance of a "flying dragon" was discussed
earlier. In another story from the days of its construction, a man named
Kideumanien flew into Nan Madol from the province of Sokehs, on the
opposite side of Pohnpei along the west coast, piloting a magical rock.

Arriving over the building site, he commanded the colossal megalith to hover in midair, then carefully lowered it into position to form the outer foundation wall at a section of the complex facing the sea known as Madol Powe, as protection against the erosional forces of wave action. To achieve this aerial engineering feat, Kideumanien uttered a spell remembered as the *Kindakan Nan Mwoluhsei*; again, the root name Mu applied to an example of ancient achievement at Nan Madol.

Additional native accounts tell of a magical pool, known as the Peirot, on the artificial islet of Peikapw. In what seems like an ancient Micronesian combination of security cameras and satellite television, the Peirot allowed Saudeleur overlords to observe whatever was taking place on Pohnpei or anywhere else in the world.

What were the origins of such myths? They are utterly unlike any others found throughout the Pacific. Could they have actually been occasioned by a lost high technology, higher even, in some respects, than our own? If so, then the Lemurians still have something useful to teach us, particularly if interpretations of Nan Madol as a weather-modification center are correct. Hurricanes and typhoons annually decimate many parts of the world, taking lives and destroying property. Perhaps a closer study of the strange ruins at Pohnpei and Kosrae may reveal the ancient secrets of a lost technology that might likewise save us from the recurring cycles of natural disaster.

TWO

Naval of the World

In Easter Island, the past is the present. It is impossible to escape from it. The inhabitants of today are less real than the men who have gone. The shadows of the departed builders still possess the land.

KATHERINE ROUTLEDGE,
EARLY-TWENTIETH-CENTURY
INVESTIGATOR OF EASTER ISLAND

On the other side of the Pacific Ocean, some 2,500 miles southeast of Nan Madol, lie the remains of another, even more enigmatic but entirely different civilization. While Easter Island's gaunt statues, known as *moai*, have been world famous for more than 200 years, its towering giants are mute witnesses to a prehistory of greater scope than most outsiders realize. Unlike Pohnpei, the island has long been and still is the focus of international scholars intent on reconstructing its past, primarily because Easter Island is an anomaly in Polynesia, not only for its monumental stonework, but also for its unique written language. Despite decades of research, however, archaeologists are still far from solving its fundamental mysteries. They are unable, for example, to convincingly explain how a material culture far beyond anything comparable in the Pacific could have arisen on just one tiny island more isolated from the outside world than any other place on Earth. The nearest inhabited landfall is Pitcairn Island, 1,242 miles to the west. In the east, nothing interrupts 2,485 miles of open water to the South American coast.

Surprisingly, the geologic provenance of Easter Island is better understood than its human origins. The island was born about 100,000 years ago, when three erupting volcanoes conjoined their disgorged lava flows to form a seven-mile-wide, fifteen-and-a-half mile-long triangle of territory. Although volcanism came to a permanent halt shortly thereafter, the resultant soil was rich and receptive to windblown seeds, which sprouted into a thick forest of toromiro and palm trees covering most of the island. Its cultural transformation came long after, when huge, finely constructed platforms, known as *ahu*, stood along the shore, surmounted by sculpted giants, their backs to the sea. So many more of the colossi littered the interior, all the way up to the lip of Rano Raraku, an extinct volcano from which they were quarried, visitors might have concluded that they had arrived at a center for the mass production of monumental statuary. Atop Rano Kao, another volcano, was Orongo, a ceremonial center of stone buildings with upper vaults built into corbeled roofs, utterly dissimilar to the fragile pole-and-thatch hovels otherwise found throughout Polynesia, but not unlike the false arches found at Uxmal and other ceremonial cities of the Maya in faraway Yucatán.

Elsewhere across Easter Island, twenty-foot-tall round towers reared amid cyclopean walls of unmortared masonry, their prodigious blocks so trimmed and perfectly fitted that a knife blade could not be inserted between them. There was a profusion of rock art in petroglyphs depicting fish, spirals, a variety of geometric designs, and the ubiquitous birdman, a cult figure without parallel in the vast Pacific. A horticultural economy prospered in bananas, pineapples, coconuts, mulberry trees, sugarcane, taro, and yam from as far away as southwest Asia in the west. *Trumfetta semi-triloba* trees, sweet potatoes, bottle gourds, and chili peppers were brought from South America in the east. Included in the native diet was a domesticated chicken of unknown provenance, remarkable—before its extinction through interbreeding with modern European varieties—for the strange blue eggs it laid.

The island had been allegedly pioneered by 300 long-eared *Hanau-eepe*, a fair-complected people who distended their ear lobes to distinguish themselves from other peoples. They alternately referred to their new home as Rapa Nui—great Rapa, or "great land of the sun-god"—and Te-Pito-te-Henua, or "navel of the world." But 300 settlers were far too few to carry out their grandiose plans for rebuilding civilization, so they imported Polynesians from among other islands to the west. These were the short-eared Hanau-momokeo, who carried out the labor directed by their long-eared superiors. For 200 years, in a period of social harmony remembered as the *Karau-Karu*, the *Hanau-momokeo* faithfully supplied the muscle-power needed to raise Rapa Nui's monumental statues and imposing walls.

Toward the close of this golden age, however, the class distinction insisted upon by the aristocratic Long Ears began to grate on proletarian sensitivities. Ill will was exacerbated by an escalating food crisis brought about by denuding the forests for *moai* production, which demanded tree trunks for rollers and vines for hawsers. A violent period known as the Huri-moai, or overthrowing of the statues, ensued. The colossi were toppled and social violence swept the island. In their last defense, the embattled Long Ears frantically excavated a great breastwork, the Poike Ditch, as a kind of Maginot Line against the rising tide of insurrection. But their attempt was no less a failure than its mid-twentieth-century counterpart. Waves of discontented Short Ears poured over the Poike Ditch, slaughtering every Hanau-eepe in a paroxysm of genocidal cannibalism.

These dire events must have transpired sometime between 1770, when a Spanish census of Rapa Nui counted 3,000 residents, and just four years later, when Captain James Cook, the famous English navigator, stepped ashore. The island had been discovered and named by Jacob Rogeveen on Easter Sunday 1722 when the Dutch admiral reported that the natives lit fires at the bases of their moai as part of a sun-worshipping ceremony, although production of the colossal idols appeared to have ceased many years before. By the time Captain Cook arrived, all the statues had been deliberately overthrown, the Long Ears exterminated, and human existence collapsed into social disarray. He counted only 600 or

700 men and fewer than thirty women grubbing among the ruins. Squalor and famine were rampant.

Beginning in the early nineteenth century, slave raids and the introduction of smallpox reduced the population still further, to just 111 survivors. These pitiful souls were easy converts to Christianity during 1868, followed shortly thereafter with their annexation by Chile, which leased out the former Navel of the World to sheep raisers from Tahiti. Dr. Thor Heyerdahl's epic voyage in a balsa raft from South America across the eastern Pacific and subsequent publication of his international best-seller *Aku Aku* during the 1950s sparked outside interest in Easter Island and an influx of tourism that continues to financially improve the inhabitants' standard of living.

Heyerdahl's intention was to show that its long-eared civilizers originated from the high cultures of preconquest Peru. Indeed, the aristocrats there were distinguished by their distended earlobes, the same practice employed by Easter Island's Hanau-eepe elite. He pointed out that Easter Island's cyclopean walls are virtually identical to the massive ramparts of Cuzco, the Inca capital, down to the mysterious knobs or protuberances and multiangled design of a readily recognizable style. Even the names—both Te-Pito-te-Henua and Cuzco—mean "navel of the world." Easter Island statues harked back to much earlier Bolivian correspondents at the pre-Inca city of Tiahuanaco. While their identification is not as close as comparisons with Cuzco's stone walls, similarity between the moai and the Andean colossi is apparent. The atypical Easter Island statue of a man squatting on his haunches was duplicated at Tiahuanaco's Poqothia Pampa. A Malanggan memorial figure from the New Ireland Province in Papua New Guinea is portrayed playing a large set of panpipes, the foremost musical instrument of the Inca.

Uru is a Polynesian place-name associated with an ancestral homeland; it is also the name of a pre-Inca tribe that once dominated the shores of Lake Titicaca, from which the totora reed was brought to Easter Island. Uru-keu, the Polynesian forebears, were portrayed in legend as golden-haired demigods; Ure was an Easter Island god who "brought fresh air from far away." The sweet potato was also native to South America, where it was known as *cumar* in Quechua, the language spoken by the Inca. In distant New Zealand, the natives called it *kumara;* it was referred to as *umara* in Tahiti and was replanted at Easter Island long ago by advanced agriculturists unknown to archaeologists.

The Polynesians used a system of record keeping that utilized knotted cords they called *tahoponapona,* not unlike the Inca version called *quipu,* except the islanders extended their use by tying them to *pipiwharauroa,* or long-voyage homing birds, which carried the messages from one island to another. In both systems, each knot, and the manner in which it was tied, together with its identifying color, represented specific numerical values and/or bits of information. The messages they carried warned of impending attacks; proclaimed significant births, betrothals, deaths, alliances, requests for or arrival of goods or military forces; and announced important religious observances.

At least four petroglyphs representing llamas have been found at Nukihiva and Oipona me'ae. The Easter Island petroglyph of a fish at Anakena Bay is executed in the same concentric, unicursal style displayed in the Nazca drawings of whales. In other words, each illustration was executed in one continuous, unbroken line, a fingerprint style not frequently encountered in the ancient world beyond the eastern Pacific and parts of South America. Rapa Nui's bird-man was depicted in rock art and *rongo-rongo,* the island's written language, as a frigate bird, whose image reappears among the enormous line drawings executed in the Nazca Desert of coastal Peru. Several other rongo-rongo figures feature the right arm pointing upward and the left downward, identical to the so-called Owl Woman portrayed on the Peruvian pampas. The same Earth–sky gesture is found in a Hawaiian petroglyph (D22-19) at Kaupulehu. Expanding this Pacific correspondence, Hawaiian myth told of the Hare a ta Ra, or house of the sun, recalling a sacred precinct of the same name, the Coricancha, at the center of Cuzco. And, of course, the sun was known as Ra in both Rapa Nui and Hawaii, while the Inti-Raimi was the Inca's great celebration of solar worship.

These and other comparisons have persuaded some investigators to conclude that culture-bearers from Peru sailed westward across the

Pacific Ocean to reestablish themselves at Easter Island. While their argument may be superficially attractive, closer scrutiny reveals some serious flaws. Long before Heyerdahl compared Rapa Nui with Andean stonework, Lewis Spence observed:

> Now, there is certainly an affinity of craftsmanship and general style between the architecture and the sculpture of Tiahuanaco and that of Easter Island. The themes of the carvers are similar, as is the treatment of these. Of course, the Peruvian work exhibits a more advanced technique, such as might be expected from a later phase of the same artistic impulse, but its general cyclopean character is the same as that exhibited in the masonry of Easter Island—and that it is not Incan Peruvian is clear from the fact that it pre-dates this style by centuries—perhaps by millennia.

Rongo-rongo was the script in use at Easter Island, but the ancient Andeans who supposedly introduced civilization there did not possess a written language. Also, the cyclopean walls of Easter Island at Vinapu are far older than their Cuzco counterparts. Mark Williams, author of one of the better books on the subject *(In Search of Lemuria)*, observes, "The Vinapu wall went up first, which means that the cultural influence was from the Pacific toward America, and not the other way around." He was preceded in this conclusion by Katherine Routledge, whose 1918 expedition resulted in some of the most fruitful archaeological research ever undertaken in the eastern Pacific. "The suggestion that Easter Island has been populated from South America may therefore, for practical purposes, be ruled out of the question," she wrote. "If there is any connection between the two, it is more likely that the influence spread from the island to the continent."

More likely still, the Rapa Nui and Andean civilizations were independently affected by an outside source common to both. Impressions made by a shared influence on two widely separated locations would explain their important, otherwise inexplicable similarities. The pre-Inca Uru of Lake Titicaca, the ancestral Polynesian Uru-keu, and Easter

Island's Ure do not prove one people was influenced by another, but rather that they were all influenced by an external power, referred to by some Polynesians as Uru, yet another name for the Pacific Motherland. To be sure, the appearance of llamas in Easter Island rock art and cultivation there of the totora reed and sweet potato clearly demonstrate important contacts with South America. But even this seemingly indisputable Andean gift to Oceania may have arrived by way of Lemurian travelers, as suggested by the name of a Hawaiian goddess. In fleeing from the grasp of her mortal lover, Lono-Mu-ku lost her leg, which grew into the first potato. After all, the Polynesians and their forebears were extraordinary mariners who visited many foreign shores and traveled throughout the Pacific world, even to Antarctica, centuries or millennia before modern Europeans.

What Rapa Nui and preconquest southern Peru did share was the traditional belief that these lands owed their organized society to a culture-bearer arriving in the remote past from a distant land, the font of high civilization, long since overwhelmed by a natural catastrophe. He was known, respectively, to the Easter Islanders and the Inca as Hotu Matua and Kon-Tiki-Viracocha. The panpipes both peoples used, their fashionable long ears, *quipu-ahoponapona* message system, statue making, tower-and-wall technology, and all the rest were said to have come from the lost homeland of their founding fathers. In other words, they originated elsewhere, and, from either necessity or design, were exported to Easter Island and Andean South America, where local factors interacted with the imported culture to create unique although similar societies.

The identity of that outside cultural influence is suggested in Easter Island's own foundation myth. It begins in a great kingdom that flourished long ago in the Pacific Ocean. According to local legend, "There was a big country, this country," known as Hiva, "a land of temples," far-spreading roads, high stone gateways, cyclopean buildings, broad ceremonial plazas, and a dense population. This "land of abundance" was rich in agriculture, but "it was so hot that in summer the sun shriveled up vegetation by its heat."

Its foremost province was Marae Renga, ruled by Haumaka. One morning he awoke with a start, the impressions of a disturbing nightmare still fresh in his memory. The bird-headed god, Makemake, had appeared to the chief while he slept. Acting on the dream, Haumaka at once dispatched an expedition of six men. Ira, Kuukuu, Mu-mona, Parenga, Ringaringa, and Ure sailed away in their ship, the *Oraorangaru*, "saved from the billows," on a voyage of discovery. Many weeks later, they discovered a small island, Motunui, off the southwest coast of a larger landfall. Sailing around its northern shore, they found the same bay described in Haumaka's dream. Their purpose now was to prepare the newly discovered island, which they named Matakite-Ra-ni, after their sun-god, for the arrival of settlers from Hiva.

They were led by Hotu Matua, the "prolific father," a descendant of Rongo, "sound" or "the Sounder," named after the conch-shell horn—the fair-complected, red-haired god who sired royal families throughout Polynesia. In a native Easter Island version of Haumaka's vision recounted by Arturo Teao, Hotu Matua assembled his family and 300 followers at Marae-toe-hau, or "burial-place bay," from whence they disembarked in a pair of huge canoes, each one a mile long. The hyperbolic details of this legend were meant to convey something of the colonizers' immense ships, capacious enough to accommodate 150 passengers per vessel, plus provisions, water, and cargo.

After 120 days at sea, the newcomers went ashore at the place Haumaka envisioned, now christened Anakena Bay by Hotu Matua after August, the month in which he arrived. His followers off-loaded everything they needed for permanent settlement, including numerous trees, tubers, and plants, plus a library of sixty-seven bark cloth–covered tablets inscribed with genealogies and histories, together with religious, agricultural, botanical, medical, and astronomical texts. But the most treasured item in his possession was the Te-pito-te-Kura, or navel of light, a sacred stone from Hiva. An oblate spheroid of dense, crystalline volcanic rock, it is predominantly gray, but with some tones grading into black. Although entirely natural, it seems to have been smoothed and slightly shaped by an artistic hand. Otherwise unexceptional in appearance, the stone is 75 centimeters across and 45 centimeters thick, with a circumference of 2.53 meters. It may still be seen near the great ahu in La Perouse Bay, on the north coast. So revered was this stone that Hotu Matua renamed Mat-akite-Ra-ni "navel of the world," Te-pito-te-henua.

No sooner had he done so than he realized another valued object had been forgotten. This was a statue of Tauto, his colleague and a great *ariki,* or chief. Two underlings were commanded to "go back to Hiva, our homeland," and return with the valuable moai. They set out at once on a long but strangely uneventful voyage: "There were no waves, big or small; there was no wind." The peculiar stillness through which they made their way was the calm before the cataclysm.

They at last arrived on the shores of Marea Renga, where they found the forgotten statue of Tauto still standing at the edge of Marae-toe-hau, just as Hotu Matua described. But as they were removing it, the god of earthquakes struck, upending great stretches of territory into the sea. As the native Easter Island account relates, *He ktu a mai e Uvoke hai akau te ua, i iti ai te kaiga*—"Uvoke lifted the land with his crowbar. The waves uprose, the country became small." Earth, sea, and sky were contorted by violence. According to Arturo Teao, "the waves broke, the wind blew, rain fell, thunder roared, meteorites fell on the island." In a frantic effort to escape the disaster with their charge, they dropped the moai, which broke into pieces. The two men scooped up the head and fled doomed Hiva in their canoe, as Haumaka witnessed the fulfillment of his prophetic nightmare: "The king saw that the land had sunk in the sea. As the sea rose, the land sank. Families died, men died, women, children and old people." *Ku emu a,* "The Earth is drowned."

Many weeks later, the hapless pair arrived back at Rapa Nui, where they were escorted immediately into the royal presence. Hotu Matua was at first overjoyed to see them. "Welcome from Hiva," he cried, "the land of abundant food and dirty lips!" This last description demonstrated his jovial frame of mind, because it signified faces smeared with eating. But the king's mood was dashed when the two men made their report by presenting the mutilated remains of the statue they had been commanded to retrieve. "Woe, the neck of the moai Tauto," he wailed, "the ariki has been broken! The body, the legs, the arms have stayed in Hiva, his homeland." Just then, Ira, Kuukuu, Mu-mona, Parenga, Ringaringa, and Ure, the scouts who discovered Rapa Nui and had prepared it for settlement, asked Hotu Matua's permission to return home. But the dejected king told them, "The sea has come up and drowned all people in Marae Renga."

During the years that followed, Hotu Matua transformed Easter Island into a lonely outpost of civilization, the last manifestation of drowned Hiva. Agriculture flourished, the old solar religion was venerated, rock art blossomed everywhere. Impressive stone walls, lofty towers, and great platforms supporting gigantic statues were the cultural adornments of Rapa Nui. To preserve their literary heritage, the islanders held an annual festival in which students of rongo-rongo had to recite long passages of the written tablets from memory in the presence of the king and his court. Perfect performances were richly rewarded with sacred statues and free food. But the slightest error merited punishment meted out not to students, who had to repeat their schooling, but instead to their teachers. Apparently, the old written language of Hiva was deemed extremely important, perhaps sacred.

Another important ceremony took place every vernal equinox, when volunteers lined the southwestern shore to compete in a very special race. They swam a mile across the turbulent, shark-infested waters separating Te-pito-te-henua from the nearby islet of Motunui. There they were supposed to find the egg of a seabird, place it in a special carrying device strapped onto the swimmer's forehead, and return with it undamaged. The first man to complete this daunting task became the most honored personage for one year, and was considered so holy that he had to seclude himself in a cave for four months without bathing or any contact with the outside world, including his wife. Until the following spring, all his wants were freely provided by a grateful society. Even after his privileged term came to a close, he was regarded with special awe for the remainder of his life and given special honors at his funeral. His victory had celebrated the mysteries of Makemake, the bird-man cult from old Hiva.

Here, too, evidence leads in a Lemurian direction. Hiva is transparently the Polynesian version of Mu, from its supremely high culture and sun-worship to the nature of its destruction, even to the inclusion of falling meteorites. One of the six explorers from Hiva who discovered Rapa Nui was called Mu-mona, and a descendant of one of the two long-eared Hanau-eepe aristocrats to survive the Poike Ditch massacre was known as Atamu. These linguistic remnants attest to the Lemurian origins of civilization on Easter Island, as well as its most sacred site. Although standard Easter Island references describe the offshore islet as Motunui, a Chilean government chart of 1918 (Number 68) and the British Admiralty Chart Number 1386 released by the U.S. Hydrographic Office Publications spell the name Mutu Nui, or the Island of Mutu, as it would have been known in aboriginal New Zealand. The Maoris there revered the memory of Mutu, who, like the Inca's founding father, Con-Tiki-Viracocha, or Sea Foam, was missing a finger. Both Mutu and Con-Tiki-Viracocha were also survivors of a terrible deluge, another shared detail that stresses the Lemurian identity of Easter Island's Mutunui.

After many years of successful reign, an aged Hotu Matua climbed alone to the top of Rano Kao, a volcano in the southwestern corner of Te-pito-te-henua. His death was described by the Oxford scholar and founding professor at New Zealand's University of Canterbury in Christchurch John Macmillan Brown: "Looking out westward, he called to the spirits that hovered round his old submerged home to bid the cocks crow, and when the cocks crew he gave up the ghost. In this tradition, we have clearly expressed the consciousness of archipelagoes to the west of Easter Island having gone down, and the submersion being the cause of ocean-voyaging immigrants settling on its infertile soil."

That Hotu Matua's account is among the most obvious references to Lemuria found anywhere seems appropriate. He was a high-ranking member of the Miru clan, known as Milu in Hawaii and Tahiti, where the eponymous founding father "dwelt beneath the sea and ruled over the regions where departed spirits were said to dwell," according to Polynesia mythographer Johannes C. Andersen, "and the direction in which this realm of Milu was situated was in the west." It was remembered as Hiva throughout Polynesia, where stories of red-haired, light-skinned survivors escaping from a drowned realm were likewise familiar. Milu, Hiva, and Mu were portrayed as excessively hot, implying that the Pacific Motherland lay near the equator.

Some Easter Island traditions have Hotu Matua arriving from the east, from the island of Sala-y-Gomez, if only because it was earlier known as Motu Motiro Hiva, or "islet in the nearness of Hiva." But the Prolific Father and his colonizers would not have needed four months to cover just 300 miles from Sala-y-Gomez to Rapa Nui. Hotu Matua's myth specifically holds that he looked in the direction of his sunken Motherland toward the west on the last day of his life. He had named the site of his landfall Anakena after the month of August; July–August is the optimum sailing season from western Polynesia to Easter Island. This is not to argue that Lemurian territories in the form of island chains or archipelagoes did not exist east of Rapa Nui. Sala-y-Gomez may indeed have been "in the nearness of Hiva," or, at any rate, among its eastern sections. But Mu originally, however disjointedly, spread over much of the Pacific Ocean from South America to Japan. Hotu Matua's roots lay in the far western provinces of that formerly immense civilization.

His hometown in Hiva was Marea Renga, or "the sacred place of Rengai." In Polynesian tradition, according to mythologist Jan Knappert, Renga, or Reinga, was the undersea realm of the dead presided over by the guardian god, Limu, from his sunken palace. Interestingly, Marae Renga drew its name from Renga, "the afterlife," just as Rome's Lemuria derived from the lemures, or ghosts of the deceased. These comparative myths clearly define Hotu Matua's origins as Lemurian.

Evidence for his successful transference of Marae Renga's sun-worshipping cult appears in some of Rapa Nui's most important place-names, such as its three volcanoes: Rana Roraku, Rano Aroi, and Rana Kao. Easter Island's earliest known name was Matakite-Ra-ni, or dwelling place of the sun god. Rapa Nui itself means great land of the sun god. Raa signified both the sun and "clan" at Easter Island, implying the same kind of solar-political relationship found among the royal dynasties of the Nile Valley. Ra figured into the royal praenomen of many pharaohs, a practice followed by most Easter Island kings, including Ta-Ra-tahi, Ra-ni, I-Ra, Matakite-Ra-ni, and Ra-pa-Re-na. Indeed, an obvious correspondence with the Nile sun god, Ra, is remarkable, even to the inclusion of hyphenated names for combined solar deities, like the Egyptian Atum-Ra or Ra-Horahkty, and the Easter Island Ra-no-aroi, Hauha-Ra, or Ra-Ra-iahopa. The Egyptian goddesses Re-nenet and Re-npet compare with Easter Island's Ava-Re-iupa and U-Re-ti'oti'o. Another solar deity worshipped there was Rangitea, just as it was 4,000 miles away on the other side of the Pacific.

The earliest ahus incorporated solar alignments of great precision, proof that their builders were astronomers on a par with architects in ancient Egypt, where many sacred structures, such as Karnac, were oriented to significant positions of the sun. The ahu at Vinapu, for example, is aligned to the azimuths of the rising or setting sun at the solstices and equinoxes. In fact, the sun was identified as Ra throughout the Pacific. The mythology of both the ancient Egyptians and the Chatham Islanders included a solar boat, referred to in the Pacific as the *Waka-Ra*. Sunrise and sunset were referred to, respectively, as Ra lik and Ra tok in the Marshall Islands, while the legendary founding fathers of Fiji were said to have built their first village near the Ra coast after arriving from the direction of the rising sun. To the Maori of New Zealand, a red sun was called Ra-ura, Manu ite Ra was their solar bird, and the Great Son of the Sun was Tama nui te Ra. The sun-god was known as Ra-Ra in the Cook Islands and signified the sun itself in Tahiti. In a popular Polynesian myth, "Maui Snares the Sun," the hero calls to his brothers, "Let us bind Ra!"

Like Andean comparisons that led some researchers to suspect South American influences in the eastern Pacific, parallels with dynastic Egypt suggest a pharaonic impact at Rapa Nui. But, as in the former case, superficial resemblances more likely indicate that both widely separated locations received independently the same cultural influences from a common outside source. This conclusion is repeated in yet another comparison with the outside world—namely, ancient India. The earliest high culture there is referred to as the Harappan or Mohenjo Daro, sprouting in the fertile Indus Valley some 5,000 years ago and roughly contemporary with the beginnings of civilization in Mesopotamia and the Nile Valley.

The ancient Indians were sophisticated surveyors, using a standard system of weights and measures in the construction of populous cities with great public baths, modern plumbing, and complex urban planning. Their port metropolis, Lothal, was home to freighters that connected a vast trading network throughout the Indian Ocean and beyond. The Sumerians knew the distant civilization as Meluhha, a name perhaps close, at least, to how the late-fourth-millennium-B.C. inhabitants of the subcontinent referred to the Indus Valley. Archaeologists have thus far identified fourteen of their urban centers, which were not loosely affiliated city-states but rather part of a single politically unified culture.

Around 1700 B.C., the Indus Valley civilization came to a violent end under the hooves of warhorses ridden by Aryan conquerors from the north. Long before, Mohenjo Daro had given birth to a written language, which has defied translation ever since it was found in the late nineteenth century. In 1932, however, a Hungarian language scholar, Guillaume de Hevesy, read a paper before the Academie des Inscriptions et Belles-Lettres in Paris, saying, "There exists a connection between the scripts of the Indus Valley and Easter Island." He found 174 identical or virtually identical glyphs from a combined total of 745, "based on two hundred twenty six Indus Valley signs and variants of signs, and five hundred nineteen signs of Easter Island—more of the latter in order to present as many variants of them as possible." His comparative investigation revealed that "both scripts use the same system of additional elements. And this, obviously, also constitutes a strong visual proof of the connection between the scripts."

Rapa Nui's rongo-rongo, like the Indus Valley script, is syllabic, or nonalphabetical, with an admixture of pictorial representations or ideograms. Both are also *boustrophedon,* or "as the ox plows," alternate lines written in opposite directions. The renowned German anthropologist Herve Heine-Geldern noted "two adjacent lines having in relation to each other their signs up-side-down, an arrangement which I have as

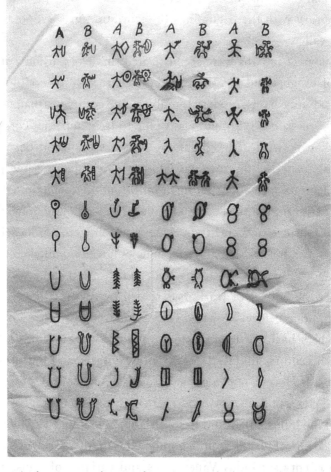

Comparison of ancient India's Mohenjo Daro glyphs (A columns) with Easter Island's rongo-rongo (B columns) demonstrating their undeniable affinity. Both cultures received the originally Lemurian script independently from their Pacific Motherland, where the first written word was inscribed.

yet been able to find only in Easter Island and in Harappa. The similarity between the two scripts with regard to the arrangement of the lines is thus really greater than Hevesy had assumed." Most of de Hevesy's colleagues echoed the Polynesian Society spokesman N. M. Billimoria when he told the Sind Historical Society that so many comparisons "cannot have happened by chance." The renowned Assyriologist Stephen H. Langdon confirmed de Hevesy's comparisons, declaring them "truly remarkable." Forty years later, Bill Ballinger, who wrote so eloquently about Nan Madol in the 1970s, could still conclude that "the number of identical characters is too large to be a coincidence. Look at the comparison of the 'characters' between the two systems of writing. If it is sheer coincidence, then it is unbelievable!"

But such parallels proved extremely problematical. The first high culture in the Indus Valley flourished from the early third millennium B.C. to the turn of the seventeenth century B.C. Archaeologists believe Hotu Matua landed at Rapa Nui sometime in the first half of the fifth century A.D. The Indus Valley civilization had been extinct for more than two millennia before he appeared, so the notion of culture bearers sailing from the Indian subcontinent across the vast Pacific Ocean to a tiny speck on the other side of the world is out of the question. Nor did Easter Islanders bring rongo-rongo to India around 450 A.D., because the script had already been dead there for more than twenty centuries. The 2,100 years separating the close of Mohenjo Daro from human beginnings on Easter Island were compounded by the 13,000 airline miles between either location. These huge discrepancies are at odds with the undeniably organic relationship between rongo-rongo and the Indus Valley script.

What particularly stung some academics who were convinced that early humans never ventured far from home was the suggestion of trans-oceanic contacts between two apparently dissimilar cultures implied by a comparison of the scripts so widely separated in both space and time. During the 1930s, when de Hevesy announced his findings, many or perhaps even most of his professional contemporaries were at least willing to concede that connections by sea between distant peoples were possible. Today, a precisely opposite view dominates American archaeology—so much so that dissenters are punished with academic ostracism, loss of tenure, and even expulsion from the profession. (For proof, see Michael Cremo's *The Forbidden Archaeologist* or Dr. Gunnar Thompson's *American Discovery: The Real Story*.) Professional deniers typically avoid arguing the facts, preferring character assassination of the cultural diffusionist and repeatedly dismissing his or her evidence until the heretic is deemed worthless by academics and public alike.

The initiator of this debunking process against de Hevesy was the internationally acclaimed establishment ethnologist Dr. Alfred Métraux, whose work at Easter Island and throughout Polynesia is still cited as authoritative by conventional scholars. In 1938, Métraux accused de Hevesy of altering and falsifying both scripts to make a deliberately fraudulent case. In truth, they bore no significant resemblance to each other, Métraux declared. Moreover, any apparent similarities were entirely accidental, and might just as well have been randomly made between any two written languages.

According to him, there is no connection between rongo-rongo and the Indus Valley script other "than that which is bound to appear automatically between two pictographies whenever and wherever they appear. I happened to compare the examples chosen by Mr. de Hevezy [sic] with the original photographs of the Mohenjo Daro seals prepared by Dr. G. H. Hunter. To my surprise, Mr. de Hevezy lacked the accuracy desirable for such work. He has taken regrettable liberties with the signs. When restored to their original proportions or outlines, identical signs in his list ceased to show any similarity. Most of the signs have been submitted to similar adjustments. If we discard these inaccuracies, the resemblances between Mohenjo Daro script and Easter Island 'writing' become extremely few and are reduced to geometrical signs."

De Hevesy's assertion was so transparently ridiculous, Métraux concluded, that no one claiming to be a professional researcher could take it seriously, and any further discussion of such impossible comparisons should be regarded as the erroneous dabbling of unqualified amateurs.

In the twenty-first century, such thinly veiled threats are enough to scare off anyone in the academic community from endorsing heretical conclusions. But during the 1930s, not everyone was intimidated by official condemnation of scientific upstarts, and some very prominent names in anthropology rushed to de Hevesy's defense. The first among them was Dr. G. R. Hunter, cited in evidence by Métraux. "It is with considerable surprise, not to say disgust," he wrote de Hevesy in a public letter, that I have read Mons. Métraux's criticism of you in the Feb.–April 1938 number of *Anthropos*. He therein accuses you, *inter alia,* of having "adjusted" certain Indus Valley signs to suit your purpose. As most of these "adjusted" signs are said to have been taken from my work on the Indus Valley script, I have taken pains to again go carefully through the list of Indus signs reproduced by you. I have found that in every case without exception when you have taken signs from my work you have faithfully reproduced them with scrupulous, and indeed remarkable exactitude. I am afraid Mons. Métraux has not even troubled to read the work of mine from which you copied the signs, viz. my article in the *Journal of the Royal Asiatic Society,* April, 1932, pp. 494–503, and this in spite of the fact that he himself refers to it in footnote 4, p. 222 of his article in question!

According to Heine-Geldren, Métraux's "unwarranted assertion that Hevesy falsified signs is based solely on his own failure to scrutinize the sources with desirable accuracy. I feel bound to say that this is the most reckless defamation of a scholar I ever came across. However, I have not the slightest doubt that Dr. Métraux, after a more careful perusal of the sources, will himself be the first to admit that his accusations were unjust, and that he will gladly offer those public apologies to which Mr. de Hevesy is fully entitled."

Heine-Geldern's confidence in the fundamental honesty of his skeptical colleague was misplaced. Métraux never bothered to reconsider the wild inaccuracy of his assertions because they were intended solely to discredit de Hevesy and render officially unacceptable such lines of research into transoceanic contacts during the ancient past. Here, Dr. Métraux was eminently successful. De Hevesy is today fleetingly recalled in archaeology's polite circles as some radical crank whose irresponsible comparison of scripts from Easter Island and Mohenjo Daro was debunked before World War II. Although Dr. Métraux disproved nothing, and was himself shown up as a sloppy researcher whose criticisms were deeply flawed, his bland accusations were embraced by ivory tower academics anxious to defend their textbook archaeology against diffusionist interlopers. They repeatedly championed his erroneous skepticism of de Hevesy until, in time, it became scholastic dogma. The process is but one example, unfortunately, demonstrating the sabotage of valid information with the potential to advance our understanding of an important mystery that continues to baffle scientists. But, because it tended toward a politically incorrect direction, a door opening on the past was shut and declared off limits to university-trained investigators.

What makes rongo-rongo's indisputable relationship with the Indus Valley even more challenging is its comparison with another ancient written language in Central America, 3,250 miles away. Two years before de Hevesy found parallels between the Mohenjo Daro and Easter Island scripts, another linguistic scholar, Erich von Hornbostel, made an equally persuasive argument on behalf of connections between picture-writing of the Cuna Indians in Panama and rongo-rongo. Though the Panamanian version possesses fewer examples of shared identity than its Indus Valley counterpart, an affiliation with Easter Island's written language is inescapable. Like them, Cuna picture-writing is boustrophedon, syllabic, and inscribed on wooden tablets, known at Rapa Nui as *kohau* boards.

Von Hornbostel pointed out:

> Precisely as was the case with the Easter Island script, so also among the Cuna it is necessary to know the text to be able to "read" it, that is, to recite it. Just as among the Cuna, on Easter Island also written texts were recited at burials. Among the Cuna, the texts in question contained the description of the road to be taken by the departed spirit after death. A priest recites the text from a picture-writing, while the corpse is taken to the grave in a boat. I take the opportunity to call attention to a remarkable and perhaps not quite insignificant conformity in the burial rites of both domains; namely, the use of feather-sticks. "For six days after his (Ngaara's) death," says Mrs. Routledge in the passage mentioned, "everyone worked at making the sticks with feathers on the top (heu-heu), and they were put all around the place."

Among the Cuna, four feather-sticks were placed together with the corpse in the grave, representing the symbol of the abode of four protective spirits that lead the souls on their pathway of death.

On Easter Island itself, feather-sticks were planted in the ground to mark off the precinct where the rongo-rongo men performed their annual recitations of the kohau tablets.

Heine-Geldern, who had publicly defended de Hevesy against his detractors, likewise supported von Hornbostel's discovery, but added that "the outer form of the Easter Island script has reached a considerably higher evolution than the Cuna script, or else—and this is probably the correct answer—the Cuna script has to a greater extent become barbarized and sunk to a lower level than that of the Easter Islanders, although it may have maintained the original form of many written signs to a better degree." Heine-Geldern's conclusion was underscored by Nele, a Cuna informant, who told archaeologists in 1928 that "the last one who knew how to draw the picture-writing proper was Memekina," a legendary scribe who had supposedly passed away long before.

Connections with a lost Pacific source went beyond any apparent Easter Island parallels to link up with the Motherland from which both rongo-rongo and the Panamanian picture writing derived. Cuna place-names and the names of their leading deities abundantly reflect Lemurian origins. The most significant and obvious among them is Mu itself. Like Churchward's female characterization of the sunken civilization, the Mu of Cuna cosmology was the Panamanian mother goddess. Mu Olokukurtlisop's creation of the sun, with whom she mated to give birth to the stars and planets, recalls the Lemurian solar cult. Other incarnations of the Cuna mother goddess included Mu Alesop, Mu Olokundil, Mu Olotagisop, Mu Olotakiki, and Mu Sobia. *Mu-olok-wit-uppu* is Cuna for "island" and *mu-olo-tup-kana* refers to islands in the sea, while Mu-lat-uppu and Tupsol-Mu-llu are islands not far from the Pacific coast. Of special significance, however, is the Great Flood that overwhelmed a vast land in the west, across the sea, from which surviving magicians sought refuge in Panama very long ago. This Cuna deluge account is appropriately known as the "Mu-osis."

Perhaps most obvious of all was Ca-Mu, literally "he from Mu," the flood hero of the Arovac Indians. They described him as a tall, white-skinned, fair-haired and bearded magician who arrived on the shores of Panama after having been driven from his kingdom far across the sea by a terrible cataclysm. Ca-Mu is regarded as the culture-bearer from whom all Arovac have since descended. So many variants featuring common aspects associated with the sunken Motherland clearly identify a fundamental Lemurian impact on prehistoric Panama, which included the importation of a script that degenerated in isolation and over time into picture-writing.

South of the Panamanian isthmus, the influence of rongo-rongo was found close to the Colombian border among a tribal people dwelling near the Sierra de Perija. They painted the glyphs on wooden sticks referred to as *tiot-tio*. J. M. Cruxent, director of the Museum of Caracas, discovered that the script was used by the Motilones Indians as late as the mid-twentieth century, and told his colleagues at the twenty-ninth International Americanist Congress in New York, "It seems curious that the manner of reading the tiot-tio, and some of the signs thereof, remind us of the Rapa Nui tablets of Easter Island." The comparison was no less intriguing to Heine-Geldern: "Dr. Cruxent announced the discovery, among the Motilones Indians of western Venezuela, of a system of picture-writing which in general character, as well as in details, so closely resembles the picture-writing of the Cuna Indians of eastern Panama and the script of Easter Island that the existence of some kind of connection can hardly be doubted."

Scarcely less surprising than rongo-rongo's Indus Valley parallels was its correspondence with the pre-Inca city of Tiahuanaco, high in the Bolivian Andes, not far from the south shore of Lake Titicaca. The ruins comprise an archaeological zone of spacious platforms, grand staircases, and colossal statuary. Although conventional scholars date most construction between 200 and 600 A.D., this suggested period has been called into question by innumerable seashells littering the *Altiplano,* or high plain, at

13,000 feet. At the far end of its raised plaza stands Tiahuanaco's most impressive feature, the famous Gateway to the Sun, a modern name given to the ceremonial arch for its solar alignment. Hewn from a single block of gray andesite, the thirteen-and-a-half-foot-long monolith is more than seven feet tall and weighs about eleven tons. Neither support of the arch is decorated; each has a rectangular niche at the center, which has a raised perimeter as though meant to hold panels, perhaps of gold to reflect oriented sunlight. Through the Gateway's lower center is cut a doorway four feet, six inches high and two feet, nine inches wide. Above it run four lines of sculpture in low relief of bird-men represented in profile on either side of a central figure, in high relief, holding a pair of staves, a belt of severed heads at his waist and tears running down his cheeks.

Similar images of bird-men recur throughout the Easter Island script and are likewise carved in relief on every available rock face at Orongo, Rapa Nui's ceremonial center. Moreover, the images of bird-men adorning Tiahuanaco's Gateway to the Sun show each carrying a vertical staff in his three-fingered hand, just as the staff-bearing rongo-rongo bird-men are missing one finger. Among the gigantic intaglios etched into the Nazca Plain of the Peruvian desert is the representation of a ringtailed monkey, its right hand minus a finger. The Inca believed civilization was brought to the Andes by Con-tiki-Viracocha, or Sea Foam after the vessel that rescued him from the flood, who had only three fingers on his left hand. On the other side of the Pacific Ocean, the Polynesians decorated their ornately carved assembly houses with a three-fingered motif they claimed was brought to them by an ancestor from the sunken palace of their chief god, Tangaroa. The transparently Lemurian name of this Maori ancestor, short two fingers, was Mutu. He was renowned throughout Polynesia as the islanders' ancestral progenitor, who came from the undersea realm of Limu. So too the Easter Islanders' written language, rongo-rongo, derived from their culture hero, Rongo, named after his emblem, a great triton shell known as the Resounder. He was the Rapa Nui version of Lono, the light-haired, fair-complected bringer of civilized ways from Hiva, his submarine homeland celebrated by the Hawaiians, who believed his descendant had returned in the person of Captain James Cook.

Easter Island petroglyphs of the bird-man Makemake.

A double-headed theme is found both on the Bolivian monolith and in the Easter Island script. The weeping-eye motif epitomized on the face of the so-called Gateway God but associated with other Andean cultures is likewise encountered inside the stone structures at Orongo, but nowhere else in the Pacific.

The Gateway's central figure wears a crescent fishtail over his chest, recalling the moon-shaped pectoral worn by Hotu Matua and all successive kings of Rapa Nui, and repeated as a rongo-rongo glyph. Although felines were unknown throughout Oceania, only at Easter Island may be found puma petroglyphs among the rock art of Orongo. The Gateway God dominating the relief sculpture wears an elaborate headdress with nineteen ray-like projections, six of them terminating in the heads of pumas. His arms are tattooed with the images of the big cats, and they compose his belt. From it hang six conventionalized representations of earless human heads with round eyes, their noses split at the upper end and branching into curving eyebrows, the same iconographic features of masks depicting Makemake, the sun god of Easter Island.

Heyerdahl concluded, "It thus appears that all the ideograms or symbolic features represented together on one monument at Tiahuanaco concur with ideograms or symbols at the ceremonial site of Orongo, where the Easter Islanders selected their yearly bird-men, and where the plumed tangata rongo-rongo, headed by the king, used to recite their tablets." Symbolic parallels linking the monolith with Rapa Nui are supported by material considerations. The statues of Easter Island and Tiahuanaco are similar, and both are portrayed wearing a stylized girdle. Rapa Nui's solar worship seems duplicated at the Bolivian Gateway to the Sun, while *tiahuanaco* is itself the Spanish corruption of Typi-Kala, or "stone-in-the-center" in the native Quechua language, suggesting the Te-pito-te-Kura, or navel of light, a sacred stone Hotu Matua brought from sunken Hiva to Easter Island.

It is hardly less difficult to accept that the illiterate Andeans carried a written language into the eastern Pacific than that the Easter Islanders taught rongo-rongo to the natives of Panama, or that someone sailed halfway around the world from Mohenjo Daro to tiny Rapa Nui. The connection between such vastly separated, although undeniably related, systems as the Indus Valley script and rongo-rongo, together with picture-writing of the Panamanian Cunas or Venezuelan Motilones, and the Gateway to the Sun's parallel symbolism at Bolivia, finds its only credible explanation in a missing sixth party from whom all the others received a common written language—a legacy inherited from some precursor civilization, the sunken homeland from which Hotu Matua brought his library to Easter Island. This conclusion is supported by traditions at Rapa Nui and Tiahuanaco, which insisted that each received the tenets of civilization from survivors arriving from some great catastrophe out at sea. The Spanish chronicler Cieza de Leon recorded a local Indian legend to the effect that "Tiahuanaco was built in a single night after the Flood by unknown giants."

Comparisons between the Mohenjo Daro and Easter Island scripts go beyond the similarity of their characters. Like rongo-rongo, "the entire collection of Indus inscriptions from seals, pottery, and copper amulets shows no development," Ballinger writes. "The signs appear fully formed, accents and all, and do not change." In other words, both the Indian subcontinent and the eastern Pacific were independent recipients of a shared written language from some external source. The original records carried from that outside location to Easter Island by Hotu Matua were said to have been written on perishable material, perhaps bark cloth. To prevent their valuable information from being lost through deterioration, it was transcribed on wooden tablets by successive generations of copyists.

As Billimoria writes, "To save the precious incisions from rubbing, the wooden tablet was slightly grooved and the letters were engraved in these grooves, the ridges between the grooves thus preventing contact with the face of the script." He additionally points out that "the tablets are made of *Podocarpus,* a tree which does not grow on Easter Island," because it can only flourish in tropical conditions that never existed at Rapa Nui. Podocarpus is, however, found in Panama, which may explain the appearance of rongo-rongo among the Cuna Indians. The tree is also found in the Moluccas, Celebes, and New Zealand. If the Easter Islanders did indeed obtain their writing materials from these distant sources, such commerce would testify to their far-flung maritime capabilities, more typical of Polynesians or earlier Lemurians than of the lubberly natives encountered by modern European visitors.

At one time, there were many hundreds, perhaps thousands, of the "talking boards," which allegedly recorded the whole history, literature, spirituality, and science of Rapa Nui and the drowned Motherland of Hiva. Tragically, early Christian missionaries at the island consigned virtually all the wooden tablets to the flames of religious intolerance. Only twenty-one examples escaped destruction, and from these pitiful fragments linguists have endeavored, mostly without success, to wrench a translation. After the Peruvian slave raid of 1862, which reduced Easter Island's population to a few dozen leprous survivors, no one was left who could read rongo-rongo.

Even more enigmatic than the kohau glyphs are those said to have been carried to the other side of the Pacific. During the deep past, the Maori hero Tamatea excavated Te Ana-whakairo, the "carved cave," a terraformed temple he decorated with carvings and paintings on the South Island of New Zealand. This holy site was intended to preserve the *tuhituhi*, sacred writing from a distant land known as Irihia, one of numerous names given to Hiva, the Polynesians' lost ancestral homeland. "The meaning of this writing is now lost," S. Percy Smith writes, quoting *Travels of Tamatea* in his *Hawaiki: The Original Home of the Maori*. "But it was treasured in the memories of the men of old." The Maori tradition relates the arrival and special preservation of a script from the same source from which Hotu Matua said he obtained the kohau records for Rapa Nui. Both versions, separated by many thousands of miles, nonetheless clearly indicate a shared experience: the transportation of a written language from lost Lemuria.

On the obscure island of Oleai, some 8,000 miles northwest of Easter Island, about 850 miles northwest of Pohnpei in the Yap district of the Caroline Islands, the natives also preserved a written language. And, like their distant Pacific neighbors at Rapa Nui, they had entirely forgotten its significance long before the early nineteenthth century, when their island was first visited by European seafarers. Although inscrutable, the glyphs were revered as heirlooms from "the gods of yesterday." By the turn of the twentieth century, the Oleai script was virtually a dead written language.

The great Scottish Atlantologist Lewis Spence personally traveled to the islet in 1914, and when he published his classic book about Lemuria eighteen years later observed that "[o]nly some half-dozen men on the island now know the script, as well as a few on Faraulep, an islet 100 miles distant. It once, however, must have been used over a wide area. It certainly is not of modern origin and is the product of many ages." In fact, a script could never have served any purpose on such small islands, so it can only be a relic from a far more vast cultural enterprise, long extinct. The same must be said of the written language of Easter Island, whose original population of just 6,000 inhabitants confined to a sixty-four-square-mile living space could not have used a written language. As Spence wrote, "There is no need for such a script on an isolated island which one could traverse in a few hours. It [rongo-rongo] was obviously intended in the first place to serve the needs of administrative communication over extensive areas, as did the *quipus* or knotted string records of the Peruvian Incas."

Spence was preceded by Brown, who hinted at a Lemurian origin for rongo-rongo:

"It is easy to cross from the coast of Easter Island to any other coast in a day on foot. The king could have taken his message himself, or, if he had sent a messenger, the few hours occupied in transit would not have shaken out of his mind any detail of a verbal message. It is clear to anyone who has visited the islet that the script could not have had any necessity for its invention or persistence there. The primary purpose of any recording method is not to preserve the memory of the past, but to communicate information or commands or advice to some part of a political unity too distant from the center to permit of frequent personal visits. As a rule, it arises or is invented when the peoples of a large territory or archipelago have been unified either by conquest or federation. It could never have appeared in the history of man as long as he lived in isolated units without commercial intercourse or war. An archipelagic empire of considerable extent needed means of communication that would enable the central authority to keep in touch with its subordinates."

Such a far-flung "means of communication" as the Rapa Nui inhabitants possessed could never have served any useful purpose on their 15-mile-long island, and was only preserved as a memorial to the drowned civilization where it had been in use.

When members of the Thilenius South Seas Expedition expanded their study of the Oleai script to include the islet of Faraulep in 1908, they were surprised to find that the few otherwise-backward natives had additionally preserved a numerical system. To the expedition members' astonishment, they learned that it ranged in figures from 100,000 to 60 million! The islanders themselves took little interest in such inconceivable sums, never engaging in any calculations that could not be counted on their fingers and toes. To them, it was little more than a child's game or curiosity from remote prehistory. Only a few old men still understood the system, and when they died no one else was interested enough to preserve it. Ballinger remarked, "The extremely high numbers have no apparent use in the daily life of a people living on a very small, sandy atoll. What could they possibly use them for? Sixty million is an incomprehensible amount or figure to an educated, sophisticated man." After the expedition members brought these high figures to the attention of the outside world, the counting system was documented by the U.S. Trust Territory Department of Education before the anomalous numerical method was lost to posterity through the indifference of future native generations.

The Faraulep numerals bear resemblance to no others anywhere else in the world. Yet they were not conceived in a cultural vacuum. Instead, they are the self-evident remnant of a long lost mathematical system that could only have arisen over a significant period of development among a large population that needed to think on a far broader scale than the few hundred inhabitants of a materially unsophisticated, obscure islet. Faraulep was undoubtedly once part of that greater enterprise, which, passing away, left behind its astronomical figures. Although they correspond to nothing on the little western Pacific atoll, they are entirely commensurate with the quarter of a billion tons of magnetized basalt that went into the construction of an immense building project on another Caroline island, at Nan Madol, or with Easter Island's 100,000 tons of megalithic platforms and colossal statues. The survival of such a numerical system is testimony to that drowned Motherland of high technology remembered across the Pacific by millions of native peoples as Hiva, Marae Renga, Haiviki, Mu, or Lemuria.

The Oleai glyphs are likewise without parallel, including rongo-rongo. Nonetheless, two Oleai figures signifying the sun are pronounced *rah-a* and *re,* comparable to the Easter Islanders' Raa. The only point of comparison, significantly, between the two sets is the Rapa Nui character for Te-pito-te-henua, "navel of the world," Hotu Matua's name for the island, and the Oleai glyph *moh-o,* for "homeland," an apparent echo of Mu, the vanished Motherland. The Te-pito-te-henua and moh-o characters are alike: the former is a circle at the center of a larger one opening at top and bottom to a couple of vertical lines; the latter is an inside circle connected at top and bottom by two vertical lines to the perimeter of a larger, surrounding circle. The Lemurian identity of both glyphs seems clear. It also suggests that more than one written language was known in Mu, perhaps because the Pacific civilization originally encompassed vast stretches of variously populated territory, since inundated.

There was, in fact, another, now lost, Easter Island script. It recorded histories, annals, and other secular matters, unlike the myths, proverbs, and genealogies preserved by rongo-rongo, and was known by the revealing name of *tau*. According to James Churchward, the tau cross—a vertical line topped by a horizontal line —"is the symbol of Mu. It symbolizes both resurrection and immersion. Resurrection, a springing into life, and immersion, the raising of land above the waters." Churchward knew nothing of the lost tau script. Nor did he know that his definition of tau would at once identify Rapa Nui with the sunken civilization in ways he never suspected, while uncovering the ultimate mystery of Rapa Nui.

THREE

The Giants Speak

*Voluntarily or involuntarily, the sojourner must hold com-
mune with those old workers. For the whole air vibrates
with a vast purpose and energy which has been and is no
more. The dweller there is ever listening for he knows not
what, feeling unconsciously that he is in the antechamber
to something yet more vast which is just beyond his ken.*

KATHERINE ROUTLEDGE

Easter Island is an anomaly in the Pacific for more than archaeological
reasons. Seismologists learned during the late twentieth century that it
is located at the intersection of two major fault lines along a rift in the
Southeast Pacific Plateau. They run contrary to each other, forming a
cross, with Easter Island positioned precisely at a central point where the
vertical fault touches the horizontal line to create a tau configuration.
While conventional investigators may dismiss this geologic feature as
entirely coincidental where Churchward's symbol for Mu is concerned,
additional considerations suggest otherwise. For example, Hotu Matua's
choice of Te-pito-te-henua, the navel of the world, is remarkably fortu-
nate, given Easter Island's placement at the meeting point of two fault
lines. Yet it seems inconceivable that he or anyone else so long ago could
have known about the geologic underpinnings of Rapa Nui—unless that
person was in possession of a technology far beyond anything for which
we are willing to give him credit. But the evidence for such a lost science

83

stands in abundance all across Easter Island in the hundreds of colossi for which this place is most famous.

Although conventional researchers are satisfied that the Easter Island statues' construction and significance have been explained in terms of Polynesian culture, the theories of mainstream scholars, and even those

Statue head, or moai, from Easter Island (Bishop Museum, Oahu).

of maverick archaeologists like Thor Heyerdahl, aimed at demystifying the moai, collapse under the weight of basic data. Almost 1,000 of the statues have been identified, and more are being found, because many were completely buried. Archaeologists believe Easter Island's prehistoric population numbered perhaps 6,000 natives, which meant one moai for every six people, if all the colossi were raised within a single generation. Their uniformity of design suggests at least that they were not made over the course of many centuries. In any case, there were always far too many of them in relation to the number of inhabitants.

The average moai weighs fourteen tons, but they vary considerably in height, from a three-foot midget to a thirty-seven-foot giant weighing ninety-eight tons. A sixty-eight-foot colossus still lies unfinished at its quarry in the crater of the Rano Raraku volcano. If completed, it would have weighed an estimated 200 tons. Some, if not all, the statues originally featured inlaid coral eyes, a few pair of which have been restored in modern times. On their heads they wore strange headgear, called *pukao*, made from volcanic tufa that could be obtained only from the exterior slope of the Punapau volcano. It was here alone that the deep crimson rock could be found and transported all over Easter Island for the production of "hats" from three feet, ten inches across and six feet high to five feet, six inches wide and eight feet high, topped with a knob from half a foot to two feet high. This red headgear contrasted nicely with the dark gray bodies of granitelike andesite, scoria (volcanic slag), or basalt.

Although only the examples wearing the pukao stood on platforms, all the statues terminate at the hips below a pronounced navel made even more conspicuous by the figure's hands framing either side, as though to emphasize "This is Te-pito-te-henua, the Navel of the World." Some moai are decorated with abstract designs—circles, concentric configurations, and crescents (perhaps astronomical or solar signs)—whereas others are more recognizable, such as the likeness of a three-masted ship, testifying to a lost maritime proficiency.

Others are depicted wearing *hami*, or ceremonial loincloths, with anthropomorphic avian designs on the back and shoulders, suggesting the swimmers who competed every spring to retrieve the first sooty-tern egg from the offshore island of Motunui in a ritual honoring Makemake, the sacred bird-man. The winner shaved his head bald, then painted it red, again associating the athlete with moai wearing their pukao of tufa. Routledge reproduces a drawing make by native Easter Islanders of a *poki-manu,* or "bird-child," a participant in the Makemake cult wearing a girdle of circles, his back adorned with heart-shaped devices, as similarly portrayed on the ancient statues. She wrote that "reasons have been given for suggesting that the images on Raraku may have been memorials of bird-men."

The swimming champion's painted pate was itself a symbolic reference to the long-eared Hanau-eepe of Hotu Matua and his fair-complected, red-haired settlers who came to Rapa Nui after the inundation of their homeland. In the first professional expedition to Easter Island undertaken by the British archaeologist Katherine Routledge in 1915, a native told her about the ancient Long Ears, "the men who came from far away in ships. They saw they had pink cheeks, and they said they were gods. The last real *ariki,* or chief, was said to be quite white. 'White like me?' I innocently asked. 'You!' they said, 'you are red,' the colour in European cheeks." Brown concurred that red is "the term generally applied by Easter Islanders to Europeans. And *urukeku* is often translated, 'red-haired'." He went on to see something other than a Polynesian physiognomy in the towering moai, "and if the fine, oval faces, the large eyes, the short upper lip and the thin, often Apollo's bow lips, are any guide to race, they indicate a Caucasoid race."

The racial identity of Hotu Matua, his family, and his followers has been a disturbing enigma since that eponymous Easter Sunday in 1772, when Captain Rogeveen welcomed on board a native who was "a whole white man." Archaeologists are still unable to explain the undeniable presence of a Caucasian people in the Pacific during prehistory. When genetic testing was initiated in the 1990s, the results were unexpected. They demonstrated the presence of Basque genes among the mixed Rapa Nui population. The Basque are not Indo-Europeans, but rather are regarded by many anthropologists as the direct descendants of a

Stone Age people who occupied the Continent and British Isles 40,000 to 3,000 years ago. They were the great cave artists of Lascaux and, later, the prolific megalith builders of Karnac. They also appear related to similar populations in northern China, where the naturally mummified remains of non-Mongoloid inhabitants have been exhumed, and among the Caucasian Ainu of Japan. It is here, strangely enough, that the closest physical comparison with the moai may be found, not anywhere throughout Polynesia. Although Easter Island lies 8,250 miles away, the northwestern coastal residents of Hokkaido, with their high foreheads and pursed lips, most resemble the type portrayed in the great statues. These atypical Japanese are themselves directly descended from the Ainu, but with an untraceable ethnic admixture. Their lineage could go back to the same people who settled at Rapa Nui and Hokkaido. If so, they may be the last vestige of living Lemurians.

There is some suggestion that at least one function of the gaunt monoliths was to memorialize this vanished ancestral people. As Brown points out, the name for the statues has not found any satisfactory etymology; perhaps the eastern Polynesian word, *moa*, "sacred," and the common Polynesian root, *i,* for "ancestry," the basis of *ivi,* might furnish an explanation for their purpose, "sacred to the ancestors." If so, *moai* is a word applied to the statues by Polynesians who arrived after the Caucasian Long Ears began setting up civilization. Although the bones of many ariki have been found in the platforms upon which the statues were erected, these discoveries do not necessarily mean that the ahu were exclusively royal ossuaries, but that they, like the moai themselves, served various purposes over time and under different cultural circumstances, from their original intentions instituted by Hotu Matua through the decline of the Hanau-eepe and the Polynesian takeover.

Most of the moai are buried deep in the ground, but some were set up on ahu of often exquisitely fitted stone leading from the land to the shore. Approximately 260 of these platforms ring the Easter Island coastline, embodying the ancient solar cult in their precise orientations to various positions of the sun. The Ahu Akivi, with its seven moai representing Hotu Matua and his six original pioneers, is aligned to sunset on the vernal equinox. These statues alone look out to sea, in the direction of the sunken Motherland. All others have their backs to the ocean from which their makers came. The Ahu Akivi's obvious Lemurian implications are underscored in Hawaiian oral tradition, which relates that Ku-Mu-honua had a son known as Ahu. The function of the Easter Island platforms as burial crypts is suggested by Ahu's murder at the hands of his elder brother, while Ku-Mu-honua's characterization as "the first man" self-evidently references human beginnings at Mu. The term *ahu,* then, was probably meant to memorialize an early Lemurian still remembered by the Hawaiians.

Many Rapa Nui platforms are more than 200 feet long, all of them built of massive blocks tooled and shaped so perfectly that a knife blade cannot be inserted between them. They show no indications of chipping or mistakes of any kind, signifying that they must have been carefully engineered, measured, and completely dressed to a precise plan before assembly. Their incorporation of exact solar alignments demonstrates a sophisticated astronomy practiced by the prehistoric architects.

The ahu terminate in two or three steep steps upon which the moai were set up by a process that continues to bedevil archaeologists. Some scholars believe their theories explain the transportation of 14- to 200-ton statues from their quarry as far as fifteen miles away. But no investigator has been able to show how the ungainly monoliths were lifted up to the top of the raised tiers without breaking or chipping both ahu and moai. Nor has anyone been able to demonstrate how the tufa-red headgear were "placed, by some ingenious device, upon the heads of figures twenty to thirty feet high," according to T. A. Joyce in *Ancient American* magazine. Brown wondered:

> How were they able to haul those brittle statues over the most uneven of surfaces, all littered with angular stones, as far as twelve or fifteen miles, without an accident in lowering them from their benches on the hillside? And here, across the stoniest, most uneven islet in the world, dozens of them were hauled without a mishap, without even a scratch. Imagine statues of material that seems no

harder than the mixture of putty and pebbles, well compressed, being dragged over even our macadamized roads, how much of them would be left before they reached their destination?

More than eighty years after Brown asked these questions, archaeologists are still unable to satisfactorily answer them, because they continue to regard Easter Island exclusively within the limitations of Polynesian material culture. They refuse to consider the more obvious truth, however objectionable: that the prehistoric inhabitants of Rapa Nui possessed a technology far greater than anything known to the Polynesians and perhaps superior to own, in at least some respects. The merest hint of this lost construction art occurs in local legend, which tells how the gigantic statues were made to walk to their assigned positions through the power of *mana*, a supernatural or psychic force, conjured by priests of the Hanau-eepe. Another tale describes a pair of enchanters who, in the deep past, flew through the air from their distant homeland to teach an old Easter Island woman the secrets of color dyeing. These stories are somewhat reminiscent of renditions told on the other side of the Pacific Ocean, at Pohnpei, to explain Nan Madol's massive stones, which were supposedly flown into place by two sorcerers from their far-off mother country. A comparison of these widely separated myths implies that some kind of high technology from an outside source was responsible for the ambitious public-works projects at both islands.

Although construction and occupation dates for Nan Madol are uncertain, most archaeologists believe that a chronology for Easter Island's prehistory has been established. It shows that the earliest radiocarbon dates for human settlement there begin around 450 A.D., after which the colossi were set up on their ahu platforms in three major phases, and rongo-rongo was transferred to wooden tablets over the next 1,300 years, until shortly after the arrival of the first modern Europeans in 1772. Credible as these time parameters may be, they contradict Rapa Nui's foundation account, which relates how its founding father, Hotu Matua, his family, and followers were forced from their homeland because it was slammed with meteorites while being overwhelmed by a cataclysmic deluge. But the geologic record shows no evidence for a natural catastrophe in the Pacific or anywhere else on Earth during the fifth century, certainly nothing involving an extraterrestrial bombardment. Our investigation of Mu traces its origins to some preglacial period more than 10,000 years ago.

In attempting to make the archaeologists' chronology conform with Easter Island myth and the story of Lemuria, could some remnant of its otherwise vanished civilization have persisted as late as 450 A.D. on some archipelagic fragment remembered as Marae Renga? Either that, or there is something fundamentally wrong with current carbon-14 testing, or at least it is incomplete. To rely exclusively on this disputable method, shown to have been far less than accurate on many occasions, may be an important mistake that has misled mainstream researchers to assume the unlikely—that Rapa Nui was a cultural anomaly utterly cut off from the outside world. David Hatcher Childress, who personally confronted the mystery of Easter Island, is one of many independent investigators convinced conventional dating procedures there and elsewhere are flawed. He wondered at "the large lichen spots on all the statues. Lichen eats living rock and grows very slowly—fractions of an inch over hundreds of years. Ages of rock are sometimes estimated by how large the lichen patches on them are. A large lichen patch would suggest that these statues were thousands of years old. In an effort to check this out, I measured lichen patches on uncut rock. They were only slightly larger than those on the statues themselves."

Lichenometry readings have taken place at Easter Island, but these were inadequately conducted for the first and only time more than forty years ago, when the method was still being developed. Results, whatever they may have been, have not been updated since and actually appear to have been lost. Opportunities for using lichen to determine the real age of civilization at Rapa Nui were dealt a serious blow during the late twentieth century, when two moai and an ahu wall at Vinapu were scrubbed clean of all growth by German archaeologists from Frankfurt's Senckenburg Museum as part of a silicon-casting project. The cost to research was especially high, because the removed lichen were among the oldest and best preserved on the island. As Jo Ann Van Tilburg lamented in *Antiquity* magazine, "Subsequent loss of these lichens due to the mould-matrix is a significant alteration of artifact data, as lichenometric studies may have potential for dating the figures."

Even so, lichenometry is by no means a final solution for determining the actual time parameters of Rapa Nui's prehistoric culture. As Shawn McLaughlin of the Easter Island Foundation explains:

Since we know that lichen growth rates vary with the species under consideration, as well as macro- and micro-environmental conditions (including air pollution, but assuming no direct or human interference; otherwise, all bets are off), it's risky to conclude a fixed growth rate for the organism, especially in a context of dating. And some debate continues to the effect of what's known as the "great period," where lichen experience an initial, rapid growth, and which can last from a few decades to, according to one critic of lichenometry, as much as four hundred years. One study, for example, revealed a growth rate curve of 14 mm during the "great period" (of one hundred years), followed by steady, linear growth of 3.3 mm per century thereafter. Another study revealed a growth curve of 3.8 to 4.5 mm per century. As might be expected, averaging in lichenometry is considered to be highly unreliable.

Other attempts to determine credible time frames for Easter Island have included obsidian hydration, based on the rate of water absorption into the surface of artifacts made from volcanic glass. But matching natural processes to human influences is problematic. More importantly, fifth-century radiocarbon dates contradict the depths at which the moai have been buried, not by human hands, but through natural deposition. Many of the monoliths stand up to their necks in soil; some are completely covered. The time needed to obscure them under twenty or more feet of earth, as Childress concluded from his comparison of lichen growth, involved millennia, not centuries, of accumulation. Also, something more than a cursory archaeological examination of the ocean floor in the immediate vicinity of Easter Island might reveal cultural artifacts that could backdate human settlement there previous to the last ice age, before surrounding tracts of territory were engulfed by a catastrophic rise in sea level caused by melting glaciers.

Whether in the deeply ancient or the more recent past, why did the Easter Islanders go to such lengths of planning and toil to manufacture and transport so many monumental statues? Establishment scientists' explanations that they were simply ancestral monuments, oversized boundary markers, tombstones, or the effigies of swimming champions do not measure up to the steep costs in physical and intellectual energy their creation required, nor do their numbers in a one-to-six ratio vis-à-vis the inhabitants. These labor-intensive demands made on the entire community could have been justified to a sophisticated, literate people only by some fundamentally urgent purpose more universally compelling than fixing borders or memorializing an elite minority. According to an 1892 article in *Nature* magazine, "The traditions in regard to the images are numerous, but relate principally to impossible occurrences, such as being endowed with power to walk about in the darkness, assisting certain clans by subtle means in contests, and delivering oracular judgments." Perhaps the "occurrences" assigned by tradition only seemed "impossible" to a late-nineteenth-century mentality that still balks at any suggestion of powers outside the parameters of Victorian archaeology. If we temporarily put aside all theories for their existence and reconsider the moai exclusively in terms of their material construction and natural environment, they may answer the question that began this paragraph.

Some of the earliest statues were made of andesite, a fine-grained rock not unlike granite in appearance but consisting of plagioclase feldspar and dark ferromagnesian materials, such as pyroxene. These are nothing more than different kinds of crystals. Other moai were fashioned from local volcanic basalt, unlike the construction of Nan Madol, which obtained its basalt from an unknown source. The prehistoric builders at Rapa Nui and Pohnpei may be related, however, in their use of crystalline rock. As mentioned earlier, Easter Island is located at the intersection of two major fault lines. The same piezoelectric conditions described at Pohnpei exist at Rapa Nui, where the Long Ears may have taken advantage of the ability of certain crystals to generate voltage when under geologic pressure.

Thanks to their crystalline materials, Easter Island's standing colossi transformed the mechanical energy of earthquakes, discharging it into electrical energy, thereby ameliorating the worst effects of seismic upheaval. The moai would have acted like reverse-energy antennas or the geologic equivalent of lightning rods, conducting and transmuting dangerous terrestrial forces into the atmosphere. Together, they formed an anti-earthquake device. If so, Rapa Nui as the site of their construction was well chosen, because the island sits strategically at the fulcrum of the seismically active Southeast Pacific Plateau. If a people wanted to build a civilization in the eastern Pacific, they had to find some way of at least lessening the worst effects of geologic violence. Easter Island is perfectly located for the installation of just such a device that would disperse or damp down terrestrial upheavals, making society possible. As long ago as the early twentieth century, the respected U.S. archaeologist Alexander Moerenhout was cited in *American Anthropologist* for his belief that the moai "had a common meaning and were all representatives of beings called *titi,* whose function it was to mark the limits of the sea and land, to maintain harmony between the two elements, and [to] prevent their encroachment upon one another." The natives themselves continue to assert that the monoliths were made and put in place to protect their island from harm.

The titi Moerenhout mentions refers to their leader, Maui-Tikitiki, or "Maui the Topknot." He alone is impersonated by the Easter Island statues, which explains why they are all alike. The red tufa headgear they wear are not hats, but rather stylized topknots in their portrayal of Maui-Tikitiki. He was the Polynesian Hercules, who, among other adventures, fished up a sunken kingdom from the bottom of the sea. His title, Tikitiki, or "top knot,"means he was a member of a privileged spiritual elite, just as Japanese samurai guarded their topknots as their most sacred badge of honor. To suffer the shearing of one's topknot at the hands of a victorious enemy was the worst form of humiliation, compensated only by *seppuku,* or ritual suicide. Buddha is usually depicted in temple art wearing a topknot, which he voluntarily cut off, then tossed to the highest levels of heaven. It symbolized his crown chakra, a psychic center connecting his soul to the Compassionate Intelligence that co-creates the universe in cooperation with enlightened beings. This was what Rapa Nui's pukao were intended to represent—the spiritual energies of human and God combined in the topknot of crown-chakra illumination. Although the fundamental utility of the moai was to act as geotransducers, their engineers were not content merely to erect them as undressed standing stones, like those of megalithic Europe, but instead fashioned them into sacred statues. In these colossi, science and spirituality are fused for complementary purposes.

World-travel writer Mark Williams observes, "The island's volcanoes do in fact produce magnetic anomalies, and a large sphere of smooth stone at La Perouse Bay radiates heat and makes compasses go haywire. If Rapa Nui is the navel of the world, this strange rock is the island's own belly button. Maybe ancient shamans similar to kahuna [Hawaiian sorcerers] geotransducers or the priests of Nan Madol used the electromagnetic field somehow to suspend gravity and render the statues weightless."

Hotu Matua's "strange rock" was the most precious heirloom carried from his sunken homeland to Easter Island, which was named after the sacred stone. If, as it appears, the polished basalt object was part of the statues' collective function as an anti-earthquake device, it would have sometimes generated the heat and electromagnetic energies Williams mentions. It would have also radiated with an occasional corona discharge of excited electrical particles to produce the Andes-Glow phenomenon still sighted at the ruins of Nan Madol. If so, then the stone's traditional identification as Te-pito-te-Kura, the navel of light, is appropriate and explicable.

A side effect of the Andes Glow might also explain why this object was esteemed with singular reverence: a curious by-product is its profound effect on human behavior. Its energies generate electromagnetic fields that can powerfully influence the electromagnetic circuitry of the brain to induce altered states of consciousness. The harnessed power of our planet was something not only directed to disperse and relieve tectonic stress, but also used in spiritual ways we are only just discovering. For example, it is now understood that granite in large volume produces relatively high levels of radiation, which alter human consciousness by inducing drowsiness and psycho-spiritual experiences, such as a sense of traveling through time and astral projection.

Better understood are the effects negative ions exert on the mind. Humans have an embedded layer of high ion content in the bones forming the walls of the sinuses, or the deep-seated sphenoid-ethmoid sinus complex, in close proximity to the brain. It reacts to high doses of negative ions by connecting with the temporal lobe, itself sensitive to electromagnetic influences. Otherwise known as the hippocampus, its functions include dreaming and memory, consciousness and subconsciousness. Consequently, a person spending any time with the Te-pito-te-Kura, especially when it was properly charged with a negative ion flow generated by tectonic action, could undergo mind-altered phenomena akin to a powerful spiritual experience. The "navel of light" may be an electrodynamic resonator at extra-low frequency that directly centers on the brain's so-called alpha frequency.

When we are passively alert—awake but fully relaxed and tending toward sleep—we are said to be in an alpha state. Medical researchers now realize that the brain generates an electrical field of its own in relation to the Earth's magnetic field. In fact, researcher Francis Ivanhoe demonstrated that the Ammon's horn of the brain actually "reads" the fluctuating field strength of the Earth's magnetosphere. As the hippocampus is stimulated with negative-ion discharge, the brain's alpha frequency deepens to generate bodily sensations of physical euphoria, while the mind may experience time-space alterations, apparitions, or other psycho-spiritual phenomena. These effects on human consciousness were probably the by-products of the moai's original collective purpose as a geologic transducer. They may have been discovered only after the statues had been set up and began to function as they were originally built to, and their tremendous fountain of discharged negative ions to relieve tectonic stress was observed to alter mental perceptions. As a secondary function to the initially mundane intentions of its builders, the moai could also have been used as objects of spiritual transformation.

To serve as the water supply of a community, a spring-fed pond is dug. But its waters have a high mineral content that produces curative or restorative effects, and it is likewise used as a site for healing. This simple analogy may be applied to the early story of the moai. Whatever they later became, they were first and foremost intended at least to mitigate the worst effects of seismic catastrophes. Major building projects in the ancient past, as today, probably served multiple functions. But the construction materials and placement of the moai match their identification as parts of a tectonic transducer far better than any other purpose assigned to them. They nevertheless represent powerful evidence for a high technology allegedly saved from some great kingdom before its watery destruction, and apparently shared with Nan Madol. At Easter Island and Pohnpei, a super science more ecologically harmonious and advanced than our own sought to control natural disasters from Earth and sky. The remains of that forgotten technology at both islands clearly define its origins in the drowned Motherland of the Pacific. The Rosicrucian author W. S. Cerve described this interaction of psychic experience with applied science as long ago as 1931 when he wrote, "The Lemurians achieved a great scientific comprehension of natural laws and at the same time [developed] inwardly certain human abilities to a degree much greater and higher than we have attained today, with all our boasted advancement in civilization."

Various traditions from several parts of the world describe Mu as a global entity, and certainly something of this characterization is suggested by the name Navel of the World. Childress points out that the Indus Valley, with its rongo-rongo-like script, and Rapa Nui "are precisely on opposite sides of the Earth: Mohenjo Daro is located at twenty seven degrees, twenty three minutes North, and about sixty nine degrees East; Easter Island is at twenty seven degrees, eight minutes South, and one hundred nine degrees, twenty three minutes West."

Exactly between Mohenjo Daro and Easter Island lie the Solomon Islands. Here alone throughout the vast Pacific, among all its thousands of islands save only at Rapa Nui, may be found examples of rongo-rongo, or the Indus Valley script. In her *Mystery of Easter Island,* Routledge reproduced five very close comparisons of Solomon Island signs similarly depicting Makemake, the bird-man, a bird holding a fish by its left wing, a spread-eagle figure with upraised arms, and a frigate bird in flight. A shared Lemurian source for these glyphs appears to have left its mark in the name of a small island among the Trobriand Group in the Solomon Sea. It is known as Mu-nawata.

A line extended halfway from Easter Island in the opposite direction from Mohenjo Daro terminates on the other side of the world in an empty stretch of the Atlantic Ocean east of the Azore Islands. It was here, outside the Straits of Gibraltar, referred to by Plato as the Pillars of Heracles, that the philosopher asserted that Lemuria's counterpart was located before it too was obliterated by a natural catastrophe. Could a former center of high civilization have been among four points of distance that measured the Earth in very ancient times? At least Rapa Nui, the Solomon Islands, and the Indus Valley were connected by 6,500-mile units and a common script. The global link suggested by that connection breaks, significantly enough, in the eastern Atlantic Ocean, where the capital of Atlantis was said to have held sway before its cataclysmic demise.

"The prospect opens up a vista of extraordinary interest," wrote the early twentieth century's premier Atlantologist, Lewis Spence. "All the evidence, preposterous or not, points to a communication of the Atlantis culture-complex to Lemurian Oceania via America. It seems to me then that we are almost compelled, whether we like it or not—and personally, I avouch myself as almost averse from such an acceptance—to agree that communication of some description must have taken place between Atlantis and Lemuria at a very early period."

Some of the evidence Spence found was preserved in oral traditions spanning the Pacific. The Maori, for example, revered the memory of Atua, the "altar of the god," a holy mountain, the original homeland of their ancestors, who largely perished when it sank beneath the ocean. Atua is also the name of a district in Western Samoa, whose inhabitants speak the oldest language in Polynesia. *At* is associated with volcanic islands throughout the Pacific Ocean, such as Atiu, an extinct volcano forming an atoll among the southern Cook Islands in the southwestern Pacific. Atauro is a small island near East Timor, memorializing, in native tradition, a larger landmass long ago swallowed by the sea.

Polynesian mythologist Johannes C. Andersen reported that natives of the Fiji Islands told of a worldwide deluge that annihilated both Atlanteans and Lemurians: "By this flood it is said that two tribes of the human family became extinct."

The Atas are natives of the mountainous central region of Mindanao, in the Philippines. They tell how the Great Flood "covered the whole Earth, and all the Atas were drowned except for two men and a woman. The waters carried them far away." An eagle offered to save them but one of the men refused, so the bird took up the other man and the woman, carrying them to safety on the island of Mapula. Here the Atas were reborn and eventually multiplied sufficiently to conquer the entire Philippines. The Atas still claim descent from these light-skinned invaders, who, over time, intermarried with the Negritos and aboriginal peoples.

An extinct volcanic mountain of the Tongatapu Group in the southwestern Pacific is known as Ata, revered by the Tonga islanders as a natural memorial to red-haired, fair-skinned gods who arrived long ago to somehow "bless" the natives.

The Marquesans regarded Atea as their ancestral progenitor. The nineteenth-century anthropologist Abraham Fornander wrote, "In the Marquesan legends the people claim their descent from Atea and Tani, the two eldest of Toho's twelve sons, whose descendants, after long periods of alternate migrations and rest in the far western lands, finally arrived at the Marquesas Islands." Like Atlas, Atea was his father's first son and a twin. With his story begins the long migration of some Atlanteans, the descendants of Atea, throughout the Pacific. Fornander saw Atea as "the god which corresponds to Kane in the Hawaiian group," and goes on to explain that "the ideas of solar worship embodied in the Polynesian Kane as the sun, the sun-god, the shining one, are thus synonymous with the Marquesan Atea, the bright one, the light."

The Marquesans' account of Atlantis is described in their oral epic *Te Vanana na Tanaoa:*

Atanua was beautiful and good, adorned with riches very great. Atanua was fair, very rich and soft. Atanua produced abundantly of living things. Atea [and his brothers] dwelt as kings in the most beautiful palaces supported on thrones. They ruled the space of heaven and the large, entire sky and all the powers thereof [astrology]. The first lords dwelling on high. Oh, throne placed in the middle of the upper heavens! The great lord Atea established in love to love the fair Atanua. A woman of great wealth is Atanua. From within Atea came forth Ono [a terrible sound, the explosion of Mount Atlas erupting]. Atea produces the very hot fire.

Atea's association, like that of Atlas, with a volcanic mountain was recognized by Fornander: "In this sense, it would appropriately convey the idea of the lurid light which accompanies an eruption of the volcano."

If Atlantis and Lemuria were in contact with each other, at least something of that relationship should have survived their passing. A combination of names does indeed appear in At-ia-Mu-ri, one of New Zealand's most important megalithic sites, regarded by Brown as evidence for builders from a sunken civilization. Its native Maori name suggests a combination of At[lantis] and Mu at this halfway location between the two sunken kingdoms. Another fusion takes place in Atamu, cited earlier as a descendant of one of Rapa Nui's two long-eared Hanau-eepe aristocrats to survive the Poike Ditch massacre. These correspondences in Oceania myth and archaeology support the distances apparently measured out around the globe from the Lemurian realm of Rapa Nui in the eastern Pacific, through the Solomon Islands and India, to the Atlantean sphere of influence in the mid-Atlantic. As the British astronomer John Wilson concluded as long ago as the late nineteenth century, "The wandering Masons, who have left their monuments in the four quarters of the world, will be found to have traversed the great Pacific Ocean, made the circuit of the globe, and measured its circumference."

But what are we to make of the often bizarre evidences for Easter Island and even more fantastic conclusions they suggest? Its foundation story is a transparent recollection of culture bearers (the long-eared Hanau-eepe) from Mu (Hotu Matua's Marae Renga, on Hiva). They worshipped sun-gods, just as the Lemurians were depicted by Churchward and other investigators as proponents of a solar religion. Their written language was not some cultural fluke, but rather a self-evident legacy from the literate Lemurians. The anomalous presence of an otherwise unaccountable Caucasian race in the eastern Pacific can likewise be explained only by the former existence of the lost Motherland, said to have been ruled by a light-skinned elite. The creation and transportation of a thousand statues, some in excess of ninety tons, was utterly beyond anything remotely comparable throughout Polynesia, but was traditionally attributed to the high technology associated with Mu.

That technology was installed to prevent or ameliorate seismic violence along an unstable rift zone in the crucial Southeast Pacific Plateau, which threatened a number of connected archipelagoes inhabited by the Lemurians. They recognized Easter Island's strategic position at the epicenter of a capital *T*, or flat-topped cross, formed by two connecting fault lines on the bottom of the sea, a configuration they used as the tau emblem of their civilization. Rapa Nui's location at its precise meeting point merited the island's designation as Navel of the World, because it was here that their world was geologically focused. Either the basalt and andesite moai failed to cope with the magnitude of the disaster that struck or they were set up too late to affect it, and Mu was destroyed.

When the first modern Europeans visited Easter Island, they saw natives still venerating the memory of their ancestral Motherland before seven statues on the shore facing the direction of the sunken civilization, and in ritual swimming contests to an offshore islet with the provocative name of Mutunui. Although the descendants of Hotu Matua survived thirty-four centuries after the cataclysm, they could not withstand internal civil unrest or imported religious intolerance, slavery, and leprosy. Within a generation after Captain Rogeveen dropped anchor off Rapa Nui on that fateful Easter Sunday in 1772, the island's science, art, and history were virtually forgotten. The Navel of the World suffered a second calamity more dire than the natural disaster that overwhelmed the Lemurian homeland it was intended to save.

Although extraordinary, it is nevertheless true that the two foremost archaeological sites in the Pacific are each located at the precise centers of meteorological or geological crossroads where their spectacular accumulations of organized basalt would tend to mitigate the worst effects of typhoons and earthquakes. Apparently coincidental relationships between Pohnpei and Easter Island vanish in light of these singular properties and unique environments. At each of the widely separated islands, we glimpse the wreck of an ancient technology powered by the same forces of nature it was designed to control, technology that ultimately miscarried. There was nothing inherently evil or weak in this lost art of applied ecological science. It collapsed instead through the shortcomings of its creators, who mastered the powers of Earth and sky but failed to control their fellow human beings.

The monumental ruins of Nan Madol and Rapa Nui are testimony to other civilizations before and since that, unable to achieve cultural balance, committed social suicide and disappeared into the void of prehistory. But enough of their achievement remains for at least a general reconstruction. As such, Pohnpei and Easter Island are microcosmic mirrors in which our own reflection is all too clear.

FOUR

Ancient Oceanic Technology

We all agree that your theory is mad. The problem that
divides us is this: Is it sufficiently crazy to be right?

NIELS BOHR

In our last several chapters, we described archaeological ruins on the islands of Pohnpei and Rapa Nui as the remains of power stations erected by the Lemurians millennia ago to effect seismic and meteorological change. If these sites were the only such evidence, they might be dismissed as the lonely outposts of some foreign civilization that established itself in isolation, utterly alien to anything known elsewhere. But additional evidence on behalf of that lost science has indeed been found, most dramatically at another obscure speck of territory in the southwestern Pacific.

Known until 1978 as the Isle of Pines, Kunie (pronounced KOO-nya) is inhabited by 1,500 Melanesian residents living on fifty-eight square miles of French Polynesia. The eight-by-ten-mile island has bewildered investigators since its discovery in 1774, because it is the only place in Oceania with stands of ancient pine trees *(Araucaria cookii)* named after the famous English explorer Captain James Cook. How they got there and why they continue to thrive on Kunie, but nowhere else throughout the vast Pacific, is an enigma that still eludes scientific explanation. They must have been brought to and planted at this Melanesian outpost in prehistory. But by whom, and for what purpose? The trees are gigantic, towering from heights of 90 to 135 feet, although their branches are only about six feet long. The titanic pines guard Kunie's rocky coastline and sprout from the tops of small hills.

The curious little island suddenly multiplied its mystery in 1961, when a university-trained archaeologist excavated some of the mounds that dot the Isle of Pines. They had never been professionally examined before, largely because the hillocks were presumed to be natural formations of some kind. Directors at the Museum of New Caledonia, in Moumea, the capital city, wanted to know if the tumuli might have been used by native ancestors for burial, so Luc Chevalier was dispatched to retrieve what, if any, artifacts he could find inside them.

Digging into the first mound he approached, Chevalier was surprised to discover a cement cylinder, two feet wide and seven feet long. Composed of an extremely hard, homogeneous lime mortar containing innumerable bits of shell, its exterior was speckled with silica and iron gravel fragments that appeared to have hardened the mortar as it set. Chevalier was inclined to dismiss the obviously man-made cylinder as a remnant of some modern historical, albeit unknown, but prosaic influences and went on to excavate another earthwork. In it he found a cement drum virtually identical to the first. With some astonishment, he gazed across the Kunie landscape, which rippled with 400 such tumuli, resembling a colony of giant anthills. Could they all hide such anomalous cylinders? he wondered.

Chevalier hurried back across the forty miles of open water with his specimens to Moumea, where they were analyzed at the museum laboratories. Researchers there verified that samples from both cylinders were artificial, but they were not prepared for the results of radiocarbon dating of Kunie's lime mortar. Repeated tests confirmed that the cement was nearly 13,000 years old. Chevalier was sent back to the Isle of Pines at the head of an archaeological team intent on a more thorough excavation. As he suspected, each of the 400 mounds contained cement pillars all alike in construction, differing only in their dimensions. They ranged in size from two feet across to more than forty inches, with lengths from three feet to in excess of nine feet. Seventeen similar mounds existed on New Caledonia itself, in an area known as Paiita, and Chevalier dug into them as well, scarcely able to imagine that they, too, concealed such strange objects. He was not disappointed, however. At the center of each earthwork was entombed a column of cement.

In comparing tumuli on the two nearby islands, the columns at the Isle of Pines differed only in their gravelly sand with high-iron oxide content from the Paiita versions with their silicaceous sand. At both locations, the hillocks stood eight or nine feet tall, averaging 300 feet in diameter. They are uniformly bare, because little or no vegetation is able to take root in their sandy construction. The hillocks contained not a single bone, artifact, or piece of burned charcoal to confirm initial speculation that they were used for burial, habitation, or ceremonial practices. Chevalier concluded that narrow shafts had been sunk vertically into the tops of the mounds. Liquid lime mortar was then poured into the pits, where it hardened in position.

Incredulous academicians refused to accept the artificiality of what Chevalier had discovered, simply because they were convinced human habitation in the southwestern Pacific before 3,000 years ago was "ridiculously impossible." Skeptics endeavored to explain away the cement cylinders by arguing they were actually nests made by some hypothetical species of extinct giant birds, a wildly ludicrous attempt to buoy up already moldy dogma banishing all considerations of early humans from Oceania. The skeptics insisted that the earliest use of cement went back hardly more than 2,000 years ago, to the engineers of ancient Rome. Yet here, in the southwestern Pacific, some maverick archaeologists were spouting scientific heresy by claiming the natives of little Kunie had been mass-producing mortar cylinders at the end of the last ice age.

Museum of New Caledonia authorities insisted, however, that their consistent testing of the cement columns unquestionably reaffirmed they were made by humans between 5120 B.C. and 10,950 B.C. These date parameters were subsequently reconfirmed with the aid of additional radiocarbon examinations of the same material by laboratory technicians at Yale University. Chevalier cited the Kunie and New Caledonian mounds as unique, and challenged conservative critics to show the whereabouts of identical or even generally similar cement pillars that had resulted from demonstrably natural processes. But answer came there none from mainstream scholars.

Neither Chevalier nor his detractors, however, were able to postulate the original utility of the lime-mortar columns. Childress, who visited the Isle of Pines in the mid-1980s, estimated their number at 10,000. Although that amount seems excessive, they might approach a tenth as many. Chevalier discovered that "three of the tumuli contained one cylinder each, and the fourth had two of them side by side. In each case, the cylinders were positioned in the center of the tumuli, set vertically." But again, why did someone go to the bother of making hundreds of cement columns on this tiny backwater of an island? What purpose could they possibly have served? Their total lack of any adornment, ritual items, or human and animal remains proves they had no funereal or ceremonial functions. However, a clue may be found in those other anomalies shared at Kunie. Could its tall, deep-rooted pines have been deliberately planted along the coast by the same people who made the cement cylinders as an effective shield to protect their tumuli against the typhoons still known to ravage the island? It does at least seem oddly coincidental that two sets of features otherwise unique throughout the Pacific should be found together on the same obscure island, unless they were specifically intended from the beginning to complement each other.

The mounds themselves were undoubtedly of special importance to have merited a protective coastline of trees. That original significance is suggested by the high iron content found in all the cement cylinders, implying they were related to the ecological technology in evidence at Pohnpei and Easter Island. While their intended function is no longer understood, we may assume they were probably powered by natural forces, perhaps seismic or meteorological, to somehow effect environmental change, not unlike the monumental structures of Nan Madol and Rapa Nui. Although the lost science of Kunie is no longer even a memory, its 400 mounds of lime-mortar columns still stand as testimony to the former technological greatness of Mu, whose people applied the energies of nature to human society in deep prehistory.

Although myth is absent from the Isle of Pines, New Caledonia, on which seventeen of the cement cylinder mounds have been excavated, does feature a Lemurian tradition to the effect that "souls of the dead float down the rivers toward the ocean, where they will live on the seabed," according to the mythologist Jan Knappert. He reports that natives believe the soul, or *ko,* becomes a small animal, such as a rat or a lizard. The animal is retrieved by a watchful priest, who plunges with it into the nearest river, where the ko infuses something of its power into a smooth round stone known as a *bao,* or spirit rock. As the soul continues on its riverine journey to the ocean, the bao is placed in a special shrine, the *mwaro,* along with other ancestral stones. These Melanesian terms parallel the ancient Egyptian division of the human soul into its primary halves, the *ka* and *ba.* But the ancestral shrine, the mwaro, appears to have received its philological derivation from Mu, whose material imprint on the island survives in New Caledonia's collection of lime-mortar pillars. Egypto-Lemurian influences also seem evident in a traditional dance, the *tamure,* still performed throughout French Polynesia.

The cement cylinders there are joined by yet another extraordinary proof of lost civilization in the Pacific, 1,400 miles east of Kunie on the island of Tonga. At just eighteen miles long, Tonga does not seem to have ever been physically significant enough to deserve special consideration, either now or in the ancient past. Yet someone on Tonga long ago commanded the construction of a 109-ton gate or arch, fifteen feet high and eighteen feet wide. The trilithon comprises a pair of rough-hewn columns, their tops cut with notches into which a nine-ton lintel was laid. How this engineering feat was supposedly achieved by a preindustrial people possessing little in material culture is difficult to understand. Likewise enigmatic is the source of the coral, which was not quarried at Tonga or, as stated in local legend, Uvea. Nothing like the Ha'amonga a Maui, or "Burden of Maui," is found anywhere else in Oceania, and its origins are no less a mystery to the islanders. All they can offer is that it was built by the Polynesian demigod Maui in the deep past with stones he brought from Wallis Island (Uvea) in a giant canoe.

As recently as 1967, however, the islanders' king noticed that a line carved on the lintel was oriented to sunrise on the summer solstice. Subsequent examination of the trilithon revealed its function, at least in part, as a solar calendar, calling to mind the massive Gateway to the Sun perched atop the Bolivian ruins of Tiahuanaco, with its thematic connections to the eastern Pacific. Could both monumental arches have been built by the same Lemurians whose influence once stretched from Tonga to the high Andes of South America? The Ha'amonga a Maui seems to imply as much, if only because the inhabitants of Mu were practitioners of a sun cult. Moreover, the trilithon is located at Heketa, near the east coast, suggesting oceanic origins, not unlike the moai of Easter Island standing along the coast in memory of Hotu Matua's arrival from his sunken homeland.

Lemurian clues may also be found in the gate's name. The Herculean Maui was a descendant of Muri-Ranga-Whenua, an apparent variant on the name of the Pacific Motherland. Was the "burden" he carried to Tonga the great stones from Mu before its inundation? In *The Lore of the Wharewananga,* a collection of Polynesian myths cited by Spence, Maui intervenes between the gods of earthquake and tempest who were trying to dismember and deluge a long stretch of primeval territory. Although Maui prevents its complete destruction, Papa is reduced to a string of islands. This tradition is the folkish memory of a former landmass broken up and partially sunk into the sea by seismic violence, a legend that accounts for the present distribution of archipelagoes stretching across the Pacific as remnants of Papa, yet another name for the lost civilization.

The Lemurian origins of Tonga's singular arch appear again at the island's prehistoric capital six miles from Heketa, located on the eastern shore of Fanga'uta Lagoon, appropriately enough for a seafaring culture. The old town is called Mu'a, with its wharf at Mu'nu, names self-evidently derived from the Motherland. The central area of Mu'a was encircled by a canal of immense proportions. Even today, after millennia of silting, this gigantic canal is thirty or thirty-six feet deep. Nearby are a number of *langi,* a local name for pyramids that rival their Egyptian counterparts. An impressive specimen is a stone platform known as the Tauhala. Just one of its blocks is more than twenty-one feet in length, weighing an estimated forty metric tons. With an engineering skill that defies belief, it was somehow inserted into a wall 666 feet long. Like its Easter Island and Peruvian counterparts, the colossal stone has been notched to fit like a puzzle piece with the matching cut of its neighbor. This unmortared arrangement was designed to make the pyramid earthquake resistant, allowing its stones to give but not separate.

The very existence of the Tauhala on the same island as that other construction marvel, the Burden of Maui, is dramatic proof that a highly advanced building technology was at work on Tonga during the ancient past. Some indication of the depth of that antiquity may be deduced at Mu'a itself, which has risen three feet since it was built, rendering the wharf useless. Oceanographers believe sea levels fluctuate over time, estimating that vessels could no longer be accommodated at Mu'nu about 2,000 years ago, although this projected period does not indicate when the wharf was made.

Another langi at Lapaha is hardly less impressive, but it bears a closer stylistic resemblance to the "citadel" found eighty feet beneath the surface of the Pacific off Japan's Yonaguni island, near Iseki Point. Each rectilinear structure features small, apparently ceremonial stairs ascending among larger, step-like layers and incorporates common solar alignments. Physical comparison of the Tonga and Japanese sites strongly argues for a shared cultural source that was responsible for building both pyramidal platforms. The chiefs responsible for these and the island's other colossal public-works projects were themselves known as the Mu'a, literally "men from Mu." A more obvious allusion to the lost Motherland seems impossible.

Tonga offers persuasive material and nominative evidence of prehistoric technology in the Pacific, but it is by no means alone. Some 3,700 miles away, equally impressive and mysterious but totally different structures are found in the Mariana Islands. Since their discovery in the early sixteenth century during Ferdinand Magellan's circumnavigation of the globe, visitors have stood in awe of the mushroomlike monuments of Guam, Tinian, Saipan, and Rota. Known as lat'te stones from the native *latde,* meaning "houses of the old people," the name refers not to elderly seniors but rather to the Taotaomona, "Spirits of the Before-Time People," characterized by the indigenous Chamoro as alien builders who arrived from over the sea during the ancient past.

Archaeologists confirm that the Marianas were first inhabited around 3000 B.C., just when the opening shot in a series of cometary catastrophes compelled Lemurians to venture throughout the Pacific, although scientific efforts to determine the age of the monoliths themselves have failed. The few other mythic traditions associated with them are less enlightening than explanatory. Masterfully hewn from a rough, metamorphosed coral, they are composed of two parts: a *haligi,* or truncated pyramidal pedestal, surmounted by an inverted hemispherical capstone, the *tasa,* five feet high and six feet in diameter. The monuments average fourteen feet high and weigh about thirty tons, although examples discovered at the As Nieves quarry on Rota are the largest known specimens at more than eighteen feet and in excess of fifty tons.

Wherever found, the lat'te are mostly lined up in double rows of a half-dozen to a dozen or more specimens, usually along riverbanks or on the shoreline, implying, as did Tonga's Burden of Maui, some vital association with water and the sea. Their two parallel rows are seven feet apart, forming configurations eleven feet wide by fifty-five feet long. Investigators speculate, based on the remains of the fallen megaliths and those still erect, that as many as 100 or more originally populated the Marianas, although they are found nowhere else on Earth. But their significance or purpose is utterly unknown. They do, however, bear a general resemblance to the colossi of Easter Island, despite the 7,750 miles separating them. Like the moai, the Marianas' standing stones are composed of a torso topped by a cap, and both versions were often set up on coastal positions. If they were all made by Lemurian technocrats, as appears likely, they probably served a similar function—perhaps, like the moai, draining off the worst effects of seismic energies, although the application of coral for such a purpose is difficult to understand.

The merest hint of such a design was suggested by the Chamoro themselves. The Spanish governor from 1855 to 1866, Don Felipe de la Corte de Calderon, reported, "In early descriptions of the islands, it is said that the natives buried their dead in the houses, and even today the people have a superstitious fear of digging up or working the ground between these rows of stones." Were the Chamoro really afraid of disturbing the dead, or did they avoid the strange monoliths because the stones would suddenly give off lethal discharges of electromagnetic energy? Their dread of the megalithic rows is reminiscent of native fears expressed at Pohnpei, where a deadly "spirit light" is believed to haunt the ruins of Nan Madol. In any case, the lat'te of Guam, Tinian, Saipan, and Rota required techniques for their construction far beyond those found among the resources of these obscure islands, and consequently seem to define an impact made on the Marianas in the remote past by an advanced population dimly remembered in native tradition as the Spirits of the Before-Time People.

But physical evidence for the existence of such a prehistoric race is scattered across the broad Pacific Ocean and found among numerous locations virtually unknown to the outside world. A case in point is Babeldaob, largest of the 343 islands belonging to Micronesia's Palau cluster. Thousands of years ago, more than 5 percent of Babeldaob's 153 square miles was terraformed into food-producing terraces. The scope of this agricultural project was so vast that its yields could have provided for hundreds of thousands of people, far more than have ever inhabited Palau. The terraces were not independently carved out of the environment over time. Rather, an army of landscape engineers sculpted Babeldaob's hills into a single immense interconnecting system according to an original, comprehensive plan. Their terraces are uniformly fifteen feet in height, ranging in width from thirty to sixty feet, and perfectly sloped inward to collect rainwater without flooding. Some hills were entirely transformed into agricultural factories, making them resemble step-pyramids.

Radiocarbon testing reveals that the terraces were in use, although far below full capacity, nearly 2,000 years ago, and eventually abandoned around 1200 A.D., but does not indicate when they were made. It is clear, however, that they belong to the same high culture responsible for the far-off Bonaue rice terraces, which differ from Babeldaob's only in the even vaster scale of the Philippine complex. Mega-planting at Luzon and Micronesia together could have fed millions of people, some indication of Lemuria's large population during the apogee of its civilization. According to Churchward, at the time of its final destruction, Mu was inhabited by some sixty-four million souls.

Babeldaob is also rich in stone statues. According to Childress, some are similar to the moai of Rapa Nui, although, at less than ten feet, not as tall. Thirty-eight have been discovered thus far, combined with examples from the fellow Palau island of Koror. They are men and women turned to stone long ago, according to local belief, a mirror image of the ancient myth of Deucalion and Phyrra, the Greek husband and wife who survived the Great Flood. After the cataclysm, which wiped out the rest of humanity, they picked up stones and threw them over their shoulders. As the stones hit the ground, they turned into men and women. The indigenous residents of Tingwon Island, twenty miles west of New Hanover in New Guinea, told J. K. McCarthy, the director of native affairs, that their ancestors had been visited long ago by giants who sailed away and were entirely annihilated at sea, only to be reincarnated as standing stones. "Often, megalithic remains in the Pacific are said to be the tombs of giants," writes Childress, "mainly because the locals can only conceive of giants having created them."

The Babeldaob inhabitants have their own re-creation story. They say that after the beginning of time, an extraordinarily voracious baby named Uab was born on the Palauan island of Angaur. He ate everything in sight, threatening the islanders with starvation, and eventually grew to such monstrous proportions that they tied him to the ground and set fire to a hut covering his head. Uab's struggles were so violent that the island shook, and his body disintegrated into hundreds of pieces to become the Palau Island cluster. In this folk tradition is recounted the seismic breakup of Mu (Angaur), accompanied by a celestial fire (Uab's hut), just as the Tingwon version identifies the ancient megaliths with their Lemurian builders. At least one of the Palau islands, Emungs, appears to have memorialized the Motherland with its name.

In her book *Palau: Portrait of Paradise,* Mandy Etpison cites most researchers, who conclude Babeldaob's statues "may have been made by a people other than the Palauans." She reports that the figures were sculpted from andesite, a hard, igneous granite not native to the island, nor anywhere else in Palau. Like the magnetized basalt of Nan Madol and the coral used to build Tonga's great arch, the source of the stone is unknown, perhaps because it came from lost Lemuria. In any case, andesite is infused with quartz crystal, giving it the same properties needed to produce piezoelectricity. Given Babeldaob's other examples of high technology in its agricultural terraces, the andesite statues may have performed a similar geotransducer function for the same seismic or meteorological purposes originally served by Easter Island's colossi and Nan Madol's 250 million tons of magnetized basalt. Interestingly, Tiahuanaco's Gateway to the Sun, in Bolivia, was made from andesite.

Babeldaob also features several sets of stone pillars arranged in rows, like the fifty-two lining a hilltop on the northern end of the island at Bairulchau, overlooking the sea, which covers more submerged ruins near the village of Ollei. The sunken site is no mere fable, as the pottery and carved stonework removed from the ocean bottom by divers prove. Native folklore about the subsurface remains or the standing stones of Bairulchau is silent, evidently because they are so old that any traditions once associated with them have been long forgotten. They nonetheless testify to the former presence of a technically sophisticated culture that once lent great importance to Babeldaob through the construction of a stupendous agrarian project and the erection of several megalithic sites.

Other examples include New Guinea's eight-foot-high obelisk fronting the rising sun and surrounded by a circle of smaller uprights. Similar arrangements of standing stones, virtually identical to western European counterparts, are found on seldom visited islands of the Schouten Group, off Wewak. A Stonehenge-like formation, adorned with concentric illustrations suggesting the sun, stands in New Ireland atop Mount Kambu. How the structure's eleven-foot-long blocks were hauled up to the summit of its 2,500-foot peak is beyond imagining. "They are so ancient," writes the Australian Keith Willey in *Assignment: New Guinea*, "that the natives do not even have legends about them." The presence of astronomical computers is an anomaly among the backwaters of New Guinea explicable only in terms of Lemurian influences during the ancient past, a conclusion underscored by their alignment with the sun, which was at the center of religious worship at Mu.

Indeed, New Guinea's Kai natives identify these megalithic sites with a race of giants who ruled the world before the Great Deluge, which changed their bodies into great blocks of stone. This is the same transformation repeated in Palau to explain the presence of ancient monoliths at Bairulchau, on Babeldaob. The Kai, however, refer to the extinct giants as the Ne-Mu. More than sixty of their naturally mummified remains were found during the mid-1930s sitting chin-to-chin in a limestone cave located in New Guinea's gold-field district of Morabe. According to an article in *Science Newsletter*, "The most remarkable feature of these mummies is their light skin."

Mixed descendants of the Ne-Mu survived at least into the early twentieth century. A 1937 *Science* magazine article told of the relatively fair-complected Tarifyroro, who dwelled in the country's virtually inaccessible hinterland. "At one time," according to the resident magistrate of New Guinea, Jack Hides, "these light-skinned people inhabited the whole of this tableland and were driven back westward by the more virile Papuans." He described Tarifyroro methods of agriculture as "the best I had ever seen. Their terraced gardens of an unusual squareness, marked off by pretty hedges of croton and hibiscus, were not unlike the Chinese market gardens we see in Australia. They grow sugar cane, ginger, bananas, sweet potatoes, spinach, mimica, and native asparagus."

Resemblances to Lemuria's terraced farming in the Philippines and Micronesia are apparent. In fact, the Kuk swamp around Mount Hagen, in the western highlands of New Guinea, shows massive soil erosion caused by an abundance of slope cultivation as far back as the tenth millennium B.C. Evidence for a sizable and agriculturally skilled population there around 4000 B.C. may be seen in surviving drainage ditches 1,500 feet long, 6 feet deep, and 14 feet wide, laid out straight and level, as though properly surveyed. Nothing of the kind has been produced by the native peoples ever since the completion of these impressive irrigation works. Around 3000 B.C., large areas of New Guinea's forests were cleared, suggesting a surge in population commensurate with the second in a series of natural catastrophes that prompted large numbers of Lemurians to leave their afflicted homeland. Its other nominative traces recur elsewhere among old place-names in New Guinea. Mumori is a highland settlement, and Budamu is in Papua's Madang District.

An important variant on the Motherland's identity appears 2,600 miles away in Mulifanua, site of the earliest known human habitation—appropriately enough, in Samoa—going back more than 3,000 years. It also features a uniquely curious structure configured into a ten-pointed earthwork referred to as a "star mound." Samoa is host to the largest pyramidal platform in the South Pacific, the Pulemelei mound at Palauli, in southeastern Savai'i. The jungle growth that almost entirely conceals it implies the ceremonial precinct's profound antiquity. According to local traditions, it was raised by the Hiti, antediluvian giants who ruled the world before "the heavens fell down" and set fire to their island. As it sank into the sea, new lands emerged from the depths to become the Samoan Islands. Fleeing from the disaster, the escapees took refuge at a cape on the westernmost tip of Savai'i, known ever since as Mulinu'u. This myth is an obvious folkish recollection of the Lemurian cataclysm triggered by a disastrous celestial event and the arrival of survivors in Samoa. It also reveals the meaning behind the name of another Pacific island, Tahiti—"of the pre-deluge giants."

Although not as big as Savai'i's Pulemelei mound, the greatest known stone structure in Polynesia was a pyramidal form located in the western part of Tahiti. Originally 267 feet long, with a base of 87 feet, broad steps of hewn coral and basalt ascended to its 50-foot-high top. The Atahura Temple was dismantled during the mid-nineteenth century on the orders of Christian missionaries, because their native parishioners supposedly undermined biblical authority by claiming that "the *marae* was built before the Flood." Although the largest of its kind, the island was home to other, similar buildings. "All were built of large stones without cement," according to W. H. R. Rivers, writing for *American Anthropologist* in 1915, "but so carefully shaped that they fitted together closely and formed durable structures."

The Tahitian word for island is *mu-tu*, apparently derived from the sunken Motherland and memorialized in Moorea, near the northwest coast. Interestingly, its reverse, *tu-mu*, means tree, which may again refer to Mu, which was synonymous with the Tree of Life. The tutelar goddess of Moorea was Tu-metua, believed to dwell in the sunken land of Avaiki, another name by which the Motherland was known in French Polynesia. Tahiti's high priest was known as the U-Mu, literally "he of Mu." In what appears to be the oldest Tahitian chant, "Strife and Reconciliation Between Heaven and Earth," the children of a primeval octopus, Fire and Water, engaged in a global battle that caused the world to be immersed beneath "a boundless sea." The name of this octopus, symbolic of a powerful center of control and influence, was "Foundation of Earthly Heaven," Tumu-ra'i-feuna, a clear allusion to Lemuria. When the floodwaters began to recede, exposing barren dry land, the sky god, Ta'aroa, copulated with Mother Earth, planting his seed in her at a place called Tumu-nui, or the "island of great Mu," from which the first human beings were born. That the Motherland is first destroyed and then becomes the birthplace of humankind is less a contradiction than a description of Lemurian vastness *(tumu-ra'i-feuna)* broken up during a struggle between Fire and Water (the fourth-millennium-B.C. comet collision) that did not destroy Mu but reduced its territory to a remnant *(tumu-nui)* of its original extent. Direct references to the lost civilization could hardly be more clear.

A find comparable to Tahiti's stone platform was made in recent years at New Zealand, immediately south of Lake Taupo. The Kaimanawa Wall is more probably a step-pyramid or terraced, ceremonial marae of immense proportions. Childress, who investigated the site in 1996, wrote that "the blocks seem to be a standard 1.8 meters long by 1.5 meters high. The bottom block runs straight down to 1.7 meters and beyond. The blocks run for twenty five meters in a straight line from east to west and the wall faces due north. The wall consists of approximately ten regular blocks that are seemingly cut and fitted together without mortar."

The wall was built by the Wai-ta-hanui, New Zealand's oldest known tribe, predating the arrival of the Maori, formerly so numerous that they made up 200 tribes. As of 1988, only 140 mixed descendants were still alive. Their ancestors were also known as the Moriori, Wai-ta-hanui, or Urukehu—"the people of the West"—fair-skinned, hazel-eyed redheads who came from a splendid kingdom utterly overwhelmed by the sea. In Wai-ta-hanui, Maori, and other western Polynesian traditions, that kingdom is still remembered as Mu-ri-wai-o-ata, an obvious reference to the lost Pacific civilization. The name reappears in the Pounamu, the Wai-ta-hanui's "green stone," a sacred relic, like Tane's "foam-of-the-ocean and white sea-mist;" Easter Island's Te-pito-te-Kura, the navel of light; and Hawaii's "light of Kane," the Pohaku-a-Kane, saved from the destruction of the Motherland.

Even without the Kaimanawa Wall, a Lemurian impact on New Zealand is undeniable. The Maoris believe that Te-Tumu was the "source" that gave birth to humankind in the land of Mataaho, known in the Marquesas' deluge chant, Tai-Toko, as Matahou. Sometime thereafter, it was overwhelmed by a killer wave, which some ancestral survivors escaped by sailing a great canoe called the Takitumu, "in remembrance of the original home they came from," according to the Travels of Tamatea, an aboriginal New Zealand chant transcribed in the late nineteenth century. It also mentions a place called Muri-wai-hou, a submarine realm reigned over by Limu, the god and guardian of the dead, from his vast palace in the depths of the sea. The chant describes the lost country of Irihia: "It was a great home of the Maori people, and in it was situated the *whare-kura* [temple of learning] of Rongo-marae-roa. It was from this land that men and tribes dispersed to the islands of the great ocean." Rongo-marae-roa was a variant of Lono, the white-skinned culture bearer from sunken Hiva (Mu), known as Irihia to the Maori.

Until the end of the nineteenthth century, the Irihia were generally considered New Zealand's first inhabitants, arriving around 1150 A.D. But in 1996, local bones of *Rattus exulans* radiocarbon dated by anthropologists told a different story. According to R. N. Holdaway in *Nature* magazine, "The data suggest that the Pacific rat was established on both main islands of New Zealand nearly 2,000 years ago. The rat is unlikely to have arrived without human assistance, on, for example, natural rafts." He was supported by archaeologist David Sutton, who

Illustration of a woman belonging to the Moriori just before their extermination in the early nineteenth century.

found "evidence of burn-offs and unexplained erosion in New Zealand that can reasonably be related to pre-Maori contacts by some unidentified people." Another archaeologist, George Cook, dated nearly 2,000 megaliths in the Waipoua Forest of the New Zealand Northland to unknown builders who preceded the Maoris. Some of their own traditions describe a light-skinned race, the Moriori, as the oldest population in New Zealand. The Moriori's existence is beyond doubt, because they were visited on their last stronghold, Chatham Island, about 500 miles east of New Zealand, by modern European explorers in the early nineteenth century. As recently as 1835, the Maoris invaded Chatham, reducing its inhabitants to slavery, followed by a period of genocide that included cannibal feasts. "No one escaped," a Maori was quoted has having said. "But what of that? It was in accordance with our custom."

The Kaimanawa Wall and nearly 2,000 standing stones of the Waipoua Forest are not the only examples of Lemurian technology in New Zealand. A far more humble but also enigmatic object was dredged up from under the ground of the Waverly District during excavation for a drain in 1925. Described by the *Polynesian Society Journal* as two and three-eighths by two inches, it was fashioned from a close-grained black stone, possibly graywacke, a nonporous sandstone containing fragments of other rock. The artifact resembles a small cue ball that has been cut on one side only to a uniform incision of perhaps one millimeter with a lozenge-like configuration opening into a one-and-one-sixteenth-inch-deep slot. A high degree of skilled machining is evident, but this contrasts sharply with the find's discovery beneath the surface of the Earth at eight feet or more, a depth that fails to precisely date it, but nevertheless confirms its prehistoric provenance. "Considerable labor must have been expended on this object," observes William R. Corliss in his *Archaeological Anomalies,* "but no one knows its purpose."

Hardly less puzzling is an absence of any tool marks, even though native New Zealanders never used implements strong enough to work in graywacke, certainly not on the level of precision in evidence here. Lack of adornment or inscriptions suggests it is not a ritual item, but more resembles a piece of machinery, impossibly fantastic as that impression may be. Nor is the item familiar to the Maori. Some of them guessed it belonged to their exterminated predecessors, the fair-complected Moriori, Wai-ta-hanui, or Urukehu, who were known for the possession of special stones like the Pounamu, or "green stone," from the old Motherland. Whatever the original function or identity of the Waverley artifact, its superb craftsmanship alone is proof that a technologically sophisticated people, at least on a par in some respects with those of the industrial age, inhabited prehistoric New Zealand.

Remnants of that scientifically proficient people are found elsewhere in the South Pacific. On the obscure islet of Raivavai, some 400 miles south of the Society Islands, monumental statues and stone walls demanding construction skills and a labor force far beyond the limitations of the present population were first documented in the 1830s by a French merchant, J. A. Moerenhout. He learned from the natives that the statues were intended to "perpetuate the memory of the most extraordinary phenomena, of the most terrible catastrophes known in the land, as the destruction of the mainland."

Nor are massive ruins or colossal statues the only proofs for the lost science of Mu. Its living legacy continues to nourish millions of people around the planet. The banana was genetically engineered thousands of years ago and is found throughout the world, testifying to the existence of a technologically advanced, global civilization in the remote past. Like other seedless fruits, including navel oranges and certain kinds of grapes that have been cultivated in modern times, the banana was produced by the same agrarian society responsible for the gargantuan rice terraces of Bonaue and Babeldaob. Its Lemurian origins are preserved in the Pohnpei myth of the islanders' ancestral god, Mwas en Leng, which explains that the first banana grew from the corpse of a divine eel. The persistence of this oral tradition at the important site of Nan Madol adds strong emphasis to its significance.

Perhaps the most astounding and certainly most cogent example of such a lost science is as timely as today's newspaper headlines, because it would appear that the Lemurians had long ago mastered what is currently known as stem-cell research. Proof for this astonishing conclusion may be found among the stone towers of Easter Island. Known locally as *pipi hereko*, they stood some twenty feet high. Behind their walls were stored the umbilical cords of every infant born on the island. Immediately after birth, a baby's umbilical cord was severed in a brief, simple ritual equal in importance to the same person's funeral. The father rushed with his child's umbilical cord to the nearest tower, where a keeper sealed it inside a gourd, which was registered with the family name, then stored for future use.

The practice was older even than the arrival of Hotu Matua, Easter Island's founding father, although it was introduced from his sunken homeland by six pioneers of Marae Renge (that is, Lemuria), who built the first of the pipi hereko at Anakena Bay. These places were considered centers of great healing, although the nature of the cures associated with the umbilical cords they preserved was lost with the extermination of the Hanau-eepe, the Long Ears, by the Polynesian Short Ears during the early nineteenth century. In any case, Easter Island's original name, Te pito te Henua, or "navel of the world," derived at least in part from native significance laid on the therapeutic qualities allegedly inherent in the human umbilical cord. The precise nature of its role in any healing practice undertaken by the islanders was lost when they were enslaved and virtually exterminated by early-nineteenth-century slave-traders. After the destruction of Mu, not all practitioners of navel healing migrated to Easter Island. Others either migrated to Hawaii or were already in residence there as part of the Lemurian polity that spread over numerous Pacific islands and was reflected in an early name for Hawaii, Ka-houpo-o-Kane, or "navel of Kane." (Kane was the god of light associated with good health and life itself.) Such a migration is suggested by Hawaii's revered goddess Pele, who was born in the deep past on Kahiki (yet another name for Mu) in a province known as Honua-mea, "the navel." After resettling in Hawaii, she renamed it after her home region, Ka Piko o ka Honua, or navel of the world, philologically echoing the Te pito te Henua of Easter Island. Variants of her myth had the name already in place before she arrived, suggesting Hawaii was indeed part of Lemuria from its beginning.

Late-nineteenth-century painting of a young Hawaiian woman wearing a represen-
tation of her umbilical cord. Was such reverence rooted in ancient recognition of the
umbilical cord's medical potential?

Even today, reverence for an infant's umbilical cord on behalf of
the child's future health is still found in some rural Japanese areas. A
Lemurian—or, at any rate, an Easter Island—connection was discovered
in December 1999 by Hiroaki Hayashi, chapter president of the Japan

Petrograph Society (JPS), atop 2,450-foot Mount Hoshigajo on the off-shore island of Shodojima. He found two stone towers, one approximately eighteen feet high with a twelve-foot base. The other stood thirty feet high and was fifteen feet wide. Their physical resemblance to the pipi hereko of Easter Island is indisputable, and associations with Mu are hardly less obvious. For example, local Shodojima legend assigns the towers' construction to the first Japanese emperor, who was known by the suggestive name Jimmu.

JPS president Professor Nobuhiro Yoshida writes that the towers were "dedicated to the deity of fertility, the so-called 'Guardian of the Red Beans.' Not only in Japan, but [in] China, Burma, Thailand, Tibet, and Korea, red beans have been the traditional components of sacred feasts. Together with boiled rice, they are consumed in memorial day ceremonies. Cakes, or *mochi,* presented as offerings to the gods, include red beans mixed with rice and honey or sugar. Interestingly, the very name, *shodojima,* means 'island of the red beans.' Perhaps it was among the most important religious centers in Asia, a suggestion underscored by traditional associations with Japan's first emperor."

A ritual in the Roman Lemuria called for the male head of each household to scatter beans from room to room as offerings to restless spirits, the lemures. And the fertility powers possessed by Shodojima's "Guardian of the Red Beans" is not unlike the longevity Easter Islanders and Hawaiians claimed to derive from the preserved umbilical cords of their infants. In any case, an ancient Japanese correspondence with Lemuria through the umbilical-cord towers of Rapa Nui seems unavoidable.

But none of the foregoing made much sense to investigators—mainstream or maverick—until the close of the twentieth century, when medical researchers discovered that the blood of a freshly removed umbilical cord possesses capacities for healing far beyond anything imagined before. According to a Detroit, Michigan, press release for April 15, 2004, "The Barbara Ann Karamanos Cancer Institute is urging expectant mothers giving birth at Hutzel Women's Hospital to donate their umbilical cords. The umbilical cords have the potential to save other children's lives. Umbilical cords are rich in blood stem cells, the building blocks of the body's bloodstream and immunity system. These stem cells can be used in place of the more difficult bone marrow transplants." Stem cells from the umbilical cord are far less likely to be rejected by the body and can be used in place of more problematic bone-marrow transplants for treating a variety of cancers."

On October 14, 2004, biology professor Mike Mathews told a gathering of physicians in Henderson State University's McBrien Hall, "Cord stem cells are adult stem cells found in the blood of a baby's umbilical cord. Adult stem cells are very rare, with only about one in every fifteen thousand cells in tissue being an adult stem cell." Even so, progress is being made, mostly in Europe, with cancer treatment using umbilical cord stem cells and for other diseases as well. British Professor Jill Hows, director of London's Cord Blood Program, announced in September 2004, "Cord blood is an exciting new source of transplantable stem cells which may be used to cure patients with leukemia." She and her colleagues believe umbilical cord stem cells already exhibit potential for opening a new therapeutic dimension currently undreamed of by most modern medical practitioners.

Was native Easter Island, Hawaiian, and Japanese belief in the human umbilical cord as a curative treasure just coincidental with today's dawning recognition of the umbilical cord's broad healing power? Or was their special reverence for it a legacy, as suggested by Polynesian myth, from the ancient science of Lemuria? Did they know something twenty-first-century researchers are only now just beginning to appreciate? As Dr. Mathews admitted, "We not even close to figuring out stem cells."

FIVE

The Colonel of Mu

Les aventures arrivent aux aventuriers (Adventures arrive with adventurers).

The story of Atlantis had two great partisans in the classical and contemporary worlds. Plato, the most influential thinker during Western civilization's early history, preserved its first-known written account from the fourth century B.C. Twenty-three centuries later, Ignatius Donnelly, the American polymath, popularized it with comparative myth and Victorian geology. Although the story of Mu lacks a similarly eminent narrator from ancient times, it does have its modern champion.

James M. Churchward was born on February 23, 1851, in England, into an old and respected Devonshire family. He was educated at Oxford and Sandhurst Military College, where he became a student of engineering. In his twentieth year, he married Mary Stephanson, and the newly wedded couple sailed to India when the young Churchward was transferred to Delhi. He subsequently earned the rank of colonel in a regiment of Her Majesty's Lancers, to which he was attached until his military retirement. Before then, he spied on potential insurgents for British Army Intelligence while aiding the Indians in famine relief. After the success of these rescue efforts, he was approached by a *rishi*, the high priest of a Hindu monastery in a valley near the headwaters of the Brahmaputra River.

James Churchward at the time he wrote his first book about the Pacific civilization of Mu.

"When he saw one day that I was trying to decipher a peculiar bas-relief," Churchward recalled fifty years later, "he showed me how to solve the puzzle of those inscriptions and offered to give me lessons which would fit me for still more difficult work." The priest told Churchward about a set of inscribed tablets purportedly describing the lost prehistory of India. Monastery regulations barred outsiders from handling these documents, but the British officer argued that their state of deterioration was already so advanced that both men should endeavor at least to copy the written narrative for the sake of preservation. Following two years of study, Churchward mastered the dead language in which the fragile texts were composed, and, together with his older mentor, over the next several months gradually teased a translation from the fragile documents. As he remembered in the first volume of *Cosmic Forces of Mu*, "In India, I found many clay tablets brought there from the Mother-land of the Naacals [the Lemurian sacred brotherhood]. They originally brought a library of over ten thousand tablets; thus it will be seen that what I found formed only a single paragraph in a long story. All except a very few of these Naacal tablets were on the creation and the workings of the Cosmic Forces."

The tale they told was like nothing found anywhere else. It related that an immense landmass had once existed in the Pacific Ocean from very ancient times. Here, humans built the first organized society, known as Mu, the Motherland of civilization. A theocracy of sun-worshipping priest-kings held sway for thousands of years, during which high levels of spiritual and cultural achievement were reached. Missionaries spread the enlightened tenets of their religion to east and west, while their fellow countrymen enjoyed generation after generation of peace and plenty. About 12,000 years ago, however, the Earth was shaken by violent convulsions, and the kingdom of Mu suffered a natural catastrophe. Its lands were broken up by a series of major earthquakes, then sank almost entirely beneath the sea. Some of the South Pacific islands are the small, scattered remnants of that once mighty empire. Its people were not annihilated, however. Some survivors sailed as far afield as the Bay of Bengal, where they sparked civilization for the first time in India. Over time, the immigrants were assimilated, but their story still survived in the crumbling tablets gingerly handled by Churchward and the aged priest.

"For seven years, during all my available time," he told a lecture audience at New York's American Society for Psychical Research, "I diligently studied under this old rishi, learning the language of Mu, her symbols, alphabet, and writings, with a view of finding out something about ancient man. At that time, I had no idea of publishing my findings. I made the study purely to satisfy my curious self. I was the only one to whom this old rishi ever gave instructions on this subject."

The artifacts he handled changed Churchward's life. "These tablets gave me the first hint about Mu," he recalled in his first book, "and sent me on a world-wide search. They had been written by the Naacals, either in Burma or in the Motherland. They told how the Naacals had originally come from the Motherland, the land in the center of the Pacific."

He resigned his commission in 1880 to begin hunting for additional evidence of Mu beyond India. But his quest was complicated by the failure of his tea plantation in Ceylon and subsequent divorce from his wife, with whom he had one son, Carlton, when the lad was just eight years old. Alone, Churchward journeyed across Southeast Asia, then throughout Polynesia when such travels were far more arduous, time-consuming, and hazardous than they are today. Through the auspices of the British consul in Samoa, who happened to be his cousin William Churchward, the colonel sailed to the remote, seldom visited Caroline island of Pohnpei, with its ancient stone city, and New Zealand, where he learned oral traditions of the lost Motherland firsthand from Maori chieftains.

During 1883, he journeyed to western Tibet, then joined an expedition to Mongolia and Siberia. Everywhere he went, he asked indigenous peoples if they had ever heard of a place called Mu. Mostly they responded with blank stares or shrugged shoulders. But sometimes his inquiry elicited hostile reactions. In Burma, he shared his discovery of India's Naacal tablets with the head of a monastery outside Rangoon. The high priest grew suddenly indignant, declaring that the tablets had been stolen from their original Burmese source. Churchward was shown to the door, as the priest spat out his contempt for the foreigner. Years later, while questioning a South Sea Islander about his tribal origins, the native unexpectedly erupted into ferocious behavior, shouting angry imprecations accompanied by violent gestures against a perceived taboo in the name La-Mu-Ra.

Startling as such encounters may have been, they nonetheless tended to confirm the fundamental authenticity of the old Indian rishi's crumbling tablets. "These rebuffs disheartened me somewhat," he recalled, "but I had already obtained so much valuable information from the tablets that I determined to study the writings of all the old civilizations and compare them with the legends of Mu." He eventually became fluent in the Tamil tongue of Sri Lanka, Maori, and various Polynesian dialects, and was thus able to converse on a familiar basis with many of the native peoples he sought out. Through the age-old stories they told to him of a Great Flood, he began to trace the cultural outlines of the sunken realm described in the Hindu records.

Arriving in the United States in 1884, Churchward continued his Lemurian search throughout Mexico and Central America. These travels having exhausted his funds, he got a job as a salesman of railroad supplies with a New York firm. The work was not steady, however, and his income fluctuated, often leaving him hard up for cash. To supplement his spotty salary, he patented and sold inventions for the Bangor and Aroostook Railroad, including innovative tie plates and lock nuts. Although he never lost interest in Mu, mere survival naturally preoccupied him at this time. His

Augustus Le Plongeon (bearded, center), the pioneering late-nineteenth-century archaeologist, who found traces of Lemuria in Mexico.

enthusiasm was rekindled, however, after meeting and befriending Augustus Le Plongeon, the controversial Mayanist, and his American wife, Alice.

Son of a commodore in the French navy, Le Plongeon was born on the island of Jersey in 1826. Twenty-four years later, after seeking his fortune in the California gold rush, he became San Francisco's county surveyor, later acquiring a medical degree. He married Alice Dixon, a twenty-two-year-old Englishwoman living in Brooklyn, when he was middle-aged. The devoted couple were true pioneers in archaeology, penetrating more of the Mayan hinterland than anyone before them. From 1873 to 1885, they explored the jungles of Yucatán, sharing hardship, adventure, and discovery while assembling large collections of invaluable artifacts that were shipped to the great museums of North America. Included were more than 500 photographs of archaeological sites never before visually documented, together with twenty paper sheets of carefully executed mural drawings.

For all their pains and achievements, however, Le Plongeon was dismissed as a crackpot archaeologist by most professional antiquarians, as they were known during the Victorian era, for his allegedly fantastic readings of the Mayan hieroglyphs. His effort to understand the complex written symbols in the context of local Indian traditions, although largely an unsuccessful procedure, was a legitimate early attempt at translation. His critics, who knew even less of the Maya's written language, were hardly justified in condemning his interpretations. Indeed, the glyphs resisted all efforts to understand them for another 100 years.

During the 1890s, Le Plongeon's guess at the glyphs' significance was as good as anyone else's, and certainly more valuable, if only because he had spent more than a decade in Mesoamerican field research, while his ungenerous colleagues speculated from the drawing room comfort of college campuses. They scoffed that his renderings of the Mayan hieroglyphs were nothing more than flights of fancy. "I have been accused of promulgating notions of ancient America contrary to the opinion of men regarded as authorities on American archaeology," he stated. "And so it is, indeed. Mine is not the fault, however, although it may be my misfortune, since it has surely entailed upon me their enmity and its consequences."

Yet Le Plongeon demonstrated his wider grasp of the inscrutable written language when he claimed to have deciphered the word Chac-Mool, together with specific directions to the location of this buried statue, from a script decorating the exterior of a structure at the ceremonial center of Chichen Itza in Yucatán. His diggers got to work at the spot he believed the inscription specified and excavated a twenty-foot-deep pit, at the bottom of which emerged one of the finest pieces of Mesoamerican art ever found. This monumental sculpture-in the-round was the masterfully executed representation of a reclining man holding a bowl over his navel, symbolizing the antediluvian Navel of the World cult as practiced in Mu and Atlantis.

Le Plongeon's engineering skill enabled the hardworking Indians to lever the two-ton monolith to the surface from its subterranean recess using only jungle vines and tree trunks. Its discovery proved Le Plongeon had correctly interpreted the Mayan inscription. Nothing could rob him of his triumph, even after the Chac-Mool itself was seized by local authorities in Merida. Shortly thereafter, a Mexican warship appeared off the coast and threatened to bombard the city unless the statue was immediately turned over to the captain. The monument was brought on board and eventually wound up on display in Mexico City, where it may still be seen.

Tragically, Le Plongeon did not live long enough to see his work verified by late-twentieth-century archaeology. He was, for example, the first researcher to determine that the El Caracol ruin at Chichen Itza functioned as an astronomical observatory, and he calculated that the ancient Maya divided a circle into 400 units. His correct translation of the Mayan word for serpent, *chan,* was crucial, because it showed that the Maya described a full circle with the term *chan-bak,* which simultaneously signifies "circular serpent" and the number 400. The same imagery recurs in the ancient Old World European Ouroboros, a snake biting its own tail, symbolizing eternal life.

These revelations would go far in determining the astro-spiritual significance of Mayan architecture. Le Plongeon's examination of the Yucatán pyramids revealed that many of them stood twenty-one meters high, while their vertical planes were inscribed in half a circumference, the diameter of which formed their ground line. He was shocked to deduce from these recurring measurements that at least some of the Mayan pyramids incorporated the physical dimensions of the Earth itself. "In this he was also prophetically correct," observed the popular author of *Secrets of the Mexican Pyramids,* Peter Tompkins.

Another word Le Plongeon claimed to read repeatedly in the Mayan script was Mu. It seemed connected to the story of a powerful island kingdom located in the middle of the Atlantic Ocean before it was obliterated by a natural catastrophe. Churchward was astonished by Le Plongeon's discovery but dismayed by its setting in the Atlantic Ocean. The tale seemed more reminiscent of Plato's Atlantis than of the Pacific Motherland he had learned about in India. He was sure the name was right, but in the wrong location. Churchward and Le Plongeon nonetheless became fast friends, and Le Plongeon was happy to have found someone who highly valued his work.

Churchward, now eager to actively take up again the quest for Mu, was frustrated by his delimiting financial condition and resolved to somehow generate enough income to support his investigations. Aware that his brilliant brother had been trying to invent reinforced steel, James joined him in the hope that he could succeed where Albert had failed, thereby making a fortune for them both. It seemed a foolish pipe dream, if only because the colonel possessed no background whatsoever in metallurgy. He had, however, spent many seasons on the railroad, was familiar with the nature of steel, and was himself an experienced engineer. Even so, his development of a superior, although cheaper, nickel-chrome-venadium alloy in 1907 seems incredible.

The alloy had an instant impact on the whole industry, so much so that Churchward's patent was stolen by long established competitors and U.S. Navy contractors intent on keeping steel production prices high; the alloy threatened to cut into their inflated profits. He took the capitalist thieves to court and won $275,000 from Carnegie Steel in 1910. Five years later, he scored a million-dollar judgment against Bethlehem Steel. The corporate lawyers savaged his original settlement, leaving him with only $135,000, but even that was a magnificent sum in the early twentieth century. He purchased a ten-acre estate in Lakewood, Connecticut, where he began compiling fifty years' worth of research and travel notes. The result was his *Lost Continent of Mu,* released in 1926, when Churchward was seventy-three years old. It became an instant popular success, eventually selling hundreds of thousands of copies. Early reviews in such prestigious publications as the *New York Times* and the *Seattle Post-Intelligencer* were fulsome in their praise.

Fame soon degenerated into controversy, however, as scientific opinion began to weigh in on the book's chief weakness. Churchward had failed to provide any sources for his extraordinary claims, a fundamental flaw exacerbated by the author's imperious attitude. "The most effective way to destroy a hypothesis," wrote renowned mythologist Lewis Spence, referring to the colonel in his own book on Lemuria, "is to advance it dogmatically and in that manner of pompous assurance and intolerance for the views of others which compares so evilly with the attitude of honest conviction." Noted Atlantologist Edgerton Sykes, while hopeful for revealing information about Lemuria, was disappointed with the book, which he deemed insupportable and needlessly confrontational. Mainstream archaeologists and geologists were predictably more severe in their criticism, scolding the unaccredited Churchward for his effrontery in gate-crashing their academic fiefdoms.

"One of the prime criticisms of Churchward," according to Florida Atlantologist Kenneth Caroli, "was that he could not provide photos of his Naacal Tablets, nor the tablets themselves, and that he refused to identify the temple where he saw them. Firstly, they did not belong to him, so he could not produce them. Secondly, he was never supposed to see them, so the temple priests could not step forward to defend him. His rishi teacher must have been dead by the time Churchward wrote his books, fifty years later. Thirdly, the tablets were supposedly stolen from Burma long before. Publicizing their location might have caused trouble. The temple in which the tablets were kept was probably Hindu, while the tablets themselves may have been Buddhist, or perceived as such, and therefore, tabu."

Undeterred, Churchward went on to release *The Children of Mu* in 1931, followed two years later by *The Sacred Symbols of Mu,* and, in 1934, *The Cosmic Forces of Mu,* volume 1, then volume 2, his last published book, the following year. Although each book was progressively less credible and more outrageous than the previous one, Churchward became something of a celebrity, being featured in radio interviews and delivering public talks about his Lost Continent. In fact, he passed away while riding the lecture circuit to a 1936 Los Angeles presentation in his eighty-fourth year. His body was interred at Kensico Cemetery, in Valhalla, New York. Just before his death he had been working on *Traces of Mu in America,* which remained unfinished; the text disappeared soon after. Another neglected work that had to wait a half-century for publication was *Books of the Golden Age,* a handwritten manuscript in his own, beautifully flowing penmanship, intended for his nephew and "adopted son," Howard William Keresey.

Had Churchward written only about his experiences at the Hindu temple-monastery and world travels thereafter in a less contemptuous tone, he would have produced a far more readable, believable series. Instead, its volumes are a tangled, turgid mess of preposterous geology, unsubstantiated claims, unconvincing opinions undifferentiated from apparently legitimate folk traditions, lost but probably authentic documents, and valid archaeological finds. *The Lost Continent of Mu* and its sequels seem to have resulted from Churchward's familiarity with a genuine Hindu document, which he struggled to explain in terms of modern science. His theory that unstable "gas belts" beneath the sea bottom brought about the Pacific continent's demise bears no resemblance to geologic reality. The tremendous technological strides oceanography has made since his day clearly reveal that no continental landmasses existed, let alone sank, during human prehistory in the south-central Pacific area he defined.

This is not to say that Mu was without any geologic foundation in reality. A relatively small continental island did exist in the South

China Sea until it succumbed to a deluge 7,000 or more years ago, when humans almost certainly occupied it. Across the Pacific Ocean, islands and whole archipelagoes have indeed risen above and fallen below the surface of the sea, even in modern times. Davies Island, in the vicinity of the better-known Easter Island, was discovered and charted during the mid-1750s. By the following century, it had vanished without a trace. While Churchward's argument for a sunken continent in the Pacific may be doubtful, plenty of sunken islands, archipelagoes, and even a continental fragment are credible candidates for the lost realm of Mu. Even so, his incredible map of a formerly continental landmass bears an uncanny resemblance to what geologists have since defined as the "super-swell." This is a vast region of shallower sea depths, volcanoes, seamounts, and seismic activity beginning at the East Pacific Rise, with its axis leading westward until it dominates much of the central Pacific Ocean. Perhaps there really was a lost continent of Mu after all.

The colonel offered a great deal more nonsense about rock-art depictions of dinosaurs in Arizona, Naacal tablets in Mexico, and other unhelpful digressions. He also tried to pass off self-evidently Buddhist, Hindu, or Aztec artworks from the last few centuries as genuine Lemurian artifacts many thousands of years old. Foremost among these transparent misconceptions was the photograph of a bronze seated figure he described as the 18,000-year-old representation of Mu, the "world-ruler." In fact, it is one of twenty-one *taras,* or "aspects" of Buddha, that could not date before the thirteenth century A.D., and is probably much more recent. Far from having anything to do with "receiving man's soul from the Creator," as Churchward would have had it, the left hand signifies Abhaya, the gesture of fearlessness; the right is Bhumisparha, or swearing by Earth Mother that the truth has been taught.

Underlying all his gross misinterpretation, exaggeration, and fantasy, however, are the bare bones of an engaging theme for which discriminating investigators continue to find better evidence. Le Plongeon's lifetime collection of materials, which Churchward inherited after the older man's death in 1908, appears to form the primary, if not always credited, source for the Mu books. They are nonetheless invaluable, because the essential story they tell can be verified by numerous outside details of the kind documented here. Churchward's narrative acts like a skeleton fleshed out by related proof. It therefore serves to unify a thousand facts into a recognizable whole, which continues to expand with the addition of new evidence. We may set aside perhaps three-quarters of his statements. But the surviving quarter demonstrates that he certainly did have access to records describing the lost Motherland of Mu.

Readers have only the author's word for the contents of the Hindu monastery tablets, which he did not directly translate, that he allegedly read in India. For all his failings, he set in motion the first serious study of the lost Pacific civilization, a quest that went on to verify many of his conclusions long after his death, and continues to this day.

SIX

The Garden of Eden?

*For over fifty years, I have been hunting these scraps and
putting them together so as to form the beginning of an
intelligent tale of the Creation of Man. It rests with those
who come after me to complete the tale.*

COLONEL JAMES CHURCHWARD

James Churchward believed that the ancient, friable tablets he saw and
translated in 1870 India had been created by "the Holy Brothers—the
Naacals—a priestly brotherhood sent from the Motherland to the colo-
nies to teach the sacred writings, religion, and the sciences. These Naacals
formed in each country colleges for the teaching of the priestcraft, religion
and the sciences. The priesthoods that were formed in these colleges in
turn taught the people": hence, the preservation of the Lemurian tablets
at the Hindu temple-monastery.

The texts were illustrated by several drawings purporting to represent some of the chief imagery associated with that high civilization
before its destruction. Its leading symbol comprised the letter tau, or
capital *T*, surmounted by a blooming lotus flanked on either side by a
smaller bush. To the left of the *T* stood a deer on its hind legs, as though
about to spring upward. According to Churchward, this composite figure represented "man's advent in the Land of Mu." The lotus signified the soul's enlightenment or awareness, as it still does in Buddhism,

Stone slab at Japan's Mu Museum representing the arrival of early humans in Lemuria, signified by a deer leaping upon a T, or tau, the symbol for Mu.

while the pair of ferns stood for spiritual and material abundance. The *T* was Mu itself emerging from the midst of the ocean. Humankind's birth and origins there were personified in the poised deer "springing into life."

Although Churchward typically offered no sources beyond his own interpretation for anything about this tau symbol, it nonetheless materializes in various cultures liable to have been impacted by the Lemurian experience. It occurs, for example, in the South Pacific realm of the lost Motherland itself, among the Marquesas Islands of French Polynesia. Kings and high priests carry a *T*-shaped baton known as the Cross of God, used, according to Leinani Melville, "on state occasions or in religious processions when officiating at temple rituals. A *tau* was hewn from a flawless piece of hard wood that had been carefully chosen and blessed by a high priest. It was usually between two and four feet long, two or three inches wide, and an inch or two in thickness." The Cross of Gold and the carefully chosen wood from which it was made signified the Hawaiians' own Tree of Life, the Puka-tala.

Pohutukawa, a Maori variant, was a sacred tree growing at the center of Limu's sunken palace "from which the spirits dropped down into the chasm that led under the sea to spirit land," according to Knappert. Both Hawaiian and Maori accounts describe the land in which this tree was venerated as the paradisiacal birthplace of mankind, from which humans spread throughout the world. They were not driven out by divine wrath, but instead forced to leave when Kahiki-homnua-kele, Kapakapaua-a-Kane, Pali-ilu, or any of the many other descriptive titles by which the Pacific Eden was known disappeared beneath the sea to become the realm of the dead. Missing from most Polynesian traditions is any association with a fall of some kind from heavenly grace. The moralistic version in Genesis seems to be a particularly Hebrew inflection, in which guilt was used by the priests to control their congregations.

Churchward's statement that "the word *tau (ta-oo)* is one of the few of the Motherland that has been handed down" appears borne out in Hora-nui-a-Tau, or "the great outstretched land of Tau," and Hau-papa-nui-a-Tau, the "hilly land of Tau." In Maori folk tradition, these were the homelands from which the Tangata-Whenua, the original inhabitants of New Zealand, arrived in the ancient past. Churchward went on to write that "among the South Sea Islanders, the constellation of the Southern Cross is called *Tau-ha*." The Hawaiians referred to the same constellation by the provocative name of Humu. Their tau-shaped Cross of God, described above, was known as the *ta-ha-oo*. Nearly 3,000 miles from Hawaii, a colossal pyramidal platform, the Tauhala, stands in Mu'a, an ancient port city on the Polynesian island of Tonga.

An elaborate *T* is repeated in Australoid bark painting. It encloses seven sparkling figures corresponding to the Pleiades. In aboriginal myth, the constellation belonged to a group of spirits, the Muramura, which combines the names of the sunken Motherland with that of the sun-god Ra. They created human beings by smoothing out the limbs of unformed beasts, then gave them the first rites of initiation into sacred mysteries. The Muramura traveled the world over before being drawn up into the night sky by a long "hair-cord." Their name, function as creators of human life, and status as world travelers emphasize their Lemurian identity.

In native oral traditions of the *keilahn aio,* "the other side of yester-day," Mwas en Pahdol was an ancestress who brought a special palm tree to Pohnpei from her distant homeland. Her story blends several important themes, not the least of which is her Lemurian name and the stupendous site of Nan Madol, described in chapter 1.

The premiere Lemurian symbol also appears among Hawaii's Puako petroglyphs. Along the Keo Trail, visitors will find several examples of the engraved *T* associated with Lono, the fair-haired, white-skinned cul-ture bearer from a lost kingdom of powerful mana. His personal emblem, known as the Lonomakua, or "Father Lono," was a tall wooden pole, at the top of which was a crosspiece forming the same tau that Churchward had insisted symbolized Mu. The portable Lonomakua was carried all over the island during the annual Makahiki festival that celebrated his arrival from a sunken kingdom in the ancient past. Lono's identification with Mu is underscored by his title, *Hu-Mu-hu-Mu-nuku-nuku-apua'a,* which indicates he could "swim" from Mu between the islands like a fish, a reference to his skill as a transoceanic mariner.

According to Leinani Melville, Lono's undersea homeland, the Poly-nesian rendition of the lost Motherland—Haiviki—derives from the root *ha* for "breath, hence, life," in Hawaiian. Remarkably, a crucial connec-tion is here made between the Pacific realm of Mu and Middle America. A *T* is also the most selectively portrayed of all Mayan hieroglyphs, fea-tured oversized and set apart among stonework at the most important ceremonial centers, such as Palenque in Guatemala and Copan in Hon-duras. It is pronounced "ik" and signifies breath, actually the breath of life. In this, the *T* glyph is remarkably close to Churchward's character-ization of the symbol as it appeared in Mu, where it stood for the begin-ning of human life. That such diverse elements from the Marquesas, Hawaii, Mesoamerica, and Lemuria so perfectly complement each other testifies to the validity of their connection.

The mysterious relationship between Easter Island and Mohenjo-Daro through their shared script was explained in chapter 3 as an inheritance both received independently from the same Motherland. But a common written language was not their only tie to Mu. Rapa

One of many T *signs symbolic of Lemuria found at the Mayan ceremonial city of Copan, Honduras.*

Nui's Lemurian *T* glyph is part of a yet indecipherable message on the Dholavira "signboard," a large display panel that stood above the north gate of Harappa at least 4,000 years ago. Mentioned as Hariyupiya in the *Rig-Veda,* the oldest and most important of the Hindu holy books, Harappa was the second city in the Indus Valley after Mohenjo Daro. The appearance of the *T* glyph here is underscored by surviving cylinder seals and apparently religious tablets emblazoned with a sacred tree, which, according to Churchward, was symbolized by the tau.

Another Mayan glyph connects with the deer image in Churchward's symbol for the Pacific Motherland. Disjointed lines radiate from a circle at the center of a rectangle to four other circles in each of the four corners, intersected by four pairs of straight lines. The glyph appears to denote a centralized location. Augustus Le Plongeon concluded it referred to legendary Mayan accounts of "the submerged places figured by the image of an animal resembling a deer placed over the legend." He writes that the hieroglyph was known as U-luumilceh, or the "land of deer." Francisco Hernandez de Cordova, the first Spanish conquistador to set foot on Mexican soil, learned of the title when he landed at a small offshore island known to the natives as Mu-geres. The appearance of this provocative name in conjunction with "the land of deer" defines a trans-Pacific connection. Indeed, *luumilceh* sounds like a Mayan version of Lemuria.

Deer imagery figures prominently and similarly in the spiritual symbolism of the Navajo Indians in the American Southwest. The animal must be killed without shedding a drop of its blood when its hide is intended for use as the costume of the god Yeibichai. He is known as the "talking god" when impersonated by an actor wearing a white-faced mask and reciting the story of creation. Yeibichai is revered as the grandfather of all the gods, who survived the Great Deluge of an island paradise in the western sea, where the first man and woman were born. So too the Navajo's sacred sand paintings could be laid out only on deerskins, and rattles used in religious dances were made exclusively from deer hooves, while the horns were revered as containers of life.

On the other side of the Pacific vastness, a deer ceremony is held annually from mid-October to early November near a path leading to the Omotesando shrine in the ancient Japanese city of Nara. There the animals are corralled and cared for at Shika-no-Tsunokiri Park throughout the year. For the autumnal Tsunokiri ritual, the antlers are sawed off to commemorate the death of a former age, simultaneously representing the rebirth of humankind in its aftermath, just as the horns, symbols of renewal, invariably grow back.

Several lines from the Boen *Rites of the Deer,* an epic poem celebrating the origins of the Tibetan people, read, "On the Earth the deer walks, the brown deer of the Mu walks. The souls of the king, his minister and vassal took on the guises of the precious cuckoo, deer, and tree." The Mu are mentioned in Boen tradition as one of the original races of pre-Buddhist Tibet.

Although deer imagery may be found in the religious symbolism of many peoples throughout the world, its appearance among the Maya, Navajo, Japanese, and Tibetans is particularly Lemurian. It combines the concept of rebirth after the disappearance of a former age, usually through the action of a great flood, thereby most closely resembling the significance of the deer in Churchward's symbol for Mu. The appearance of a people bearing this name in connection with the sacred deer in Tibetan tradition could not be more clear.

As mentioned in the Tibetan *Rites of the Deer*, the soul of the king's vassal took on the guise of a tree. Referring to his *T* representation of the sunken civilization, Churchward wrote, "Mu was symbolized by a tree, the Tree of Life." Its glyph was the *T,* or tau, which simultaneously signified the configuration made by the sea-floor fault lines crossing at Easter Island, as we learned in chapter 3. This was the same Tree of Life mentioned in the account of humankind's creation as described in Genesis in the Hebrew scriptures. The colonel's insistence that the first earthly paradise was actually in the South Pacific naturally aroused intense opposition from traditionalists in both science and religion.

His conclusion seems affirmed, however, by numerous Polynesian creation accounts that describe Te tumu o te pohoe as literally the Tree of Life, which nurtured the first human beings in Haiviki. Wood was, after all, sacred to the trans-Pacific Tane, known as Kane in Hawaii, the divine patron of all who worked with wood, especially canoe builders, because his light-skinned people were renowned sailors from the sunken homeland of Haiviki. But Tibetan connections between a Tree of Life (reincarnated life) and people from Mu are not the only outside support for the colonel's characterization of a Lemurian Garden of Eden. Interestingly, the Chinese word for wood or timber is *mu*. It also means to immerse, suggesting the Lemurian flood.

Ancient China's most important deity was Xi Wang Mu, the goddess of immortality, worshipped from at least Shang dynasty times, beginning around 1600 B.C. The date is provocative, because the last vestige of Lemuria appears to have slipped beneath the surface of the sea about the same time. Xi Wang Mu's migration to China from her fabulous palace in the east implies the arrival of culture-bearers carrying an important mystery cult to the Asian mainland. She originally resided in the Happy Isles, until Shoulao, Fuxing, and Luxing took their leave. A porcelain dish from the early-eighteenth-century reign of Yong Zheng (presently at London's Victoria and Albert Museum) depicts Xi Wang Mu, as she follows these gods of long life, happiness, and prosperity across the sea from her former Palace of Immortality, being engulfed by angry waves. The scene appears to represent the evacuation of Lemuria, an implication reinforced by a bronze mirror from the Han dynasty. It is decorated with the likeness of Xi Wang Mu accompanied by spirit guardians mounted on deer, the animal already associated with Lemuria in various circum-Pacific cultures. The Japanese counterpart of Shoulao, the god of longevity, was Jurojin, whose animal was the deer, upon which he rode.

Xi Wang Mu's chief duty was to tend a peach tree that grew in her garden. Its fruits bestowed eternal life on anyone who ate them. The tree was known as the Jian mu and was regarded as an *axis mundi,* the center of the world around which all earthly life revolved. Variants of her myth spoke of Fu Sang mu, a Tree of Life originally found across the eastern ocean at the center of a legendary island kingdom known as Tai Shan, an apparent reference to the Pacific Motherland, where the inhabitants were said to be white, not Asian. After Xi Wang Mu left Tai Shan, she replanted the Fu Sang mu at the center of her new palace beyond Mount Kunlun. It was known then as the Ruo mu tree. In other words, the Lemurian mystery cult had been relocated to China after the "immersion" of Tai Shan. Appropriately, Xi Wang Mu was also venerated as the goddess of disasters. Recalling the Maya's hieroglyph with breath, *ik,* identical to Churchward's *T* for Mu, she was synonymous with the *yuanqi,* or the primal breath that breathed humankind into existence. Here, too, the Hebrew scriptures' version of Jehovah's creation of Adam by breathing life into him seems parallel.

Ancient Chinese cosmology defined a sacred tree, the *kien-mu,* where heaven, Earth, and hell met at the center of the universe. The identifiably Lemurian concept of spiritual balance is apparent in China's kien-mu.

The Tree of Life is a motif recurring in cave art, bronze drums, and murals throughout Southeast Asia, such as the ceremonial cloths, called *tampan,* from Lampung in southern Sumatra. The Dyak natives of Sarawak and north Borneo combine the deluge story with their belief that the first man and woman were born on a paradisiacal island, at the center of which was a holy tree guarded by a dragon. At the woman's request, her husband stole one of its forbidden fruits, precipitating a global flood. H. Ling Roth's late-nineteenth-century monograph on the Dyak, cited by Stephen Oppenheimer in his *Eden of the East,* demonstrated that their account predated missionary contacts. It lacks specific reference to the lost Motherland, but Kumu-Honua, the Hawaiian Adam, is an inescapably Lemurian name.

Mu was known throughout central Polynesia as Bolotu, where the Pukatala Tree of Life stood at the island's very center. Fruits of the Pukatala were said to have bestowed immortality on the first humans. Throughout Polynesia, the sacred red pine was known as *rimu,* which sprang from Mumu-hango. According to Churchward, "Mu was symbolized as a tree, the Tree of Life. One of the names given to Mu was Tree of Life. The sacred writings tell us that Mu was the Tree of Life and that Man was its fruit."

Oppenheimer demonstrated that the Tree-of-Life myth originated in the Moluccas and spread outward as far as the Near East and the Valley of Mexico in a manner that uncannily paralleled a genetic outflow of migrating human populations. His conclusion was foreshadowed by Churchward, who believed that "Mu—the Garden of Eden—was dead and buried beneath the waters." In his 1970 reappraisal of the colonel's work, the popular science writer Hans Stefan Santesson concurred: "The Garden of Eden was not located in the Valley of the Euphrates, but instead this selfsame Mu, 'The Motherland of Man'." His conclusion was supported by Polynesian myth, like that of Pali-uli, the Hawaiian Garden of Paradise, where the earliest humans were created. The name of the first woman in Hawaiian myth was Iwi: literally, "the bone." In the Samoas and at Rotumah, she was remembered as Iwa. Premissionary traditions such as these made modern conversion of the islanders to Christianity easy. Their story of the Garden of Eden had come back full circle from its deeply prehistoric origins in the South Pacific to the ancient Near East and nineteenth-century evangelism.

Among the Sumerians, the Garden of Eden became Dilmun, in which at least some reference to Mu was not lost. Much later, authors of the

Hebrew scriptures transformed it into a moral fable to explain the origin of sin and downfall of humankind. The Hebrew Eden clearly derives from the Sumerian *edin,* meaning fertile plain. But even Genesis hints of the comet that sparked the evacuation of Lemuria, when Jehovah sends an angel wielding a flaming sword to drive Adam and Eve from paradise. "In Egypt," Le Plongeon pointed out, "the eating of a quince by two young people together constituted betrothal. . . . In this custom, we find a natural explanation of the first seven verses of the third chapter of Genesis."

Throughout the nineteenth century, evolutionists were convinced a lost continent had existed south and west of India to explain the dispersal of lemures from Madagascar to Ceylon. A leading theorist of the age, Ernst Haeckel, first argued that protohuman development actually began in Lemuria. "The distribution of the human species," he concluded, "from a single, primeval home, may be approximately indicated. The probable primeval home, or 'paradise,' is here assumed to be Lemuria, a tropical continent at present lying below the level of the Indian Ocean, the former existence of which in the Tertiary Period seems very probable from numerous facts in animal and vegetable geography." His proposal was eventually dismissed, but in the closing decades of the twentieth century, it enjoyed a revival when the hitherto unsuspectedly close relationship between lemures and early hominids became clear. Haeckel's proposition received additional impetus from a new theoretical trend that no longer confined the beginning of human evolution to southern Africa. The concept of parallel evolution, roughly simultaneous in various, sometimes widely scattered parts of the world, gradually gained general respect, as physical evidence from Asia and even America began to surface.

Homo sapiens sapiens (neanderthalis) is believed to have evolved about 120,000 years ago, and mainstream archaeologists insist that the first humans crossed over a former land-bridge from Asia into North America no earlier than 12,000 years ago. Yet bones of modern humans have been found beside well-made spearheads dated to a quarter of a million years ago in a high mountain valley near the small town of Hueyatlaco in the

Valsequillo region of south-central Mexico. Remains at the site proved that early hunters were killing and butchering large mammals, such as the extinct American camel, glyptodont, mastodon, and mammoth, as far back as Pleistocene times. The discovery came as a shock, not only to evolutionists, but also—and especially—to anthropologists.

Thirty-two years later, two men attending a boat race on the Columbia River near Kennewick, Washington, found a skeleton police assumed belonged to a recently murdered Caucasian man. Subsequent testing showed that the homicide investigators were correct as to the man's race, but their time frame needed adjustment. The victim was more than 9,000 years old. Moreover, he was racially unrelated to Native American tribal peoples, whose Mongolian ancestors had crossed over the Bering Straits land bridge into Alaska perhaps three millennia earlier. If Kennewick Man did not join their trek from Mongolia, where did he come from?

But he was neither alone nor the oldest of his kind. That status belongs to Penyon Woman III, a specimen at Mexico City's National Museum of Anthropology, discovered during the excavation of a well at the nearby international airport. Inadvertently unearthed was the skull of a female Caucasian who died when she was twenty-seven years old, between 13,000 and 12,700 years ago. At that time, according to mainstream archaeologists, Mongoloid peoples migrating out of Asia over the Bering Strait into Alaska were the only inhabitants of North America. Their cranial remains are short and broad, like those of modern-day Indians. In sharp contrast, the Mexico City skull is long and narrow, identifiably Caucasoid, according to geologist Silvia Gonzalez. A teacher at John Moores University in England, she received a grant from the British government to conduct her research, and wondered if the skull, found back in 1959, was older than its museum designation in the sixteenth century. She sent it to Oxford University for carbon-testing. Results confirmed that the young woman to whom it belonged was part of a fair-skinned population that resided in the Americas during the last ice age.

But Penyon Woman was not unique. On October 9, 1993, an ice-age grave was found in Browns Valley, on the Minnesota border with North Dakota. Although some 1,000 years younger than the Mexican find, Browns Valley Man is the oldest Caucasian thus far recovered in the United States. Artifacts taken from his grave are not associated with the Yuma or Folsom types, which flourished toward the close of the last ice age. For lack of any other explanation, these artifacts were categorized by conventional scholars as transitional between the Yuma and Folson types. In fact, however, these grave goods are more likely the products of some foreign, overseas source, a supposition reinforced by the Browns Valley Man's discovery near the eastern bank of the Minnesota River.

A more recent find occurred in 1965, when the remains of a female Caucasian were excavated from a waterway in Colorado. The 9,700-year-old Gordon Creek Woman had a smaller, narrower face than those of comparative indigenous peoples. It also displayed alveolar prognathism, which causes the tooth region to jut out slightly, a characteristic not found in tribal Americans but typical of modern Europeans. Interestingly, Gordon Creek Woman's bones and nearby tools had been sprinkled with hematite at the time of her burial. Hematite is a blood-red pigment manufactured in powdered form for funerary purposes by the Red Paint People, unknown mariners who traveled along the eastern seaboard of North America 7,000 or more years ago.

A no less remarkable find was made in 1940, when the excellently preserved body of a 9,400-year-old Caucasoid male was discovered inside a Nevada cave. The upper part of his body was partially mummified, and some scalp with red hair was still attached to the crown of his head. His grave was lined with sagebrush, upon which the corpse was laid, indicating that his people were sophisticated enough to use burial rites. Known as Spirit Cave Man, he had been placed on his left side with legs flexed upward to bring the knees level with the hips, a posture similar to the fetal position (suggesting rebirth) found in predynastic Egyptian interment. Well-made leather slippers, a rabbit-skin blanket, and beautifully woven mats were still in good condition. Tragically, Spirit Cave Man disappeared forever after he was handed over to the Nevada Indians.

Minnesota's 7,800-year-old Pelican Rapids Woman was found in 1938, but was eventually presented to local Indians for anonymous reinterment, even though she displayed Caucasoid features. The same fate befell Browns Valley Man. And Gordon Creek Woman, nearly forty years after her discovery, has never been DNA-tested. Nor has the ten-year-old female at Nevada's Grimes Point Burial Shelter been subjected to scientific examination, despite the location's 9,740-year-old origins. Oregon's Prospect Man, more than 6,800 years old, likewise remains untested. Testing is under way, however, on Arlington Springs Woman, a contender for the oldest known inhabitant of the Americas after the quarter-million-year-old Hueyatlaco site. Her discovery was also unique because it was made on an island, Santa Rosa, off the southern California coast, thereby proving her people's ice-age maritime skills. DNA research is also planned for Nevada's Wizard Beach Man (10,500 Years Before Present, or Y.B.P.), the Wilson-Leonard site in Texas (10,000 Y.B.P.), and Montana's 10,800-year-old Anzick burial of a young child. Such testing is important, not only to determine the racial backgrounds of these individuals, but also to compare the genetic makeup of the various human population groups that first peopled America, their origins, and the times of their arrivals.

During the summer of 2002, Dr. Theodore Schurr told the American Association for the Advancement of Science that DNA research at the Southwest Foundation for Biomedical Research (San Antonio, Texas) was able to trace four major lineages of American Indians to Siberia and northeast Asia—specifically, in Baikal and Altai-Sayan. These findings tallied with conservative theories of Mongoloid peoples arriving in North America over the Bering Strait land-bridge before rising sea levels engulfed it after the close of the ice age, about 9,000 years ago. However, Dr. Schurr and his colleagues were able to trace a fifth, numerically minor, lineage with ancestral roots among Caucasian groups. Known as Haplogroup X, it was present among some Algonkian-speaking tribes, such as the Ojibwa, long before Columbus or even Vikings arrived in America. Haplogroup X comprises about 4 percent of modern Europeans, but it also occurs to a lesser degree in the Near East.

A second, smaller group of Indians—the Blackfoot, Iroquois, Inuit, and lesser tribes from Minnesota, Michigan, Massachusetts, and Ontario—although they have some Mongolian blood, nonetheless stem from yet another ancient Caucasian branch that produced the Jomon, the earliest culture creators in Japan, beginning about 10,000 years ago. Silvia Gonzalez, who was responsible for the redating of Penyon Woman III, concluded, "If this proves right, it's going to be quite contentious. We're going to say to Native Americans, 'Maybe there were some people in the Americas before you, who are not related to you.'" In reporting these revelations in 2002, in Washington, D.C., science editor Roger Highfield stated that sufficient DNA evidence now exists to show that America was "colonized" by Caucasians 30,000 years ago. They did not come over any long-since-sunken land-bridges from Asia; they were already in possession of a maritime technology sophisticated enough to carry them across the vast, hazardous stretches of open sea.

In July 2001, an international team of researchers headed by the University of Michigan's Museum of Anthropology found evidence of Caucasians in North America more than 15,000 years ago. University of Michigan spokesman C. Loring Brace announced that native inhabitants dwelling south of the U.S.–Canadian border are directly descended, although racially mixed, from an early Caucasian people. Brace and his colleagues from the University of Wyoming, the Chinese Academy of Sciences in Beijing, the Chengdu College of Traditional Chinese Medicine (Sichuan Province), and the Mongolian Academy of Sciences in Ulaanbaatar compared craniofacial measurements of twenty-one prehistoric and modern human skulls. Their analysis showed that the earliest Americans were not associated with any Asian population.

The genetic strain in the indigenous inhabitants of the Pacific Northwest, Brace said, was a match for the Caucasian people who occupied Japan 15,000 and more years ago. Science staff reporter for the *Wall Street Journal* and assistant editor of *Forbes Magazine* Priscilla Meyer told *Ancient American* readers, "Already evidence is stacking up to support the ancient scenario of an enormous migration of millions of people by boat across the South Pacific as early as 5,000 years ago. Nothing in the official story would allow for such a migration, but the genetic evidence is clear and unmistakable." According to the Naacal tablets Churchward was allowed to read, the population of Mu at the time of its inundation numbered sixty-five million inhabitants.

Meyer continued:

> The great pilgrimage came many thousands of years after the first Americans crossed over from northern Asia, presumably by the Siberian–Alaskan land-bridge. But the late population waves across the South Pacific appear to account for the lion's share of the American Indian or Amerind population that inhabited Mesoamerica and South America when the Spanish Conquistadors arrived in the early 1500s. For now, mainstream archaeology is dealing with this new genetic evidence by looking the other way. Eventually, the results could force archaeologists to rewrite America's ancient history. Most recently, scientists tracked a mutated human gene across the South Pacific from Southeast Asia to Easter Island, off the coasts of Peru and Chile. The unique mutation has even permitted archaeologists to date the large migrations, placing the first to 2500 or 1700 B.C. . . . They found four genetic flukes that were shared only by current residents of Southeast Asia and the South Pacific island chains. . . . Modern Amerind tribes with the tell-tale genetic markers include the Maya of Guatemala, the Pima and Hopi of the American Southwest, and the Ticunas of the Brazilian rain-forest.

Meyer's early date for a trans-Pacific mass migration to the Americas nearly coincides with complementary astrophysical evidence indicating the final destruction of Mu in 1628 B.C. The genetic markers she mentions, tracing South Pacific influences to the American Southwest, confirm Hopi oral traditions of partial origins from over the sea in the west, just ahead of a rising tide that engulfed their ancestral realms. Memory of the flood has been perpetuated by a ceremonial group, the Water Clan, with the revealing name Patkinya-Mu. Its members conduct their commemorative rituals at a *kiva,* a circular, subterranean shrine.

According to Frank Waters's authoritative study, rafts in which the Hopi forefathers, remembered as the Patki, or water people, fled the inundation of their Pacific homeland are signified by layered cedar poles stacked crosswise in the kiva between stone blocks.

The Patkinya-Mu oral tradition holds that flood refugees in North America were met by Massau, a native guide, who directed them to the Southwest, where they could live in peace. The sole object the immigrants were able to preserve from their sunken homeland was a stone tablet broken at one corner. Massau prophesied that some day in the distant future their fellow survivors would find them, and the tablet must be presented to the visitors as a means of identification. A lost white brother would then deliver the absent fragment, signaling the beginning of a new age. Over the millennia, the stone was in the special care of the Fire Clan. In the 1500s, when their representative gave it to a conquistador, the dumbfounded Spaniard did not know how to react, save to get on with the colonization of the American West. The Hopi are still waiting for their white brother with the missing piece.

Meyer traces the same trans-Pacific impact on Mesoamerica to validate Colonel Churchward's contention that a Lemurian priestly class, the Naacals, actually became the Maya elite. The Maya, however, date only from the second century B.C., far more than 1,000 years after the ultimate immersion of Lemuria. Churchward was actually referring to a preceding culture as yet undiscovered in his time. This was the Olmec, from which the Maya inherited the basis for their own urban society. Olmec civilization began around 3000 B.C., followed by two cultural and population surges in the seventeenth and thirteenth centuries B.C., which correspond, respectively, to the Lemurian and Atlantean catastrophes.

"In the Americas," *Ancient American* writer Martin A. Grundy points out,

> four basic mtDNA lineages have been identified and normally labeled A to D. Lineages A, C and D are also found in Siberia, which is not surprising, if Native Americans originated in Asia.

The B lineage, however, is confounding researchers, because it is lacking in the Siberian populations. Just as the degree of change in a language can be used to estimate its age, so the amount of variation within a given genotype can be used to estimate when a population first arrived in a particular geographical region. Using this approach, it has been estimated that the A, C and D mtDNA lineages arrived in the Americas some 41,000 to 20,500 years ago with linear B appearing only 12,000 to 6,000 years ago. The B lineage is found predominantly to the south of the Americas, and is rare or absent in the NaDene and Eskimo-Aleut languages groups to the north.

The geographical distribution of the B mtDNA lineage causes a problem: If this lineage represents a later migration across the Bering Land-Bridge (as suggested by its age), then why is it predominant in the south, and why does it not exist among the people of Siberia? The answer seems to be that some genetically distinct group independently colonized the south. The estimated age of the B lineage is greater than 4,500 years, and so it should not come as a surprise that the language of these people, if different from that spoken by peoples of the other American mtDNA lineages, should now be unrecognizable. The B lineage does exist in some Polynesian groups, and it has been suggested that these people might have reached the American continent in prehistory. . . . Genetic analysis has revealed the enigmatic B mtDNA lineage, which suggests the presence of a distinct racial group to the south.

The arrival of this B lineage from the South Pacific 12,000 years ago roughly coincides with the late-ice-age flood that dramatically raised sea levels, inundating all the low ground of Lemuria, and compelled the mass migration of its inhabitants to higher places of refuge. Genetic proof is bolstered by fresh linguistic evidence. Gaining greater scientific credence is the belief that Hohokan dialects spoken by North America's Pacific coastal and Southwest Indians ultimately stem from Austronesian languages known across Oceania.

Excavation of a buried
moai reveals deposition
up to its chin, suggesting
a far greater antiquity for
the statue than assigned
to it by conventional
investigators.

A member of the Ama cult
impersonates a survivor from
sunken Mu wading ashore
in ancient Japan, holding a
branch from the Tree of Life.
Photo by Professor Nobuhiro
Yoshida.

Re-erected in modern times,
moai line the beach at Easter
Island's Anakena Bay.

Entrance to the pre-Inca city
of Tiahuanaco, in the Bolivian
Andes.

A monolithic statue at the city of
Tiahuanaco resembles an Easter
Island moai.

The Philippines' Banaue rice terraces, the ancient breadbasket of Lemuria.

The same ancient farming technology "fingerprint" appears in Ena, Japan (pictured left), and at the Incan sky-city of Machu Picchu, high in the Peruvian Andes (pictured below).

The colossal Candelabrum of the Andes, coastal Peru.

Top of a buried arch at Tiahuanaco.

One of Tonga's monumental pyramids.

Japan's prehistoric stone towers closely resemble Easter Island and South American counterparts, because all were once part of Lemuria. Photo by Professor Nobuhiro Yoshida.

Mid-nineteenth-century illustration of Easter Island's stone tower before its destruction.

One of the Silustani towers near the shores of Lake Titicaca in the Andes Mountains of Bolivia. Its similarity to Japanese and Easter Island versions points to common Lemurian origins.

Japan's sunken monument off the shores of Yonaguni Island.

This artist's rendition of a Hawaiian heiau, or ceremonial platform, demonstrates its similarity to the underwater discovery near Yonaguni Island. (Keaiwa Heiau, Oahu)

A stone arch's neatly fitted blocks at Yonaguni Island's underwater citadel.

A corridor and flight of short steps cut into Yonaguni's subsurface structure demonstrate its artificial nature.

A scuba diver swims along the spiral stone staircase winding around an immense tower underwater near Okinoshima Island, Japan.

Bronze emblem at Tokyo's Shinobazu Temple portraying the lands of Mu engulfed by the sea.

California's Hemet Maze Stone emblazoned with the sacred symbol of Mu.

The symbol of Mu copied by Colonel James Churchward from monastery records he studied while serving with the British army in India during the 1870s.

As some indication of the very large-scale mass migrations generated by the ice-age deluge, these South Pacific genetic influences were not confined to Mesoamerica and the American Southwest. Indeed, the Haida Indians of Pacific coastal British Columbia more often resemble modern Japanese than most other Native Americans. Mixed descendants of the Japanese, today's Ainu recall a time when the sea suddenly rose over the land, drowning a majority of humankind. Only a few survivors escaped by climbing to mountaintops. The Ainu are the last surviving remnants of the original Caucasian inhabitants of Japan, which they dominated until little more than 2,000 years ago. From 480 to 221 B.C., Chinese society disintegrated during a period known as the Warring States. The empire suffered a major brain drain, as most of its intellectuals and many aristocrats fled the bloodshed for the relative safety of Korea. When conditions began likewise to deteriorate on the peninsula, the former leaders of Chinese culture migrated once more, this time to Japan. There they intermarried with the resident Caucasians, known as the Jomon, creators of the world's first pottery, to form the modern Japanese people. These events are mirrored in the simultaneous elite flight from China during the time of the Warring States, termination of the Jomon, and start of Japan's first mixed culture, the Yayoi.

The appearance of Ainu-like Caucasians on the other side of the vast Pacific Ocean has come as a shock to American archaeologists. Most of the deeply prehistoric skeletal remains are being found by professional excavators and amateurs alike in the western part of the United States—often, as with Washington state's Kennewick Man and Arlington Springs Woman on the California island of Santa Rosa, near or on the Pacific Coast, where arrivals from Lemuria would be most expected to have taken place. These discoveries are by no means confined to North America, however. In 1962, the mummy of a six-foot-tall blond woman was found in a pre-Inca grave near Chancay, among the central-coastal mountains of Peru. Lima's Herrera Museum features a room given over entirely to well-preserved preconquest mummies displayed behind glass cases. About a half-dozen specimens have light-colored, wavy, fine-textured hair ranging from brunette and red to sandy and reddish blonds. Colonel Churchward wrote that Mu was a multiracial state, but dominated by a native Caucasian people.

Kahiki was the Hawaiian Lemuria, as described in the creation chant the *Kumulipo:* "A land with a strange language is Kahiki. Kanakas [men of our race] are not in Kahiki. One kind of man is in Kahiki—the Haole [white man]. He is like a god. I am like a man." Kahiki's inhabitants did not immigrate from outside the Pacific, but originated there, hence the story of their autochthonous creation in the Garden of Eden. With the loss of that earthly paradise, they moved throughout Polynesia and Southeast Asia, across the Indian Ocean, up the Persian Gulf, and into Iraq, leaving traces of their myth among various peoples along the way. They finally resettled between the Tigris and Euphrates Rivers, where their tradition was preserved but distorted over the millennia by local influences. Tracing their long trek, Oppenheimer followed specific Eurasian genetic marker lines, both nuclear and mitochondrial, spreading from an area of ocean south of Thailand, across India and into Mesopotamia, and beyond to central Europe.

Oppenheimer was preceded in 1933 by Lewis Spence:

It may be that the fair race of Lemuria, after the submergence of the main land-masses of that continent, seeking refuge from an area tormented by cataclysm, made their way northward and westward by slow degrees by Micronesia, to Japan and thence to the Asiatic mainland. . . . It appears as much more probable that the fair race colonized the north of Europe from Lemuria via Siberia then it advanced from that latitude to Oceania. This fair race, coming from Lemuria, may have entered Japan and China at a very early period where yet the Mongolian had left his center of dispersal in western Asia, and may have pressed onward or have been driven by circumstances into southern Siberia, which, it is generally agreed, is the point whence the fair peoples of the north of Europe commenced their migration to the countries they now occupy.

Spence's tracking of a fair-complected people migrating from Lemuria across Asia seems confirmed by the prehistoric remains of Caucasian men and women found in China during the last decades of the twentieth century. From the mid-1970s to the late 1980s, first dozens, then hundreds of mummified bodies were discovered in northwestern China's Takla Makan Desert. The desiccated corpses were mummified by the region's exceptionally dry conditions, resulting in an astonishingly high level of preservation. The men, women, and children were often attired in superbly woven textiles, sometimes including felt, comparable in style and sophistication to the finest Scottish tartans. More remarkable still, the remains were unquestionably Caucasoid, with red or blond hair and other, distinctly non-Mongoloid physical traits. They also preceded China's first historical civilization, the Shang, by five or more centuries, with date parameters from 3,800 to nearly 5,000 Y.B.P. These predynastic inhabitants were not numerically insignificant transients but instead formed a large community, as evidenced by more than 500 specimens found so far in the desert.

Modern residents in the vicinity of the mummies are the Uighurs, a Turkic-speaking minority in western China, where their partial Caucasian origins suggest genetic links to the prehistoric inhabitants. The Uighurs consider themselves so racially distinctive that they are seeking independence from the People's Republic of China. Forensic anthropologists can only speculate on the origins of this anomalous people, but James Churchward claimed as long ago as 1926 that inscribed tablets he read while an officer in India recounted that the Uighurs were once part of "the principal colonial empire belonging to Mu." They spread, the inscriptions reported, across northern China and southern Russia, into Europe as far as Ireland and Spain, at a time when "the Gobi Desert was an exceedingly fertile area of land. The history of the Uighurs is the history of the Aryans."

In other words, the Caucasian mummies found in Uighur territory are the remains of immigrants whose own ancestors fled the inundation of their Pacific homeland by moving across China and into the Gobi when that region was still inhabitable. With deterioration of the climate and desiccation of the land, they migrated westward into India and

Europe in what historians came to call successive waves of Indo-Aryan invasions from the late fourth millennium to the twelfth century B.C. Churchward's statements seemed utterly bizarre at the time he published them and for more than fifty years thereafter. But with the discovery of an ancient Caucasian population in western China, his characterization of a powerful Lemurian influence among the Uighurs seems credible. Nor did he alone associate the Gobi region with civilizers from the Pacific.

Belief in a pre-Polynesian white race from some idyllic homeland is widespread throughout the Pacific. The natives of Male Kula greeted late-eighteenth-century Europeans as Ambat, the same name applied to an "aboriginal" race of fair-skinned people in New Hebrides. Knat was the legendary white hero of Motu Island, in the Banks Group. The *agalo i mae* were red-haired, light-complected "ghosts of war" described as "immigrants" who arrived at North Mala in the Solomon Islands—the same tradition preserved at Vanua Leva in the Banks. In the Pumotus and Tahiti there are traditions of red-headed women with blue eyes who rose up from the floor of a lagoon, the mythical rendition of a historical occurrence: the emergence of survivors from the Lemurian flood.

Papua tribesmen cited by Knappert conduct a coming-of-age ceremony suggesting human origins in Mu. Adolescent boys are confined in a huge wickerwork affair made to resemble a fish, from which they emerge reborn as men. Their effigy basket is referred to as the Vai-Mu-ru. New Guinea cosmological myth tells of a murdered female wallaby from whose corpse lice emerged to become the first men and women of a white race, able to communicate among themselves without recourse to speech. Only much later did they develop a language. A second batch of lice to crawl from the decomposing wallaby were black. In time, they too become human, today's dark-skinned aboriginals of New Guinea. Being older, the white people were more culturally advanced, and invented a fleet of canoes in which they sailed away toward the sunrise, never to be seen again.

According to the Kumulipo, Hawaii's oldest and most important oral tradition, the Mu originated in Helani, "the unstable land in the deep blue sea," an apt characterization of geologically unstable Lemuria. A story from the Hawaiian island of Kauai relates that the king of the Mu opposed mixed marriages between his people and the Polynesians. Having failed to discourage these relations, "he called the men and their first-born sons together and told them that on the next night all the Menehune would leave the island, so that their racial purity would be maintained. The Menehune men were not allowed to take their Hawaiian spouses or their younger children with them."

The tale recalls an admonition by the Polynesian sea god Tangaroa, who exhorted his people to "keep their skins white like their minds." As late as the mid-nineteenth century, blond children were sacrificed on Mangaiia, the southernmost island of the Cook Group, to Tangaroa. The Menehune-Mu were not mythical creatures; they actually appeared in a census during the reign of Kaumuali around 1820, when sixty-five out of 2,000 residents in the Wainiha Valley were counted as Menehune. They lived away from others in their own community called Laau, or "forest."

The ubiquitous Polynesian demigod Tane is described in numerous oral traditions as red-haired. His people were characterized by the Maori as *karakako*, "white." Spence quotes an old Maori who remembered traditions of the Iwi Atua, original inhabitants of New Zealand: "In appearance, some of them were very much like the Maori people of today; others resembled the *paketa* [whites]. The color of most of them was *kiri puwhero* [ruddy complected], and their hair had the red or golden tinge which we call *uru-kehu*. Some had black eyes, some blue, like fair-skinned Europeans."

The Iwi Atua were remembered as the guardians of sacred places, a function apparently connected with recent archaeological discoveries in New Zealand. Located immediately south of Lake Taupo, on North Island, the Kaimanawa Wall is a step-pyramid or terraced ceremonial platform of the kind found throughout Polynesia, although among the very largest examples.

For lack of any datable material, the Kaimanawa Wall's age is elusive. Century-old trees growing through the structure date it to prehistory, but the Maori, who arrived in New Zealand 700 years ago, were not its builders, because they never erected anything of the kind. It may have been raised in the ancient past by the Waitahanui, whose elders apparently preserve some knowledge of the ramparts even today. The Kaimanawa Wall's Lemurian identity is underscored by the Maori's own tradition of a people that preceded their occupation of New Zealand. The light-skinned Moriori were allegedly the builders of irrigation terraces, hilltop fortifications, and monumental stone walls like the Kaimanawa. Indeed, ancient terracing faced with embankments of stone may still be visited in the district of Pelorus Sound.

According to tribal elders of the Ngatimaniapoto, a blond people, the Patupaiarche, spread throughout the world from their sunken homeland in Hawaiki. New Zealand's Mount Rangitoto was said to have been the Patupaiarches' sacred center. Similarly, the Gilbert Islanders of Micronesia have traditions of a blond-haired people, the Matang, who spread across the ocean following a terrible cataclysm that destroyed their opulent homeland during the ancient past. Genetic traces of the Matang resurface occasionally among natives of the Solomon Islands, especially in Malaita, where light-haired natives may yet be encountered. Spence hastens to add that these atypical individuals represent the recurrence of a recessive type, and "are indigenous, and not European hybrids."

Spence was supported by a Christian missionary who lived among various South Seas natives during the nineteenth century. "All through the race, wherever we meet with it," Percy Smith observed, "we find a strain of light-colored people who are not albinos, but have quite light hair and fair complexions. With the Maoris, this strain often runs in families for many generations. At other times, it appears as a probable revision to the original type from which this strain was derived. There are also traditions among the Maori of a race of 'gods' called Pakahakeha, who are said always to live in the sea and are white in complexion—hence the name Pakeha they gave to the white man on first becoming acquainted with us in the 18th century." Pakeha bears a striking resemblance to Pahana, the Hopi Indians' "lost white brother," possessor of a missing piece from the stone tablet their ancestors managed to salvage from the oceanic homeland before its inundation. It seems likewise similar to Pakoyoc, the light-skinned hereditary class of Inca rulers, who traced their lineage back to Viracocha, or Sea Foam, the fair-complected, red-haired culture-bearer who arrived in Peru following a great flood. The New Zealand Pakeha, North American Pahana, and South American Pakoyoc, despite the vast distances separating them, appear to have been nothing more than local linguistic inflections on the identity of the same Caucasians from an undersea realm.

The Maori Pakahakeha is even more cogent to our investigation of that lost Pacific civilization. Churchward stated that *keh* in the Lemurian language signified the people of Mu, as symbolized by the image of a deer beside the *T* glyph for the Motherland. In Maori, Pakahakeha means "moonlike," or "skin like moonlight." Another early-twentieth-century mythologist specializing in New Zealand prehistory, James Cowan, believed that the infrequency of light-haired individuals among the native inhabitants represented "the remnants of an immeasurably ancient fair-haired people who have left a strain of uru-kehu, or blondness, in mostly Maori tribes." The Pakahakeha were said to have been great builders of monumental stonework, like that of the Kaimanawa Wall. On the islands of Kosrae and Truk, they were revered as the Kona, or the Pinari, the "first men," native to the Buka Passage Area. By whatever name they were known across the Pacific islands, Haiviki was their sunken homeland, according to, for example, the elders of Ngatimaniapoto.

The fair-complected Niwareka, wife of the Maori god Mataora, belonged to a golden-haired people who introduced weaving and woodworking. "That this myth applies to the remnants of an old civilization whose peoples dwelt in a remote, or submerged, island," Spence emphasized, "can scarcely be questioned."

Across the Pacific and around its bordering continental shores of Australia, Asia, and America are the scattered skeletal remains, living remnants, and native traditions of a lost Caucasian race. Its member groups include the Ainu of Japan; British Columbia's atypical Indians, the Haida; Kennewick Man and numerous other ice-age non-Mongoloids from Washington state down the western coasts to Peru; together with universal folk memories recited by Polynesians, Micronesians, Melanesians, and Australoid Aborigines of fair-skinned culture bearers from a sunken Motherland long ago. Genetic and cultural evidence for the existence of such an antediluvian people is abundant. "We are therefore thrown back on the hypothesis," Spence concluded, "that the Lemurians were a white race having an extremely ancient development within the Oceanic area." The Garden of Eden described in Genesis, although presented as a fable by authors of the Hebrew scriptures, is a mythic parallel of human origins in the South Pacific, as traced by modern science.

The same evidence indicates that these early humans raised the world's first civilization in their oceanic birthplace. Many were forced to migrate by the calamitous consequences unloosed at the close of the last ice age. Waves of immigration spread east, where their remains are beginning to be recognized by anthropologists shocked by the discovery of non-Mongoloids in ancient America. But most went to Southeast Asia, where a native people, the Hmong, form an anomalous group. A persistent creation myth described their origins as a Caucasian people, a folk tradition confirmed only by recent DNA testing. Hmong oral traditions also tell of a great deluge, after which their ancestors, the Hmu, arrived in Southeast Asia. The Hmong still refer to themselves as Hmu. Oppenheimer correctly observed, "Much of the geographic distribution of modern languages—at least until the major colonizations of recent times—dates from the end of the Ice Age."

Generations after the Late Pleistocene deluge, the flood survivors and their descendants migrated across northwestern China, where their mummified remains are still being discovered throughout the Gobi Desert region. They eventually settled in the steppes of central Russia, but centuries of harsh conditions transformed the traditionally peaceful Lemurians into cattle-herding warriors known as the Aryans. Deteriorating climate conditions during the mid-fourth millennium B.C. rendered the steppes increasingly uninhabitable, so mass migrations erupted into the Indian subcontinent, Asia Minor, the Near East, the Mediterranean, and continental Europe. These large-scale incursions produced the early civilizations of the Indus Valley, Mesopotamia, and the Nile Delta. Newcomers mixed with indigenous people, who contributed local inflections to the resulting high cultures. This synthesis accounts for the fundamental similarities and individual differences of the first city-states at the start of the ancient world.

All included a lost Garden of Eden with its Tree of Life. Although synonymous with the Pacific Motherland itself, such a tree may actually have been revered in Lemurian times, and it still exists. In the story of Easter Island, a sacred tree was entrusted to Hotu Matua before he left Maere Renga with a company of colonists. Prior to making landfall at Anakena Bay, the kingdom had vanished into the sea. He replanted the toromiro, and its descendants flourished on Easter Island for centuries thereafter. By 1956, however, the last specimen, which grew nowhere else on Earth, was close to death. But the controversial archaeologist Dr. Thor Heyerdahl collected some of its seeds. These were sent to Sweden for replanting at Gothenburg's botanical garden. Just as the Easter Island toromiro died, three new examples sprouted under the care of Professor Carl Skottsberg, a leading authority on Polynesian flora. He gave their seeds to Danish botanists, who planted them on Easter Island as part of a Chilean reforestation project.

Today, hundreds of toromiro are again flourishing across Hotu Matua's second homeland. Their ancestor may have been the original Tree of Life in Lemuria's Garden of Eden.

SEVEN

Hawaiian Motherland

The carvings confirm Polynesian myths of a golden race
of people, who somehow survived the disappearance into
the sea of a lost continent we call Mu.

MAUI LOA, CURATOR,
HAWAIIAN ETHNIC ART MUSEUM, OAHU

Particularly gratifying moments for students of the past occur when a story long regarded as nothing more than legendary turns out to be true. Such a moment came in October 2004 with a discovery that not only radically altered present understanding of human origins, but also brought to life a myth repeated by native Hawaiians. Four hundred and sixty-two years before, they had told a Spanish explorer, Enrique Gaetano, the first modern European to visit their islands, that they were not the original inhabitants. Their ancestors had been preceded by the Menehune, a race of dark-skinned dwarves who stood just hip-high to the six-foot-plus newcomers. The naked little people were primitive hunters, even by Polynesian standards, and furtive forest dwellers who lived on small animals killed with simple clubs. Ever the elusive aboriginals, they withdrew under the immigrants' growing population pressures, retreating to the mountains of *pu'ukapele,* "the hills of Pele," where the Menehune practiced secret magical arts.

Menehune was probably a title similar to "sorcerers," because *hune* means magic. They were likewise remembered as the *kama'aina*, or "children of the land," indicating their native status at the Hawaiian Islands in pre-Polynesian times. The Society, Cook, and Tuamotus Islanders knew this same early people as the Manahune, *mana* suggesting that they were a race of spiritually powerful practitioners. While conventional scholars dismissed all consideration of the Menehune as entirely legendary, Bulletin 203 of the *Bernice P. Bishop Museum Newsletter* reported that "in the reign of Kaumualii, the last independent ruler of Kauai, a census was taken of the population of Wainiha Valley in which sixty five of the two thousand people counted by the king's agent were Menehune. All sixty five lived in a community named Laau in the depths of the valley forests." Undertaken during the early 1820s, the census documented the last vestige of the Menehune in the Hawaiian Islands they had once dominated. A Menehune leader on Oahu, Ku-leo-nui, or "Ku of the loud voice," was supposed to have conducted funeral games of spear- and disk-throwing, boxing, wrestling, and foot races after the death of royal personages. In fact, the recorded names of the winners are still preserved and venerated by native Hawaiians.

Even so, archaeologists and anthropologists alike were unanimous in their assessment of Hawaii's little people as fairies, sprites, or brownies, not unlike the leprechauns of Irish legend. In 1964, however, scientists found suggestions of unusual early human habitation at Liang Bua, a "cool cave" in the local Manggarai language, extending 130 feet into a hillside on Flores, a remote Indonesian island east of Java and northwest of Australia. Thirty-four years later, they discovered what appeared to be an extremely old man-made stone tool at the site. Carefully pursuing this lead, excavators eventually revealed a virtually complete human skeleton unlike any they had seen before. Beginning in September 2003, they undertook the laborious task of reassembling and identifying each of its bones in a Jakarta laboratory. Thirteen months later, the restored skeleton represented "a fundamentally new being," according to Joseph B. Verrengia, science writer for the Associated Press, "a discovery that could rewrite the history of human evolution. It would be the eighth species in the *Homo* category."

Homo floresiensis, or Flores Man, declared George Washington University anthropologist Bernard Wood, "is arguably the most significant discovery concerning our own genus in my lifetime." He was seconded by Chris Stringer at London's Natural History Museum, who described the find as "the most extreme figure to be included in the extended human family. Certainly, she is the smallest." University of New England's Peter Brown, who authored the study of the Flores discovery, stated, "This is the first time that the evolution of dwarfism has been recorded in a human relative."

The proportionally formed adult female stood just three feet tall, weighed no more than fifty-five pounds, and had a brain less than a third the volume of a modern human's, small even for a chimpanzee. Although far smaller than any other member of the genus *Homo,* her brain was complexly convoluted, suggesting a higher level of intelligence that belied its grapefruit size. Dean Falk, a paleoneurologist at Florida State University, declared that the creature's brain "has features I've not seen in anything this size." The tools and other man-made artifacts found with her and her six similarly dwarfish companions could not have been crafted by anyone less than a fully competent human. She was not "some kind of 'freak' that we just happened to stumble across," added Richard G. Roberts, from Australia's University of Wollongong, but an example of the first-known human dwarf species, as additionally confirmed by six other specimens found in the Liang Bua cave. They range in age from 12,000 to 9,500 years old, although the best-preserved skeleton belonged to a woman who lived 18,000 years ago. Nicknamed "Hobbit" after J. R. R. Tolkien's *Lord of the Rings* trilogy, she inhabited a real-life Middle Earth populated by giant tortoises large enough to ride, midget elephants no bigger than ponies, and monster rats the size of full-grown black Labrador hunting dogs.

The Flores people not only were toolmakers but also knew how to light fires and hunted in groups, implying they lived in communities and communicated effectively. But "the specimen's baffling combination of slight dimensions and coarse features bears almost no resemblance either to modern humans or to our large, archaic cousins," observed Verrengia.

"The lower jaw contains large, blunt teeth and roots like *Australopithecus,* a pre-human ancestor in Africa more than three million years old. The front teeth are smaller than modern human teeth. The eye sockets are big and round." In light of this new discovery, however, Africa, the supposed cradle of humankind, no longer holds "all the answers to persistent questions of how—or where—we came to be."

However, the sudden disappearance of humanity's real-life Hobbit 12,000 years ago is a question credibly answered by geologists. They know now that the ice ages were not peacefully superseded by some gradual warming trend, a theory generally accepted well into the last century. Instead, the last glacial epoch ended amid scenes of catastrophic volcanism and seismically generated super tsunamis that brought about the extinction of creatures like the monster rats and midget elephants, including Flores Man.

But maybe he did not completely disappear after all. DNA testing of the Liang Bua cave bones reveals that *Homo floresiensis* traveled beyond their Indonesian island, journeying eastward into the Pacific. Verrengia writes that even *Homo erectus* precursors "migrated from Java to Flores and other islands, perhaps by bamboo raft, nearly one million years ago." Genetic traces and disparate islander accounts extending throughout Oceania suggest the little people reached Hawaii ten millennia or more before the earliest known settlement in the islands. Mike Morwood, a research team member at Liang Bua, observed that *Homo floresiensis* must have possessed at least enough seafaring skill to negotiate the fifteen miles of open water from the Asian mainland to Flores. Only humans with enough brainpower to build boats could have made such a crossing, according to Morwood. Could these Indonesian Hobbits have traveled farther, island-hopping all the way to Hawaii, where Polynesians knew them as the Menehune?

If so, then either the Hawaiians maintained a factual memory over an astounding 12,000 years or examples of *Homo floresiensis* lingered on in the islands until less than 200 years ago, as indicated by the early-nineteenth-century census mentioned above. In any case, the existence of a species hitherto unrecognized and unsuspected by science was already known in the folk traditions of preliterate peoples. Native islanders did, in fact, tell of a half-size, hairy people with flat foreheads who long ago resided in the remote corners of Flores, an oral tradition spanning the Pacific from Indonesia to Hawaii.

The scientific confirmation of old legends can be as thrilling as psychic visions proven correct. The actress Shirley MacLaine, during one of the "past-life dreams" she experienced while on pilgrimage in Spain, learned that the capital of Lemuria was called Ramu and was located in the Hawaiian Islands. She was unacquainted with the works of Colonel James Churchward, but her vision closely paralleled his explanation of the Motherland's political power center, as described by his biographer, Hans Stefan Santesson: "When elected to be the king-emperor, this hieratic head assumed the title of Ra—the Sun—Ra being the king's symbol. To this title, Churchward tells us, was added the name of the land, Mu, so that the king's full title—the reference here is presumably to his dynastic title—was Ra Mu." In Hawaiian myth itself, the firstborn of Ra'i ra'i, a sun goddess, was Mu Re, ancestor of the islands' earliest inhabitants. A simple transposition from Mu Re to Ra Mu, and the solar identity of both versions defines a credible connection. A Melanesian tale recounts that a man went to the plains of the Ramu River, where a goddess in the guise of an old hag gave him a coconut that turned into a beautiful woman. After she became his wife, all the bachelors obtained similarly magical coconuts, and thus New Guinea was populated. Ramu not only features the name of the Pacific Motherland, but that of the sun god worshipped there as well.

Combining Shirley MacLaine's "past-life memory" with Churchward's research and native traditions suggests that Lemuria's capital was so identified with the king that they shared the name or title. If coincidence is discounted, the actress and the author tend to validate each other's statements, separated as they are at either end of the twentieth century. But they assume far greater significance when we learn that the Hawaiian Islands in which Ra Mu once supposedly held sway are extraordinarily rich in evidence on behalf of the lost civilization. As Leinani Melville, the Hawaiian historian, has written, "There has been, of course, much controversy over the existence or non-existence of the fabled land of Mu. It was accepted as fact among the educated Hawaiians. The white newcomers generally chose to regard it as myth. But so many things that the natives accepted as fact, the westerners regarded as fiction."

According to Hawaiian oral tradition, the islands were already inhabited long before the first Polynesians arrived during the second or third century A.D. by two very different groups: the dwarfish Menehune and a people whose very name confirms the existence of the lost Motherland, because they are known in Polynesian myth as the Mu. A more unequivocal connection with the Pacific civilization could not be clearer, and everything about the Mu, beginning with but not limited to their eponymous identity, suggests Lemurian origins. Over time, as both of these peoples declined toward extinction, Menehune and Mu became increasingly intertwined and synonymous with the same pre-Polynesian inhabitants of Hawaii. This confusion appears in some native accounts ("A Maiden from the Mu," Puku'i), in which the Mu are uncertainly described as a possible "tribe" of the Menehune.

The Menehune-Mu were remembered as great shipwrights and seafarers who sailed in fleets from Helani, formerly located far to the east and recalled as "the unstable land lying in the deep, blue sea," described by the Kumulipo. The catastrophe depicted in this chant of creation was at the center of Hawaiian religious ceremonies, wherein the gods were prevailed upon with offerings at their shrines to prevent the recurrence of the Deluge that had drowned Helani. Oppenheimer notes, "The Pacific versions of this story have one brother as a dark-skinned hunter-gatherer, whereas the other is a pale-skinned coastal fisherman who invaded from the sea"—respectively, the Menehune and the Mu.

The latter appear in several other Hawaiian accounts, such as the appropriately entitled *Ku-Mu-honua*. It describes them as the light-skinned, fair-haired construction engineers of cyclopean *heiau* (temples), *loko-ia* (fishponds), and "ditches," the only kinds of excavation known to the Polynesians. In "A Maiden from the Mu," the heroine's hair is described as shining "like the feathers of the 'o'o' bird." According to Mary Kawena Puku'i, the o'o' *(moho nobilis)* were "much prized by early Hawaiians for their few yellow feathers." But the real purpose of various megalithic projects assigned by legend to the Menehune, not unlike the ruins of Easter Island or Pohnpei, has never been satisfactorily determined. As the renowned British Atlantologist Edgerton Sykes wrote, "We are still uncertain as to the precise ritual function of the fish ponds."

In any case, the Mu achieved great architectural feats, because they were renowned for their mastery of spiritual forces known as mana, which they received from their god, Ha-Mu-ka. Here too is suggested the otherworldly powers said to have been used at Nan Madol and Rapa Nui to move the tons of basalt logs and towering moai. *In Search of Lemuria* author Mark R. Williams visited a stone temple on a high bluff overlooking Waimea Bay on the northern shore of Kauai. "According to local lore, *Pu'uo Mahuka Heiau* was built in a single night by the Menehune, who must have used some powerful mana to erect this massive, low-walled platform that's larger than a football field." Another public-works project attributed to the Mu is Kauai's 900-foot-long Alekoko fishpond. To travel writer Jim Rodgers, the Menehune "were marvelous stonemasons, and anthropologists agree that the Hawaiians were not capable of building such sophisticated cut and keyed masonry."

Later, Williams examined the so-called Menehune Ditch. Although currently used as an irrigation canal, "it once stood more than twenty feet tall, built of carefully dressed and fitted stone slabs like something ancient Romans would have erected. Today, the site lies unheralded next to a swinging bridge across the Waimea River. But it's still enough to conclude that the building technique is really different from the piles of rough lava I've seen throughout the islands. These stones have been finely cut and shaped like intricate puzzle pieces to withstand the most violent cataclysm." The building style Williams describes is reminiscent of monumental stonework found at Easter Island and Tiahuanaco. The Lemurian identity of these Hawaiian temples surfaces in their holy-of-holies. Known as the *paehe-mu,* it is an enclosure within the heiau set apart for sacred and ancestral images.

As might be expected of a deeply ancient, long-lived civilization remembered by numerous native peoples throughout the Pacific, the drowned kingdom from which the Menehune came still goes under a variety of names. They are nothing more than different cultural inflections on a single source known to Polynesians, Micronesians, and Melanesians—various tribal and ethnic responses to a shared place of origin known as Hiva, Haiviki, Kahiki, Mutuhei, and so forth. Honomu is one of several place-names in Hawaii commemorating the lost civilization of the Pacific; it means "sacred Mu."

As Leinani Melville pointed out, "The Mu knew their motherland by several names. Havai'i, now pronounced Hawaii, was only one of them. Tradition has handed down the knowledge that a few of the Mu survived the cataclysm which pulverized their ancient civilization. Those few preserved the traditions of their forefathers and handed them down to the next generation. This pattern went on for centuries, even for thousands of years, until Captain Cook, the English navigator, discovered the remote descendants of the Mu living in the jungles of Hawaii."

The Islands' most ancient and important oral tradition is the Kumulipo. The renowned Hawaiian scholar Bernice Bishop, in her authoritative translation, indicated its extreme antiquity: "The language is often archaic, containing many words completely unknown to modern Hawaiians." This "Song of Creation" was divided into numerous chants, the first one of which clearly defines Lemurian origins in the Pacific as Ku-Mu, the source. According to mythologists Martha Ann Imel and Dorothy Myers Imel, Ra'i ra'i, the goddess of sunshine, "came from heaven to Earth to be the mother of the Mu, the first humans." The earliest of these, Ku-Mu-honua, used the power of mana to build the premier temples from great stones. Some of his descendants were Ka Mu Lewa, Ka Mu Lani, Lolo Mu, Heku Mu, Nana Mua, Haleku Mu, Ku Mu lea, Mu Liele-alii, Ko Mu koa—names that embody their ancestral homeland. They were a white people, according to the Kumulipo: "Born was Hakea, fair-haired, a male."

Through Ku-Mu-honua, the lineage of every great chief and high priest was traced back to the supreme god, Te Tu Mu Nui, the "great builder" or "master teacher" who made the world. Over many generations, the chiefs and priests originated all those things eventually used by human-kind and some spiritual arts since lost. Mu-eu introduced cloth-beating, and Mumu-hango showed how to use totora reeds for making boats and roofs. Kahiki entered a golden age of productivity and prosperity. But it was not to last. "The era of overturning," the Po-au-huliha, was ignited by the famous volcano goddess: "From Kahiki came the woman, Pele. Lo, an eruption in Kahiki! A flashing of lightning, O Pele! Belch forth, O Pele! The phosphor burns like the eye of Pele, or a meteor-flash in the sky. The heavens shook, the Earth shook, even to the sacred places. The Earth is dancing. The heavens are enclosing. Born the roaring, advancing, and receding of waves, the rumbling sound, the earthquake. The sea rages, rises over the beach, rises to the inhabited places, rises gradually up over the land."

The Po-au-huliha grew more violent, escalating into the Kai-a-ka-hina-li'i, the "flood that caused the downfall of the chiefs," who fled "in crowds from the vanishing isle on the shoulders of Moanaliha" (the ocean): "Ended is the line of the first chief of the dim past. Dead is the current sweeping in from the navel of the world. That was a warrior-wave. Many who came vanished, lost in the passing night. The swirling, shifting ocean climbed the mountains, sucked in and swallowed up life as it climbed higher and higher above the homes of the inhabitants. The swelling sea, the rising sea, the boisterous sea, it has enclosed us. O, the overwhelming billows in Kahiki! Finished is the world of Haiviki."

Henceforward, the west, where Kahiki went down, was referred to as *he ala nui o ka make*, "the great road of death or the dying." The vanished Motherland itself was renamed yet again, as Kahiki-ho-nua-kele, "the divine homeland going down into the deep blue sea." Despite its destruction, there were many survivors. One of them was Nuu, who, with his wife, Lilinoe, and three sons and their wives, escaped in *He waa Alii o ka Moku,* a royal vessel that carried them safely to Hawaii. Although the Chant of Creation was recited by skilled and highly trained speakers, the Kaiakahinalii, or Great Deluge, was similarly recalled in ritual performances by hula dancers. They were led by a teacher known as a *kumu,* yet another name evocative of the drowned Motherland.

Wooden tiki statues stand guard on Hawaiian shores against a repetition of the Great Flood that overwhelmed the Polynesian Motherland.

That these accounts did not evolve as the result of contact with nineteenth-century missionaries was made known by the experience of William Ellis, who was personally involved in the Christian conversion of native Hawaiians. "After a succinct account of the deluge," he recalled,

I endeavored to exhibit the advantages of faith, and the consequences of wickedness and unbelief, as illustrated in the salvation of Noah, and the destruction of the rest of mankind. After the conclusion of the service, several persons present requested me to remain till they had made some inquiries respecting the deluge, Noah, etc. They said they were informed by their fathers that all the land had once been overflowed by the sea, except a small peak on the top of Mouna-Kea, where two human beings were preserved from the destruction that overtook the rest, but they said they never before heard of a ship, or of Noah, having always been accustomed to call it the *kai a Kahinarii* (sea of Kahinarii).

This and related native versions of the deluge story feature a superabundance of materials unquestionably describing the existence and subsequent annihilation of the Motherland. As Lewis Spence observed, "It is self-evident that these myths of destruction had their origin in Lemurian tradition, as by the period of Polynesian settlement in Oceania its greatest time of seismic violence had long passed." Remarkably, the Kumulipo tells of a deadly "current sweeping in from the navel of the world," the same title by which Easter Island was originally known. In the previous chapter, we learned that Te-pito-te-henua referred to the midpoint or epicenter of two fault lines crossing at a geologically unstable rift in the Southeast Pacific Plateau. The Lemurians were aware of its potential danger and tried to limit the worst of its consequences by erecting the basalt moai as component parts of a telluric transducer that would dissipate the extreme energies of seismic violence. But the Kumulipo tells of a tsunami, a "warrior-wave," that came from the direction of Easter Island and overwhelmed Kahiki.

Another connection with Rapa Nui is an early name the Mu gave to Hawaii: Ka-houpo-o-Kane, or the navel of Kane. Kane was the god of light, reminiscent of Te-pito-te- Kura, the navel of light, Easter Island's most holy artifact, brought personally by Hotu Matua from his sunken homeland, Marae Renga. The Maori of the western Pacific told of their primeval ancestor, Tane, who carried Foam-in-the-Ocean and White Sea-Mist to New Zealand from the land of Hiva before its disappearance.

Replicas of these sacred stones were placed in every *whare,* or chanting school, and students stood on them to absorb their mana when reciting on graduation day. It appears that the Motherland bequeathed several such relics to its escaping culture bearers, who used them as symbols around which the old mystery-cult might be revived on foreign shores. The Pohaku-a-Kane, located in Puna, coastal Hawaii, on Cape Ku-Mu-kahi, are a pair of stone pillars allegedly retrieved from Kahiki before it sank beneath the sea. Similar cone-shaped stones by the same name served as altars within the *hale mu-a,* or men's eating house. Ka-houpo-o-Kane appears to have signified that Hawaii was just as much a center ("navel") of Lemurian spirituality as was Rapa Nui.

Traditions of a Great Flood from which the Mu arrived centuries before the Polynesians to accomplish outsized feats of architecture like the Menehune Ditch are contradicted by archaeologists. They argue that no physical proof of human occupation in the Hawaiian Islands goes back further than 1,800 years ago. Even so, accidental finds beginning in the early nineteenth century suggested a far more profound antiquity than arrived at via carbon-14 testing. For example, during excavation of the first wells on Honolulu in 1822, a shaft was sunk eight to ten feet through surface loam and volcanic sand. Beneath this, the diggers were obstructed by a hard level of coral rock in which a human skull and several bones were found. When Honolulu Harbor was being dredged in 1858, the tip of a spear point, together with a worked stone, was recovered from similar depths of mud and black volcanic sand. The next year, a human skull was discovered in a deep substratum of volcanic mud at Molakai. The circumstances of these finds dated them by more than a millennium before the second- or third-century arrival of Polynesians at Oahu.

Occasional material evidence for earlier human impact on the Hawaiian Islands is supported by cultural confirmation in the form of navigation methods allegedly inherited from the Mu. The Mu were said to have built huge catamaran vessels in which were undertaken the first transoceanic voyages plotted on ingenious star charts. One of their ancient maritime techniques was related in 1891 to W. D. Alexander, a professor of anthropology fluent in various Hawaiian dialects, by a Kauai elder, who provided the following sailing directions, as useful as they were ancient:

"When you arrive at the Piko-o-wakea, the equator, you will lose sight of *Hoku-paa* [the North Star], and then Newe will be the southern guiding star, and the constellation of Humu will stand as a guide for you."

"The constellation of Humu" was known to Dr. Alexander and his culture as the Southern Cross. In the night sky, it forms a *T*-configuration, which, according to James Churchward, was the national emblem of Mu. "The *Tau* is a picture of the Southern Cross," he wrote. "The reason for its adoption as the symbol of resurrection was: when the Southern Cross appeared at a certain angle in the heavens over Mu, it brought the long-looked-for rain. With the rain, seeds in the ground sprang to life, drooping foliage revived and sent forth fresh shoots, upon which flowers and fruit grew. Then it became a time of plenty and rejoicing in Mu—life had been resurrected." A viable connection between the Hawaiian Humu and Churchward's Tau through the Southern Cross to the lost Motherland seems inescapable.

One of the most provocative pieces of evidence on behalf of the drowned Motherland was traced by Mark Williams to Honolulu's Bernice P. Bishop Museum, the renowned institution for Polynesian archaeology. On a tip, he learned that its basement archives contained a "Chart of the World" compiled at the behest of Hawaii's last reigning monarch during the late nineteenth century. It was alleged to have made some references to Mu. Following a prolonged search among the dusty records, the old document was found and spread out for Williams. "It is a large and colorful rendering of the Earth's surface," he explains, "with lands denoted as 'rising' or 'subsiding', and showing an enormous continent between Fiji and Madagascar called Lemuria! The map is signed 'Rex Kalakaua,' and dated 1886." That preceded by forty and more years popular books about the lost "continent" by Brown, Churchward, and Spence, none of whom suspected the chart's existence, judging from their works, which make no allusion to it.

An accompanying manuscript, part of the Marques Papers, reports that the map was drawn by an unnamed ship's captain, whose handwritten journal also survives. In it, he describes Pacific geology, stone ruins, and dozens of islands, together with information about their myths and native populations. "We are on the threshold," the anonymous author concluded, "and Lemuria may be raised again in all its glory." Williams was "amazed that an obscure, unpublished manuscript could contain the precise detail used repeatedly in later accounts of the sunken Pacific continent. But the identity of the captain died with Mr. Marques, who was the French consul in Hawaii around 1900."

Though the descendants of Mu in the Hawaiian Islands did not welcome their Polynesian guests in the second or third century, they refrained from making war against them, but kept their distance, refusing any kind of social intercourse. They were a private populace determined to hold themselves aloof from all outside influences. According to native tradition described by Leinani Melville, the Mu were a "secretive people who preserved what they knew in silence. They were sworn never to reveal any of the rites of the Mu to those who did not belong. Secrecy was their motto." Their very name forms the expression *ho'omu*—"to sit in silence; to refuse to answer; speechless," according to the Hawaiian lexicographer Mary Kawena Puku'i.

But as the newcomers' population swelled, the Mu were crowded out from one island to the next, until they had to evacuate even their beloved Kauai. A small minority, most of whom had taken Polynesian spouses, refused to leave and hid in remote wooded areas.

Their last-known points of refuge were hardly more than two small outposts in the west, beyond sight of land. Even so, the uninhabited islands are one of Pacific archaeology's most challenging enigmas. Nihoa, from the Hawaiian word for "serrated," refers to its jagged profile, and lies some 170 miles from Kauai. Its 156 acres of barren rock form a windswept track just one mile long and a quarter-mile at its widest point, with its eastern end rising nearly 900 feet. Necker Island, at thirty-nine acres and about 320 miles away, is even smaller and farther off. Neither outcropping possesses trees or soil in which to grow crops. Freshwater springs do not exist, and annual rainfall in the form of passing squalls amounts to no more than twenty or thirty inches. Both islands are continuously battered by high seas that make any landing along their rocky coasts perilous. While the immediate vicinity of Nihoa was visited from prehistoric into modern times for its turtles and seabirds, Necker Island was unknown until its European discovery in 1789.

Two more inhospitable locations could scarcely be imagined. Yet they are covered with nearly 100 stone buildings, including at least two cemeteries, together with fishhooks, sinkers, fiber fishing lines, cowrie-shell lures, hammerstones, grindstones, adzes, and innumerable other tools—physical proof of large, settled populations in an environment unable to support life. Forty-five of the sixty ruins on Nihoa are houses, walled storage or holding areas, bluff shelters, agricultural terraces, and other utilitarian structures for daily life; all but one of Necker's thirty-four archaeological sites are temple platforms or heiau. P. V. Kirch, who visited the islet during the early 1980s, reported that the "marae are amazingly consistent in plan and architectural style and consist basically of a low, narrow, rectangular platform adjoining a paved rectangular court or terrace. Arrayed along the platform are a series of upright stone slabs, while other slabs are positioned at certain points in the court." The arrangement of these standing monoliths was probably based on astronomical orientations with various positions of the sun.

Most of the stone statues, the largest one at sixteen inches, have been recovered from Necker, suggesting a link with Nihoa and a division of purpose for a single population. While its members resided on Nihoa, Necker was set aside as a place of pilgrimage by sea. Flotillas of catamarans carrying crowds of devout worshippers across threatening waves toward their sacred isle makes for an impressive vision. All indications are that this hardy people not only survived but prospered for an indefinite period as well, although how they sustained themselves against such daunting odds, where they came from and when, and the nature of their fate are questions scholars have been grappling with unsuccessfully for more than 200 years. Hawaiians believe the prehistoric residents of Nihoa were the *kanaka maoli,* "men unlike ourselves," another reference to the Mu. Some of the finer examples of stonework at Necker do indeed resemble Kauai's Menehune Ditch and the Alekoko fishpond.

Nihoa's stepped terraces (again suggesting Lemurian farming methods) testify to the agricultural know-how of the vanished inhabitants and their determination to live amid hostile surroundings. But their incomparable seamanship may have granted them a measure of abundance in contrast to their arid environment. The immediate waters are rich in whales, reef fish, turtles, sharks, pearl oysters, and sea cucumbers. The little island itself is home to monk seals and many species of seabirds, including albatross, boobies, finches, frigate birds, petrels, shearwaters, and numerous other tropical birds. The Miller-bird is found only at Nihoa. The same folk genius who caused a holy city to rise on remote Necker Island was capable of wrenching prosperity from adversity.

Nihoa and Necker were the last refuges of survivors whose heritage was greatness and destruction, a legacy that toughened them and polished their civilized brilliance for centuries after the catastrophe that annihilated the Motherland. But in this transient world, even the redoubtable Mu could not hold out indefinitely against the inertia of time. Like the reticence for which this people were renowned, the stone ruins of two deserted islands have stood in silence ever since their builders vanished into the vast Pacific unknown centuries ago.

EIGHT
Lemurians in America

*Known to literally hundreds of native peoples, from the
Arctic Circle to Terra del Fuego, long before Christian
missionaries arrived with their own tale of the Flood,
the fundamentally consistent tradition of a Great Deluge
is undoubtedly the tribal memory of some very ancient
natural cataclysm their various ancestors experienced in
common during the deeply ancient past.*

WILLIAM ALEXANDER,
NORTH AMERICAN MYTHOLOGY

A volcanic event of cataclysmic proportions exploded across New Zealand thirty-six centuries ago. Known as the Taupo Valley Center eruption, it coincided with the final destruction of Lemuria and was witnessed by the ancestors of today's Maori natives. They still recollect that crucial catastrophe in their myth of Rongo-mai—"sound-warrior"—a sky god who long ago attacked the world in the guise of a comet. After decimating humanity, he transformed himself into a gigantic whale that sank into the sea. This myth is not only descriptive of the final destruction of Mu, but also remarkably similar to Lemurian versions on both sides of the Pacific. The ancient Chinese *Huainanzi* relates that a gargantuan whale, symbolic of a large island, perished in the Sunrise Sea after the beginning of time when "a broom-star" (an extraordinarily large and brilliant comet) appeared in the sky.

Meanwhile, the Koryak, Kamchadal, and Chuckchee Indians of coastal British Columbia recall Quikinna'qu, "the first man" and only survivor from an island that had been transformed into a whale by the Thunderbird. To escape attack from its talons, the whale dove to the bottom of the sea, drowning everyone on its back except Quikinna'qu, who floated on a log to what is now Vancouver Island. There he married an indigenous woman, whose children became the tribes of the Pacific Northwest. The Haida likewise told of a killer whale upon whose back humankind first resided, until it sank beneath the waves under savage attack from the sky. Many drowned, but some floated to the shores of British Columbia, where they became the ancestors of today's native peoples, referred to as the Killer Whale People. Significantly, the whale-island was remembered as Namu.

These flood stories are retold in oral tradition and preserved in the famous wooden obelisks erected by various native Pacific peoples of western Canada. However, these tall structures were not worshipped as idols, but are more accurately defined as heraldic monuments symbolically depicting the lineage of the family before whose home or lodge they stood. The poles begin narrating their story from the top, signifying the remote past, usually ending with the portrait of a recent, the latest, or the current head of the household at the bottom. As the totem-pole specialist Edward Keithahan made clear:

These myths cannot be read in the strict sense of the word. Rather, it should be said that they may be recognized, for they contain nothing more or less than a system of memory devices which, taken in their proper sequence will recall a myth. The legends of these totem carvers are principally made up of tales of migrations, the flood, inter-tribal wars and early contacts with white men. All groups have accounts of a flood that inundated all of the land save the highest peaks. The story is the inspiration for several totem poles, notably the Bear totem mortuary pole of the Nanyaayi at Wrangell and the Devil's Thumb pole of the same place.

In Northwest coast myth, a bear led survivors of the deluge to the shores of British Columbia. The Devil's Thumbpole was sacred to the Talqoe-di tribe because it was meant to have been a stylistic representation of Talth Qua Na Sha, the holy mountain on which their ancestors found refuge from the flood. More commonly positioned at the top was an effigy of the Thunderbird grasping Namu in its talons, thereby boasting of a family's allegedly antediluvian descent. The same whale was famously portrayed on the front of Chief Johnson's house in Alaska, and as a large petroglyph at the Hetta Inlet. Haida belief held that the souls of those who drowned at sea joined the Killer Whale People in their ancestral home on the ocean floor.

The first totem pole was introduced by Alaska's Kaigani Haida, originally from Langara Island; their story of its Lemurian origins was paraphrased by Keithahan: "The birthplace of the totem pole is a sunken land where hilltops become islets, and mountains rise sheer from the water's edge. Its valleys are bays and inlets, while its farmland is presently inundated." A Haida folk story recounted how some fishermen

Thunderbird, the personification of celestial violence, attacks Namu. Haida painting at the Field Museum of Natural History, Chicago.

Haida totem pole outside the Field Museum of Natural History, Chicago.

went down to the beach early one morning long ago, where they were surprised to find a waterlogged totem pole floating in the tide. They took it to their village, where it was recognized as a post from one of the Killer Whale People's undersea temples. The Northwest Pacific Coast inhabitants henceforward erected carved poles after the example found by the fishermen. Their first post-deluge pole was set up on Dall Island, at Cape Muzon, whose name memorialized the lost Motherland. As Churchward wrote in 1926, "These legends and carvings on the totem poles strongly confirm the fact that the forefathers of those Indians came from Mu."

Refugees arriving from the cataclysm were depicted in local myth as fair-skinned, red-haired seafarers who took wives among the ancestors of the Indians. This legendary portrayal seems to have been borne out by the natives themselves, who exhibited a high incidence of white characteristics that perplexed early European visitors. British explorer George Dixon marveled that an indigenous woman of Yakutat he saw in 1787 "had all the cheerful glow of an English milk-maid; and the healthy red which flushed her cheek was even beautifully contrasted with the whiteness of her neck; her forehead so remarkably clear that the translucent veins were seen meandering even in their minutest branches—in short, she was what would be reckoned handsome even in England." The following year, another British visitor, John Meares, said the Nootka women of Vancouver Island "not only possessed the fair complexion of Europe, but features that would have attracted notice for their delicacy and beauty in those parts of the world where the qualities of the human form are best understood."

In 1817, Camille de Roquefeuil, a French navigator, recalled, "We saw several men and a greater number of women whose complexion differed from white only by a tinge of pale yellow. The greater number of the Indians have black hair, the remainder a light red." Among the Kaigani Haida, who originated totem-pole construction after discovering the first example, "red hair is still quite common," according to Keithahan. These anomalous physical traits appear to be genetic traces of Killer Whale People who, as stated in native myth, arrived on British Columbian shores after the inundation of their homeland. So too in stories of a great flood repeated throughout Oceania the survivors are often, if not usually, characterized as light-skinned and red-haired. Native tradition and a mixed racial legacy combine to offer persuasive evidence on behalf of survivors from Lemuria in western Canada.

Many Northwest coast accounts identify the lost realm of the Killer Whale People as Dzilke. Also known as Dimlahamid, its story is preserved by the We'suwet'en and Gitksan in northern British Columbia. For many generations, they recall, the inhabitants of Dzilke prospered and spread their high spirituality to the far corners of the Earth. In time, however, they yielded to selfish corruption and engaged in unjust wars. Offended by the degeneracy of this once valiant people, the gods punished Dzilke with terrible earthquakes. The splendid Street of the Chiefs tumbled into ruin as the ocean rose in a mighty swell to overwhelm the city and most of its residents. A few survivors arrived first at Vancouver Island, where they sired the various Canadian tribes. Researcher Terry Glavin, relying on native sources, estimated that Dzilke or Dimlahamid perished around 3,500 years ago, the same period assigned by geologic evidence for the final destruction of Lemuria, in 1628 B.C.

Similar versions are known down the West Coast and into the American Southwest. California's Chemehuevi and Mohave Indians believe Hawichyepam Maapuch was responsible for keeping the Great Deluge from obliterating all life on Earth. The sea goddess spared the last two creatures, Coyote and Puma, who sought refuge at the summit of Charleston Peak. As the flood receded, they descended the mountain to repopulate the world. The creation myth of the Yokut, a southern California tribe, recounts that humankind originated on an island in the middle of a primeval sea, where Eagle and Coyote fashioned the first men and women. The Maidu, another California Indian tribe, told of Talvolte and Peheipe, the only survivors of a natural catastrophe that destroyed their earthly paradise after its inhabitants, grown corrupt, had offended heaven.

The Lemurian identity of this lost homeland is suggested in Mu-ah, Shoshone for "summit of Mu," a sacred mountain in California, which may have been chosen by Lemurian adepts for the celebration of their religion, and which has been regarded as holy ever since by native peoples. So too Pimugnans, the original name of coastal southern California's Gabrielino Indians, echoes the same sunken civilization. Mythographer Joseph Wherry cites a native myth that told of Hokan-Siouan origins: "In the dim and distant past, the forebears of many California Indians lived on an island somewhere in the Western Ocean. This island was Elam, and they worshiped the powerful god named Mu." Like Haida stories of the Great Deluge, the Hokan-Siouan version includes a bear as flood hero.

William Donato, president of the Atlantis Organization, wrote of the "Western Whites" for *Ancient American:*

In the 16th century, Cabrillo described the people of Gha-las-Hat (California's San Nicholas Island) as being more advanced than those of the mainland. He described the women as having "fine forms, beautiful eyes and a modest demeanor," and the children as being "white, with light hair and ruddy cheeks." Their culture seems to have been a variant of the Chumash-Gabrieleno. Old ship logs and other contemporary written accounts also refer to the "white-skinned" Native American communities on Santa Catalina Island. A study of human crania cited by Dr. Jeffrey Goodman showed that the ancient Channel Islanders had the greatest affinity with a group label "archaic Caucasoid."

Catalina was called "Pimu" by the original inhabitants, while Santa Cruz Island was known as Limu. Incidentally, Limu means "in the sea." The fact that two of the California Channel Islands have "Mu" as part of their names may not be coincidental. According to Yurok Indian traditions, before their ancestors arrived at the Klamath River, the land was occupied by a white-skinned people they described as moral and civilized, and shared what they had with the Yurok, who remembered them as the Wah-gas. Were they descendants of Mu?

Coastal Peru is no less rich in native traditions of the Lemurian catastrophe, as recounted in the Yurukare Indian story of Tiri. It tells how their ancestors hid in a mountain cave during two worldwide cataclysms that destroyed a former age. All other humans were killed in a fire that fell from the sky, followed by an all-consuming deluge. Tiri alone of all the deities took pity on the survivors of a sinful humankind by opening the Tree of Life, from which new tribes stepped forth to repopulate the world. As described in chapter 6, Mu itself was known as Tau, the Tree of Life.

The Motherland's name lived on in the identity of another great people, the Chimu, who raised a powerful civilization, Chimor, that dominated the Peruvian coast from circa 900 A.D. until their defeat by the Inca in 1476. Their capital, Chan-Chan, lies just north of Trujillo. At the zenith of its power, the eighty-square-mile city was home to nearly a quarter-million residents, master irrigationists whose *pozos*—stone-lined reservoirs—held up to two million gallons of fresh water carried from mountain streams by aqueducts more than 100 miles long. The high technology and social organizational skills necessary to build such a huge population center were brought to Peru, according to Chimu historians, by Taycana-Mu. He had been sent on a culture-founding mission by his superior, who ruled a kingdom in the Pacific Ocean.

Another important Chimor city was Pacatna-Mu, christened after an early Chimu general who became the regional governor. The so-called Palace of the Governor at Chan-Chan is surrounded by an immense wall decorated with a sculpted frieze depicting a sunken city: fish swim over the tops of linked pyramids. The scene appears to memorialize the drowned civilization of Mu, from which the ancestors of the Chimu—literally, the "children of Mu"—arrived on Peruvian shores after the catastrophe.

The premier pre-Inca city of Bolivia and its apparent relationship to Lemuria through Easter Island have already been mentioned. That connection could be more than cultural and might signify a clue to Tia-huanaco's inexplicable location atop one of the great mountain ranges of the world. During my first visit to the ruins, in 1994, I wondered how such a metropolis could have functioned, to say nothing of having been built, at 13,300 feet, where it is difficult to breathe, as well as impossible to grow a variety or sufficiency of crops necessary to feed its estimated 40,000 inhabitants.

The steps of the Kalasasaya, or sunken plaza, are each single blocks of rectangular stone some thirty feet broad and weighing an estimated forty tons. The Gateway to the Sun alone was cut from a single fifteen-ton stone. Back in Peru, outside the ancient capital of Cuzco, I had examined the gargantuan ruins of Sacsayhauman. Officially labeled a fortress, the site's alleged military attributes were not apparent, despite its 300-ton blocks. At Tiahuanaco itself, stone slabs in excess of 130 tons were moved from quarries fifty miles away. How could such tonnage be transported over exceptionally arduous distances, up and down mountains and valleys, then manipulated with uncanny precision at an altitude where just breathing is difficult, even for natives?

Some magnitude of the difficulty posed by this question has been revealed by modern construction experts. They calculate that moving a single 130-ton block would have required the concerted effort of 8,450 able-bodied men. Expecting so many workers to pull a 130-ton weight in perfect unison seems far beyond probability even under ideal conditions, and utterly impossible in view of the site's mountainous environment. Yet against all logic, Tiahuanaco exists where it does. Harold T. Wilkins, an extensive world traveler and popular archaeological writer in the mid-twentieth century, was likewise unable to reconcile its construction with its location: "That this city of the dead—probably the oldest in the world—was originally built in the clouds, in rarefied air where breathing is a torture, and a waste of scrub on a bleak mountainside, where nothing grows that is edible or can grow, is most improbable."

Today, Aymara residents in its general vicinity eke out a subsistence existence on stunted maize, frozen potatoes, and *chicha,* fermented from cornmeal to produce a powerful alcoholic drink in which they drown their misery. The Altiplano is dry, desolate, and pockmarked with scrub bush, an unsupportive environment contrasting illogically with the obvious architectural genius responsible for Tiahuanaco. These contradictions between the ancient city and its natural setting have long puzzled investigators. In 1920, the renowned British geologist C. Reginald Enock wondered:

> How did the large population which formerly existed there subsist in a region so lofty, where few food products grow and [with] a large population such as must have been required to furnish workers to move the great monoliths and construct the colossal buildings encountered there and in the Titicaca basin? The suggestion has been made, even, that the Andes have reached their final elevations since the time of man's habitation of them, and since the epoch of

the great megalith structures. Whilst it is doubtful if this explanation could be accepted, it is, nevertheless, remarkable that these works and the evidences of a former population exist at an elevation above sea-level where corn did not grow.

Approximately 800 feet lower and almost twelve miles away, Lake Titicaca is the highest saltwater lake on Earth, and, at 1,214 feet, one of the deepest. It is also about half as large as Lake Ontario, with a surface area of some 3,200 square miles. Natives around its shores have long spoken of an ancient city beneath its waters, despite the condescending smiles of establishment archaeologists. In 1955, a former U.S. Marine scuba instructor, William Mardorf, followed up on these resident accounts by conducting several dives beneath Lake Titicaca. At depths of ninety-five feet, he claimed to have found several stone ruins similar in style to Tiahuanaco, but attempts to photograph them were frustrated by poor underwater visibility and the relatively primitive condition of subsurface photography at the time.

Llamas lounge before the pre-Inca "fortress" of Sacsayhauman, outside Cuzco, Peru. Like other monumental structures found in the high Andes, its very creation seems miraculous.

In November 1980, Hugo Boero Rojo, a Bolivian expert in Andean cultures, located sunken man-made structures off the shores of Puerto Acosta. Unlike conventional scholars, who failed to find anything in the lake because they exclusively trusted their purely scientific methods, the scuba divers were led to their discovery by Elias Mamani, an elderly resident Indian. Underwater photography documented what Rojo described as "temples built of huge blocks of stone, with stone roads leading to unknown places." Although these structures were found between forty-five and sixty feet beneath the surface, Rojo said that "flights of steps whose bases were lost in the depths of the lake amid a thick vegetation of algae" indicated greater, unknown depths for their foundations, thereby tending to confirm Mardorf's sighting at ninety-five feet down twenty-five years earlier.

Clearly, the underwater buildings must have been built before the lake existed, which would date their construction to an impossible antiquity. Worse, geologists know that Lake Titicaca has been gradually receding over the last 4,000 years, a fact that multiplies the sunken city's already incomprehensible age. Yet Tiahuanaco itself may be at least as old.

While walking toward the Kalasasaya, I noticed an ornately carved horizontal stone block rising less than three feet from the ground like a monumental croquet hoop. Only gradually did I realize it was the top of an arch, the rest of its length buried in the earth. I later learned that even though only 10 percent of the archaeological zone's 400 acres had been excavated, archaeologists had identified a number of partially or fully buried structures at depths of more than six feet. Only severe winds operating over many thousands of years or an immense deluge could have washed so much soil over them. Helmut Zettl correctly observed after visiting the site during the 1960s, "The mountain ranges which surround the area are not high enough to permit sufficient run-off of water or wind erosion to have covered the ruins to such a depth. A large amount of water had to have inundated the city; when it receded, it left the silt covering all evidence of an advanced civilization, leaving only the largest statues and monoliths still exposed." It would appear that local Bolivian legends recounting Tiahuanaco's construction at the time of the Great Flood have some basis in fact.

In the 1930s, when the well-known archaeologist Julio Tello was excavating at Chavin de Huantar, then the oldest known ruins in Peru, he found that the arches were deeply covered under prodigious amounts of dirt and rock. As nothing in the immediate environment could account for such deep deposition, Tello concluded it must have been brought to the site by a series of super tsunamis that had swept over Chavin de Huantar, perhaps bringing about its abandonment, leaving behind great quantities of sediment. If this event corresponded to the age of the ruins, it occurred about 3,000 years ago.

About a mile north of the Kalasasaya, toward Lake Titicaca, is a radically different site. While Tiahuanaco is still standing, the superbly machined blocks of Puma Punku lie scattered around the area as though they were Styrofoam instead of multiton blocks of andesite, a fine-grained rock resembling granite. At twenty-seven feet in length and as much as 300 tons, they dwarf even the megalithic masonry at Tiahuanaco. The relative conditions of the two locations and Puma Punku's superior tonnage are not all that separate them. They are so stylistically dissimilar from each other that the same culture could not have been responsible for both. In contrast to Tiahuanaco's dry-wall construction of various-sized stones neatly fitted into each other like a cyclopean puzzle, the monstrous slabs at Puma Punku had molds cut into their edges; when precisely matched, block to block, molten metal was poured into the depressions, hardening into clamps as it cooled. This construction method, utterly unlike anything found throughout Andean civilization before or since, was the expression of a sophisticated technology investigators are at a loss to explain.

Tiahuanaco is rich in statuary, but no statues exist at Puma Punku. Its builders preferred to sculpt recessed crosses-within-crosses and triangles-within-triangles into the extraordinarily hard andesite as though it were soft butter. The intricacy and precision of these geometric designs far exceed anything comparable in South America, or perhaps anywhere else in the world. Yet the stones into which they were cut with such

The ruins of Puma Punku.

great skill have been haphazardly thrown about by what might have been the most violent natural upheaval to have ever shaken Bolivia. As *Reader's Digest* described it, "A jumbled heap of stones looking as if they were hurled to the ground by some great natural catastrophe, is all that remains of Puma Punku." Aside from its foundation, the only original structure left relatively intact is what appears to be a canal, another anomalous feature some investigators believe proves the site was originally a port for Lake Titicaca when its waters extended this far. But the discovery of man-made ruins under the lake renders that supposition untenable.

Childress addresses the contradiction by asking, "If a massive earthquake tossed down the three hundred-ton stones of Puma Punku, scattering them about the plain like a bunch of toys, then why were not the buildings of Tiahuanaco likewise destroyed? Is it because they were built at a later time, after the cataclysm?" These challenging questions are not easily answered. Still, it is no less difficult to understand how Tiahuanaco could have been built or flourished in such an unsupportive environment. Just as difficult to grasp is why one site was reduced to ruins by the same upheaval that left the other, with its inferior tonnage and construction, still standing.

Strangely, Puma Punku bears far less resemblance to nearby Tiahuanaco than it does to another pre-Inca city some 300 miles across the border, in Peru. While climbing the mountains above Ollantaytambo, I was amazed to find the ground littered with seashells. Not all of them appeared to be fossilized, because they crumbled almost to powder at the touch, implying they were several thousand, not millions, of years old, as claimed by official scholars. If these mountains really had been covered by some ocean long before humans evolved, the organisms left behind would not still be unfossilized. I recalled my first view of the Andes from the open window of a venerable train that laboriously wound its way from Cuzco to Machu Picchu at the base of the sky-reaching peaks. They seemed very different from the Rockies, Appalachians, and Alps, all of them obviously weathered with the passage of long geological eras. The steep-sided Andes radiated a freshness that made them appear as though they had just been thrust up from the earth the previous night. My rational mind fought down the impression, which went against current geological theory, but has been nonetheless echoed by many other independent observers.

According to David Scarboro, earth sciences faculty member of the Open University:

The plates whose collision is uplifting the Andes Mountains are the South American plate and the Nazca plate. The Nazca plate is moving eastwards from the East Pacific Rise. The South American plate is moving westward from the Mid-Atlantic Ridge. Where these two plates meet, the Nazca plate is being subducted beneath the South American plate. The Andes mountains lie above the subducted zone. The subducted slab is heated by friction and by the hot mantle into which it is descending. This heating causes partial melting of the slab and the overlying mantle, generating magma that rises into the crust. Most of the magma cools and solidifies in the lower crust, adding to its volume—a process known as underplating. The high heat flow above the subducting slab also reduces the density of the crust, causing the crust to become isostatically buoyant. Both underplating and the isostatic uplift of the region contribute to the formation of the Andes.

Scarboro's succinct explanation of South American mountain building is eminently comprehensive, depicting a gradual development over the last fourteen million years. But could that process on occasion have been greatly accelerated somehow, forcing this high range, second in the world only to the Himalayas, to rise far more rapidly than scientists believe? These mountains themselves are rising much faster than once thought. According to the British documentary writer Charles Allen, "A leading authority in Himalayas geomorphology (Adolf Gansser) has gone so far as to suggest that some sections of the Himalayas may have risen as much as nine thousand feet and more within the last half-million years—and that the rise may be continuing at the rate of some thirty inches a century."

As recently as 1992, during relatively moderate seismic activity (5.7 on the Richter scale) in southern California, sections of the San Gabriel Mountains rose more than a foot. Exactly 300 years before, the Caribbean island of Jamaica was seized by an earthquake so powerful that more than eight hectares of territory fell into the sea and two mountains moved nearly a quarter of a mile in three minutes. In the early nineteenth century, the New Madrid earthquake forced the Mississippi River to flow backward and radically changed its course through southern Illinois. Events such as these show that Earth's otherwise incremental changes are sometimes interrupted by episodes of swift movement on a colossal scale. Enock believed that "the Andes have been up-heaved in recent geological times, perhaps by successive stages. It may even be that aboriginal man beheld some of the changes in these regions, and in this connection the conditions encountered on the great uplands give rise to certain interesting reflections regarding the epoch of their elevation to their present high altitude."

The millions of seashells underfoot at Ollantaytambo, Lake Titicaca's saltwater and pre-lake sunken ruins, Tiahuanaco's uninhabitable natural environment and six-foot-plus deposition of sediment, Puma

Punku's widely scattered megalithic blocks—all bespeak the establishment of sophisticated urban centers built at sea level during the deeply ancient past before they were suddenly thrust to the tops of newly formed mountains. Wilkins observed that Lake Titicaca "has a chalky deposit of ancient seaweeds, with lime, about two yards deep, which indicates that the ridge where it is found was once an ancient seashore. The remarkable unevenness of forces would account for the curious fact that the shore or strand lines found on mountain slopes and walls of the Bolivian Altiplano, and denoting the beaches of ancient seas or ancient lake levels, are not level either with the present level of Lake Titicaca, or with that of the modern Pacific Ocean."

But what was the mechanism for such an inconceivably violent change? Even the most potent earthquakes could not have pushed up the Andes to over 13,000 feet in a short period.

A map of the eastern Pacific Ocean's tectonic disposition shows that the Nazca plate abutting Peru–Chile, where it is gradually forcing up the Andes, is squeezed between the South American plate in the east and the Pacific plate from the west while being blocked in the north by the Cocos plate. Tiny Easter Island sits at the precise midpoint where the Nazca plate's southern boundary, the Nazca Rise, running east to west, meets to form a T with the north-to-south East Pacific Rise. Hotu Matua's Navel of the World was well named. In any case, these interacting plates explain how mountains are made in South America, incrementally over vast stretches of time at about the rate of human fingernail growth. But that process might be greatly accelerated if the Pacific plate suddenly brought extraordinary pressure to bear on the East Pacific Rise against the Nazca plate, forcing the Andes to rise rapidly, even instantaneously.

The key words here are "suddenly" and "extraordinary pressure." They do, however, accurately describe conditions during a glacial epoch climatologists call the Boelling interstadial. It occurred when 600,000 square miles of ice collapsed, flushing a million liters of fresh water into the South Pacific every second. Sea-levels jumped by sixty feet to overwhelm vast territories across Polynesia and literally push them down to the ocean floor. If the early-nineteenth-century New Madrid earthquake had taken place in the Central Pacific instead of the Saint Louis area, many billions of tons of water would have inundated an island the size of southern Illinois. The abrupt surge of weight on the Pacific plate caused it to press against its East Pacific Rise connection with the Nazca plate, which responded by increasing the rate of subduction beneath the upward-moving edge of the South American plate. The Andes Mountains shot toward the sky.

The cataclysmic rise of lands produced by the sinking of others recurs throughout circum-Pacific folk traditions and finds examples in documented geologic events. During an 1885 expedition to Falcon Island, off the coast of Tonga, American surveyors found that it stood 290 feet above sea level. Thirteen years later, it disappeared into the ocean. During 1927, Falcon Island broke the surface and continued to rise to its present altitude of 100 feet. That even a two-mile-wide oceanic territory could sink and reemerge in just forty-two years—a geologic nanosecond—demonstrates that the abrupt rise of land does occur in the Pacific region.

Churchward quotes contemporary earth scientists on Japan's devastating earthquake of 1923, when 156,984 lives were lost: "An island which existed off Yokohama was submerged, and near it another island emerged at the same time. The bottom of the sea was raised around Yokohama, so that the depth of water was reduced." He wrote in his second volume of *Cosmic Forces of Mu,* "Against the foregoing, we have to take into consideration what took place in the Malay Archipelago during the [1880s], with various similar phenomena reported from various parts of the Earth along the lines of the gas belts, where volcanic elevations of as much as ten thousand feet were made overnight."

Churchward's mention of Malaysia recalls my encounter with a cultural representative from that country in the early 1990s, when she told how the sinking of her ancestors' ancient homeland simultaneously "raised" the archipelago they sought refuge on and settled. "What goes down must come up, geologically, too," she said.

A similar version repeated by the Selung natives of another archipelago, the Mergui, off southern Burma, recounts that their ancestors came from a huge land far out across the Pacific Ocean, where the sun rises. After many generations of happiness, the daughter of an evil spirit unexpectedly appeared in the sky, from which she hurled flaming boulders into the sea. The flood this attack generated arose to engulf virtually the entire Earth, and all living things perished except for a few men, women, and animals who repaired to the top of a high mountain that still stood above the waves. From its summit, the remaining sorcerers exerted their magical powers to make the waters abate. As they did so, new lands arose, including the Mergui Archipelago, where the survivors found salvation and intermarried with the indigenous people to produce the Selungs. Their foundation myth not only describes the rise of one immense territory caused by the sinking of another, but also associates the deluge responsible with a comet's meteoric barrage, a common feature in other traditions about the destruction of a homeland in the Pacific Ocean.

Missionaries like Rev. William Ellis heard the following typical example firsthand in the early nineteenth century, before such foundation myths were demonized or obliterated by proselytizing Christians: "As Haiviki went down, Rua pushed up the Tuamotu Islands from the ocean bottom. The creatrix, Rua papa, produced Tahiti in a similar fashion." Mention of Rua and Rua papa in this Tahitian version is particularly cogent, because Rutas was one of the names by which Mu and/or its people were remembered, particularly in Asia. Wilkins cited Indian accounts of "Rutas, in the pagoda traditions of old Hindustan, and which, they say, was disrupted by a series of terrific earthquakes and a deluge, sinking it far under the ocean, in a day 'before the Himalayas existed'."

These disparate recollections of a discernibly Lemurian disaster associate it with the sudden appearance of new land and the abrupt upsurge of mountain building. Could they be folk memories of an immense cataclysm actually experienced by the ancestors of peoples from Asia, Malaysia, and the Pacific?

It would seem that only the extreme catastrophism of the Boelling interstadial would have been powerful enough to force the rapid rise of the Andes. If so, then Lake Titicaca and its ancient cities were built at sea level more than 10,000 years ago. Mainstream scholars find this conclusion unacceptable in the extreme, because they believe Tiahuanaco dates back no earlier than 600 A.D. They are at a loss, however, to credibly explain why most of its archaeological zone is buried under more than six feet of sediment. Until recently, they taught that the earliest traces of civilization in South America began with Chavin de Huantar, about 3,000 years ago. But in 2001, excavators found a sprawling urban center 120 miles north of Lima in the Supe River Valley, fourteen miles from the Pacific coast. Known as Caral, the city, formerly inhabited by 30,000 residents, was dated more than sixteen centuries older than Chavin de Huantar. Another Peruvian site, the pyramidal Huaca de los Sacrificios, is even more ancient, dated to 2857 B.C. Yet its level of sophisticated construction proves it is not the first of its kind, only the oldest so far unearthed, and was doubtless preceded by an extensive development well into the fourth millennium B.C. Though both Caral and the Huaca de los Sacrificios flourished long after the end of the last ice age, their recent discovery nonetheless demonstrates that archaeologists are still far from establishing a basal date for the beginnings of Andean civilization, which might very well find its roots in the Late Pleistocene.

Paul Dunbavin believes that the cataclysm of 1628 B.C. was sufficiently powerful to have left an enduring geologic legacy. "The emergence of the Pacific coral islands may also have occurred only since 1600 B.C.," he wrote. "Other radiocarbon dates quoted by Fairbridge suggest a date of between 1500 and 1800 B.C. for this Pacific emergence." While "this Pacific emergence" was very likely associated with the final destruction of Lemuria, the catastrophic scope of the 3100-B.C. natural disaster was probably greater. Whether it or the seventeenth-century-B.C. event was earthshaking enough to have actually compelled the sudden rise of the Andes Mountains is less certain, however, than the superior violence of the Boelling interstadial. But, as the archaeologists insist, ice-age roots for either Tiahuanaco or Puma Punku seem far too early, just as their origins before 1628 B.C. strike independent investigators as too late. Indeed, Caral and Huaca de los Sacrificios predate the final destruction of Mu; neither bears the marks of catastrophism. "If this continent sank at the same time that the Amazon basin rose," Childress postulates, "then the canal at Puma Punku could have been built before the upheaval to serve the same purpose which the Panama canal serves today."

Tiahuanaco's rectangular ground plan and extended forecourt do bear stylistic resemblances to ceremonial centers raised by builders of the Salavarry culture, a coastal civilization that curators at the Trujillo Archaeological Museum contend is more than 5,000 years old, a time frame rejected until recently by most conventional scholars outside Peru. But if the Salavarry structures do hearken back to late-fourth-millennium-B.C. beginnings, then they just predate the global catastrophe of 3100 B.C.

But a great deal of new research unhindered by the limits of academic preconceptions needs to be pursued before any one of the cataclysms now known to have shaken the world between the end of the last ice age and the close of the seventeenth century B.C. may be singled out as the event that pushed the Andes Mountains to their present altitude. More certain, however, is the impact Lemuria had on ancient South America, whenever it took place, as evidenced in the so-called Nazca lines. They comprise many dozens of outsized illustrations created in the Peruvian desert, rendering it, quite literally, the largest art gallery on Earth. Its artists were members of a culture archaeologists have labeled Nazca less for accuracy than for convenience after the southern coastal area in which the terraglyphs are found.

The Nazca was one of many sophisticated societies that preceded the better-known sixteenth-century Inca empire, officially flourishing from circa 200 B.C. to 400 A.D. Some revisionists bracket the Nazca period from the early first century A.D. to as late as 750, with the drawings making their appearance toward the close of that time parameter. These estimates are almost entirely arbitrary, however, because the lines themselves cannot be dated, although pottery shards in their vicinity lend themselves to carbon-14 testing. Conventional archaeologists make a significant leap of faith, however, in assuming that the same people who used the pottery also made the lines.

In truth, little is known about the Nazca, although hundreds of their mummified remains and the ruins of extensive irrigation projects combine with the gigantic geoglyphs to produce a prodigious body of physical evidence. Their origins and fate are unknown, despite the Nazca's undeniable influence on Andean civilization. The focus of their mystery, of course, is the famous collection of colossal desert drawings. They sprawl over 400 square miles of southern Peru's desert coast and are divided into groups of geometric designs (mostly spirals and trapezoids), bioglyphs (representations of plants and animals), and 762 lines, some of them extending dead straight for more than twenty miles through mountains and valleys, over all kinds of terrain, some of it formidable.

They were etched into the arid plain, or pampa, by clearing aside the grayish brown desert patina to reveal yellow sand just beneath. As such, they are intaglios, or slight depressions in the ground. The greatness of their creation may be appreciated when we know that the vast majority of them are unicursal—in other words, the figures are formed of unbroken lines—and are so enormous that their true configurations can be understood only from an altitude hundreds of feet overhead. At ground level, they cannot even be discerned. Obviously, these remarkable geoglyphs could only have been designed by way of a mathematically sophisticated grid system executed by skilled labor. No other Andean culture before or after the Nazca produced such immense illustrations. Their only counterparts in the outside world may be found among south Britain's hill figures outlined in chalk. But the Cerne-Abbas Giant, a rendition of Hercules outside Dorchester, and the Bronze Age Uffington Horse, near Oxford, share no apparent relationship with the Peruvian drawings, which are much larger.

One of the Nazca trapezoids is over 3,000 feet long. All the biomorphs, mostly of birds, are likewise of colossal dimensions. A cormorant or its close relative, the anhinga, for example, is 2,100 feet long. Since their accidental discovery by a pilot in the 1930s, numerous attempts have been made to demystify the Nazca lines, from fantasies of ancient astronauts who used them as runways, to astronomical interpretations in which the terraglyphs were supposed to represent various celestial phenomena. All these theories folded long before the end of the last century, although at least some sky significance on behalf of the images was established. About that same time, however, the giants of the pampas began to speak for themselves.

David Johnson, who investigated them with his geologist colleagues from the University of Massachusetts, suspected some kind of relationship between the desert illustrations and water. They found that the Nazca trapezoids corresponded to subterranean water sources. The trapezoids occurred at the exact points where aquifers enter the valley at geologic faults in the rock formations. Some of the straight lines paralleled water courses that dried up many centuries ago. Another large trapezoid clearly pointed downstream. About the same time Johnson began noticing the Nazca lines' apparent association with water, an archaeological team from the University of Illinois headed by Helaine Silverman working at Nazcas' biggest site, Cahuachi, established an unequivocal relationship between underground water sources and rayed lines extending outward from a common center. These centers were positioned just where water spills into the river valley next to the pampas. The Silverman group also discovered that many of the lines themselves were parallel to the direction of the flow of water.

After reviewing these findings, Michael Aveni, a leading archaeo-astronomer, concluded:

> I have no doubt that some sort of ritual on the ray centers and trapezoids, wherein people assembled for reasons connected to the ritual acquisition of water, was involved. The patterns of lines also speak of relations among people who manufactured them, and possibly of astronomy via the connection between sunrise/sunset positions and the date of arrival of water in the valleys adjacent to the pampa. . . . With so many lines pointing to the sun's place on the horizon at the beginning of the rainy season, is it possible that they were created as some sort of offering to the rain gods?

The biomorphs themselves appear to answer in the affirmative. Most if not all of them signify moisture (and, hence, fertility) in one form or another. Apparent Nazca illustrations symbolic of water include seaweed, the frigate bird and pelican (both birds bloat the sac of their lower bill with water), together with the above-mentioned cormorant, or anhinga, another fishing bird that, plunging into the sea, always emerges with a water-filled bill. Even more obvious are the representations of three whales, two of which are shown pregnant, a pointed statement on the necessity of water for life. The Nazca drawing of a fox does not seem connected to water, until we learn that it is a leading character in local native traditions of a great deluge in the ancient past. The flood rose over the entire world, except the summit of Mount Villcacoto, where humans and animals sought refuge from the lapping tide. The fox was the last to arrive, and so was crowded by the numerous survivors to the edge of the flood, where the end of his tail dipped into the water. After the deluge receded and everyone came down from Villcacoto to build a new civilization, they saw that the tip of the fox's tail had been stained by the water, a mark he passed down to all his descendants, who came to symbolize life's survival of the world flood.

Two other animal figures likewise seem out of place: the hummingbird and the spider. However, the former is the only bird that exclusively drinks for nourishment. Because of its grotesquely extended right leg, the Nazca drawing of a spider was regarded by archaeologists as the representation of an entirely fabulous creature. As recently as 1991, however, just such a specimen as depicted on the pampas was discovered—not in Peru, but on the other side of the South American continent, in the Brazilian rain forest. Known as a *Ricinulei,* the elongated right leg features the male spider's sex organ, which it also uses to drink beads of moisture collected in morning dew. Unable to be seen with the naked eye, *Ricinulei* is the smallest spider in the world. The hummingbird is likewise the smallest of all birds. Yet both are portrayed on the desert canvas in gigantic form. How could the ancient artists have known about or even seen *Ricinulei,* appropriate as it was for the symbolic representation of water? Any connections between coastal Peru and the distant Amazon, separated by the Andes Mountains, seem unlikely in the extreme.

But there are Inca and pre-Inca traditions of Viracocha, or Sea Foam, a semi-divine man who traveled far, sometimes by boat, as his name implies, carrying the benefits of civilization throughout South America. In fact, his emblem appears at least twice on the Nazca Plain, and in both instances it is associated with underground water sources. The 180-foot-long image of a monkey has only four fingers on his right hand; reputedly, Viracocha was likewise missing a finger. The monkey's tail is formed into a spiral that is directly over a subterranean aquifer. Another spiral, 270 feet across, lies on the southern bank of the nearby Ingenio River, placed with similar precision above a water source. The so-called Baby Bird geoglyph points to an extinct aquifer with Sea Foam's four-fingered right hand.

With one hand, a ninety-foot anthropomorphic hill-figure points at the ground; with the other, it points toward the sky, as though appealing to heaven. This interpretation is emphasized by its bird-shaped head, identifying the effigy as Owl Woman, a powerful shaman still venerated by some native tribal peoples in the region as the bringer of fertility. At Cerro Unitas, in northern coastal Chile, 500 miles south of the Nazca lines but stylistically related to them, sprawls the world's largest representation of a man. Discovered as recently as 1967 by Eduardo Jensen, a general in the Chilean air force, it is a 270-foot image of a deity or shaman with rays of spiritual power (the crown chakra?) radiating from his head. He is also known among the Fox, Kickapoo, and Sauk Indians—some 7,300 airline miles away in Illinois, Michigan, and Wisconsin, respectively—as the divine personification of irrigation.

Another connection between South and North America is the so-called Candelabrum of the Andes, a gargantuan geoglyph cut into the slope of a hillside at Pisco Bay, fronting the Pacific Ocean at Paracas, from which it may be seen from more than twelve miles out to sea. Its name derives from early Spanish explorers, who regarded it as an omen for their conquest of Peru. To them, the image depicted a stand with holy candles used in the Catholic high mass. However, among the Navajo sand-painters of the American Southwest, about 4,000 miles to the north, the same image is revered as the Tree of Life positioned above

The world's largest geoglyph, Chile's Cerro Unitas Giant.

a static rain cloud, from which it receives nourishment. Like the other Peruvian earth effigies, the Paracas terraglyph was synonymous with water, while its undoubted identification as a Tree of Life—the same name by which, according to Churchward, Mu was known—points up the Candelabrum's Lemurian origins.

Its 596-foot length is not only colossal, but revealing as well. In the mid-1950s, after twenty years of laboriously surveying the Nazca lines, the German immigrant and mathematician Maria Reiche determined that they were precisely laid out in a common unit of measurement—5.95 feet—used by no other Andean culture.

Although it is true that many Nazca drawings require the perspective of altitude to be seen properly, an out-of-body experience, hot-air balloon, or spaceship is not required to appreciate their true configurations. An accurate picture of the bioglyphs eventually develops in the minds of people who walk the unicursal lines while concentrating on them and collecting details of their shape and form. It seems clear that they were ritual pathways used by the ancients to visualize and pray for water through the imagery of sacred moisture-related symbols.

Such a theory should not offend mainstream scholars, but they are

sure to find its implications unsettling. The Nazca's gigantic, rain-induc-
ing geoglyphs and their skilled construction of truly monumental irrigation projects suggest a people obsessed with diminishing fresh-water supplies in an increasingly dry environment. Obviously, they did not settle in
southern coastal Peru to initiate a sophisticated civilization under devel-
oping desert conditions. They arrived when the valleys were fertile with
nurturing rivers. The numerous ruins of deep, skillfully built aquifers and
dozens of water-related drawings spread across the pampas bespeak of a
culture in crisis and transition, engaged in a desperate losing struggle to
maintain society against an advancing desert. Yet geologists know that
southern coastal Peru did not become the driest place on Earth, which it
is today, only thirteen or sixteen centuries ago, when, according to conventional archaeologists, the Nazca were still flourishing. On the contrary,
the Nazca Plain was transformed into a desert region between 6,000 and
5,000 years ago, at the latest. This would make the Nazca at least partially
contemporary with dynastic Egypt's first pharaohs, who were likewise
renowned irrigationists concerned primarily with water management.

Perhaps a worldwide climate change brought about South America's
ecological transformation. If so, then a late-fourth-millennium-b.c. cultural level for Andean civilization has already been identified (at least
among Peruvian scholars), known as the Salavarry period. Around 3100
b.c., ceremonial mud-brick platform mounds surrounded by rectangular
walled enclosures, very much resembling the earliest dynastic ceremonial centers in the Nile Valley, appeared along southern coastal Peru.
It would appear, then, that the massive line drawings and magnificent
aquifers of the Nazca Plain could not have come into existence less than
twenty centuries ago, as mainstream archaeological opinion insists.
They resulted instead from the desperate efforts of a people to save their
civilization from the inexorable desert through subterranean engineering in search of new water sources and ritual appeals for rain. However,
living conditions continued to deteriorate, until society could no longer
be sustained against the growing aridity. After circa 2000 b.c., all that
remained were the great aquifers collapsing under the sand and the mute
images of vain prayers to heaven.

Members of the Salavarry culture may have laid out the geoglyphs and biomorphs, but who created the Salavarry culture? Throughout the twentieth century, archaeologists believed the population of coastal Peru 5,000 or 6,000 years ago was insignificantly small and divided into disconnected tribes of primitive farmers and hunters. Yet this conclusion was contradicted by coastal Peru's contemporary ceremonial centers and particularly the Nazca lines. Both sets required advanced surveying, a unified system of measurement, and grid geometry on a gigantic scale. Of any preliminary evolution that led up to their application—which must have required a long period of maturation—there is. no indication. Ceremonial centers and the Nazca lines appear in full-blown development, implying that the technology responsible for their monumental creation originated elsewhere before its importation, in an already advanced condition, to South America. Moreover, these outsized public-works projects were created by and for large populations conventional scientists were reluctant to admit existed, until excavation results of a broad archaeological zone known as the Norte Chico area, about 120 miles north of Lima, were made public in December 2004. Even a few reputable mainstream Americanists, like Michael Moseley, had previously argued for the "maritime foundations of Andean Civilization" along the Pacific coast.

Digs at Norte Chico confirmed Moseley's suspicions with the discovery of twenty-four buried sites, all featuring monumental architecture in the form of spacious walled plazas, step-pyramids, and population centers. An abundance of hemp used to make hawsers for ships indicated these lost cities were ports or, at the very least, intimately connected with a seagoing people. A profusion of carbon-datable material established that Norte Chico was flourishing as long ago as 4900 B.C., finally giving place to the Salavarry culture about eighteen centuries later. This surprisingly profound antiquity, combined with the arrival of Norte Chico's urban development on the Pacific coast in an already fully mature condition, with no sign of previous cultural evolution, strongly suggests that civilization was imported to South America from Mu.

The Lemurians were the only conceivable candidates for the ancient irrigationists who left behind the world's largest art gallery. They were already in possession of a high culture long before western Peru's lush valley was transformed into the driest location on Earth, and much later tried to fend off the advancing desert with a combination of spiritual and technological powers in an era when science and religion were inseparable and indistinguishable. Indeed, a large, unknown number of mummies excavated from the Nazca Desert and associated by archaeologists with the Paracas culture responsible for the drawings are red-headed, just as the Lemurians are famous in the folk traditions of Polynesia and British Columbia for their red hair.

An outstanding collection of these mummies is preserved at Lima's Herrera Museum, where they are on public display in their own room. About a third have bright red hair; a smaller fraction are blond to reddish blond and light auburn—this among a native Andean population of black-haired people. Heyerdahl's inquiries established that hair loses its sheen after death, but its color remains unchanged. The glass-encased mummies allow close inspection of the hair roots, which, under the scrutiny of a magnifying glass, show no indication of having been dyed red or blond. Unfortunately, Herrera Museum curators interrupted my photography of the fair-haired human remains and tried to sell me a book about them instead. It contained a few images of one mummy, but these were copyrighted and could not be legally reproduced. Such are the limitations on research in modern Peru!

The Andean mummies tell of more than their racially anomalous identity and indicate an antiquity far deeper than the first-century-B.C. origins assigned to them by conventional archaeologists. Water workers laying pipes through a 120-foot-high mound near the Chilean city of Arica in November 1983 accidentally excavated a necropolis of ninety-six mummified corpses in excellent condition. They were subsequently carbon-dated by Dr. Marvin Allison, an American pathologist, to almost 8,000 years ago. His findings radically contradicted establishment academics convinced the first civilizations began in Mesopotamia just fifty-five centuries ago. According to them, the first South American civilization came later by almost 1,000 years. Yet Dr. Allison's repeated testing, confirmed by his peers, dated the oldest Arica mummy to circa 7,810 Y.B.P., some twenty-six centuries previous to the earliest known Egyptian mummies. If their Chilean counterparts predated both Mesopotamian and Egyptian cultures, then what could have been their origins, if not Lemurian?

Not coincidentally, the Arica mummies were uncovered in the same country as the Cerra Unitas Giant hill figure of the Atacama Desert. At the time of the Spanish conquest, the Molle Indians there wore a false beard made of ceramic by inserting it through a hole cut into their own jawbone. It was worn in painful imitation of ancestors who arrived from over the sea long ago after the Great Flood—a curious commemorative adornment for a people unable to grow facial hair.

Though it is almost impossible to come up with a firm timeline for the creation of the giant geoglyphs in Chile and Peru, settlers from Mu had to have arrived on South America's Pacific coasts more than 5,000 years ago, probably no later than 3500 B.C., conceivably much earlier, perhaps by as much as several centuries or even millennia.

Indeed, physical evidence was discovered for just such a profound antiquity nearly 500 miles south of the Nazca lines, at Monte Verde. Dated to 13,000 years ago—just when the first humans to reach North America were supposedly beginning their trek from Siberia across an Alaskan land bridge some 3,000 miles away—a settled community of herbalists was already flourishing in southern Chile.

They erected more than a dozen rectangular wooden framework apartments, each from nine to fifteen feet long, covered with mastodon hides and laid out in parallel rows east and south of the Chinchihuapi Creek. Although each building featured its own pit furnace, a large, outdoor hearth served communal cooking. The site was unusually advanced for its time, but was more remarkable still for its function as an herbal center.

In a peculiar, wishbone-shaped structure, archaeologists found the remains of twenty-seven medicinal plants. While some were locally grown, others came from hundreds of miles away, far up the Pacific coast and high in the Andes Mountains. Apparently, Monte Verde was a planned community of health-care specialists who gathered, prepared, and dispensed curative substances. Their knowledge and their collection of herbal flora were nothing short of prodigious.

This pharmacological know-how, plus everything else about the twelfth-century-B.C. inhabitants, defines them as outsiders enjoying a material culture unlike that possessed by contemporary Chilean natives. Moreover, these ice-age Monte Verdeans could not have wandered down toward the bottom of South America from the far north; undoubtedly arrived across the ocean in the west. Their Pacific origins, necessary maritime skills, expertise as herbalists, and social organization all describe medical practitioners from an overseas culture well versed in the high arts of civilization.

Whenever they arrived, the first Lemurians in Peru probably came as missionaries, but the physical attractiveness of the Nazca Valley made them forget about any return voyage. They were eventually joined by other kinsmen, and their population in the new, agriculturally rich land grew sufficiently large to support an urban society, the ruins of which appear in the Norte Chico and Salavarry cultures' ceremonial centers. Sometime around the turn of the fourth millennium B.C., a deteriorating climate brought about the steady worsening of living conditions. The Lemurians tried to keep ahead of the widening ecological crisis with an ever-more-complex irrigation network. But when they began to retreat before the encroaching desert, they bolstered their aquifer technology with sympathetic magic and communal spirituality. Huge Earth images symbolic of water became focal points of mass pilgrimages, harnessing the accumulated psychic energies of the entire population. As thousands of men, women, and children walked the mazes of frigate birds, whales, spiders, lizards, monkeys, seaweed, cacti, and other moisture-related geoglyphs, their prayers and meditation combined with the effigies themselves to manifest the appearance of rain or artesian springs.

In fall 1994, while in pursuit of some liquid refreshment of my own at the Kamikaze Bar in Cuzco, the former imperial capital of the Inca, a Quechua Indian shaman told me that the Nazca terraglyphs were not surveyed originally to mark the aquifers; rather, the intaglios were initially laid out in the middle of the desert where there was no sign of moisture, then trod by the "ancient ones." In so doing, they conjured the underground water from nothing. It was, he said emphatically, the simultaneous visualization of a whole community, using the colossal, suggestive images as evocative tools, that first brought the aquifers into existence. That was the real meaning, he said, of the desert's ninety-eight-foot Owl Woman, her one hand raised toward heaven, the other pointed at the Earth. She personalized the perennially magical axiom "As above, so below." "The owl is a symbol of wisdom for our ancestors, as it still is the West, and for the same reason," he said. "Namely, its great eyes allow it to see things in darkness which are hidden to others. The Ancient Ones who drew Owl Woman's shape and all the other designs not only meditated as they walked them, but danced and sang along the Nazca lines to achieve altered states of consciousness, the only means by which the energies of the universe may be summoned and controlled."

Hearing this very ancient tradition from the mouth of a man whose life belonged to such folk legacies made me recall the famous rain dance known in its myriad versions to every Native American tribe from Canada to Chile. I thought as well of similar communal psychic experiences alleged to have originated among the spiritual adepts of Mu. Perhaps the paranormal powers first mastered there attempted to preserve South America's oldest civilization amid a deteriorating environment. If so, then the massive but fragile images still adorning the Nazca Plain might represent the only surviving testimony to a battle fought and lost by Lemurian colonizers in prehistoric Peru against the inexorable forces of nature that would later, in a different fashion, overwhelm their forsaken Motherland.

NINE

Asia's Debt to Lemuria

It is now a recognized principle of philosophy that no religious belief, however crude, nor any historical tradition, however absurd, can be held by the majority of a people for any considerable time as true without having in the beginning some foundation in fact. We may be sure that there never was a myth without a meaning; that mythology is not a bundle of ridiculous fancies invented for vulgar amusement; that there is not one of those stories, no matter how silly or absurd, which was not founded in fact, which did not hold significance.

H. H. BANCROFT,
LATE-NINETEENTH-CENTURY
AMERICAN ANTHROPOLOGIST

Various native peoples of the American Southwest are renowned for their sandpaintings. These are graphic if ephemeral masterpieces in grains of corn pollen, charcoal, crushed flower petals, and red, yellow, and white sand trickling between the thumb and forefinger of Hopi, Apache, Papagos, Zuni, and Navajo artists. The grains are expertly strewn upon a background of white buckskin spread across the floor of a simple dwelling place known as a *hogan*. Their numerous designs,

209

varying in size from two to twenty feet in diameter, are mostly traditional forms repeated over unknown centuries with only occasional and slight variations. Some sandpaintings narrate important folk memories, while others, known as "sings," are believed to possess curative qualities. The patient is seated at the center of the design, where he or she is empowered by the surrounding mythic images, which absorb pain and evil. The excellence of the painting's execution is meant to attract healing spirits, with whom the patient identifies following a preparation of ceremonial purification through confinement in a sweat lodge, ingestion of herbal medicines, taking ritual baths, refraining from sexual intercourse, and the induction of vomiting.

Sand painters are all members of a tribal guild in which they are taught the techniques, significance, and mystical power of their craft, as handed down from generation to generation. When their ancestors migrated into the Southwest about 700 years ago, they may have learned dry painting from resident Pueblo peoples, perhaps the Anasazi cliff dwellers at Canyon du Chelley or Casa Grande. But mythic tradition assigns the origins of this art to the Holy People. Long ago, before the Great Flood, these unseen spirits shared their spiritual powers with the Wind People, who passed on such knowledge to the Navajo. The story is depicted in the Te-o-sol-hi, or "water creature" sandpainting, named after the sea-god. When his daughter was stolen by Coyote, he commanded the ocean to rise, forcing everyone to evacuate the Third World for refuge in the Fourth, in an effort to isolate the kidnapper. Thus, humans were compelled to find salvation in America from the advancing tide. As soon as they found Coyote and turned him over to Te-o-sol-hi with the missing child, the waters receded.

Another sandpainting recounts the Tsil-ol-ni, or "whirling logs," story, wherein the hero and his followers are abducted by the Water People to their home at the bottom of the sea. He prays for help from the Black God, who responds by threatening to send a fire from heaven. The Water People release their captives, and, as some compensation for their trouble, share their healing secrets with the flood protagonist and his family, who become ancestors of the Navajo. The hero later beholds a configuration of whirling logs with pairs of black and white *yeis,* or wise spirits, standing at the outer ends of the formed cross. They give him seeds and instruction in the ways of farming, which become the traditional basis of agricultural life in the Southwest.

The Tsil-ol-ni is the most transparently Lemurian sandpainting. It and the Te-o-sol-hi together portray the deluge that was responsible for bringing tribal ancestors to America and mention the Black God, a clear reference to a cloud menacing the Water People's homeland with fire from heaven. Such imagery recalls the cometary destruction of Mu, as described in numerous oral accounts spanning the Pacific, from the Easter Island version of Hotu Matua's meteorite-blasted homeland, to New Guinea folk memories of some celestial flame that preceded a global inundation. The Water People, with their sunken realm and superior medical skills, are self-evidently Lemurian precursors.

The Tsil-ol-ni is often used in healing ceremonies, its "whirling logs" with attached yeis configured into a swastika. The Hopi tell of two world-class floods, one from the east, the other in the west, each represented by its own variation of the hooked cross. The left-oriented

Navajo shamans create a swastika design at the center of their sand painting.

version signifies the arrival of survivors from the destruction of the east, a direction some investigators believe indicates the former position of Atlantis. But an earlier migration across the ocean from the west is symbolized by a right-oriented variant. These two migration accounts are most dramatically combined in the Hemet Maze Stone, a gray boulder emblazoned with the intricate design of a labyrinthine maze enclosed in a three-and-a-half-foot square.

The petroglyph is located on a mountainside just west of Hemet, California, some ninety miles southeast of Los Angeles. Accumulation on its surface of a light patina known locally as "desert varnish" suggests the incised carving was executed between 4,000 and 3,000 years ago, despite the insistence of mainstream archaeologists, on tenuous physical evidence, that it could be no more than a few centuries old. The maze itself is in the form of a swastika. But in the bottom-left corner of the square outline of the Hemet Maze Stone is a simple, much smaller, reversed or right-oriented hooked cross, known in Buddhism as the *sauvastika*. Swastikas and sauvastikas are common images throughout Asia, where they denote Buddha's right and left foot, respectively, and refer to his missionary travels throughout the world. As such, the Buddhist swastika-sauvastika and the California petroglyph appear to share a parallel symbolism, which both Asians and ancient Americans may have received independently from a common source.

Churchward identified the swastika as a Lemurian emblem decades before he learned that the same sign was used by the Hopi to identify their ancestral influences from refugees of a great flood. He stated that it was originally one of the most important symbols in Mu, embodying as it did "the four great primary forces" of the universe, "the key of universal movement," a characterization complementing both Hopi and Buddhist symbolism. The same sentiment appears in other Navajo geo-art, such as the swastika-configured Whirling Rainbows, described by the Otomi Indian sandpainter David V. Villasenor as representing "the most powerful force in the creative spirit of evolution."

The rainbow guardians, or Na'a-tse-elit yei, are protectors against a recurrence of the deluge that wiped out a former world. No less cogently, Churchward wrote that the Lemurian swastika signified a power "working from west to east," just as the Hopi ascribe their west-to-east ancestral migration to the rightward-hooked cross. A neighboring tribal people revere Poshaiyankaya, who led Zuni ancestors into the American Southwest following their near annihilation in the Great Flood. Zuni pottery commemorating that mass-migration is decorated with a swastika motif.

If this allegedly Lemurian symbol was missing from the Pacific realm, we might have cause to doubt its association with Mu. In fact, however, it was singled out for special reverence by Hawaiians as the Cross of Teave, signifying, according to Leinani Melville, "the Supreme Father, a 'God of Flame', often referred to as 'The Almighty Flame of Creation' from whom all forms of life that inhabit this Earth originated." Not only does her definition aptly characterize Lemuria as the source of civilized existence, but it also shares the meaning with the Greek swastika, the sign of Prometheus, whose fire-drill stick was his gift of technology to a primeval humanity. On the other side of the ocean from Hawaii, in the western Pacific, when asked to endorse documents proffered by late-eighteenth-century European explorers, illiterate Micronesians often signed with a rightward-oriented hooked cross, because it was the mark used by their ancestors around the time of the Great Flood.

A sauvastika was likewise fashioned into ornamental featherwork made by late-fifteenth-century Aztecs to symbolize Chalchiuhtlicue. As her descriptive name implies, Our Lady of the Turquoise Skirt was their sea-goddess, depicted in temple art seated on a throne around which people are drowning in huge whirlpools. Chalchiuhtlicue's myth is a self-evident evocation of some seminally important natural catastrophe at sea. Like the Hawaiian Cross of Teave, the Mayan *kak* was a hooked cross symbolizing fire.

The hooked cross was believed to have been introduced to India by Aryan invaders during the eighteenth century B.C., but it was already revered as a sacred symbol in the Indus Valley civilization—whose Easter Island connections were mentioned in chapter 3—1,000 or more years earlier. The famous Mohenjo Daro cylinder seal depicting a bison eating from a feeding tray features a sauvastika on its reverse.

That this sign has featured prominently in numerous diverse cultures over the millennia is not as surprising as the virtual uniformity of its meaning among such otherwise dissimilar peoples. The creative flame and the mass-movement that it connoted in so many mythic traditions around the globe implied a shared source from which the hooked cross was carried throughout the world. Common origins are likewise suggested by its ancient appearance high in the Himalayas, where a swastika on the tongue of Nyatri Tsenpo was enough to secure him the throne of Tibet as its first king; this unusual feature of his myth signified that he spoke words of mystical potency. The sign was universally recognized as the mark of supreme spiritual power and is described by the symbolist writers Tatjana and Mirabai Blau as "a remnant of the early Tibetan Bon religion."

Bon was actually an all-encompassing term for Tibet's different mystical traditions before they were absorbed and blended by Buddhism in a polytheistic synthesis beginning in the mid-eighth century A.D. It derives from *bon pa,* which means to recite magical formulas, implying an emphasis on spirit possession, controlling demonic forces, and the transmigration of souls, which infused matter in all forms. The practitioners of this animistic faith believed that reciting or chanting certain syllables or sounds, known as mantras, could influence energy patterns for powerful effects in both the spiritual and physical planes of existence. In one, the fabric of individual human destiny might be rewoven, while multi-ton stone blocks could be levitated in the other through voice-induced altered states of consciousness.

The mystery-religion of shamanic ecstasy and manipulated sound, according to the Tibetan historian Namkhai Norbu, had been introduced at the beginning of the second millennium B.C. by a foreigner, Shenrab Miwoche, or the Great Supreme Man of the Shen, his clan. Like the Buddhists who came centuries after him, Miwoche combined the various native mystical cults under his own to fashion Bon, or Boen. He settled in Shang Shung, presently known as western Tibet's Guge region, between

A Hawaiian priest of the Kahuna mystery cult wears headgear resembling that worn by the Yellow Hat adherents of Tibetan Buddhism. Native traditions of missionaries arriving from an antediluvian kingdom are still current in both Hawaii and Tibet.

Mount Tise, or Kang Rinpoche (better known as Kailas), and Lake Mapham, or Manasarovar, still the two most sacred places in the world for millions of Asians. As Norbu observes, this area "can in all respects be considered the cradle of Tibetan culture." Tise/Kang Rinpoche/Kailas is called the Swastika Mountain because it is the axis mundi, or navel of the world, around which the Earth seems to revolve for pilgrims who experience spiritual illumination. The term was previously encountered during our quest for Lemuria at Easter Island, originally known by the same title, Te-Pito-te-Henua, as was the Inca capital, Cuzco.

Norbu writes of Miwoche, "The main aim of his mission was to renew and reform the pre-existent cognitive and ritual traditions," not abolish them, as demonstrated by his substitution of human and animal sacrifices with clay or butter effigies, a practice still observed by the Dalai Lama and his followers. From Miwoche's concern for all life, we may infer that the principle of compassion for all sentient beings at the core of Tibetan Buddhism likewise derived from the Great Supreme Man of the Shen. Something of the mystical idea he brought echoes in the name of the place he chose to live. While *shang* is merely a term of respect, like *dear* or *beloved, shung* is the Tibetan Garuda eagle, the mythic personification of fire, whose emblem is the swastika. "Miwoche's fire," however, was the kundalini possessed by every sentient being—an internal energy form residing in a coil at the base of the human spinal column. It may be either fanned into flame by a cathartic experience or aroused through meditative procedures to generate spiritual enlightenment and connection and dialogue with the Great Compassionate Mind that is the universe. This "fire" is regarded as the most active of Boen's five "elements."

In converting the regional king, Triwer Sergyi Charuchen, Miwoche's mysticism spread over eastern and central Tibet, where its popularity became so deeply rooted that all subsequent efforts to ban it failed. Even after the royal temple and *gompa,* or lamasery, at Totling were destroyed in the seventeenth century and abandoned, Boen compelled Buddhism to evolve very differently in Tibet than it did in other lands. "Enshrined at Kailas-Manasarovar are the elements of the ecstatic and the anti-orthodox in Indian and Tibetan religion," according to Charles Allen in his history of Mount Tise. Tibetan Buddhism's uniqueness is the result of its synthesized Boen influences.

Among their enduring contributions that set Buddhism in Tibet apart from its development elsewhere is ritual sandpainting. Appearance of this sacred art among two peoples half a world away from each other in geography and culture has long mystified anthropologists reluctant to join their mainstream colleagues in dismissing comparisons between central Asia and southwestern America as mere coincidence. While admittedly significant differences separate the two versions, there are nonetheless some striking similarities. Among the most fundamentally important is the hooked cross that Buddhist monks and Navajo shamans alike incorporate in their designs, because to both practitioners it is the foremost symbol of spiritual power. The Tibetan counterpart of the Tsil-ol-ni is the Kalachakra, or "wheel of time," a body of wisdom concerning the recurrence of teachers like Buddha, as expressed in a sandpainting. It is a *mandala,* the symbolic representation of cosmic energies with which its creators seek identification, just as the Navajo "dry painters" become one with the same forces. Making the mandala is in itself a form of meditation on the theme of infinite compassion.

Like Native American artists, the monks are specially trained by a master, who sees to it that the traditional designs are perpetuated with a minimum of variation. The Kalachakra is a visual idealization of the celestial city, a place of perfect harmony, where the supreme goal of enlightenment is found. On either side of the world, sacred chants and prayers accompany completion of a sandpainting. At the conclusion of ceremonies, disposal of the sand is an important ritual in both cultures. The Navajo scoop up the grains and carry them a distance north of the hogan for burial in a direction associated with escape to the next world. Tibetans throw the sanctified sand into the ocean (a lake or stream, if they are too far from the seashore) in honor of the Dalai Lama, whose name means "ocean of compassion." But the Boen origins of Tibetan sandpainting equally suggest references to lost Lemuria.

In any case, not only the practice of this peculiar art, but also the identical solemnity with which it is revered by Tibetans and Southwest American Indians, both of whom use sandpainting to achieve altered states of consciousness, is remarkable. Different colors signify the cardinal directions for both peoples, who each conduct sunrise circumambulations of their dry paintings featuring representations of one central and four cardinal mountains. Nor is the Tibetan prayer stick unknown to Navajo shamans. These analogies are beyond mere coincidence. They are also powerfully underscored by the hooked cross commonly configured as the foremost sacred symbol in both central Asian and southwestern American versions.

Parallels are drawn closer still in a comparison of the foundation myths of each culture. Tibetans have their own version of the Water People, the pre-Navajo masters of spiritual healing. In the *chog rabs,* or origin myths, the birth of Shenrab Miwoche in 1917 B.C. signified, in Norbu's words, "the beginning of Tibetan history." The master, as mentioned, was not one of the indigenous Se, but belonged to the first of five different races that arrived over time in successive waves of immigration. These were, from the most recent to the earliest, the Ra, Dru, Tong, Dong, and Mu. Each, together with the indigenous Se, is symbolized by six rays streaming from a rising sun depicted on the Tibetan national flag. The rising sun indicates the direction from which these foreigners came, and also suggests the solar mysticism of the Lemurian Motherland.

Like the pre-Polynesian inhabitants of distant Hawaii, Miwoche's people were called the Mu, and were regarded, according to Norbu, as "an ancient class of celestial deities" who commanded great spiritual powers. At the head of their pantheon was a sky god with the self-evidently Lemurian name of dMu-bDud Kam-Po Sa-Zan. But finding Miwoche connected to the lineage of Tibet's founding father confirms the seminal impact made on central Asia by culture bearers from Mu. He was born during the early second millennium B.C., putting him in Mu 276 years after the cataclysm of 2193 B.C. and 289 nine years before the final catastrophe in 1628 B.C. In other words, he lived at a time long after his Motherland had recovered from its penultimate destruction but centuries before its climactic demise. The date assigned to Miwoche's birth is particularly credible in Lemurian terms because, unlike so many other traditions of a flood-hero finding refuge in some foreign land, his myth does not include any natural catastrophe at a time when Mu itself was free from exceptional geologic upheavals.

During this 565-year hiatus between natural disasters, Lemurians were spreading their enlightened mystical principles to many foreign lands. Miwoche was one of these seafaring missionaries, and among the examples of the spiritual discipline he carried is one still remembered as the *dmu dag,* or *rmu thag*—the Mu cord—by which initiated adepts flew through the sky to any place on Earth or in the heavens. It was an infinitely expanding silver tether connected to the solar plexus, allowing human consciousness to range throughout the universe without risking separation of the soul from the body, which would result in death. Familiar today as astral projection, its origins with the Mu, regarded by native Tibetans as "an ancient class of celestial beings," seem appropriate.

Miwoche also told how humanity came to be. He said that at the beginning of time, the gods, bored with the vast emptiness of space, created a cosmic egg, which eventually hatched of its own energy. From its yolk, they fashioned the first expression of civilization, the *khro ch dmu rdzong,* or "cast-iron fortress of the Mu." Then from the egg appeared Sidpa Sangpo Bumtri, a fully mature, divine manifestation of the gods themselves in human form—a white man (*dkar,* literally, "white"), "the king of existence, of plenitude, of goodness and of virtue," according to the mythic texts translated by Norbu. Now another egg, this one of blue light, broke open to reveal a beautiful woman whom Sidpa Sangpo Bumtri named Koepa Chuchag Gyelmo because of her aquamarine skin. Her shoulder-length hair fell in seven blue plaits, which he compared favorably to his seven turquoise jewels. From their union were born the *srid pa pho dgu* and *srid pa mo dgu,* Earth's primordial males and females, the ancestors of humankind, including Thum thum rnal med rje, the "Awakened Lord of the Mu."

This cosmological story is an obvious description of the birth of not only civilization, but also early humanity itself, the Mu, Miwoche's own people. It is also reminiscent of the Easter Islanders' most important ritual activity, their annual swimming contest to the offshore islet of Mutu, where the first man to return with a sooty-tern egg received top honors. Perhaps their springtime ceremony commemorated the same cosmic egg mentioned in Tibetan myth. In any case, the Lemurian identity of Sidpa Sangpo Bumtri is transparent, although Koepa Chuchag Gyelmo's significance is less obvious. The woman's emergence from a blue egg and her aquamarine skin may be metaphors for the ocean, since Lemurian civilization developed from the close human interaction of land and sea. Or the blue of her origins and physical appearance could symbolize the third eye, or brow chakra, an indigo-colored energy center associated with the perception of spiritual truth. Less ambiguous is Thum thum rnal med rje's identification as Awakened Lord of the Mu, a title prefiguring the Buddha, likewise the Awakened One, and referring to a master of spiritual enlightenment. By all accounts, Mu was the Motherland of not only humankind, but of the mystical arts as well.

During his travels through central Tibet in the early 1980s, Childress visited the village of Purna with its cliffside monastery, the Phuktal Gompa. Its library, according to a resident monk, contained information about Mu, also referred to as Rutas, where public education supposedly consisted of twelve grades roughly equivalent to modern American grammar and high schools. A Thirteenth School, however, taught people of exceptional abilities the esoteric wisdom of Lemurian mysticism, enabling them to become its elite practitioners and teachers. Long before the final destruction, the monk said, these initiated masters were already voyaging to many other parts of the world as proselytizing representatives of an elevated belief system. It would appear that Shenrab Miwoche, the Great Supreme Man of the Shen, was one of these missionary Mu.

When the end finally came, the Thirteenth School did not perish with Rutas. Instead, its members immigrated to the Himalayas, where they could preserve their spirituality in the isolated, pristine conditions of the highest landmass on Earth, free from the cataclysms that destroyed their Motherland. Lhasa, the Tibetan capital and palace of the Dalai Lama, was originally their religious retreat, where Lemurian mysticism—referred to by the native population as Boen po—eventually melded with eighth-century Buddhism.

Though the monk's story is unverifiable, internal evidence tends to affirm its credibility. For example, he stated that the Thirteenth School of Lemurian mysticism was headed by supreme masters who formed a council of seven. This septuple arrangement recalls the seven plaits of Koepa Chuchag Gyelmo's blue hair and Sidpa Sangpo Bumtri's seven turquoise gems. Both sets were stressed in the Boen myth of the cosmic egg, emphasizing their significance. Her blue-plaited hair was equated with the seven paths to enlightenment—mindfulness, observance of the law, effort, joy, tranquillity, concentration, and equanimity. The treasures of the ideal ruler—the queen (feminine energy; i.e., intuition), the jewel of clear thought, the wheel (proper use of time), the elephant (willpower), the minister (wise counselors), the general (loyal followers), and the horse (speed, mobility)—found their counterparts in the seven turquoise jewels of Sidpa Sangpo Bumtri. Rutas's Council of Seven seems part of this same septuplicate symbolism.

Although the Lemurians made their most indelible impact in Asia on Tibet, they did not pass unnoticed through China, where Tien-Mu was remembered as a mountainous land far across the Pacific Ocean. While most of the Motherland lay low near the sea, at least some of its archipelagoes were mountainous. It was also known as Chien-Mu, described in the *Chou-li,* an ancient Chinese book of rites, as a place where Earth and sky met at the cosmic axis. Here time and space became irrelevant, the four seasons merged into each other, pairs of opposites were resolved, and the opposing principles of yin and yang no longer strove against each other, but instead grew peaceful in balanced harmony. Chien-Mu signifies the sacred center, the still-point reached in deep meditation. Its name implies that these concepts are to be associated with the Pacific Motherland of Mu, the original navel of the world where they were first developed and reached high levels of spiritual attainment.

The Motherland was known in ancient China by various titles, including Peng Sha. Spiritual powers were said to have reached their fulfillment there, as sorcerers mastered human levitation and other psychic arts.

Peng Sha was ruled by Mu Kung, king of the gods, who dwelled in a golden palace beside the Lake of Gems. Here a blessed peach tree provided fruit from which was distilled the elixir of eternal life. This same theme reappears in the Japanese tale of Urashiro Taro, whose adventures under the sea led him to a sunken kingdom from which he returned with the Peach of Immortality. In Chinese myth, the drowned realm was known as Shen Chou, a very ancient empire, preceding the creation of China itself. Before Shen Chou disappeared beneath the Pacific Ocean, the goddess of mercy, Xi Wang Mu, carried away the Tree of Immortality to her fabulous palace in the remote peaks of the K'un-lun Mountains. There she tends it for the gods and only the most virtuous human beings. At a periodical banquet, the P'an-t'ao Hui, or Feast of the Peaches, these select individuals achieve immortality by eating the blessed fruit. Shen Chou is an apparent Chinese reference to the lost Pacific civilization, as underscored by the goddess's name, Hsi Wang Mu, and the Tree of Life with its sacred peaches. At London's Victoria and Albert Museum is an early-eighteenth-century porcelain dish painted during the reign of Yong Zheng. It depicts Xi Wang Mu and a mortal attendant led by the gods of happiness (Fuxing), longevity (Shoulao), and earned wealth (Luxing) away from Shen Chou, portrayed as a magnificent temple sinking into the sea. The Lemurian implication of these mythic motifs is apparent.

Chronologist Neil Zimmerer writes that Mu King "formed a special group of eight humans, who were given fruits from the Tree of Life. They were known as the 'immortals'." According to Churchward, the Tree of Life, the embodiment of immortality, was Lemuria's chief emblem. Fu Sang Mu was envisioned as a colossal mulberry tree growing above a hot "pool" (sea) in a paradise far over the ocean, toward the east. The land itself was hot. No fewer than nine suns perched in Fu Sang Mu's lower branches. White women renowned for their beautiful long hair tended the *li chih,* or herb of immortality, in a garden at the center of the island. The Lemurian climate was said to have been very hot. Di-Mu was the Chinese Earth Mother, who gave life to all sentient beings at the birth of time, just as Lemuria was known as the Motherland because it was considered the birthplace of humankind. The theme of human beginnings in a lost oceanic realm is recurrent through many circum-Pacific cultures, such as the Chinese story of Lao-T'ien-Yeh. This "Heavenly Master of the First Origin" sired the first boy and girl children, according to a mythic account cogently entitled *The Emperor of Mu.*

The natural catastrophes that battered the Motherland and eventually overwhelmed it were dramatically documented in ancient China. Its imperial library featured a colossal encyclopedia alleged to contain all knowledge from ancient times to the fourteenth century, when additions were still being made. The 4,320-volume set included information about a time when Tien Ti, Emperor of Heaven, attempted to wipe out sinful humankind. He commanded She-Mu, the Destroyer of Life, to strike the world with a celestial cataclysm: "The planets altered their courses, the Earth fell to pieces, and the waters in its bosom rushed upwards with violence and overflowed the Earth." Another god, Yeu, taking pity on the drowning human beings, caused a giant turtle to rise up from the bottom of the ocean, then transformed the beast into new land. Remarkably, this version is identical to a creation myth repeated by virtually every tribe north of the Rio Grande. Native American Indians almost universally refer to their continent as Turtle Island, after a gigantic turtle that had been raised up from the sea floor by the Great Spirit for their salvation from the deluge.

Another Chinese text explains how "the pillars supporting the sky crumbled, and the chains from which the Earth was suspended shivered to pieces. Sun, moon and stars poured into the northwest, where the sky became low; rivers, seas and oceans rushed down to the southeast, where the Earth sank. A great conflagration burst out. Flood raged." The *Shan Hai Ching* tells of a prehistoric catastrophe that took place when the sky tipped suddenly, causing the Earth to tilt in the opposite direction. The resulting flood sent a vast kingdom to the bottom of the ocean. One of its many descriptive titles was Pu Chou Shan, the "Imperfect Mountain." After the primeval goddess Nu Kua Shih created humanity, she had worked with men and women to build the first kingdom at Pu Chou Shan, where a golden age of greatness spread around the Earth. Many years later, one of her divine princes, out of envy, fought to overthrow her. During the heavenly struggle that ensued, his fiery head struck the Imperfect Mountain. It collapsed into the sea, resulting in a global flood that obliterated civilization and most of humankind.

It is not possible to determine which of the several natural catastrophes that afflicted Lemuria are described in these accounts. However, the defining cataclysms left indelible scars on the history of China. The Paleolithic, or Old Stone Age, came to an abrupt end 12,000 years ago, just when Mu was broken up and much of its territory overwhelmed during an exceptionally violent geologic period, known as the Boelling interstadial, at the close of the last ice age.

Enduring myth assigns the first Chinese civilization to Emperor Fu Hsi, whose overseas arrival was supposedly preceded by a great flood traditionally assigned to 2950 B.C. His date roughly coincides with a major global catastrophe known to have occurred around 3100 B.C., as discussed in chapter 12. In archaeological terms, the Neolithic Yangshao and Hongshan cultures came to a sudden end after 2,000 years. They were replaced by the far more advanced Liangzhu state-form that introduced city planning and organized agriculture. Remarkably, the peanut was cultivated for the first time in China during the Liangzhu. Peanuts are not native to Asia and could only have been obtained from America. The implication here is that arriving Lemurians had already established important contacts on the other side of the Pacific.

The Liangzhu was closed down and the Xia dynasty winked on with the late-third-millennium-B.C. Lemurian catastrophe. Caroli believes the Chinese story of ten "suns" falling from the sky is mythic imagery for a major cometary event. Emperor Shun saw them as he was about to ascend the throne and witnessed a large meteor strike the Earth, followed by a devastating deluge. "The whole world was submerged," he wrote, "and all the world was an endless ocean. People floated on the treacherous waters, searching out caves and trees on high mountains. The crops were ruined, and survivors vied with fierce birds for places to live. Thousands died each day." These calamitous events took place around 2240 B.C., corresponding roughly to the penultimate Lemurian catastrophe. The earliest phase of Chinese civilization documented in the archaeological record sprouted about seventy years after the Motherland was finally destroyed. The sudden appearance of the sophisticated, bronze-working Shang dynasty on the plain of the Yellow River suggests it was the mixed offspring of native Asians and refugees from Mu.

That same ancient immigration is still commemorated in Thailand with a unique relic from their vanished homeland. A flood myth also known in Laos tells how a semi-divine people long ago dwelled on a distant island of great splendor and renown until celestial powers threatened it with a global deluge. Three wise men were able to remove a central pillar from the chief temple and carry it away in their ship before rapidly rising waters engulfed the entire island. Sailing toward the setting sun for many days, they finally reached the shores of Southeast Asia. There they erected the pillar and named it after the sunken realm: Lak Mu-ang, or holy stone of Mu. Around it, they built a new kingdom, Ayodhya, the magnificent result of native labor directed by imported genius. During centuries of subsequent imperial expansion followed by wars and invasion, the city was sacked and its holy relic spirited away yet again from imminent destruction.

In 1782, King Rama I set up the Lak Mu-ang at the precise center of the new Ayodhya, one of several since the original capital's overthrow. He traced his royal descent from the three flood-heroes who landed in Southeast Asia, but even these distinguished origins could not discourage his enemies from eventually laying waste to the city and carrying off the sacred column, which was never seen again. Rama VI replaced it with a faithfully executed replica and installed it in its own shrine at the center of Bangkok.

Ever since, the duplicate Lak Mu-ang has been decorated with gold leaf (commemorating the Motherland's ancient solar religion) and surrounded with precious gifts (mostly ivory tusks and golden bowls filled with flowers) by anyone wanting to pay homage to the Pillar of the City. The building in which it stands is decorated with symbols and images of the drowned homeland, where it was originally part of an antediluvian temple. These include stylized swastikas and scenes of a tropical island suggesting Lemuria itself. The Lak Mu-ang shrine is an elaborate

Thailand's Lak Mu-ang, sacred memorial to the lost Motherland.

pavilion with intricate gold-inlay doors, and is set, atypically, below ground level in a sunken court, suggesting the undersea condition of the kingdom from which the upright was rescued. Its name recurs at other important monumental sites in Thailand: Mu-ang Fa Daet, Ban Mu-an Fai, Mu-ang semay, and Mu-ang Bon, where the original sacred

Painted ceramic scene at Bangkok's shrine of the Lak Mu-ang depicts Lemurian themes.

stone of Mu may have been installed by immigrants from that vanished civilization.

Reverence for the lost Motherland survives in more than Thailand's holiest monument. Every November, thousands of celebrants gather under a full moon at the shore to launch huge armadas of model boats made of dried banana leaves. Each little flower-bedecked *krathong* carries a votive candle and trails plumes of incense on its way over the ocean in homage to Suvarnamacha, queen of the sea, and the spirits of an ancestral people who long ago perished when she sank their splendid kingdom. The Loi Krathong is similar to Japan's nocturnal Bon Odori, with its own flotillas of candlelit model boats sailing in the general direction of a sunken realm. Both annual ceremonies are not unlike the Roman Lemuria, which was also celebrated to propitiate ghosts of the restless dead, victims of a great deluge.

Thai myth and ceremony are wonderfully supported by physical evidence brought to light by a paradigm-smashing discovery accidentally made in the mid-twentieth century by an American college student, Stephen Young. Until this son of a former U.S. ambassador to Thailand tripped and fell over an exposed root near the farming town of Ban Chiang in 1966, archaeological dogma held that this part of the world was a cultural wasteland, where bronze making was first imported from China no earlier than 800 B.C. and human affairs had always been conducted on a rather low order of civilization. But while Young lay sprawled on the ground, he noticed fragments of some unusually attractive earthenware protruding from the soil. He sent them to the University Museum at the University of Pennsylvania in Philadelphia for testing by a new dating process, thermoluminescent dosimetry, specifically designed for pottery analysis and highly regarded for its accuracy. It revealed that the Thai shards were 6,000 years old, 500 years before the birth of urban cultures in Mesopotamia, where civilization was supposed to have begun. Unwilling to accept even the thermoluminescent data, museum director Froehlich Rainey sent Young's samples to Oxford University for review. The results were identical.

At the same time, bronze ax heads, along with the molds in which they had been cast, were being excavated near Ban Chiang at Non Nok That by Wilhelm Solheim, from the University of Hawaii. He also found carbonized bits of cucumber, bottle gourds, pepper, and water chestnuts, as well as other evidence for agriculture 2,000 years before the onset of Mesopotamian farming. These finds were accompanied by pottery thirty-three centuries older and more advanced than anything ever recovered from the Tigris–Euphrates region. In addition to advanced metallurgy, agriculture, and pottery making, Thai silk manufacture was also in full swing centuries before it began in China.

But the first real examination of the site near Ban Chiang did not get under way until 1974, when a joint excavation codirected by Chester Gorman of the University Museum and Pisit Charoenwongsa, curator of Bangkok's National Museum, investigated a man-made mound twenty feet high and a mile around. Over the next five years, they retrieved eighteen tons of artifacts, or more than 30,000 vases, bronzes, and iron relics skillfully manufactured 5,600 years ago. At the lowest and most ancient level, the archaeologists found a beautifully crafted spearhead dated to 3600 b.c., the oldest known bronzework in the world.

The more than 400 ceramic vessels removed from the artificial hill had been made in an astonishing variety of designs, shapes, colors, and sizes, all attesting to an artistically appreciative population. Of the 126 intact skeletons found there, many wore bronze jewelry; one had a bronze ring on every finger and toe. There were bells, bracelets, weapons, tools, and ornaments—all of bronze, centuries before the technique of combining the proper proportions of copper, zinc, and tin were known in the Middle East. Bronze was the nuclear fission of its day, superior to stone or any other metals previously worked. One of the bronzes was an agricultural implement for harvesting rice, the production of which was yet another first for prehistoric Thailand. There were also domesticated animals, including buffalo, pigs, chickens, and dogs.

But who were the ancient civilizers of Ban Chiang? They appear to have been direct descendants of a people whose bones archaeologists found in the extreme northern end of the country at a site known as Spirit Cave, first used as a hunting camp 12,000 years ago. Its residents were tall, muscular outsiders, physically different from the native population. According to University of Hawaii anthropologist Michael Pietrusewsky, "They definitely do not seem to be closely related to the present population of Southeast Asia, nor were they particularly Mongoloid." He

The traditional temple architecture of Bangkok's Wat Phra Keo mimics the sacred homeland ruled over by Suvarnamacha at the bottom of the sea.

A section of a mural at Bangkok's Wat Phra Keo depicts the ancient deluge that overwhelmed the Motherland.

added that their skeletal remains resemble those of Polynesians more than any other racial group.

They deliberately chose the Ban Chiang area for settlement, because, as scholar Ronald Schiller writes, "They lived in one of the few places on Earth where copper and tin are both plentiful." In other words, they were already metalsmiths before their arrival, and Ban Chiang's mid-fourth-millennium-B.C. spearhead had been preceded by centuries of bronzework. Large numbers of seashells discovered in the mound not only indicate commerce along the coast but bespeak maritime skills as well. Everything about this atypical people suggests they were in possession of the civilized arts previous to their arrival in Southeast Asia, because no traces of early development are apparent. Orderly burials, cloth manufacture, and design arts all belonged to a sophisticated culture far in advance of contemporary local societies.

So far, Ban Chiang is the only one of some 300 related mounds to have been studied. Excavation of these other earthworks might reveal the best physical evidence for Lemurian civilizers in Thailand. Spirit Cave's 12,000-year-old date coincides with the first large-scale emigrations from the geologically stricken Motherland, a correspondence underscored by the physical resemblance of its inhabitants to Polynesians. Bronzework did not begin in Southeast Asia but was imported by sailors from some outside culture where metallurgy, weaving, pottery making, and all the rest had obviously enjoyed long-term development before coming to Ban Chiang. It would seem, then, that catastrophic rises in sea level at the end of the last ice age forced some Lemurians to seek higher ground across the ocean. Only this conclusion adequately explains the anomalous appearance of a high civilization in the midst of what was otherwise a cultural desert.

Bangkok's Lak Mu-ang is not the only Asian monument commemorating the lost Motherland, however. Japan's modern Mu Museum is unique in the world, with an origin as strange as the lost realm it showcases. It began one day just after the Second World War in the mind of Reikiyo Umemoto. While the young monk was deep in meditation at the seashore, he experienced a life-changing vision. It revealed a vast panorama of Lemurian history and spirituality spanning many thousands of years. His inner eye beheld the birthplace of humanity, the rise of early civilization, its florescence around the world, its final annihilation, and the fate of survivors throughout the Pacific. And he was presented with a parting gift—the high wisdom of Mu's Thirteenth School. After his reverie, this forgotten mystery-cult was refounded as the "World's Great Equality" in Hiroshima Prefecture, where its esoteric principles were shared with a few initiates.

One of the initiates was able to interest some wealthy patrons in volunteering funds for the construction of a fifteen-acre temple-museum. The surrounding grounds were made to reflect the sacred architecture and ceremonial landscape revealed in Umemoto's vision as closely as possible. In 1976, the red-and-white complex, decorated with life-sized statues of elephants and dramatic murals, was completed. The location in Kagoshima Prefecture had been determined as much for its strong physical resemblance to Lemurian topography as for the area's perceived geo-spiritual properties. The large, professionally staffed facility features a modern research laboratory, and the museum's displays of authentic artifacts and quality re-creations are the only collection of its kind on Earth. Although spiritual services at its temple are restricted to initiates, artifact halls are still open to the general public. The ninety-year-old monk had lived long enough to see his postwar vision of Lemuria brought to life before he passed away in 2002.

Although his Mu Museum is the most modern living memorial to the ancient Motherland, it is not the only one in Japan. Chikubujima is a shrine to the goddess Benten, or Benzaiten, a mythical idealization of culture bearers who brought civilization to Japan from over the sea. Chikubujima's location on the coast of Biwa-ko, or Lake Biwa, near Kyoto, is not entirely legendary. Along its shores are found the earliest material evidence for human habitation in the islands, suggesting the first arrival of Lemurians in Japan.

With that country's political and spiritual shift to Tokyo in the seventeenth century A.D., leaders at the new capital landscaped their own version of Chikubujima from an inlet of Tokyo Bay, since known as

The Mu Museum, Kagoshima Prefecture.

Shinobazu. It is an artificial island sitting at the center of a large pond
fringed with rushes, inhabited by varieties of waterfowl and connected
by causeways to the shore in imitation of the Chikubujima original.
Both are representations of the homeland from which Benzaiten sailed
away, a clear reference to Mu, symbolized by statues of fish and emblems
of either three pyramids in the sea or a single, disintegrating pyramid
engulfed by high waves; perhaps both are implied. In a remarkable comparison, a similar scene is portrayed on the walls at Chan Chan's Palace
of the Governor, a pre-Inca megalopolis in northern coastal Peru.

The Lemurian features of Benzaiten's myth appear in her function
as the goddess of civilization, who carried the gifts of music, eloquence,
fine arts, and maritime skills aboard a great "treasure ship" from Horaizan before the splendid kingdom sank beneath the surface of the sea. Its
name is derived from the island's highest mountain, Horai, on the summit
of which grew the Tree of Life, with which, according to Churchward,
the Motherland was commonly identified. Like Benzaiten, the Chinese
Xi Wang Mu kept a Tree of Life whose peaches granted immortality

to anyone who tasted them. The allegorical "fruits" of its knowledge refer to understanding of kundalini, that innate psychic energy able to spiritually empower us as it spirals up the human spinal column, the real "tree of life." Something of this originally Lemurian concept echoes in the biblical Garden of Eden, with its trees of knowledge and immortality.

The Tree of Life is found in oral traditions of Japan's pre-Asian inhabitants, the Ainu. Their oldest creation story tells of Chikisani-kamui, who assumed the form of an elm, the first tree. From her branches, the various races of humankind emerged. Her children were Aeoina-kamui and Pa-kor-kamui, whose incestuous relationship gave birth to the universe. Its dominant sky deity was Chuh Kamuy. A sun-goddess, she brought warmth and light to a cold, dark world. The Earth itself became the body of Kamu-mimusubi, the mother goddess, who bore Kamui-fuchi, the supreme ancestress of the Ainu people. These most important deities are all inflections on the name of the lost Motherland of Mu.

Today's Ainu are mixed descendants of a Caucasian population so thoroughly described by native peoples throughout the Pacific region. They are modern remnants of this lost race, which also appear among 9,000-year-old skeletal remains found in Washington state (the so-called Kennewick Man), the atypically bearded Haida of coastal British Columbia, and which left traces of their DNA in parts of Polynesia. The great British Atlantologist Edgerton Sykes wrote that the Ainu "represent a racial complex which is completely different from that of either Japan or China, and, as such, they were probably the remains of the population of the northernmost culture of the disaster period." Complementing his conclusion, the Ainu recall a time when the sea suddenly rose over the land, drowning most humans, only a few of whom survived by climbing to mountaintops.

Sykes also wrote of their flood-hero, Okikurumi-Kami, who was said to have escaped the deluge in a *shinta*, or "flying cradle," that landed at Haiopra in the northern Japanese island of Hokkaido. Was this myth a folkish memory of another example of the Lemurians' super-technology, like that of their weather-control science at Nan Madol?

Revealingly, *shinta* is just one letter different from Shinto, the name of Japan's pre-Buddhist religion, practiced by the Ainu before the arrival of Sino-Korean immigrants in the mid-eighth century A.D. Like Tibetan Boen mysticism and the Thirteenth School of Mu from which it derived, Shinto is the animistic worship of nature, reverence for the sentient in all forms, and recognition of the *kami,* or soul, in everything. "Oddly enough," wrote Sykes, "Shinto is not only an Ainu word, but what is more, it seems to have been an Ainu religion before the Japanese arrived. The words for 'god', 'prayer', and 'offering' are the same in both languages, and it seems that the Japanese adopted them from the Ainu after settling in the islands." Professor Yoshida writes that "most old Japanese words were originally Ainu."

The Ainu are not alone, however, in remembering a global flood that drove their ancestors to Japan in the distant past. The Ama are an obscure, numerically insignificant tribal people who believe they are direct descendants of foreigners from a high civilization across the sea. The visitors preached a solar religion, and one of its symbols, a rising sun, became the national emblem of Japan. It also signified the direction from which they came—the eastern Pacific Ocean. Their island kingdom, Nirai-Kanai, was eventually overwhelmed by a great flood and lies at the bottom of the central Pacific Ocean. To commemorate these events, the Ama still conduct an annual ceremony at the eastern shores of Japan, held in early April or October. At dawn, the celebrants gather on the beach to face the dawn and pray for the souls of their ancestors. After purification with seawater, a designated leader walks into the ocean up to his neck bearing a small tree branch in his hand. After a pause, he turns to face the shore. Emerging from the sea, he is greeted with the wild beating of drums and joyful chanting, as though he has survived some terrible catastrophe. The branch he carries is an obvious reference to Lemuria as the Tree of Life.

A related Japanese myth describes Sagara, the dragon god of an undersea kingdom, where he owns a "pearl" able to cause catastrophic floods. He also possesses a magical weapon. The Kusanagi sword passed for some time among various members of Japan's royal household, to

In a dawn ritual honoring the sun-god worshipped at Mu, Ama celebrants pay homage to the arrival of their Lemurian ancestors on the eastern shores of Japan.

A man carries a branch from the Tree of Life in an annual Ama ceremony commemorating the arrival of Lemurian survivors in Japan.

whom it brought victory, but it was eventually returned to its rightful owner. Henceforward, Japan's military exploits were no longer invariably invincible. Perhaps the Kusanagi was a mythic symbol for some forgotten technological heirloom from the lost Motherland.

Even though over time the process of mythmaking transformed Japan's antediluvian culture bearers into sea-gods, something of their Lemurian roots still persists in present-day veneration for the Munakata-No-Kami, revered by initiates of the Jingu-Kogo sect, as the first inhabitants of Japan after the flood. Their main sanctuaries in Osaka,

In this late-nineteenth-century painting of an Oahu princess, she carries a branch symbolic of the sacred tree revered by her ancestors at Hiva, the sunken homeland of the Hawaiian people.

the Sumiyoshi Taisha and Munnakata-Taisha, allegedly preserve written accounts of the Mu-nakata-No-Kami preceding officially recorded Japanese history by many centuries.

Although today's Ama reside mostly in the area of Ohita Prefecture's Saheki Gulf, their oldest-known settlements occurred at some of the country's most ancient habitation sites: Minami Amabe-gun (Ohita Prefecture), Amabe-cho (Tokushima Prefecture), Kaishi-cho in Sado (Niigata Prefecture), and Itoman-cho (Okinawa Prefecture). These locations are also archaeological zones where members of the Jomon culture blossomed. Their appearance signaled a sharp break with Japan's Paleolithic or Old Stone Age by introducing the earliest-known pottery together with town planning and deep-sea fishing. Invention of the toggle harpoon, an advanced weapon for hunting sea mammals, proved they were acquainted with long-distance voyages. Northern Honshu's Komakino Iseki and Oyu stone circles show that archaeoastronomers flourished in ancient Japan. These sites are hardly unique, however, because a rich variety of standing stones, many of them oriented to significant celestial phenomena, are found across the country.

An outstanding example was uncovered from thick foliage that had concealed its location atop a steep hill near the northwestern town of Nabeyama in the late 1990s. Featuring obvious if faded solar symbols on their eastward-facing flanks, the twin eight-foot-tall uprights are precisely spaced so a narrow gap allows a brief sunburst on the morning of each Midsummer's Day.

This orientation demonstrated the enduring impact made by Neolithic astronomers in Japan, because even today Midsummer's Day is commemorated throughout the country. Known as the Bonmatsuri, it is a celebration of the dead, who, before gaining entrance to heaven, must cross the river Sanzu no Kawa. To do so, they have to pay a spectral ferryman for passage, and to that end, relatives of the deceased still place a sachet containing a few coins around the neck of the dearly departed. The striking resemblance of this traditional Japanese custom to the ancient Greek practice of burying the dead with coins for the ferryman at the banks of the River Styx seems linked to the Nabeyama megaliths on which the

Japan's Nabeyama twin megaliths were precisely oriented to sunrise of Midsummer's Day by its Lemurian astronomer-priests. Photograph by Hideyuku Suzuki.

Bonmatsuri Festival still takes place, which are set up and oriented to commemorate Midsummer's Day. We are reminded of Euhemerus, the Greek philosopher, who claimed to have actually visited remnants of a Lemuria-like kingdom during the late fourth century B.C.

Common astronomical functions and resemblance of these structures to foreign counterparts like Britain's Stonehenge and France's Karnac suggest the spread of megalith building from the Pacific Motherland into western Europe six and more millennia ago. Additional physical proof indicates the Lemurians voyaged in the opposite direction to South America, where Betty Meggers (Anthropology Department, National Museum of Natural History, Smithsonian Institution, Washington, D.C.) and archaeologists Clifford Evans and Emilio Estrata found Jomon handiwork at Valdivia, Ecuador. The ceramic artifacts they retrieved in the mid-1960s were decorated with the distinctive chevrons, bone motifs, and stipples that confirmed a Jomon connection.

"Having been taught in graduate school that cultural development in the Americas was independent of that of the Old World," Meggers recalled,

> we did not think to look for more distant antecedents until Estrada pointed out some remarkable resemblances to Jomon pottery in Japan. . . . In 1963, we traveled from Tokyo to southern Kyushu, examining collections of sherds from Jomon sites. Comparing details of Jomon decoration with enlarged photographs of early Valdivia examples revealed an astonishing degree of similarity. Moreover, the contexts fulfilled the requirements that had been specified for distinguishing diffusion from independent invention: A complex of traits existed on each side of the ocean; the traits were free from functional constraints that might favor their independent duplication; the Early Middle Jomon assemblage was the product of some 6,000 years of elaboration from simple beginnings, whereas the earliest Valdivia pottery had no local antecedents; the dates for Early Middle Jomon and early Valdivia were contemporary; and the Japan Current provided a feasible route from west to east.

Archaeologist Dr. Gunnar Thompson wrote that the "presence of the Jomon ceramic tradition in Ecuador is evidence of a migration consisting of several ships or a whole village. Excavations also uncovered toy houses, panpipes, and headrests—all made from ceramics." His illustrations comparing Jomon and Ainu cultural details with those of America's Pacific Northwest peoples affirm their intimate connection. Stephen C. Jett, from the division of textiles and clothing at the University of California at Davis, writes, "It is generally thought that the carriers of Jomon Culture were ancestral to the historically known Ainu of northern Honshu, Hokkaido, southern Sakhalin, and the Kurile Islands, rather than to the modern Mongoloid Japanese." The same may be said of the Ama, whose genetic links to the Ainu are apparent. Jomon, Ainu, and Ama are only post-deluge, even modern, names for the Lemurians who traveled around the Pacific Rim during the ancient past.

But it is in their guise as the Jomon that tales and traces of anomalous Caucasians throughout Oceania find archaeological confirmation. Solheim writes that "Jomon" or "Jomon-like" artifacts have been found in Taiwan, the Philippines, Micronesia, northern Melanesia, New Guinea's northern coast, and eastern Indonesia. "Actually, by 1972," Jett declared, "even older Jomon-like cord-marked pot-sherds had already been reported from much father afield, the island of Efate in the New Hebrides (now Vanatu). In conformation of the visual impressions of that time, later a scientific team definitely tied these fourteen sherds (from twelve to thirteen separate vessels) to the Early Jomon of northernmost Honshu, of circa 5200 to 3600 B.C., a time of rising sea-levels. . . . Too, Ainu and Polynesian cranial and facial features showed affinities."

Jett was supported by artifactual evidence cited by the Swedish anthropologist Bengt Anell as long ago as 1955, when he observed, "Polynesian hooks have their closest counterpart precisely in Japan." The Jomon spur has led to a conciliation of archaeology and myth that affirms Lemuria's far-flung impact throughout the Pacific, from Asia to the Americas.

Jomon culture appeared suddenly in Japan at the conclusion of the last ice age, about 12,500 years ago, somewhat before a similar immigration left its mark at Thailand's Non Nok That and Spirit Cave, the result of catastrophic flooding that ravaged the low-lying lands of Mu and forced at least some of its population to find higher ground elsewhere. Even Glyn Daniel, the ultraconservative editor of *The Illustrated Encyclopedia of Archaeology*, admitted, "Jomon Japan seems to have been remarkably isolated, particularly from its great neighbor, China, and it may have had more in common with the islands of the Pacific." Indeed, early, middle, and late cultural surges correspond, respectively, to the three Lemurian inundations, beginning in the late fourth millennium B.C., followed by a 2193-B.C. cataclysm, culminating in the catastrophe of 1628 B.C.

These catastrophic events were documented in one of Japan's earliest historical documents, the *Fudoki*, or Records of Wind and Earth. Its companion volumes were the *Kojiki*, or Records of Ancient Matters, and

Nihongi, Chronicles of Japan. Although they only date back to 712 A.D., 713 A.D., and 720 A.D., respectively, all were based on a much earlier set of records that disintegrated over time. Their transcription was completed during a surge of national creativity known as the Nara period, when scholars took renewed interest in the past. The *Kojiki* and the *Nihongi* both record that Japan's first emperor was Jimmu, descended from a sea king, the ruler of a great land across the Pacific, from whom he derived his name, the *jim,* or Son of Mu. The location of his palace, with its medicinal well, is still revered at Sai Jinja. He was followed by Kammu, who fell ill while still the crown prince. People successfully prayed for his recovery at the Muro-Ji Temple, perhaps Japan's oldest sacred site, where a reclusive sect of holy men preserved the esoteric mysticism introduced by the Son of Mu. Kammu's successor, Temmu, was renowned for having transcribed the *Kojiki, Nihongi,* and two earlier books lost to memory. These sources report that the last of Japan's prehistoric kings was Mumayado, born in 593 A.D., who converted from Shinto to Buddhism before his death, just twenty-eight years later.

The Lemurian root identity of these royal names is self-evident. They are consistent with the impact made by formative influences from Mu not only on Japan, but throughout Southeast Asia and the entire circum-Pacific as well.

TEN

What's in a Name?

Ko gub ni du war gag, I have come to ask.

A POPULAR MICRONESIAN EXPRESSION

When searching for missing persons, detectives begin by inquiring about their names in the vicinity where they were last seen. The same procedure is applied by archaeological detectives looking for a lost civilization in the Pacific Ocean. If such a power was in fact great enough to seminally influence literally millions of people residing around the Pacific Rim—from Asia and Australia, across Oceania, Micronesia, Melanesia, and Polynesia, to the Americas—then its name should continue to echo in the folk memories of numerous surviving societies. And that identity would surely have been stamped indelibly into their national psyche, had that civilization been snuffed out by some dramatic catastrophe.

Indeed, the recurrence of this name among various peoples unknown to one another and otherwise separated by many centuries, vast distances, racial backgrounds, or cultural differences is persuasive evidence for a genuine experience independently shared by them all. If, additionally, that name is associated with similar themes found among these diverse human population groups, then it undoubtedly belonged to an actual place and event, however much steeped in myth and legend.

Unfortunately, conventional archaeologists and anthropologists denigrate the mythic traditions of humankind, dismissing them as useless fables and limiting the quest for prehistory to spade and pottery shard. Yet myth

243

is the only means by which preliterate peoples preserve the truths most important to them, like extinct insects in ancient amber. Myths endure over time because they carry at their core some perennial recognition that strikes a resonant chord in generation after generation. It seems remarkable, then, that variants of the names Mu and Lemuria are indeed found precisely among those circum-Pacific peoples on both sides of the ocean where investigators expect to find them, like flocks of birds circling around a vacant stretch of sea formerly occupied by their sunken nesting ground.

An important pioneer in Polynesian archaeology, Abraham Fornander, understood the value of making cultural comparisons, especially in the Pacific. "Were every other trace of a people's descent obliterated by time, by neglect, by absorption in some other tribe, race or tongue," he believed,

> the identity of the nomenclature of its places of abode with that of some other people would still remain an *a priori* evidence of the former habitants of the absorbed or forgotten people. Were every other record and tradition of the descent of the present ruling races in America, North and South, obliterated, the names which they have given to the headlands, rivers, cities, villages, and divisions of land in the country they inhabit, would primarily, and almost always infallibly, indicate their European descent—English, Spanish, Portuguese, French, etc., etc. The practice of naming new abodes in memory of old homes is a deep-rooted trait of human nature, and displays itself alike in the barbarous as in the civilized condition of a people. We find it in the wake of all great migrations, from the most ancient to the most recent. History is full of illustrations to this effect, to prove the presence of the mother race, through its migrations in foreign lands where every other vestige, except this one, has been trodden out by time or by succeeding migrations of other peoples and races.

Though variants of *mu* are common enough in many languages, whenever they are associated with known aspects or leading themes of the Motherland—such as specific references to a sunken homeland, the Tree of Life, an ancestral people, the Great Flood, and so forth—they identify the lost civilization, describe it, trace its surviving influences in the world, and help confirm the credibility of its former existence.

A case in point is the Hawaiian word for seaweed, *limu*. While its exoteric meaning seems only to define a common plant *(Sargassum echinocarpum)*, its esoteric significance refers to the flowing hair of a goddess from the bottom of the ocean, where she dwells in a kingdom that long ago sank during a natural catastrophe. Hina-lau-limu-kala is the divine mother of the Hawaiian people and patroness of *kahuna,* the antediluvian medical wisdom preserved from drowned Kahiki. Her derivation from Lemuria, in both name and myth, is apparent.

The Roman Lemuria was a festival of the dead, commemorating and appeasing the spirits of those who died prematurely or violently, and aimed at encouraging them to return to a sunken kingdom by the same name. Something of that funereal quality persisted in the Hawaiian "water of purification," the *wai huikala*, in which ground-up *limu kala* was sprinkled on mourners after the burial of the deceased. Scott Cunningham, an authority on Polynesian mysticism, stated that "*Lei limu kala* (wreaths of seaweed) are still offered at fishing shrines by those who work the waters or by anyone grateful for the sea's gifts. I've also seen *lei limu kala* draped around upright stones on temples throughout the islands, even those in the mountains."

The same theme recurs in the Horiomu, which is, like the Roman Lemuria, an annual ceremony to appease souls returning from the afterworld as ghosts, but conducted by the Ki wai people of Melanesia. The Puka-Mu-ni is likewise a funeral rite conducted by the Australian Aborigines of Melville Island, off the coast of Arnhem Land. An annual Chinese ceremony to propitiate She-Mu, the Destroyer of Life, and the ghosts of people drowned in the Great Flood was conducted on the ninth day of the ninth moon, just as the Roman Lemuria opened on the night of every May 9.

In the American Southwest, the Hopi ceremonial calendar includes the Powamu, which features a "bean dance" to honor troublesome ghosts and distract them from hurting young children during their initiation into the tribe. A dancing actor known as the Mu-yin-wa, or maker of all life, appears during the ritual event, a white line signifying his skin color painted down the front of his arms and legs. In the Mu-yin-wa's personification of the Direction Below (sunken Mu?) and the recurrence of Mu in his name, the Lemurian origin of these ceremonial details is apparent.

Caroli writes, "The Hopi claim to have crossed the Pacific after the Flood, in which continents were torn asunder. They island-hopped in reed vessels, stating that many islands also sank, or became much smaller. Their path in the south was either blocked by high mountains, or the mountains arose as they came to the Americas. The Keresian Pueblo peoples remembered 'Hawaiku' as an ancient homeland across the Pacific somewhere." The story of their ancient migration is still preserved by members of the Dwelling-on-Water Clan, whose ancestors crossed the Great Sea from the west. In the Hopi language, the Dwelling-on-Water Clan is known as the Patkinya-Mu, a self-evident reference to the lost Motherland.

On either sides of the world from Arizona, beans were ritually cast by the head of the household in each of his rooms to propitiate restless spirits in the Roman Lemuria and the Japanese Obon. Ceremonial (and, in some cases, philological) correspondences among Hawaii's Wai huikala, Japan's Obon Festival, Melanesia's Horiomu, China's She-Mu, Australia's Puka-Mu-ni, the Hopi Powamu, and Rome's Lemuria are beyond coincidental, and testify instead to an outside source independently responsible for them all.

On the distant island of Tonga, Lihamui was a period corresponding to May, the same month in which the ancient Romans celebrated Lemuria in memory of the deceased. Throughout much of Polynesia, the divine guardian of the dead was Limu, who dwelled in a splendid kingdom on the bottom of the sea. Among the Ha'apai Group of islands, his palace is still known as Limu.

Many thousands of miles away, the indigenous Chumash of southern California's Pacific coast knew the offshore island of Santa Cruz as Limu, or "in the sea." Today's Pismo Beach derives from their Pismu. *Beach* in Chumash actually refers to a sacred site on the shore known as Muwu. Just north of it, lying near the sea, is another revered location, Wene Mu, and

Nipumu was a village for the celebration of ritual activities. These revealing place-names preserve the identity of the lost homeland from which the
Chumash ancestors arrived in southern California during the deep past.

On the other side of the world, long before the Romans celebrated
their Lemuria, Dumu was the earliest recorded dying-and-reviving deity,
who set a pattern for subsequent resurrection gods from Osiris to Christ.
Dumu appears in the Hebrew scriptures as Tamuz and is familiar to
students of ancient Sumer as Dumuzi. Like the Lemurian Tree of Life,
Dumu's date palm was revered by fourth-millennium-B.C. Sumerians as
sacred. Originally worshipped as a goddess, like most mythic personifications of the Motherland, Dumu became syncretized with a god as a
bisexual, ultimately single male personality. His/her capacity as a deity
of rebirth is in keeping with the survival of refugee culture-bearers in
Mesopotamia from a natural catastrophe in the Pacific. Even Dumu
may have been preceded by the Sumerian birth goddess "of the watery
deeps," Nammu, from whom sprang not only the gods, but all mortal
life as well. Dilmun, the lost land from which Dumu came, is suggestive
enough of Lemurian origins, but more so in its earlier name: Mu-Ati.

These discernibly Lemurian themes on fundamental concepts in early
religious thought is particularly significant because Sumer is, after all, still
generally regarded by conventional scholars as the earliest documented
civilization. In other words, traces of Mu are apparent not only in this
presumably first high culture, but also in its own very beginnings.

Lachamu and Lachmu were worshipped during the late fourth millennium B.C. by the Sumerians. The heavenly pair were revered as creation deities, the first gods, children of Tiamat, the "bitter ocean." At
that same remote period in the Nile Valley, the oldest divine creator was
Temu, "maker of gods and men." Like Lachamu and Lachmu, his home
was in the sea, where he was responsible for stirring up a great flood that
largely obliterated a former humanity. Temu was portrayed in temple art
wearing the double crown that identified him as the progenitor of dynastic civilization, and implied that Egypt was founded by culture bearers
from Mu. Temu was worshipped as Egypt's foremost deity by the intel-
lectually renowned priests of Anu, known to the Greeks as Heliopolis,

or City of the Sun, its name reminiscent of Lemuria's solar religion.

Lemurian influence in Africa was not confined to Egypt. The supreme deity of Buganda, in Uganda, was Mu-kasa. His oracular shrine, forbidden to all but the tribal chief, was set up on Lake Victoria's sacred island of Bubembe in imitation of the god's original homeland, overwhelmed during the deep past by the Great Flood. Another Ugandan god with watery associations, Mu-gizi, was the Bunyoro guardian of Lake Albert. His fellow immortal, Mu-nume, was invoked during periods of drought or, appropriately enough, deluge. Elsewhere in East Africa, Mu-lungu was the Swahili god from which all creation spread around the world. In South Africa, Mu-jaji is still the goddess of destructive tempests, recalling the catastrophic destruction of her distant homeland. She has long been represented by a lineage of mortal queens, high guardians of Mu-jaji's secret of eternal life. It was upon her cult that the writer H. Rider Haggard based his famous novel *She.*

On the other side of the continent, in western Africa, Mu-so Koroni is "the pure woman with the primeval soul" to the natives of Mali. The mother of life, she introduced humankind to the principles of agriculture. Her consort, the sun-god Pemba, assumes the guise of the Tree of Life, yet another theme encountered in Lemurian symbols around the world.

Even the Pygmies of central Africa tell of Mu-gasa, who, in the ancient past, presided over a paradise in the distant east where the first human beings were created. Due to their disobedience, a great tempest arose, and Mu-gasa departed before his homeland was utterly destroyed, eventually settling, unseen, among the Pygmies.

At the edge of the Lemurian sphere of cultural influence, a pre-Hindu people remembered as the Redin by natives of the Maldive Islands in the Indian Ocean left extensive ruins and place-names associated with the lost Motherland. The Redin worshipped a mother goddess, Ham-Mu-Mata, still revered by the Hindu Bhils, a tribal people of western India. Laamu, referred to locally as the "first land sighted," was initially glimpsed by the Redin on their long-distance arrival from the east in large, fast, oar-driven ships. A people of seafarers and builders, they are described as blue-eyed with red hair and sharp noses, a characterization brought back to life in 1980, when fair-complected American visitors were greeted by the natives as "Redin." Even today, some residents on the Maldive island of Baara exhibit occasional physical features reflecting those of the prehistoric civilizers.

Modern Maldivian sailors still honor the Redin by placing a pair of limes at the stern of their canoes whenever departing Rasgetimu, in memory of the compassion shown by the ancient inhabitants to a stowaway aboard one of their vessels. Rather than punishing him, so the story goes, for trying to get away from the island, they comforted the boy with fruit. The preservation of this tradition over the millennia proves that the Redin are not in the class of fairies or spirits but are still regarded as a real people, however long vanished, by today's islanders.

Laamu features the largest *hawitta* (a pyramidal stone-and-earth mound) in the Maldives. It is surrounded by a cluster of other islands, all populated by ruins, said to have been the Redin's earliest settlement, but their first landfall was made at Utimu. On nearby Gamu have been found numerous artifacts adorned with sun symbols, implying that the Redin understood and appreciated the significant location of the Maldives in the middle of the equatorial channel. The glyphs also underscore James Churchward's description of Mu as the center of a solar cult. Redin worship was supposed to have centered on a sacred flame. In fact, all their hawitta were oriented toward the east, with a ramp ascending the western flank to the apex. Reverence for the sun is evident in the name of another island important to the Redin: Rasgetimu. It combines the Egyptian word for sun—Ra—found throughout Polynesia and that of the sunken Pacific homeland, Mu. In Oivehi, the Maldivian language, the word for king is *rasage,* apparently descended from the Redin, whose monarchs traced their lineage from a sun-god, just as Churchward depicted the solar inheritance of Lemurian kings in Ra-Mu. The connection becomes yet more sharply defined in the Oivehian word for "island"—*timu.* The combination of *mu* in these words and names clearly reveals their origins in the lost kingdom of the Pacific.

Another language parallel suggests that the Redin introduced civilization into the subcontinent more than 5,000 years ago. The Oivehi *bara'baro* for "good" or "fine" means the same in Urdu, an Indo-Aryan language derived from a lost dialect spoken throughout the Indus Valley during the fourth and third millennia B.C. In Hindu myth, the mother of the gods was It-Mu, a non-Indo-Aryan name with roots in the fourth-millennium-B.C. Indus Valley. The implications of these comparisons are supported by material evidence. An otherwise unique red-and-black mosaic bead removed from a hawitta on the Maldive island of Nilandu is identical in all respects to specimens found at the Indus Valley port city of Lothal, where a bead-making factory has been excavated. These complementary linguistic and physical clues point to the Redin as builders of India's first great cities at Harappa and Mohenjo Daro.

If they were indeed responsible for Indus Valley civilization, then resemblances between its script and Easter Island's rongo-rongo come into sharper focus. In chapter 2, those correspondences were explained by the arrival at the subcontinent and in the eastern Pacific of culture-bearers from Mu, who instituted their written language in both widely separate locations. Only highly skilled mariners of the Redin's reputation would have been capable of carrying such knowledge around the world. Their legacy left among the place-names, terms, artifacts, and archaeological sites in the Maldives and the Indus Valley credibly identify them with literate sailors from an outside source that cannot be found because it no longer exists. The Redin and Lemurians were one and the same seafaring civilizers who brought the tenets of their lost kingdom eastward to Rapa Nui and westward to prehistoric India.

They were also known as the Rutas, according to the French scholar Louis Jacolliot, who spent much of his life from 1837 to 1890 researching the temple records of ancient India. Indeed, the word Redin could very well be a philological twist on the name Rutas. During the course of Jacolliot's studies, he was surprised to discover that Sanskrit was not the oldest language of the subcontinent; it had been preceded by an earlier tongue known as Samsar. He learned that Abbé LeLuc, a fellow countryman, while traveling through Tibet in 1845, was shown Samsar glyphs etched on the leaves of an artificial tree preserved at the Kunbun monastery in Sinfau, on the border with China. The monks claimed that the characters belonged to the written language of the Rutas, sun-worshippers on a great island kingdom far across the sea in the east, very long ago, before it was engulfed by a terrible catastrophe.

Following up on Abbé LeLuc's Tibetan visit, Jacolliot found the Rutas cited in early Hindu literature, where their sunken home was identified as a lost "Motherland, the font of civilization," originally one moon's voyage east of Burma. Both investigators were somewhat confirmed in the early 1980s, when World Explorer president David Hatcher Childress found references to Rutas at another Tibetan monastery, near the village of Purna. It was here that a Phuktal Gompa monk told him about a school of mystics who long ago escaped from the destruction of their country by seeking refuge in the Himalayas.

While neither Frenchman mentioned that Motherland by name, Abbé LeLuc's encounter at the Kunbun monastery with its artificial tree and leafy Samsar glyphs remarkably complemented the Tree of Life Colonel Churchward stressed was synonymous with Mu itself, an assertion seconded by Polynesian oral tradition and Chinese myth. The *Huainanzi*, an original collection of cosmologies from ancient China, describes the Ruo mu tree, a counterpart to the Fu Sang mu, or sacred mulberry, associated with cleansing or purifying the sun in primeval times, recalling the Lemurian solar religion. The Ruo mu stood west of an axis mundi, the center of the world, at the Jian mu, where spirits came to Earth, just as the Roman Lemuria, Melanesia's Horiomu, the Hopi Powamu, and so forth were associated with the passage of ghosts. Together, Fu Sang mu, Jian mu, and Ruo mu signified the passage of the sun from east to west, originally delineating the vast extent of the Motherland.

In 1879, Jacolliot published *Histoire de vierges: Les Peuples et les continents disparus,* in which he concluded:

> One of the most ancient legends of India preserved in the temples by oral and written tradition relates that several hundred thousand years ago there existed in the Pacific Ocean an immense continent which was destroyed by geological upheaval and the fragments of which must be sought in Madagascar, Ceylon, Sumatra, Java, Borneo and the principal islands of Polynesia. According to the Brahmans, this country had attained a high civilization, and the

peninsula of Hindustan, enlarged by the displacement of the waters at the time of the great cataclysm, has but continued the chain of the primitive traditions born in this place. These traditions give the name Rutas to the peoples which inhabited this immense equinoctial continent, and from their speech was derived Sanskrit.

Caroli writes, "Jacolliot's Rutas brought the Brahman faith with them to India when they fled their sunken homeland, whose demise resulted in the Sub-Continent's rise from the depths. The ancestral Aryans came, not from the north, as mainstream archaeologists insist, but from the lost land of the Rutas."

One of the sources that provided Jacolliot with information about the Rutas' deeply prehistoric country was the *Surya Siddhanta,* according to Professor H. T. Colebrook "the most ancient treatise on astronomy in India. Prince Maya [Asura Maya, its author] is represented as receiving his science from a partial incarnation of the Sun." He told of not one but two antediluvian civilizations. These were Saka Dwipa, identified with Plato's Atlantis by William D. Whitney, professor of Sanskrit at Yale, in 1854, and Ruta, which was divided into another island, Daitya.

Native correlations between the Rutas and Lemuria are found across the Pacific. In Mangaian myth, Ru was the god of Avaiki, the undersea palace of the dead, and creator of an island at the center of the world, Rangi-motia, yet another name for the sunken civilization. Fornander researched a "Polynesian legend from Raiatea, Society group, which states that the Deluge was occasioned by the wrath of Rua-Haku ["Rua, the Lord"], the great ocean-god of that group." The deluge itself was known as Te tai o Rua-tapu after its flood-hero, Rua-tapa, in pre-Christian New Zealand. He was a legendary craftsman from Avaiki who taught the Maori ancestors the art of woodcarving. As Haiviki went down, Rua pushed up the Tuamotu Islands from the ocean bottom, and the creatrix, Rua papa, produced Tahiti in a similar fashion. In the Cook Islands, Ruange was the mother of tribes. All these mythic associations, spread over great distances from each other, define various aspects of the far-flung ancestral kingdom they all had in common.

Among many other names in Hawaii, this kingdom was known as Ta aina o Rua, or simply Ta Rua, in either case meaning the "land of the Rua," said to have been the original home of the Mu people before their pre-Polynesian arrival in Kauai. If, as Melville writes, they knew their country as the Pit or Crater of Heaven, Ta Rua o Rani, then referring to themselves as the Rutas makes some sense. She tells us that the root, *rua*, signifies "growth and development from fire," an apparent allusion to the technological and cultural creativity of the Mu, "who composed the world's first civilization." The name is close to the Sanskrit (or Samsar?) root for Rutas, *rta*; it means to be ritually or cosmically fit, appropriately enough, in view of the strong spiritual focus attributed to this vanished people.

Spreading across Polynesia and beyond, they imprinted the identity of their Motherland in numerous place-names that still survive to mark their impact on Oceania. Indonesia's native Sarawak worship Munsumundok, who created all life after she emerged from a great "rock" (i.e., island) in the middle of the sea. The Mulinu'u Peninsula is believed to have been the spot where flood survivors landed at 'Upolu, in Samoa. On its southern coast are Salamumu Beach, Mulivai, and Si'umu. Namu'a Island stands just off Upolu's eastern shore from the village of Samusu, opposite Muli-fanua Wharf, in the west. The seaside position of these locations indicates their Lemurian significance, as do Tahaa's Tapamu Bay and Faatemu Bay on Raiatea, largest of the Leeward Islands, in French Polynesia.

Nomuka and Nomuka'iki lie among the Ha'apai Group in the kingdom of Tonga, while Mu'umu'a and 'Umuna belong to the Vava'u Group. Munawata is found among the Trobriand Islands in the Solomon Sea, and Tumu-te-Varovaro is the spiritual title of Rarotonga. On the Indonesian island of Flores, where scientists found the dwarf species remembered in Hawaiian tradition as the Menehune, the giant but now equally extinct volcano that snuffed out the lives of these little people at the close of the last ice age is still known as Keli Mutu.

As might be expected, given Lemuria's supposed former location, the concentration of place-names incorporating Mu is greater in the South Seas than in any other area on Earth. The Motherland died long ago, but its name still echoes across the islands of the Pacific Ocean.

ELEVEN

The Sleeping Prophet of Lemuria

> *Edgar Cayce is thought by many to have been the great-est clairvoyant and prophet since the days of apostolic revelation.*
>
> BRAD STEIGER

Of our era's alleged "psychics," one name stands out. Edgar Cayce's status as a genuine seer not only survived his mid-twentieth-century death into the next millennium, but has grown considerably beyond his lifetime reputation as well. The cause is not difficult to understand. His forty years of subconscious health pronouncements form a body of recorded medical information sought out by sufferers from around the world as effective countermeasures to invasive surgical procedures. His reputation as a healing intuitive aside, the far fewer utterances he made about Lemuria are not, as skeptics might expect, statements of wild fantasy, but instead remarkably consistent, and well within the scope of archaeology and geology. More valuably, they shed new light on the people, spirituality, and destiny of Mu otherwise unavailable from conventional sources. Whether or not we give any credence to psychics, renowned or otherwise, his characterization of Lemurian people and events is surprisingly credible and illuminating if viewed through the lens of neither preconceived belief nor unbelief.

Edgar Cayce, the "Sleeping Prophet,"
who envisioned Lemuria.

Born in 1877 in Kentucky, Cayce was known as the Sleeping Prophet because he offered cures while in a deep trance. Until his death in Virginia sixty-eight years later, Cayce dictated thousands of "life readings" allegedly obtained from a kind of spiritual record he claimed to be able to read while experiencing an altered state of consciousness. His formal education was meager, and points of reference were for him more spiritual than historical or academic. His grasp of the world was often biblical, not scholastic. It seems clear, then, that considerations of a sunken civilization were beyond the scope of his rural background, his fundamentally Christian worldview, and even his interests. Nonetheless, he inexplicably began talking about sunken cities one day during the course of giving medical advice after nearly twenty years without mentioning a lost civilization. Awake, he knew virtually nothing about Atlantis and less concerning Lemuria. Yet their sudden appearance among the life readings was entirely in keeping with his therapeutic counsels.

During the early 1920s, in the course of listing and describing the root causes for various inexplicable ailments afflicting his clients, Cayce stated that these apparently baseless health problems were the subconscious residue of negative behavior carried over from previous lives in Atlantis a very long time ago. Unresolved at the time of its cataclysmic destruction, their "bad karma" carried over millennia of incarnations, inflecting each one into the present lifetime as guilt complexes, resulting in so-called psychosomatic conditions—actually, physical reflexes or reactions to spiritual pain, hence their suffering from incarnation to incarnation. "There can be no physical healing," Cayce often repeated, "without spiritual healing, because the soul is the seat of our being."

For more than twenty years after first startling his clients with their former lives in the sunken capital, Cayce went on to discuss Atlantis in many hundreds of life readings, though far less frequently mentioning Mu or Lemuria. When asked why, he responded that the Atlanteans had behaved very badly, accumulating enormous karmic debt that needed to be set right over the course of numerous reincarnations. The virtuous Lemurians, spiritually solvent (for the most part) to the end, had incurred less soul debt and were subsequently freer from the soul-cleansing round of birth-death-rebirth.

America's renowned medical intuitive often mentioned Atlantis during his altered states of consciousness. But his description of the lost civilization was less for historical purposes than to provide a setting for past-life behavior. According to Edgar Cayce, important ethical decisions acted on in the ancient past contributed over subsequent reincarnations of a particular soul to its development, down to the present time. He believed that the predicaments or circumstances of the individuals who sought his counsel during the early twentieth century sometimes found their karmic roots in prehistory. Cayce was chiefly interested in Atlantis only insofar as it helped shed light on the spiritual condition of his clients. And since the Atlanteans were supposed to have been a morally challenged people, most of his life readings concerned men and women who long ago dwelled in the doomed oceanic kingdom.

He found far fewer with a Lemurian background. Because the Pacific Motherland missed the materialism and wars that characterized its Atlantic counterpart its more peaceful inhabitants had less karmic repercussions. What he did say about Lemuria, however, illuminated the lost realm from a unique perspective. Beyond any psychic or karmic considerations, Cayce's readings about Mu or Lemuria are self-evidently plausible, because they often contain information that made little or no sense at the time they were made, but have been since confirmed in many instances by subsequent discoveries in geology and archaeology.

A case in point was his description of a forgotten civilization he claimed flourished in what is now the Gobi Desert many thousands of years ago, when it was created by "those from the land of Mu" (1273–1 M.40 10/16/36). Living conditions then were utterly unlike the hostile environment for which the region is infamous, Cayce said, and it began to deteriorate rapidly to its presently uninhabitable status immediately following the Great Flood. Recalling the Lemurian Garden of Eden, he spoke of "the first appearances of the Adamic influence that came to Asia and the Near East through that now known as the Gobi land" (1210–1 M.54 6/29/36).

When Cayce made these statements in the mid-1930s, few people knew what he was talking about. One who did was James Churchward, whose several volumes about the Pacific Motherland had been recently published. In his first book, *The Lost Continent of Mu,* he declared, "At the time of the Uighur Empire, the Gobi Desert was an exceedingly fertile area of land." The Uighur was the principal colonial holding belonging to Mu at the time of the biblical "Flood, which destroyed its eastern half. Eventually, the Uighurs extended themselves into Europe around the western and northern shores of the Caspian Sea, as related in a very old Hindu record; from there, they continued on through Central Europe."

During the lifetimes of Cayce and Churchward, and long after their deaths, both men were almost universally ridiculed by professional geologists and archaeologists for such statements. The Gobi Desert was generally believed to have always been an immense wasteland, never the "exceedingly fertile area" portrayed by the psychic and the colonel. Scanty records referred to a twelfth-century Uighur "kingdom" of sorts in inner Asia, but nothing earlier. Today's Uighurs are a sedentary people whose social organization revolves around village life in northwestern China, where they subsist on *kaoliang,* a kind of sorghum. "There seems to be little direct connection between the medieval people and those now bearing the name," according to Rudy Evermann, a specialist in the history of the Gobi Desert. A Uighur impact on Europe appeared ludicrous, and a crazy reversal of European influences on the East deemed incontrovertible by scholars.

In 1962, however, geological opinion was turned on its ear by abundant physical evidence proving that the Gobi region had indeed alternated between extended periods of fertility and aridity over the last few million years. The most recent environmental events occurred at the close of the Pleistocene epoch, 12,000 Y.B.P., and again around the turn of the fourth millennium B.C. As recently as 3,000 years ago, shepherds were tending flocks of sheep where today an ocean of sand spreads beyond the horizon. An even greater shock to conventional wisdom occurred in the following decade, when the corpse of a fair-complected, red-haired adult male was found in central Asia. Almost perfectly intact because he had been naturally mummified by arid conditions of the Takla Makan Desert, the man was dated to nearly 10,000 years ago, millennia before the arrival of the first Chinese.

Nor was he alone. The remains of other contemporary as well as later white-skinned men, women, and children were excavated, more than 500 alone in the Uighur areas of Ueruemchi and Tarim. Discoveries continued into the early twenty-first century, when a cemetery of several hundred more Caucasian mummies was unearthed in the eastern Gobi during summer 2004 by Chinese archaeologists. Investigators were especially struck by the advanced state of attire worn by many of the corpses. They were dressed in beautifully made felt shirts, tailored trousers, elaborate skirts with handsome belts, silk scarves, and leather jerkins, and they were shod in deerskin shoes or slippers.

The profusion and consistently skillful execution of their remarkably well-preserved clothing underscored Churchward's comments made fifty years before: "The Uighurs had reached a high state of civilization and culture; they knew astrology, mining, the textile industries (!), architecture, mathematics, agriculture (!), writing, reading, medicine, etc. They were experts in decorative art on silk (!), metals and wood, and they made statues of gold, silver, bronze and clay; and this was before the history of Egypt began." Archaeologists traced some of the Ueruemchi mummy styles and design patterns to central Europe, again as Churchward had indicated decades earlier.

"*The history of the Uighurs,*" Churchward stressed in italics, "is the history of the Aryans," foreshadowing the anomalous discovery of ancient Caucasians in northwestern China, just where Cayce also spoke of an "Adamic" civilization in "the Gobi land."

My first book about the Sleeping Prophet, *Edgar Cayce's Atlantis and Lemuria,* compared his statements regarding both sunken civilizations

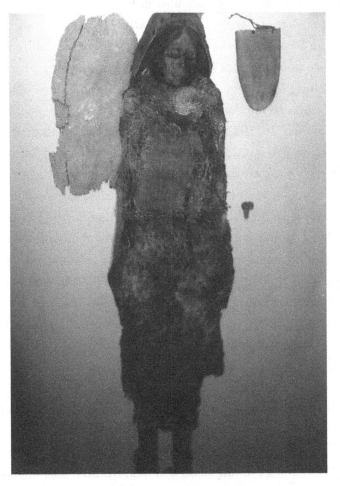

One of China's Caucasian mummies.

with archaeological and oceanographic discoveries made since his death in 1945, findings that tended to confirm the correctness of his accounts. In trying to arrive at a convincing compromise between science and the psychic, however, I was led to conclude that his concept of time while in a trance state was uncertain. His visions were akin to vivid dreams, wherein the sleeper, on waking, may recall many details with great clarity, but his sense of time is invariably hazy. In sleep, consciousness moves from our familiar concept of time into a twilight zone of timelessness. Cayce was not, after all, referred to as the Sleeping Prophet for nothing. He will be excused then, if his physical description of the lost kingdoms, while credible, is chronologically unreliable.

Some readers of *Edgar Cayce's Atlantis and Lemuria* insisted that he be taken at his word, however, and objected to my suggestion that these civilizations flourished not hundreds of thousands of years ago but into the late Bronze Age, around 1500 b.c. A close examination of his words, however, leaves us unclear about his concept of time.

On February 16, 1932, Cayce said, "Lemuria began its disappearance —even before Atlantis . . . ten thousand, seven hundred light-years, or Earth years, or present setting of those, as set by Amilius—or Adam" (364–4). Could he have really meant "light years" in the same sense we understand the speed of light? A "present setting" of 10,500 light-years means that Lemuria was more than sixty-three thousand trillion years old, a figure predating by far the creation of the universe. Whatever kind of calendar Adam may have known is anyone's guess. And what could "Earth years" have meant? Ours is a solar calendar, less than twenty centuries old. During Roman times and before, numerous and often radically different calendrical systems were employed by many various cultures. They were additionally based on the phases of the moon, the rotation of the stars, the appearance of certain constellations, the zodiac, the number of royal generations, the foundation of cities, natural events, and so on and so on.

Whatever Cayce's concept of time might have been while he was unconscious, it had nothing to do with years as they were understood in the twentieth century. Clearly, he was struggling to describe a genuine chronology for Lemuria, but he was prevented from doing so by the very nature of the dimension into which his consciousness had been elevated. It must be remembered that he envisioned the world and the passage of time not from the perspective of everyday life, but through the magnifying lens of an Otherworld, a trance or dream state that broadened and colored his point of view. To clearly explain what he saw to other mortals not blessed with such a vision was difficult, because they had nothing in their experience with which to compare it.

Although Cayce's chronology is uncertain, his brief references to Lemuria are far less ambiguous and more convincing. A case in point is among the first statements he made about the lost Motherland, when he touched on Lemuria only briefly in his lengthy response to a question concerning geographical and geological conditions on Earth at the time *Homo sapiens sapiens* came into being. "The Andean, or the Pacific coast of South America," he said, "occupied then the extreme western portion of Lemuria." Sixty years after he made this statement, California's Scripps Oceanographic Service published a series of maps revealing the latest discoveries in sea-floor research. One such map details and names the Nazca Ridge, a former land bridge of more than 200 miles long that once connected the Peruvian coast at Nazca with a sunken archipelago. In 1932, Cayce appears to have identified an underwater feature unknown to science until the 1990s, thereby providing substantive evidence for Lemuria's existence.

Ironically, his first mention of the Pacific civilization, nine months after prophetically alluding to the yet undiscovered Nazca Ridge, details the beginning of its demise. He stated that a "portion" of "Lemuria began its disappearance" 10,700 years ago. This time period coincides remarkably well with the final moments of the last ice age, when melting glaciers generated dramatic increases in the global sea level, drowning coastal regions and far-flung lowland territories around the world. Lemuria and its culture continued to survive and prosper long after some territories were lost in the ice-age deluge, just as Cayce said. But related archaeological evidence tends to confirm his rough date for this early flood.

Simultaneous with dynamic sea-level rises and Cayce's eleventh-millennium-B.C. date was the sudden emergence of the sophisticated

Jomon culture in Japan and the contemporary drowning of Yonaguni's sunken ceremonial structure. These two apparent consequences of the concluded ice age imply that Lemurian refugees migrated to places like Yonaguni from the larger Japanese islands of Honshu and Hokkaido. After the ice-age flood, according to Cayce, the Lemurians began long-range voyages—at least their missionary representatives traveled throughout the world on behalf of spreading the Lemurian gospel. He describes their temple-building activities in Yucatan, and representatives from Mu were said to have been on hand for opening ceremonies of the Great Pyramid at the Nile Delta.

These and other events come into sharper focus through the names Cayce provided of the men and women who actually participated in them. In life reading 1159–1 F.80 for May 5, 1936, he spoke of Amululu, "a priestess . . . who came west from the activities of the Lemurian land." The civilizing influences she helped bring into Peru formed "what later became known as the Incals." Amululu taught and supervised the production of "metals, crockery, woven cloth, the use or application of these in the services not only for the places of abode, but for the places of amusements or for places of worship."

Many of the Lemurians he mentioned by name, like Amululu, were deeply involved in civilizing South America. Om-muom appears to have been among the first, when he labored in Peru at "the beginnings of the communications with those of many other lands" after the onset of geologic trouble threatening to break up the old Atlanto-Lemurian world. During the seismic violence of those times, the best and worst in human beings, then as now, emerged. Omuld and Oumu were cited by Cayce as Om-muom's contemporaries who lost their nerve during the Peruvian experience, while Ulmu lost something more—his life, while trying to rescue others imperiled by the natural catastrophes bedeviling South America and much of the rest of the world.

Lemurian spiritual greatness, Cayce observed, was superior even to the high levels of paranormal power developed in Atlantis. Here he is richly validated by an abundance of Asian, Australian, Pacific islander, and pre-Columbian American traditions that define their versions of

Lemuria as the sunken Motherland of sacred wisdom. Australian Aborigines believe that the tenets of their Dream-time cult arrived from the "land of Perfection" before it was engulfed by the sea. Burotu is remembered as the sunken realm of powerful priests who spread the secrets of their high magic from Tonga to the Fiji Islands. The Chumash Indians of southern coastal California believed that the ancestors of their medicine men were missionaries from Lemuria, after which one of their offshore islands was originally named.

But most of Cayce's recorded statements about the lost Pacific kingdom follow its people to other parts of the world. During his life reading of April 17, 1936, Edgar Cayce told of immigrants from a global catastrophe arriving in the Near Eastern "lands of Zu." Interestingly, Har-Sag-Mu was known 5,000 years ago as "Mu of the Mountain Range," where Zu, the Sumerian sky-god, settled after causing a terrible cataclysm. Thereafter, "stillness spread abroad, silence prevailed." In the later Babylonian version, as preserved in the Assyrian library of Ashurbanipal, Zu stole the Tablets of Destiny from his fellow gods and brought them to Har-Sag-Mu. His self-transformation into a bird of prey to fight off a serpent guarding the tablets recurs in worldwide imagery of an eagle battling a snake, from the Greek Delphi and Norse Yggdrasil to Aztec Mexico and pre-Columbian Colombia.

Zu's myth is also associated with the chakra system of spiritual conflict between the kundalini serpent wound around the base of the human spine and Garuda, the eagle of an enlightened crown chakra. The myth implies that this metaphysical concept was brought directly from heaven to Har-Sag-Mu, a sacred mountain on the Pacific island of Mu. Zu's theft of the Tablets of Destiny, which first described kundalini yoga, parallel the Western myth in which the brother of Atlas, Prometheus, stole fire from the gods and gave it to humankind. That "Promethean heat" appears to have been no less analogous to kundalini energy, because the Greek Titan suffered the daily digestion of his liver by an eagle.

Cayce portrays the people of Mu as far-ranging travelers, sailing mostly to Peru, but also to Yucatán and the American Southwest, as far afield as the Nile Valley, and even to Atlantis. They went there, Cayce said, mostly to study the sciences, of which alchemy was one he singled out for special mention (274–1 M.34 2/13/33). The Lemurians apparently left something of themselves behind, because their religious ideas made converts among the spiritually divided Atlanteans (1273–1 M.40 10/16/36).

Atlantis was to suffer four natural catastrophes, each one sparking waves of migration to other parts of the world, before the final destruction. Survivors from all of these calamitous events, save the last, sometimes sought sanctuary in the Pacific kingdom, perhaps because it was so far removed from the geologic violence of the mid-Atlantic world, or due to ancient kindred ties of common spirituality with the gentle Lemurians. Describing a client's past life as an Atlantean refugee during one of these upheavals, Cayce remarked, "The entity was among the last to leave for what was then Mu" (557–2 F.52 5/23/34).

Indeed, relations between the two widely separated oceanic civilizations may have been more than cordial, at least in a few instances. Cayce refers to a half-Lemurian, half-Atlantean as Mufuti (2850–1 M.18 11/14/42), and a female spiritual adviser in Atlantis was called Muglo (2454–3 F.43 7/15/42). He mentions an Atlantean ruler in Yucatán with the distinctly Lemurian name of Zurumu (1632–3 F.38 8/9/38). These hybrid Atlanto-Lemurian personal names are complemented by identifiably Atlantean place-names and ancient heroes or gods found throughout numerous Pacific island cultures.

According to the Tanimbar Austronesian people of southeast Maluku, Atuf separated the Lesser Sundras from Borneo by wielding his spear while traveling eastward with his royal family from a huge natural cataclysm that annihilated their distant homeland. It supposedly took place at a time when the whole Earth was unstable. The chief cultural focus of the Tanimbar is concentrated on the story of Atuf and his heroism in saving their ancestors from the disaster. "Thereafter they had to migrate ever eastward from island refuge to island refuge," writes Oppenheimer. "As if to emphasize this, visitors will find huge symbolic stone boats as ritual centres of the villages" (page 278). North of Maluku, a similar account is known to the islanders of Ceram and Banda, north of

Maluku. In their version, their ancestors are led to safety by Boi Ratan, a princess from the sunken kingdom.

Profound impressions were likewise made in early pharaonic Egypt, where at least two important gods revered during dynastic times bear the stamp of Lemurian influence. Temu is described by archaeologist Anthony Mercatante as "the oldest of the creation gods in Egyptian mythology." Temu was an undersea deity, dwelling in the primeval ocean he brought about. His thoughts made the heavens, animals, plants, mortals, and the gods themselves, who were expressions of his will. He was responsible for a catastrophic deluge that long ago covered the entire face of the globe, destroying all life, except for a few virtuous men and women who joined the gods in a "solar boat." Landing at the Nile Delta, they began civilization anew. Appropriately, the ancient Egyptian word for *ocean* was Mu. Beyond Temu's self-evident name, his myth implies the arrival in Egypt of culture bearers from Mu, which suffered several major flood events. In later dynasties, his name changed as a consequence of large-scale immigration from Atlantis, and he was known henceforth as Atmu.

Another Lemurian deity worshipped throughout the Nile Valley from a very early period was Khnemu. His name means literally "the Molder," because he shaped the cosmic egg, from which all life hatched during remote prehistory. This was the omphalos, or navel stone, leading symbol of Atlanto-Lemurian spirituality. Khnemu was portrayed in temple art with the body of a man sprouting four ram heads. These signified the dissemination of his navel-of-the-world cult from its place of origin across every sea to the four cardinal directions; the ram has, since ancient times and in many cultures, personified oceanic voyagers. Khnemu's popularity was so deeply rooted that his veneration continued well into the second century A.D., when gnostic gems bearing his image were still being made. The worship of these two gods from the beginning of Egyptian civilization supports Cayce's contention that adepts from Mu contributed to the foundation of its powerful religion (1353–1 F. Adult 3/26/37; 2697–1 M.48 3/11/42).

Some of the overseas immigrants he described bore unmistakably

Lemurian names, like Shu-Su-Mu-Lur-r (1695–1 F.32 9/29/38) and Mu-Elden (2513–1 F.70 6/12/41). As representatives of the old mystery-cult, they attended the completion of the Great Pyramid at the Giza Plateau. This was accomplished when "the crown or apex . . . of metal that was to be indestructible, being of copper, brass and gold with other alloys," was fixed to its summit. The "Earth building," as he referred to the pyramid, functioned in part as a place of spiritual transformation and initiation.

According to Cayce, its official opening set an unremembered precedent for similarly spiritual events in the future. "The ceremony was long," he recalled,

> the clanging of the apex by the gavel that was used in the sounding of the placing. Hence, there has arisen from this ceremony many of those things that may be seen in the present; as the call to prayer, the church bell in the present may be termed a descendant . . . the sound as of those that make for mourning, in the putting away of the body; the sounding as of ringing in the new year, the sounding as of the coming of the bridegroom; all have their inception from the sound that was made that kept the earth's record of the earth's building. (378–14 M.56 9/26/33)

Cayce said a lasting impact was made on the American Southwest, "in particular that portion of Arizona and Nevada that [is] as a portion of that brotherhood of those peoples from Mu" (812–1 F.48 2/4/35). Cayce told how a client, in a former Lemurian incarnation, journeyed to what is "now known as Arizona and Utah . . . those portions that were then a place of refuge from Mu" extended as far as Missouri (816–3 M.51 2/17/35).

These states are especially pertinent to our discussion of Lemuria, because the tribal peoples who have inhabited them for time out of mind preserve rich oral traditions of the vanished Pacific civilization. For example, the Ute Indians, who gave their name to the state of Utah, revere Mu-sinia as their sacred white mountain. It is among the Hopi and Zuni in Arizona and Nevada that tribal accounts of ancestral wanderings from the Pacific Ocean are well preserved in oral tradition and ceremonial ritual. Both are combined in annual dramas reenacted at the *kiva,* a circular structure built over a subterranean chamber connected by a ladder. As initiates emerge from the underground room, they are doused with copious amounts of water by fellow participants loudly reminding them of the terrible deluge their forefathers escaped in the distant past.

Cayce's special reference to southern California for its Lemurian past is particularly underscored by the testimony of its native peoples (1473–1 F.49 11/10/37; 5750–1 Hugh Lynn Cayce 11/12/33). According to California's Salinen Indians, humanity perished in a world flood. Only a single diving bird survived. It dove deep into the ocean and fetched up a beak-full of muck from the bottom of the sea. Seeing this performance, Eagle God descended from the sky to fashion a new race from the retrieved mud.

The Washo are native Californians who recounted an early golden period of their ancestors. For many generations, they lived in happiness on a far-off island, at the center of which was a tall stone temple containing a representation of the sea god. His likeness was so huge that its head touched to the top of "the dome." It seems remarkable that the Washo, whose material culture never exceeded the construction of a tepee, would have even known about an architectural feature as sophisticated as a dome. Their deluge story tells of violent earthquakes that caused the mountains of their ancestral island to catch fire. The flames rose so high they melted the stars, which fell to Earth, spreading the conflagration around the world. Some plummeted into the sea and caused a universal flood that extinguished the flames but threatened humanity with extinction.

The Wintun tribe of California told of a shaman who stole the magic flute of Katkochila, the sky-god. With this instrument, he could make his people the most powerful in the whole world. Katkochila, in a rage, showered the Earth with fire from heaven but doused the conflagration before humanity was exterminated.

In the Wiyot tribal account of Above-Old-Man, the Creator (Gudatri-Gakwitl) sent a worldwide flood to extinguish humankind and most animals. Condor survived to find only his sister, a few birds, and a single raccoon left alive. A new humanity was born from his incestuous relationship. Wiyot custom mandated that a chief take his sister as bride, if only ritually, to commemorate his people's descent from the ancestral pair that escaped the Great Flood.

Southern California's Yokut Indians recount that humankind was born on an island in the middle of a primeval sea. Here Eagle and Coyote fashioned the first men and women.

Volcanic Mount Shasta is described in several local Indian myths as the only dry land to have survived a worldwide flood. Building a raft, Coyote-Man sailed over great expanses of water to arrive at its summit. There he ignited a signal fire that alerted other survivors, who came to Mount Shasta, from which they repopulated the Earth. Into modern times, mysterious lights sometimes seen on the mountaintop are associated with ceremonies of a Lemurian brotherhood, whose initiates allegedly perform rituals from the lost civilization.

Lemurian influences dominated the development of Mesoamerican civilization until waves of immigration arrived from the east. "There had been the upheavals also from the land of Mu, or Lemuria," Cayce said, "and these had their part in the changing, or there was the injection of their tenets in the varied portions of the land—which was much greater in extent until the final upheaval of Atlantis" (5750–1 Hugh Lynn Cayce 11/12/33). His statement is reflected in the Mayan word for flood: *mu-luc,* literally, "drowned Mu" or "drowned like Mu." Mu-tul was a Mayan city founded by Zac-Mu-tul, whose name means, "the white man of Mu." Mu-tul seems philologically related to the Polynesian Mu-tu (Tahiti) and Mu-tu-hei (Marquesas), all defining a Lemurian common denominator.

The deluge-hero of the Caribs (who gave their name to the Caribbean Sea) was "the man from Mu." Described as a fair-complected, light-haired and -bearded sorcerer, Ta-Mu escaped a natural catastrophe at sea. The Caribs compared their sixteenth-century Spanish conquerors to Ta-Mu. A similar flood survivor was known to the Arovac Indians. They remembered Ca-Mu, "he from Mu," as a tall, white-skinned, fair-haired and -bearded magician who arrived on the shores of Panama after having been driven from his kingdom far across the sea by a terrible cataclysm. Ca-Mu is regarded as the man from whom all Arovac have since descended.

When Cayce said that "the Andean, or the Pacific coast of South America, occupied then the extreme western portion of Lemuria," he accurately portrayed the extent of its influence, which appears to have spanned the islands between Japan and the shores of Peru (364–13 11/17/32), for Mu or Lemuria was not so much a specific land as it was a people and their culture spread over a number of territories more or less connected to each other across thousands of miles.

Cayce's particular life reading is supported by a wealth of physical evidence among the extensive ruins of Chan Chan, just north of the Spanish colonial Peruvian city of Trujillo. It was the pre-Inca capital of the Chimu, with numerous other philological references to the vanished Motherland of Mu. Chan Chan had been built, the Chimu recounted, at the behest of "a great lord from across the sea." Its founding father was Taycanamu, followed by another culture bearer, Pacatnamu. These important names must have derived from the sunken city actually depicted on the adobe walls of Chan Chan's Palace of the Governor. The monumental mural still portrays a long line of step-pyramids with fish swimming over their summits, obviously depicting a sunken city, perhaps that of Taycanamu's "great lord from across the sea." His story compares with Hotu Matua's account of having been ordered away from Marae Renga by his superior before Hiva sank into oblivion.

This evocative imagery appears to depict Colombian native traditions of a great oceanic kingdom destroyed by some natural catastrophe from which the culture hero A-Mu-Ra-Ca led his followers to South America. In Akkadian, the language of Sumer's Semitic conquerors at the close of the third millennium B.C., A-Mu-ruu means "western lands." The name, in both Colombian Muysica and Akkadian, refers to the lost Pacific Ocean civilization of Mu. A related flood account was current at the time of the Spanish conquest among the Karaya Indians, whose ancestors were led by Kaboi into a massive cave as a place of refuge. After the waters retreated, they followed him back into the world

Part of the Chimu's sculpted mural depicting a sunken city at Chan Chan's Palace of the Governor, outside Trujillo in northern coastal Peru.

and were guided by the song of a bird. This bird motif recurs in several deluge traditions around the world, not only in Genesis. Kaboi is known throughout South America, referred to as Ka-mu by the Arawaks, Ta-mu by the Caribs, Kame by the Bakairi, and Zume by the Paraguayans.

Of Lemuria's demise, Cayce said little, except that it took place before the final destruction of Atlantis. He was more concerned with the implications of the Pacific kingdom's peaceful accomplishments, which continued to shape the reincarnated lives of men and women seeking his spiritual guidance. Karma is the consequence of our behavior, he explained. By striving for social balance and individual harmony, the Lemurians largely avoided any need for reincarnation as a means of correcting the consequences of former indiscretions and went on to fulfill their spiritual destiny in levels of being beyond the Earth plane.

TWELVE
The Destruction of
Lemuria

*It is obvious that those Polynesian myths of submergence
and cataclysm had their origin in Lemurian tradition.*

LEWIS SPENCE

Native Hawaiians told Captain James Cook, who visited them in the late eighteenth century, about a former homeland overwhelmed by some world-class natural catastrophe very long ago. The story was so meaningful to them that they preserved it over countless generations in their most important creation-chant and had it recited during only the most significant occasions by professionally trained speakers before the king and his assembled court. The title of this lengthy oral account—the *Kumulipo*—at once incorporated the name of the lost kingdom—Mu—and the nature of its annihilation, a global flood. But it was not unique. Variations of the tale were repeated across the Pacific realm by population groups separated from one another by a vastness not only of physical distance, but of race, culture, and language as well. Polynesians differ as much from Melanesians and Australian Bushmen as Peru's Aymara Indians do from Tibetans or Aleuts. Yet all these otherwise dissimilar peoples, and every one in between, possess a common account of some defining moment in prehistory when a former world came to an abrupt end, searing its original glory and violent passage into their collective consciousness forever after.

James Churchward's painting of Mu about to be overwhelmed by a super-tsunami.

While the universality of this perennial recollection suggests that a natural catastrophe of some kind probably took place, the function of myth is to describe and encapsulate such an event, truth, or memory of special significance in poetry or legend, not to date or document it in a historical survey. That is the job of archaeology, geology, and oceanography. Alone, these scholarly disciplines may reveal much of the past, but without complementary folkish traditions they risk becoming removed from human experience and fail to make much impact on our times. When science and myth combine, however, the story they tell in their own way rises above both dubious fable and bloodless analysis. They are brought into sharper focus than either is individually capable of achieving.

Science is fact; myth is metaphor. The two are not necessarily exclusionary, even though the former uses data made successively obsolete by investigative progress and the latter has nothing more to go on than hearsay. In each other's service, however, inherent weaknesses are mutually canceled out by their fundamental strengths to produce something neither was capable of generating alone.

When scientists are able to validate myth, an earthshaking break-through takes place. Narrative, hardly more than folktale, is confirmed by research, which itself is fleshed out with the details of physical evidence. The result is recognition of a powerful, self-corroborating truth: the transformation of legend into reality—a supreme discovery. Such a dramatic realization occurs in the quest for Mu, when its formerly uncertain existence and the nature of its sudden demise merge to confirm each other. Only as recently as our own epoch, however, has science reached a sufficiently high level of technological sophistication to verify the Lemurian myths that have persisted in the folk memory of numerous indigenous peoples for millennia.

Cutting-edge science has begun to cross-reference a story that begins about 12,000 years ago. By that time, Mu was already more than thirty centuries old. Most of that very long era was uninterrupted by serious geologic upheavals until the end of our planet's most recent glacial epoch. Caroli describes

the collapse of one of the vast Antarctic ice-sheets, comparable in size to one-third to one-half the Laurentide sheet of eastern Canada, which was centered upon Hudson's Bay. That means roughly a million square kilometers of ice of unknown thickness. It may have poured a million liters of fresh water per second into the South Pacific, forcing the warm, tropical currents north into the temperate zone. The scale of the resultant land-slides and seismically generated waves would have been difficult to imagine.

Something of that prehistoric catastrophe came to life the day after Christmas 2004, when the most powerful seaquake in forty years (9.3 on the Richter scale) unleashed a tsunami across the vast Indian Ocean. Spreading outward from its epicenter 155 miles off the coast of Sumatra and 5,280 fathoms deep, twenty-foot-high waves traveling 500 miles per hour claimed some 200,000 lives in a dozen countries from Somalia in East Africa to Thailand and Indonesia. Millions were made homeless and whole communities obliterated. Michael Dobbs, a writer for the *Washington Post* and himself a surviving eyewitness in Sri Lanka, reported that "the beach and the area behind it had become an inland sea, rushing over the road and pouring into the flimsy houses on the other side. The speed with which it all happened seemed like a scene from the Bible—a natural phenomenon unlike anything I had experienced before."

Strung out from the tip of the Indian subcontinent toward the equator, the low-lying Maldive Islands were completely swamped; many had to be abandoned. Archipelagoes spanning the south-central Pacific, across which the culture and people of Lemuria had distributed themselves, were also mostly flat continental shelves and lowlands, especially vulnerable to an increase in sea level, particularly if it took place in sudden surges, as happened about 12,000 years ago. According to Enzo Bosci, director of Italy's National Geophysics Institute, the Indian Ocean seaquake of 2004 even disturbed the Earth's rotation. What kind of impact the far more powerful violence of postglacial times had on our planet, to say nothing of its low-lying archipelagoes, truly boggles the mind. But well-publicized, horrific images of the monster wave that inundated places like Thailand's Phuket provide a parallel glimpse of the greater deluge that overwhelmed Lemuria.

"In the last two decades, evidence has accumulated showing that the rise in sea-level after the last Ice Age was not gradual," Oppenheimer writes "Three sudden ice-melts, the last of which was only 8,000 years ago, had a catastrophic effect on tropical coasts with flat continental shelves. Rapid land loss was compounded by great earthquakes, caused by cracks in the Earth's crust, as the weight of ice shifted to the seas. It is fairly certain that these quakes set off super-waves in the world's great oceans." His characterization of more than one cataclysmic deluge was foreshadowed in the 1970s by geologist Caesare Emilliani at the University of Miami, who documented a series of floods lasting between a decade and a century that greatly raised sea levels, but centered around 9600 B.C. for their occurrence.

Supporting evidence has been described recently by the British researcher Paul Dunbavin: "Off the Hawaiian Islands, for example, a sequence of submerged shorelines has been detected down to a depth of eleven hundred meters [3,400 feet]. The high beaches can usually be dated to the Pleistocene [contemporary with the appearance of modern man, concluding about 10,000 years ago] or even earlier; but oscillations during the Holocene [present geologic epoch] are of a lower order than this. The published sea-level curves generally agree on an average rise of sea-level of about thirty five to forty meters [110 to 123 feet] between ten thousand and five thousand years ago, with only a slight decline, if any, since that time."

Large tracts of Lemuria must have been broken up by a "sudden warming that occurred about 10,500 B.C., known as the Boelling Interstadial," according to Caroli.

> It was the most intense and sudden such oscillation at the end of the last Ice Age, and resulted in a massive surge in sea-level by about sixty six feet. There were more major oscillations of the Earth's magnetic field between about 9700 and 9100 B.C. The field strength suddenly shrank fivefold, then increased again, and later the magnetic pole shifted thousands of miles from its previous position for between twenty and one hundred years. Solar flaring and celestial bombardment can effect [sic] the magnetic field, so both could have occurred about the same era, circa 12,700 to 9100 B.C. There may have been multiple catastrophes, not just one. No one knows, however, what caused this warming, nor why it proved so intense.

As Oppenheimer points out:

> Some catastrophists see in this evidence of a sky-ripping disaster such as a meteoric bombardment. Tsunamis have big brothers, sometimes called super-waves, that may follow visits by large bodies from outer space. . . . Waves from these may arise to hundreds of meters and may travel hundreds of kilometers inland. The superfloods thus caused would inundate vast areas of coastal lowland and would even travel up small mountains. Depending on the size

of the asteroid or comet, and where it landed, there could be catastrophic conflagrations and rains of fire as a result of volcanic matter thrown into the atmosphere. Increased seismic activity would also inevitably follow. After the initial destructive effects of the waves and the increased volcanic activity, there would probably be a prolonged winter as a delayed result of the volcanic matter thrown up into the atmosphere through the breached crust. A short ice age could even occur.

Caroli admits that "Indo-Pacific tektites seem to date to between sixteen thousand and nine thousand years ago." Tektites are small, glassy bodies originating in outer space, the debris of asteroid or meteorite collisions with the Earth. *Watermark* author Joseph Christy-Vitale likewise concludes that a series of celestial cataclysms coincided with the end of the last ice age. "Within the last fifteen thousand years," he writes,

> "our immediate galactic neighborhood has witnessed five supernovae explosions. One, the star Vela, is believed to have self-destructed between eleven thousand and fourteen thousand years ago at a distance of forty five light-years from Earth. In cosmic standards, that is just around the corner. A piece of flaming star matter, not much smaller than the planet Earth, rocketed in our direction and, traveling anywhere between one-fiftieth and one-one hundredth the speed of light, could have entered the outer limits of our solar system less than a thousand years after the explosion. The event we are remembering occurred around twelve thousand years ago and, falling within the dates for Vela's final convulsion, suggests this piece of star shrapnel was the source of the local disaster."

Despite the horrific scope of the catastrophes, Mu largely survived, despite the inevitable loss of territories, because its island populations were spread out over archipelagic chains that almost linked the Americas with Asia. The upheavals did have the effect, however, of uprooting many Lemurians, forcing them to abandon their sunken or battered homelands and seek new lives in other parts of the world, where their influence was profoundly felt. As Oppenheimer observes, "Much of the geographic distribution of modern languages—at least until the major colonizations of recent times—dates from the end of the Ice Age."

But if a celestial cause for these calamitous events is conjectural, the next three global cataclysms were undoubtedly generated by what the ancient Greeks referred to as an Ekpyrosis, a universal conflagration, or "burning of the world." As recently as 1997, a general consensus concerning the likelihood of an ancient Ekpyrosis was reached at an international symposium of archeoastronomers, geologists, physicists, climatologists, paleobotanists, and leading authorities in other related fields meeting at Britain's Fitzwilliam College, Cambridge. They concluded that the early history of civilization had been punctuated by the close pass of a killer comet that pushed humanity to the brink of extinction. Known as Encke, after the eighteenth-century Swiss astronomer, its first near miss took place around 3100 B.C. and rained down a barrage of debris in a fiery swath around the world. Meteoric collisions ignited widespread volcanism, earthquakes, and tsunamis that ravaged the oceans. Civilizations fell and were succeeded by new kingdoms. As mentioned in *Survivors of Atlantis,* "Massive flooding forced ancestral Austronesians, who belonged to an archaeological culture known as the Dawenkou in southern Shandong and Jiangsu, to migrate from Taiwan to the Philippines." The Paleolithic age closed abruptly and simultaneously in China, Korea, and Japan.

"It would appear then that the volcanic activity and the climate changes around 3100 B.C. must be seen as only evidence of a much wider malaise," Dunbavin states. "That malaise should rather be viewed as the aftermath of an impact event, the resultant wobbling of the Earth on its axis, and an inexorable change in the axial tilt. . . . Before this date evidence suggests that the world was very different from the one we inhabit today. . . . The map of the world would have had an unfamiliar look about it, with many islands that do not exist today."

Scars of Comet Encke's late-fourth-millennium-B.C. passage still exist in north-central Australia's Henbury Craters and in drilled ice cores filled with contemporary ash-fall from both sides of the Pacific Ocean. While California's Mount Shasta erupted, Japan's Hakone and Numazawa volcanoes, on Honshu, and Rishiri, on Hokkaido, exploded. The cause of their generally simultaneous activity has been found among numerous tektites dated to the same period.

"In the Andes," Dunbavin observed, "the San Rafael Glacier began to advance after 3000 B.C., reaching its maximum advance around 2500 B.C. This date comes from the bottom sediments of a pond that formed on the terminal moraine." Only an extremely powerful influence could have restarted the advance of a glacier, an event contemporary with the disastrous appearance of Comet Encke.

Evidence of massive flooding during this period is beginning to reveal the scope of the late-fourth-millennium-B.C. catastrophe. Dunbavin explains:

> Prior to about 1000 B.C., the mangrove forests covered the entire coast south of Manta (Equador), as far as the Gulf of Guayaquil. The maximum southern extent seems to have occurred at about 5000 B.C., when they extended as far as Talara, in Peru, some three degrees of latitude further south. These changes imply variations in the nature of the ocean current, allowing the tropical rainfall to move further south. . . . A submerged forest near Wellington in Hutt Valley, New Zealand, is also prime evidence. Dated at around 3200 to 3000 B.C., it shows a good correspondence with the similar submerged forest deposits of this age in western Europe. . . . Along the west coast of Australia, a prominent "fresh" submerged beach platform has been noted by divers at a depth of three to four meters [nine to twelve feet] below sea-level, which has also been tentatively dated to about five thousand years ago. . . . Along the nearby Japanese coast the range of warm water mollusks retreated some 6 degrees C further south at about 3000 B.C., indicative of a temperature up to 5 degrees C higher than today and synchronous with a local fall in sea-level.

Dunbavin is seconded by Christy-Vitale:

> Spread across the vast stretches of the Pacific are thousands of iso-
> lated islands. Widespread throughout these islands are land shells
> from the mollusk family *Clausiliacea*. They have a natural aversion
> to salt water, and their distribution and close relationship has con-
> vinced a number of botanists that a large, continental land-mass once
> existed in this vast oceanic region. . . . The idea of being separated by
> the slow, gradual process of continental drift is called into question,
> because they are too closely related. The evidence creates the impres-
> sion all these animals were stranded by some sudden and dramatic
> event in the recent geologic past.

The late-fourth-millennium-B.C. cataclysm that literally rocked the
world savaged much of the Motherland, although its people continued
to preserve their culture on the islands and archipelagoes left to them.
Over the next 1,000 years, they prospered and developed the civilized
gifts their ancestors had so long nourished, until the natural catastrophe
that drove Mu to the precipice of oblivion was hardly more than a dim
memory. That awful recollection came rushing back to life in 2193 B.C.,
when Comet Encke yet again showed its terrible face in the night skies
of Earth. It vomited flaming boulders at the Pacific, igniting volcanoes
in Japan from famous Mount Fuji to Hokkaido's Mount Mashu, and
farther north at Mount Mendelev, in the Kurile Islands.

On the other side of the ocean, Alaska's Mount Hays blew up,
accompanied by major eruptions in the Sand Mountain Field of Oregon,
Colorado's Mount Dotsero, and Hell's Half-Acre, in Idaho. The hundreds of cubic miles of ash these outgassings disgorged into the atmosphere caused a climate regression that registered worldwide in the peat
bogs and tree rings identified by dendrochronologists. Global temperatures plummeted, and the sun was darkly obscured. Crops failed, famine
ensued. Caroli states that "the last known mega-tsunami in the Indian
Ocean hit western Australia around 2000 B.C." Jett writes of the "severe
climate change in Asia about 2000 to 1000 B.C."

The Chinese chronicled these calamitous events in myth. Their Shanhaijing told of K'ung-Kung, a horned monster that tore a hole in the sky and blotted out the sun as a flaming red dragon 1,000 li long—virtually from horizon to horizon. Spitting hot boulders at the world, K'ung-Kung set it afire. As recounted by Caroli, "The heavens were deranged, causing darkness, earthquakes and waves that overtopped the mountains and filled the valleys. That was no riverine flood! It was said that humanity needed nine years to recover from the disaster, which supposedly took place around 2200 B.C." At the same time, Emperor Shun's ascent to the throne took place when "ten suns appeared at once and threatened to burn up the world."

K'ung-Kung is an obvious reference to the killer comet that returned with devastating effect on our planet. Once more Mu persevered, its civilization battered and more islands lost beneath the sea or ravaged by volcanism. The Lemurians were a resilient people, however, and used even their worst misfortune as a foundation on which to rebuild society and regain their former happiness in fresh opportunities. But the next cataclysm would be their last. Five hundred sixty-five years after K'ung-Kung "attacked the Earth," Comet Encke swept its meteor-strewn tail across our orbit again, doubling the fiery destruction inflicted around the world by its late-third-millennium-B.C. passage. The best-remembered effect of Comet Encke's early-seventeenth-century-B.C. sortie was the detonation of the volcanic mountain of Thera, an Aegean island known today as Santorini. Its collapse spawned a 500-foot-high tsunami that rolled up the whole eastern Mediterranean, toppled Minoan civilization on Crete, shattered cities all along coastal Asia Minor and the Near East, and claimed countless numbers of drowning victims from Egypt's Nile Delta.

The Pacific area did not escape chastisement, however. As before, Japan suffered with the caldera eruption of Mount Sanbe in southern Honshu, while, far across the sea, the Alaskan Akiachak exploded. "It was one of the most severe post-glacial eruptions," Caroli remarks, "at half the ejecta produced by Tambora, but more than Thera. The Aegean volcano put out thirty to thirty three cubic miles of material, but

Akiachak disgorged fifty cubic miles of ash." Oregon's Blue Lake Crater and Newberry volcano blew up, as did the infamous Mount Saint Helens in Washington. The South Pacific island of Rabaul erupted with extraordinary violence but was surpassed by more massive outgassing from the Hawaiian Mauna Kea. Elsewhere in the Pacific, as the renowned catastrophist Immanuel Velikovsky recounts, there is a Samoan tradition of a former landmass said to have included Borneo, Fiji, and Tonga, suddenly engulfed by the sea during this same period.

The outstanding volcanic event of 1628 B.C., however, was the blast produced by New Zealand's Taupo Valley Center. Caroli says, "The Taupo volcanic zone is quite large, about two hundred fifty kilometers long by forty to fifty kilometers wide, encompassing more than just New Zealand's north island. It is also broken down into sub-regions. Via carbon-14 dating, it could be exactly contemporary with Akiachak." More potent than Thera's nuclear-like outburst, it generated a 200-foot-high wall of water traveling several hundred miles per hour like an all-encompassing shockwave throughout the Pacific. Islands standing in its way were overwhelmed and swept clean of every obstruction. Whole archipelagoes vanished or were depopulated. Others abruptly sank beneath the surface of the ocean in accompanying earthquakes.

"During one big quake in Chile, in 1960," Caroli observes, "some coastal areas dropped by more than four feet." Similar downfall would have drowned the flat, low-lying continental shelves that made up so much of Mu. If they fell suddenly by just fifteen feet, as did broad portions of southern Illinois during the early-nineteenth-century New Madrid earthquake felt over 1.5 million square miles, billions of tons of water rushing over the territory would have pushed it to the bottom of the sea. David Sandwell, professor of earth sciences at the renowned Scripps Oceanographic Institute, headquartered in La Jolla, California, believes parallels between the great New Madrid earthquake and a possible geologic mechanism for the Lemurian deluge are valid. "During an earthquake," he says, "you could have the land shift up and down by ten meters [thirty feet], and that would be enough to drown some exposed areas. I think probably there was a civilization that did get wiped out."

The combination of volcanism, meteor falls, mega-tsunamis, and seismic upheaval rippling in earthquake swarms across the Pacific tore the Motherland limb from limb. What remained of her territories was smashed beyond repair or rebuilding, and groups of shell-shocked, struggling Lemurians melted into the foreign populations of Oceania, Asia, and the Americas. Not coincidentally, what archaeologists call the Lapita culture, characterized by sophisticated pottery and far-flung voyages, appeared throughout the western Pacific about this time. Its representatives were survivors of the natural disaster that destroyed Mu.

Although their plight is currently being verified by archaeologists and geologists, it has been known to half the native peoples of the world for millennia. As Oppenheimer notes, "Stories of a civilization-destroying catastrophe are older than writing." He cites the work of Stith Thompson, the renowned American folklorist, who categorized a "World Fire" as part of Pacific myths recounting a global calamity. For example, the pre-Buddhist Tibetans told of a time

> once in the past, in the first time cycle, when all living beings, from the peak of existence down to the depths of the hells, were about to be destroyed and annihilated. Standing upright on the peak of the seven gold mountains, Kunzang At Muwer brandished a flaming gold stone as big as a wild yak. And, twirling it in space, hurled it unto the Earth. It fell into the outer ocean [the Pacific], and the immense sea boiled and contracted. The four continents and the minor ones caught fire from the borders, and Mount Meru [the *axis mundi,* or sacred center of the world] was about to collapse. Then the deities and the demons of the nine dimensions trembled with fear, fainted and were paralyzed.

A people who never knew the written word, yet preserved a vivid knowledge of the Lemurian catastrophe, are the Australian Bushmen. They tell of Mu-Mu-Na, the flaming rainbow serpent, also known as Mu-It, that fell from heaven to cause a world flood. When recounting the story, even today, Australoid speakers swing a bull-roarer named after their mythic rendering of the deluge-inducing comet, because it imitates the fearsome sound produced by the falling rainbow-serpent. Their narrations often include descriptions of an ancestral paradise before it sank beneath the sea, remembered as Baralku.

In verification of its historical validity, the lost homeland was similarly recalled by Fiji Islanders as Burotu, and as Buloto in distant Samoa and Tonga. It is here that oral tradition claims that the 105 tons of coral limestone used for the monumental arch called the Burden of Maui, described in chapter 4, was ferried by survivors from Burotu. The Tonga islanders believe Buloto was destroyed when the "heavens fell down" and fire married water to produce the Samoan islands. The Fiji Burotu may be philologically related to Rutas, another name by which Mu was known in Asia. In Melanesian tradition, Makonaima was the last king of Burotu before it sank beneath the Pacific Ocean. He was said to have been a leader among the Vue, an extinct race of fair-haired foreigners who passed through Melanesia in the wake of a cataclysmic flood. Described as the possessors of powerful mana, or magic energy, the Vue are believed to have built the megalithic structures scattered throughout the Pacific islands.

According to the Tanimbar Austronesian people of southeast Maluku, Atuf separated the Lesser Sundras from Borneo with his spear while fleeing eastward with his royal family from a ferocious cataclysm that annihilated their distant homeland. These events supposedly took place at a time when the whole Earth was unstable.

References to the death of the Motherland are known throughout New Guinea. The Ne-Mu are characterized by the Kai tribal peoples as having been much taller and stronger than today's humans and are said to have ruled the world before the Great Deluge. They introduced agriculture and house building to Kai ancestors. When the flood came, all the Ne-Mu were killed, but their bodies turned into great blocks of stone. This final feature of the myth betrays the Kai's reaction to megalithic structures found occasionally in New Guinea, often composed of prodigious stonework they identify with the preflood Ne-Mu. The Nages, a New Guinean tribe residing in the highlands of Flores, tell

of Dooy, their light-skinned, red-haired forefather. He alone survived
the Great Flood that drowned his distant kingdom. Arriving in a large
boat, he had many wives among the native women. They presented
him with a large number of children, who became the Nages. When he
died peacefully in extreme old age, Dooy's body was laid to rest under
a stone platform at the center of a public square in the tribal capital of
Boa Wai. His grave is the focal point of an annual harvest festival still
celebrated by the Nages. During the ceremonies, a tribal chief wears
headgear fashioned to resemble a golden seven-masted ship, a model
of the same vessel in which Dooy escaped the inundation of his Pacific
island kingdom.

According to the British writer Chris Ogilvie-Herald, "Even in the
mountains of Tibet there survives a tradition of a cataclysm that flooded
the highlands, and comets that caused great upheavals."

A particularly graphic portrayal of the Lemurian catastrophe is
found among the Shans, a tribal people inhabiting northeastern Burma
(Myanmar). Offended by the immorality of his human creations, Ling-
lawn, god of the sky, dispatched lesser deities to punish humankind.
"They sent forth a great conflagration," his myth tells us, "scattering
their fire everywhere. It swept over the Earth, and smoke ascended in
clouds to heaven." His wrath appeased, Ling-lawn extinguished the
burning world in a universal flood that killed off all living things, except
a man and woman provisioned with a bag of seeds. The couple survived
Ling-lawn's deluge in a boat, and from this husband and wife the world
was repopulated and replanted.

Another pair of seaborne heroes were said to have built the strange
Micronesian city of Nan Madol on the Micronesian island of Pohnpei, described in chapter 1. The twin sorcerers allegedly came from a
splendid kingdom thereafter destroyed by falling stars and earthquakes.
These forces sank Kanamwayso to the bottom of the sea, where it is
inhabited by the spirits of those who perished in the cataclysm, and who
still preside over the ghosts of all individuals who subsequently drowned
at sea. This same sunken realm is known throughout Polynesia by its
more obvious name, Mu-ri-wai-o-ata.

Nan Madol was built to save the Lemurian breadbasket of the Philippines from typhoons, and it is here, in the mountainous central region of Mindanao, that the Ata natives tell how the Great Flood "covered the whole Earth. All were drowned except for two men and a woman. The waters carried them far away." The Ata still claim descent from these light-skinned survivors, whose children intermarried with the Negritos and aboriginal peoples.

Thousands of miles to the east, on the opposite side of the Pacific Ocean, Maya residing along the western coastal regions of Mexico, at the ceremonial center of Monte Alban, told the late-nineteenth-century archaeologist Augustus Le Plongeon that Homen, the god of cataclysms, brought a former world to an end: "By his strong will, Homen caused the Earth to tremble after sunset; and during the night, Mu, the country of the hills of mud, was submerged. Twice Mu jumped from its foundations. It was then sacrificed with fire." Not coincidentally, some of the Monte Alban pyramidal structures, with their twin pylons, bear a discernibly close resemblance to the terraced formation found underwater off the shores of Japan's Yonaguni Island.

The Klamath Indians of south-central Oregon and northern California believe that Kmukamtch, a shining demon from the sky, endeavored to destroy the Earth with his celestial flame, followed by a worldwide deluge. This self-evident reference to the comet that destroyed Lemuria is underscored by the appearance of the Motherland's name in Kmukamtch. To another California tribe, the Modoc, Kmukamtch means, literally, the "ancient old man from Mu," the creator of humankind. According to California's Ute Indians, "The sun was shivered into a thousand fragments, which fell to Earth causing a general conflagration." Their name for this celestial explosion was Ta-wats, who ravaged the world "until at last, swollen with heat, the eyes of the god burst, and the tears gushed forth in a flood which spread over the Earth and extinguished the fire."

The cometary theme recurs in the creator deity of the Sinkaietk, or Southern Okanagon Indians, in Washington state. Angered by the ingratitude of their ancestors, Qoluncotun hurled a star at the Earth, which

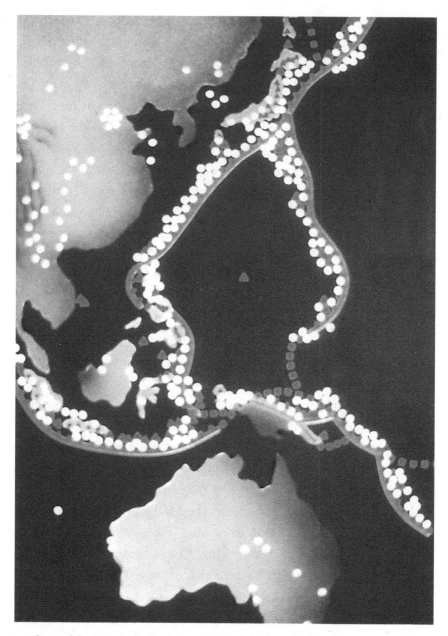

Outlines of the lost Motherland are defined by dots signifying volcanoes along earth-quake fault lines in this map from the Milwaukee Public Museum.

burst into flames. Just before the entire planet was reduced to ashes, he extinguished the conflagration by pushing "a great land" beneath the sea, making it overflow into a world flood. From its few survivors, he refashioned humankind into various tribes.

Mythographer William Alexander cited horrific imagery describing an ancestral cataclysm preserved by the Haida, Tlingit, and G'tskan peoples of coastal British Columbia. They recall a flaming monster that fell from the sky with "a whistle in his mouth. As he moved forward, he blew it with all his might, and made a terrible noise. He came flowing and blowing. He looked like an enormous bat with wings spread." Like China's horizon-spanning K'ung-Kung, the monster's fiery feathers "grew til they could touch the sky in both sides." After it crashed into the world, there was "nothing but waves of flames. Rocks were burning, the ground was burning, everything was burning. Great rolls and piles of smoke were rising. Fire flew up toward the sky in flames, in great sparks and brands. The great fire was blazing, roaring all over the Earth, burning rocks, trees, people, burning everything. Water rushed in. It rushed in like a crowd of rivers, covered the Earth, and put out the fire, as it rolled on toward the south. Water rose mountain high."

Ntlakapamuk Indians in British Columbia's Thompson River area likewise speak of a time when the Earth was consumed by a fire so universal that only a worldwide flood succeeded in extinguishing it. Farther north, Alaska's Cree Indians of the sub-Arctic Circle preserve traditions of a catastrophic deluge that destroyed most of the world long ago. Wesucechak was a shape-shifting shaman who escaped the catastrophe he caused when he got into a fight with water monsters that murdered his brother, Misapos. Aleut Indians of the Aleutian Archipelago revere the memory of Iraghdadakh—literally, "the old man"—who repopulated the world after it had been overflowed by the sea.

Shared universal accounts among widely diverse peoples around the Pacific Rim commonly describe a ferocious comet that long ago caused their ancestral center to disappear beneath the middle of the ocean. As already touched on, traditions among inhabitants of this exceptionally broad region where the event supposedly occurred likewise spoke of Oceania's own Ekpyrosis. In the Easter Island version, Hiva, Hotu Matua's vast homeland, sank under a combined earthquake and meteor assault. Samoans tell how the "heavens fell" on Hiva, setting it afire and pushing it beneath the waves: "Then arose a terrible odor. The odor became smoke, which changed into great, black clouds. The sea rose suddenly, and, in a stupendous catastrophe of nature, the land sank into the sea." To Tahitians, the sky god, Tagaroa, was so angry with humans for their disobedience to his will that he "overturned the world into the water," drowning everything except a few mountain peaks rising above the surface. Like Easter Island's rendition, which related that an eerie calm preceded the disaster, the Tahitian myth recounts how "the wind also died away, and when all was calm, the stones and the trees began to fall from the heavens."

Natives of the Sandwich Islands described the Tai-a-kahina'rii, or "Sea of Kahina'rii," which inundated their place of origin after it was incinerated by the celestial Ta-poha-i-tahi-ora, as an "explosion in the place of life."

Mangaia Island's leading culture hero, Ngaru, unleashed a flood so powerful that it extinguished the fires of hell. His story and the Lemurian name of the lost homeland are preserved in a popular creation chant, the Dirge for Vera: "Alas, the death-knell of Mueu is beating! How desolate is our home! The band of Vera shall safely reach their home beneath the glowing tide."

New Zealand's Maori tell of a priest who prayed for salvation from a great celestial flame that threatened to incinerate the world when it was still new. His prayers were answered with a colossal flood that quenched all the fires but wiped out a once-splendid kingdom, killing most of its inhabitants.

A lengthy account of the cataclysm occurs in the Marquesan *Te-Tai-Toko*, or Chant of the Deluge. It begins:

O, Mutu-hei was a spirit pervading and vast. The Lord Ocean was going to pass over the whole dry land *[A taha ta te Mu oa]*. Here is confusion among the generations of animals. Sounding excitedly is the voice of the birds. Creaking is the voice of the trees in the forest. Unstable are the heavens. Bursting forth is the voice of the thunder [Ono]. Striking are the lightning-bolts. Shaking the world is the earthquake. Coming is the dark cloud and the rainbow. Wildly comes the rain and the wind. Whirlwinds sweep over the Earth. Rocks roll down into the ravines. The red mountain-streams [of molten lava] are rushing to the sea. Here the waterspouts. Tumbled about are the clustering clouds of heaven. Greatly revered be the voice [Ono] of my god in the sky.

The tabu of Lono [the fair-haired flood-hero] has passed to Kahiki [Lemuria]. It has passed thither and overthrown the tabu [against harming Lemuria] of Kahai. The tabu of Kahai [the god of natural disasters] has been sacrificed on the altar [of destruction]. It has fallen and tumbled into confusion. The flood is roaring, and it will fall over the valleys, pass over the plains. It will bury the mountains, and envelop the hill-sides. Dead are the fish, fallen in their flight; fallen, disfigured, all through Kahiki.

The flood is roaring. God wills it. Noise, god, noise *[Mu Etua mu]*. Here is manifest trouble. Shaken and mixed up is the Earth. Moving are the gills, the fins and the head of the Earth. My god has assumed the shape of a shark. O, the god of destruction! Turned is the bosom of my god to the sky, turned and treading on Kahiki. Doomed is the image of Lono to destruction. Standing, it falls to the foundation of the land. Cracking is the voice of the thunder, cracking inside the shining black cloud. Whirling up is the dust in the sky.

Who would have thought that the great Earth could be buried under a roaring flood? Fallen has Makakulukahi [an ancestral holy place]. Broken are the Kamahele branches of the god. Shattered is the brittle stone [temples]. Strewn are the pieces in Haehae [a sacred center]. Ono [thunder] ruled the sound, and broke up Mutu-hei. The land which I enjoyed and rejected and forsook, it has gone before. It is forgotten. It has gone, both back and front.

Although Lemuria suffered a series of natural catastrophes, the foregoing traditions describe the 1628 B.C. cataclysm that finally destroyed it. They not only complement the scientific evidence for such a climactic event, but also bring this moment back to life in language as graphic as it is imperishable.

The Great Flood that destroyed the Pacific Motherland, as dramatized in the temple murals of Thailand's important spiritual center, the Wat Phra Keo, Bangkok.

THIRTEEN

The Discovery of
Lemuria

Their architectural remains, so far from being the
wreck of legend, even now litter the abysses of the sea,
awaiting discovery by processes of archaeology as yet
unguessed.

LEWIS SPENCE, 1924

In 1971, a research vessel for Decca Survey out of Houston, Texas, was plunging through the high swells of the Pacific Ocean about fifty-five miles off Peru, parallel to the coastal city of Callao. On board was Thomas Vanderveer, a young navigator whose job was to operate his remotely controlled television camera with external lamps mounted on an underwater sled played out behind the ship by several thousand feet of cable. He and his mates were searching for oil seepage from the ocean floor with bottom-profiling instruments, including side-scan sonar, which transformed echoes bouncing off hard features on the ocean bottom into electronic images.

Vanderveer's television was equipped with an early video camera that recorded everything it detected on a tape reel. Between 6,000 and 9,000 feet down, with the vessel cruising at three or four knots, it detected nothing but a flat wasteland of sand and mud. After several long hours of uneventful observation, the camera revealed a steep formation that rose too fast for Vanderveer to maneuver the sled out of harm's way. "All of a sudden, we got a real fast rise," he recalled, "and I couldn't get the sled up fast enough, because the ship was doing about three or four knots; we had a lot of cable out. As the sled was coming up over the rise, it hit ground and then tumbled. But as it recovered, we saw buildings like something you'd see at Chichen Itza, with columns along the front, about the same size; rectangular buildings."

Vanderveer's monitor suddenly filled with the ghostly form of a large edifice standing apparently intact under several thousand feet of water. The lamps of the sled illuminated a pale structure, making it resemble the Maya's Temple of the Warriors in Yucatán. Significantly, it is also known as Kukulcan's Temple of a Thousand Columns. Kukulcan, or the Plumed Serpent, was the title of the Maya's fair-haired, light-skinned founding father, who arrived from over the sea in the ancient past, bearing all the gifts of the high civilization he left behind.

Vanderveer's camera quickly passed over two or three other similarly monumental buildings nearby, then revealed nothing more but typical ocean bottom. The chance encounter had lasted less than one minute. In all the excitement of its surprise discovery, however, bearings were neglected and positioning forgotten, frustrating repeated attempts to relocate the sunken city. But the videotapes had faithfully recorded the sighting. Renewed viewing convinced Vanderveer and his shipmates that the structures were not only artificial, but very similar in design to Mesoamerican architecture as well.

Their unintentional find had been preceded by another oceanographic vessel, the R.V. *Anton Bruun,* on October 29, 1965. While its crew took bottom core samples and collected specimens of small mollusks along the same stretch of Peruvian coast at a similar depth as the Decca Survey ship in the Milne-Edwards Deep off the Peru–Chile Trench system, their underwater cameras automatically clicked off a photographic survey of the sea floor. Only hours later, after dozens of individual shots were being developed and cataloged, did the researchers notice a very peculiar image among them.

The official report for the *Anton Bruun's* eleventh cruise reads:

Off Callao at a depth of two thousand meters (Sta. 158) some exceptionally interesting photographs were obtained. Figure 11 shows two columnar structures projecting from the sediments. These were represented in only one exposure out of the seventy five to eighty that were taken at this station. This station was re-occupied in an attempt to obtain more clues regarding the origin of the structures. One exposure showed a block-like rock similarly exposed on the surface of the sediments and another showed what is possibly another buried columnar structure. It is tempting to suggest that these represent evidence of submerged man-made structures. The apparent "inscriptions" on the columns is suggestive as is also their upright condition. The absence of typical submerged rock exposure is further suggestive that these photographs have recorded more than just sedimentary rock exposures. The possibility certainly exists, even if the possibility is low, that these photographs do show evidence of submerged man-made structures. Whether they were dropped into the sea or gradually submerged remains to be determined.

In the opinion of geologist William Hutton, a former director of U.S. government-funded geoscience research programs, the structures "certainly look more like man-made columns than natural rock formations on the sea-floor." The photos showed groups of stone pillars protruding some five feet above the mud. Others had fallen over, but all were about two feet in diameter, and none stood perfectly upright, but often leaned at a common angle. As the report noted, at least one of the standing columns was inscribed with an apparent glyph unlike any written language with which archaeologists were familiar. A caption beneath one of the submerged images reads, "Photograph of the bottom at 2000 meters showing two columnar structures projecting from the sediments. Note the inscription resembling the figure 9."

The Decca Survey and *Anton Bruun* discoveries opposite the Peruvian city of Callao were long preceded by an interesting parallel on land. "In 1576," William Donato wrote for *Ancient American,* "when sailing out of his course between Callao and Valparaiso, Juan Fernandez encountered what he thought was the coast of a great southern continent. He claimed to have seen 'the mouths of very large rivers . . . and people so white and so well clad and in everything different from those of Chile and Peru.'" Some investigators wonder if a final remnant of Lemuria could have possibly persisted as late as the sixteenth century, before it was at last engulfed by a powerful earthquake known to have shaken much of South America's Pacific coast shortly after Fernandez's sighting. In any case, the *Anton Bruun*'s oceanographers did not find any sunken buildings, although their photographs of stone pillars in the same vicinity and at the same approximate depth as Vanderveer's discovery of column-fronted structures suggest that both ships visited the same area of ocean. Moreover, the Milne-Edwards columns do bear at least some resemblance to the Chichen Itza Temple of the Warriors he used as a comparison. Dr. Robert J. Menzies, Cruise 11's chief scientist, told reporters, "Although the idea of a sunken city in the Pacific seems incredible, the evidence so far suggests one of the most exciting discoveries of the century."

The evidence suggests something else as well. Vanderveer and Menzies each made his find at roughly 6,000 feet. This is also the average depth of unusual submarine volcanoes known as guyots. These underwater mesas are unusual for their almost perfectly flat tops, typically six miles in diameter, which were formed by wave action when they stood at the surface of the ocean, as proved by fossil corals found at many guyots. Coral cannot live below 450 feet, so they must have formed when the sunken mountaintop was still at sea level. Ripple patterns commonly observed at the summits were made by millennia of waves brushing the uppermost section of the volcanoes before they were engulfed. About 160 guyots have been identified in the Pacific basin between Hawaii and the Marianas, occupying more than a million square miles of ocean floor. Remarkably, many of them appearing in groups or clusters have identical elevations. It would appear they together experienced a process or event responsible for their inundation. Are these guyots—or, at any rate, those at a common level—the former lands of Mu? Buildings and pillars found off Peru at the same depth imply as much.

A guyot approximately 270 miles off the coast of Washington state has, in fact, yielded physical evidence of a sunken civilization. Discovered in 1950, the Cobb Seamount is part of a chain of sunken mountains extending into the Gulf of Alaska. Relatively easy exploration of its twenty-three-square-acre flat top has been afforded by comparatively shallow 120-foot depths, making it one of the most thoroughly studied guyots in the Pacific Ocean, and, in the words of David Hatcher Childress, "a star program of the University of Washington for years." He cites a September 10, 1987, issue of the *Seattle Times,* which described man-made artifacts retrieved from the Cobb Seamount. They included pottery dated to 18,000 Y.B.P. and the mummified remains of porpoises and whales. Little more has been published about these finds since they were made, probably because they contradict academic doctrine purporting that North America was uninhabited until just 13,000 years ago. In any case, evidence for human occupation of the Cobb Seamount suggests that Lemuria was more of a culture and a people than a specific territory, one that spread across the Pacific from coastal America to Japan on numerous islands, some of them now under water.

Another discovery made under the ice might have defined the northernmost limits of that antediluvian culture. In 1938, American archaeologists Magnus Marks and Froelich Rainy began surveying the outlines of what they assumed was a typical Eskimo community, at most 500 years old, as dimly suggested in the permafrost of Ipiutak in northern Alaska. Into their third season, however, they noticed the outlines expanded far beyond the limitations of a tribal fishing community. To their astonishment, they could discern not a primitive village, but instead an urban center of long boulevards flanked by square foundations spreading east and west along the northern shore of Point Hope. The larger square structures had been regularly arranged along five main avenues and down shorter cross-blocks, where smaller structures, suggesting houses, stood at right angles to the thoroughfares. Here was city planning, not a primitive village.

More than 600 buildings were surveyed, and at least another 200 identified within an archaeological zone almost one mile long and somewhat less than a quarter-mile wide, although these were not the actual city limits, which were never precisely determined. Marks estimated an original population in excess of 4,000 residents, larger by far than anything known to the Eskimos, who, in any case, never built such structures or laid out an urban center. Of the twenty-three buildings excavated in June 1940, no artifacts resembled local native crafts. "One of the most striking features of the Ipiutak material," Rainey observed for the prestigious *Natural History* magazine, "is the elaborate and sophisticated carving and the beautiful workmanship, which would not be expected in a primitive, proto-Eskimo culture ancestral to the modern." Researcher Rene Noorbergen added that the inhabitants "had a knowledge of mathematics and astronomy comparable to that of the ancient Maya."

Ipiutak is located 130 miles north of the Arctic Circle, where ferocious temperatures blasted by windstorms make it today one of the most desolate and uninhabitable places on Earth. Yet it was not always so. Geologists calibrating the depth at which the ruins were found dated their origins to 30,000 or 40,000 years ago, the last time Point Hope was temperate enough to allow the establishment of such a population center. Archaeologists convinced the first cities were built in Mesopotamia around 3500 B.C. recoiled at such contrary evidence. Yet this period corresponds to drastically lowered sea levels that allowed the populating of new landmasses such as Australia. More relevant to our investigation, the Naacal tablets that Colonel Churchward examined in India stated that civilization first arose on Mu about this time.

Lemurian identity for the ancient townspeople was further indicated by a spiral composed of two elements carved in the round, a preferred artistic design found on Ipiutak artifacts. It is encountered nowhere else in America, but it can be traced to, of all peoples, the Ainu, whose transoceanic voyages to Ecuador were discussed in chapter 9. Their Caucasoid connection to the Point Hope site reappeared in a cemetery excavated by Marks and Rainy. The human remains they unearthed belonged to individuals taller and more slender than the indigenous inhabitants, with cranial details similar to contemporary Cro-Magnon skulls. They also had blond hair. According to F. S. Pettyjohn in *Ancient American* magazine, "Some scientists remark on the resemblance of this vanished people to the Ainu." His article features the photograph of a red-haired mummy belonging to the prehistoric Alaskans, "one of perhaps thousands unearthed over the course of nearly three hundred years. The Eskimo, who over-ran the entire Catherine Archipelago from the Alaskan mainland, intermarried with the original inhabitants, and inherited much of their physical characteristics, as well as their culture, to become the historic Aleut, very few of whom still exist. . . . There were still a few members of this mysterious race surviving on the Northern Kurile Islands when the Russians arrived in 1741."

He writes that these Caucasian inhabitants

> hunted in the sea for subsistence, practiced mummification of the dead, operated a decimal system that could tabulate up to one hundred thousand, and used a twelve-month calendar. They had a working knowledge of astronomy and anatomy, human and animal, setting simple fractures and performing operations, one in particular being the removal of eye abscesses. Experts at sea, they were fearless in their pursuit of whales, walrus, sea-cows, sea-lions and seals. Combustible sulfur was used to start fires, with sparks being struck from rocks containing pyrite. They also mined copper and iron sulfides, oxides, synite, slate, sandstone, pumice, greenstone and many other minerals, which they used as paint for their lamps, dishes, tables, tools and weapons.

Recalling the Lemurians' Micronesian weather-control station at Nan Madol, Pettyjohn writes, "They had the world's first weather bureau: After a hunter grew too old to pursue the chase, he was often trained in the art of weather forecasting. Atmospheric pressure, air density, wind velocity and temperatures were used along with centuries of observation of local weather conditions to enable the observers to render competent daily forecasts."

Despite the depredations of religious fanatics and the indifference of conventional scholars, physical evidence of the ancient Alaskans still exists. As Pettyjohn remarks, "The Smithsonian Institution, in Washington, D.C., is the only official repository for the few remaining Alaskan mummies. Large numbers of them were burned by early Christian missionaries jealous of all forms of 'paganism'. But there are doubtless many more yet to be unearthed in the frozen northlands. Perhaps enough will be found in future excavations to determine once and for all the identity of this fair-haired people who long ago dominated what has since become the largest state in the Union." They were almost certainly the same Caucasians who built the metropolis at Ipiutak, with its Lemurian implications, which may be found in the Eskimo name for Alaskan's ancient inhabitants: the Ta-iagu-*mu*it.

These suspicions were supported by Marilyn Jesmain, writing for the same *Ancient American* issue in which Pettyjohn's article appeared.

On-going research at an ancient rock art site in Alaska appears to preserve the visually symbolic record of a world-class natural catastrophe. The project area of investigation is located atop a mountain in the central portion of the Tongass National Forest, in a southwestern section of the state. Two sites, King's Mill Mountain on Kupreanof Island and Devil's Thumb on the mainland east of Petersburg, suggest that early humans sought refuge in this area during a period of extreme high water. Southwest Alaska consists of a narrow strip of mainland coast and hundreds of islands known as the Alexander Archipelago. It was the maximum westward extent of Late Wisconsin glaciation [25,000 to 10,000 Years Before Present]. The Holocene [current geologic epoch] shorelines at the close of the Pleistocene [last ice age] stabilized near their modern positions in an area now referred to as the Tongass National Forest. Recent evidence indicates that a catastrophic dissolution of the Cordilleran ice sheet happened approximately sixteen thousand years ago.

The petroglyphs she reproduces depict possible representations of a comet and people fleeing in a large boat. Included is the spiral motif prominent among the adorned artifacts of Ipiutak.

As part of her research, Jesmain visited the indigenous village of Kake, where she learned about local deluge traditions from a native elder. "Although Kake is Tlingit," she writes, "the Haidas, Bella Colla, Tsimshian, and other, modern coastal tribes are new-comers to the area [5,000 Y.B.P. +/–]. Since they are linguistically related to the interior Athabaskan, they probably arrived from the inland via various rivers that cut through the coastal range. But the Tlingit speak of an earlier people living in the vicinity when they arrived. What became of those original residents in unknown. Their story of a terrible deluge that destroyed them but made way for the tribes which today inhabit Alaska may be contained in the rock art of King's Mill Mountain."

The Arctic city beneath the ice is perhaps the oldest metropolis in the world. Even so, every indication argues that all the building skills and urban planning that went into its construction manifested themselves in full bloom, as though imported from a society already long acquainted with urban development. Nothing at Ipiutak suggests local evolution of the standardized measurements, large-scale division of labor, or surveying technology. Since these civilized arts seem to have been imported by a people racially dissimilar from the native population, we may infer that the only conceivable candidate for such an outside source was the lost Motherland richly described in the oral traditions of numerous cultures around the Pacific Rim.

A paradigm-busting find announced in November 2004 showed that the Ipiutak civilizers were not alone on the continent, when the Topper site was found by Albert Goodyear from the University of South Carolina's Archaeology and Anthropology Department. Contemporary with the Arctic city under the ice, "Topper is the oldest radio-carbon-dated site in North America," he said. Goodyear made his announcement only after beginning excavations in the 1980s. He would not have achieved his discovery even then had he followed established procedure. Mainstream archaeologists do not probe beneath the Earth's surface for evidence of early humans in America any deeper than levels corresponding to 13,000 Y.B.P., because they refuse to believe humans arrived here any earlier.

Going four meters deeper than his conventional colleagues, Good-year found hundreds of tools made from locally obtained chert. The flintlike stone chisels and scrapers were used to skin hides, butcher meat, or carve antlers, wood, and ivory. He speculated that the area's mild climate 50,000 years ago and abundant natural resources made it the ideal setting for an active society. Indeed, the large number of stone implements and their variety of purpose recovered from Topper suggests a populous community of craftspeople who had already attained a hierarchy of skills. And their presence on a major river in South Carolina, far from the alleged migration of Mongolians across a theoretical land-bridge from Siberia, implies arrival by boat. Although establishment scholars absolutely reject any evidence of Paleolithic maritime skills, especially for ancient Americans, *Scientist* magazine's Marsha Walton and Michael Coren wrote in their coverage of Goodyear's and similar finds, "These discoveries are leading archaeologists to support alternative theories—such as settlement by sea—for the Americas."

As Marks and Rainey began their excavations in the Far North, an American explorer well known in his own time, Harold T. Wilkins, met "a haciendo (Munoz) who owns an estate on the seashore not far from Guayaquil, Ecuador, close to a place called Esmeraldas. He sent a diver to fish up statuettes from a drowned and very ancient city lying underwater just off the shore." Munoz told him some of the artifacts were covered with hieroglyphs no less inscrutable than the single example photographed decades later by researchers aboard the *Anton Bruun.* His divers supposedly found "ancient convex lenses under water there, and also reflectors. They were made of obsidian. . . . They [the former inhabitants of the sunken city] must have been scientific opticians, even astronomers."

Wilkins was deeply impressed by the haciendo's collection, which he was allowed to examine personally. He concluded:

The artifacts of this unknown nation, whose city is beneath the sea off Ecuador's shores, are singular. Besides fine obsidian mirrors, carved like lenses in a way to suggest that the race had a knowledge of optics, there are queer, oblong-shaped prisms, on whose facets are carved animals, hieroglyphs or symbols. They may have served the same purpose as the *chop* or personal seals which every Chinese mandarin used formerly to affix to documents, which were not legal without such a seal. . . . An imaginative man or woman might, therefore, have some warrant for theorizing that the queer remnants of old races who met in out-of-the-way or dangerous regions of this continent were survivors from some post-paleolithic, or antediluvian age of the world's history.

Because these artifacts were not retrieved by university-trained specialists under scientifically controlled conditions, mainstream archaeologists dismissed the haciendo's finds as worthless. Yet they may be revealing pieces of the Lemurian puzzle. The optics indicated by the items are in keeping with the Motherland's high technology. More immediately relevant, Wilkins reported that the statues brought up from the waters off Guayaquil appeared to portray Japanese faces. Jomon pottery finds, as described in the previous chapter, were discovered in Valdivia, Ecuador, twenty years after he saw the Munoz collection.

Another, although quite different, undersea location has been found more than 3,500 miles southeast of Palau, at Fiji. A cave, its walls covered with rock art and apparent inscriptions, lies in twenty feet of water at Yasawa-i-Lau. The last time ocean levels were that low was around 1600 B.C., just when Lemuria suffered her final destruction.

Fiji tradition does, in fact, describe such a cataclysm, remembered as the Ualuvu, or Great Flood, that overwhelmed a former kingdom known as Nakauvadra, yet another name for the drowned Motherland. Survivors of the Ualuvu were said to have settled throughout the islands to become their first inhabitants. The small island of Koro was entirely dedicated to memorializing the Great Flood and lent its name to the Fiji deluge-chant, the annually performed Ngginggi-tangithi-Koro, because Koro was another name for the sunken Motherland. Fornander wrote that the Ngginggi-tangithi-Koro "conveys the idea of a little bird (the Qiqui) sitting there (atop Koro's highest point) and lamenting the

302 The Discovery of Lemuria

drowned island. I have heard a native chant, *Na qiqi sa tagici Koro ni yali*—'The *qiqui* laments over Koro, because it is lost.'"

Complementing the Ngginggi-tangithi-Koro are outsized structures found on Rotuma. They were described for the *Royal Anthropological Institute Journal* by W. W. Wood, who visited the remote Fiji island in the 1870s. "The megalithic monuments on the principal island were not far from the beach," he wrote, and were

> composed of masses so large that it was difficult to conceive the means by which the natives had been able to arrange and move them. The tombs consisted of a low platform of earth enclosed by slabs of stone set vertically, and in the centre of one or more huge stones of irregular shape—mere masses of rock—some of which must weigh many tons. The remarkable point was that these simple people should, without the aid of machinery, have been able to raise and arrange these great masses of rock. The natives [of Rotuma] are of a different race and lighter colour than those of Fiji's *[sic]*.

This suggests past admixture with foreigners, perhaps the megalith-builders. Childress doubts the structures were actually tombs, as Woods presumed, and speculates that they were "meant for some other purpose."

The fabled giants who allegedly built these "tombs" after the Ualuvu stepped from legend into reality as recently as 2002, when the skeleton of an exceptionally tall man was exhumed on Fiji. University of the South Pacific radiocarbon testing of baked-clay grave goods, mostly pottery, found with the burial site yielded a date 3,000 Y.B.P. In life, the man stood six feet, four inches, far above the average height of Fiji natives in the second millennium B.C. or now. "Officials wanted to keep the strange discovery a secret," reported *The Times of India*, "but that hope quickly disappeared, as word of the discovery spread."

The find proved something of an embarrassment to conventional anthropologists, because the skeleton belonged to a Caucasian individual, one of the lost white race of the Pacific recounted in folk traditions throughout Oceania—from New Guinea to the Alaskan Islands. The date of his interment more than thirty centuries ago does roughly correspond to the final destruction of Mu, in 1628 B.C., although he may have been a Lemurian who lived 600 years after that event, unless further dating is unable to push him back before 1000 B.C. In any case, discovery of the skeleton is yet another validation of myth as verifiable history, lending additional credibility to native Fiji accounts of the Great Flood.

By far the most dramatic underwater discovery of its kind during the twentieth century was made in Okinawa Prefecture by a local dive-master on the south shore of Yonaguni, Japan's westernmost territory, at the end of the Ryukyu chain of islands extending south from Honshu. The fewer than 2,000 inhabitants of the six-mile-long, almond-shaped island make their living from farming, fishing, and tourism. It was to encourage the latter industry that Kihachiro Aratake was exploring the crystal-clear seas approximately 300 feet off Arakawa-bana in 1985, when he stumbled on more than he had bargained for. Standing under seventy-five feet of water was what seemed to be a flat-topped stone pyramid. Nearly eighty feet high, its uppermost part rose about three feet above the waves. Impressed by what he believed was a man-made structure of deep antiquity, he began referring to the location as Iseki Point, or place of the ruins.

News of Aratake's find spread rapidly throughout Japan, attracting scuba-diving enthusiasts from all over the country, despite strong local currents and schools of hammerheads patrolling the shores of Yonaguni. The sharks represent the first of many enigmas associated with the sunken structure, because they congregate en masse at very few other locations in the world's oceans. What instinctual impulse or behavioral memory prompts them to select this particular spot no one knows.

Most observers were impressed by the subsurface feature's man-made appearance, although skeptical archaeologists, relying only on hearsay and amateur photography, dismissed it as a natural, if unusual, formation. Those who should know better—professional geologists—were not quite so certain, however. One of the best, marine seismologist Masaaki

Kimura, led his students in a professional survey of the underwater structure to determine its real identity. "After a preliminary investigation in
1992," he said, "the University of the Ryukyus has been conducting a
consistent, continuous program of research [at Yonaguni's submerged
site]. In 2000, we made measurements using lasers, multinarrow beams,
airplanes and Be-10 [sonar]. It (the survey team) consists of instructors at
the University of the Ryukyus and students."

With no preconceived notions of any sunken civilization, the physical evidence the team members accumulated gradually persuaded them
of the subsurface enigma's artificial character. When Professor Kimura's
conclusions were finally published, the meticulous presentation of his
scientific proof persuaded a large majority of his critical colleagues that
the thing off Iseki Point was indeed a monument fashioned by human
hands.

A fellow geologist who was not entirely convinced flew in from the
United States to examine it for himself in September 1997, returning
the following summer for additional dives. Dr. Robert M. Schoch is an
associate professor of science and mathematics at Boston University's
College of General Studies. Earlier in the decade, he became internationally known for demonstrating that the telltale marks of water erosion on
Egypt's Great Sphinx dated its oldest sections to circa 5000 B.C., some
2,400 years earlier than mainstream archaeologists claimed and about
twenty centuries before the official beginning of dynastic Egypt itself.
Having already bucked the academic establishment, he seemed open-
minded enough to pass professional judgment on Yonaguni's underwater
mystery with welcome impartiality. At first sight, according to Schoch,
"the submarine cliff appeared to be cut in a series of immense, geometric
terraces, their surfaces broad and flat, separated by sheer, vertical stone
risers." They looked like impossibly huge steps in a titanic staircase only
a giant could climb.

On closer examination, Schoch noticed that the entire structure was
composed mostly of medium to very fine mud-stone and sandstone, with
clearly defined bedding planes crisscrossed by parallel joints and fractures; they made natural formations seem artificial. Back on Yonaguni,

exposed sandstone outcroppings along the southeastern and northeastern coasts bore a striking resemblance to the pyramidal structure under water. "The more I compared the natural, but highly regular weathering and erosional features observed on the modern coast of the island with the morphological characteristics of the Yonaguni Monument," he explained in *Pre-Columbiana,* "the more I became convinced that the Yonaguni Monument is primarily the result of geological and geomorphological processes at work."

His conclusion seemed to contradict Professor Kimura's assessment of the sunken feature as artificial, but really defined it more clearly. "We should also consider the possibility," Dr. Schoch stated, "that the Yonaguni Monument is fundamentally a natural structure that has been enhanced or slightly modified by humans in ancient times." In other words, the prehistoric islanders may have cut and shaped an outcropping of rock into a citadel, temple, quarry, or cultural center of some kind. If so, their transformation of a preexisting form was entirely in keeping with ancient, ongoing East Asian traditions of subtle alterations in natural surroundings as exemplified in Zen gardening, ritual Japanese landscaping, and Chinese feng shui. These terraforming practices, aimed at establishing a harmonic relationship between humans and the environment, could stem from the construction technique apparent at the Yonaguni Monument; they are certainly rooted in Lemurian nature worship.

While Dr. Schoch was willing to concede the possibility of human influences on the structure, he was not convinced they had actually been at work. Professor Kimura agreed that it had been "carved out of an entire knoll or rocky outcrop," hewn from the solid bedrock at a time long past when it stood as dry land above a lower sea level. But he felt sure the numerous surveying studies and physical proof his teams collected during nearly ten years of research unquestionably established its artificial nature. Among the most persuasive pieces of evidence were ancient hand tools recovered not only from the island but at the structure itself as well. Known throughout the Ryukyus as *kusabi,* the tools were made from an igneous rock that is not found on Yonaguni, so it must have been imported specifically for cutting and modifying the softer sandstone formation from which the Yonaguni Monument was fashioned. Its surface shows tool marks that have been matched to several kusabi discovered by divers.

Another set of drilled holes ran across the top of the structure. "They are about twenty centimeters apart," observed Celine Shinbutsu in her book with Professor Kimura, "and aligned as if they had been laid out with a ruler. It is conceivable that shellfish carved the holes, but not likely. The best digger is the sea-urchin, but sea-urchins create a differently shaped hole from the ones at Iseki Point. It is very likely that the shellfish efforts to enlarge the holes to their own specifications are responsible for the slight variations in size."

Just how these holes were made and for what purpose was explained by Kotara Maja, the master stonemason chosen to head up restoration of Okinawa's historic sites damaged during World War II. His expertise in traditional forms and construction techniques uniquely qualified him for these extensive projects. When shown the peculiar line of evenly spaced holes atop the Yonaguni Monument, he immediately recognized them as part of an ancient block-breaking procedure still in use. Holes are drilled to a roughly uniform depth and at prescribed intervals near the edge of a natural rock formation, then large poles are inserted and forcefully worked back and forth in unison by a team of workers. The rock soon fractures in a straight line and breaks off in the desired building block. Mr. Maja's conclusions were paralleled by the statements of another master stonemason at Okinawa, Koutaro Shinza. He and his colleagues agreed that the underwater structure near Iseki Point was an artificial quarry and refused to believe it was the exclusive result of natural forces.

Even more unequivocal are small rectangles found under sheltered areas of the Yonaguni Monument, away from the action of strong eroding currents. The three-inch-long, straight-angled openings could not have been formed by natural processes. Moreover, they were not cut facedown, but laterally and level into the rock.

Yet one more set of completely different holes was found on top of the structure. They are far larger and deeper, about three feet in diameter, cut four feet into the solid rock, and separated by a flat, extremely artificial-looking partition. Maja was also acquainted with these holes. He recognized them as the same kind in which were rooted tall, sturdy props as part of a primitive yet effective brace or crane to lift heavy stone blocks. Although a traditional design of unknown antiquity, such wooden hoists were still functioning in remote rural areas, far from electrical hookup, as late as World War II.

The identification of holes for making and lifting stone blocks enforces theories of human influence at the Yonaguni Monument and tends to support its characterization as an ancient quarry. Other details, however, define it more as a work in progress, its construction long ago interrupted by a sudden rise in sea level. Holes are found only on the structure's uppermost portion; its lower two-thirds appear finished and features more architectural details. These include what Kimura and other divers at the site describe as a "loop road," a stone feature resembling a man-made path or causeway winding around from the base of the structure connected to the top by a drainage canal. Its surface is smooth and regular, as though paved.

Professor Kimura surveyed "a stairway-like structure, not just on the south side, but all around. The north side shows the strongest indication of having been man-made. Furthermore, one part of it is a stairway." At its base is a formation resembling a massive, freestanding gate not unlike Andean stonework on the other side of the Pacific Ocean. The joints formed by its blocks are level with each other on either "leg," stressing comparisons with preconquest Peru.

No less surprising is a huge, egg-shaped boulder sitting on its own plinth, or low platform, upon which it has very obviously been set with precise deliberation. The ovoid megalith seems far more at home among French or British standing stones of Neolithic Europe than on the sea bottom near a small Japanese island.

Yonaguni's underwater monument displays many details beyond the purview of geologists to explain adequately. One such enigma is a large intaglio of an hourglass figure beautifully cut into the surface. Not far away is a long, dead-straight channel terminating in a short flight of seven steps. Below it is a low, narrow tunnel, artificial in appearance for its regular courses of stone blocks with matching joints. Divers entering at one end emerge to find themselves confronted by the so-called "twin towers." Such an orientation seems to have been purposely built into the tunnel, implying its original function as a sacred way.

Granite slabs rear up before scuba-equipped visitors emerging from the tunnel like two nineteen-foot-long books of unguessed but undoubtedly high tonnage. A three-inch gap separating them calls to mind the same configuration found at Japan's pair of standing stones in the thickly forested area of northwestern Honshu, as described in chapter 9. The two Nabeyama megaliths likewise form a slot through which the sun is seen to rise on the morning of each Midsummer's Day. Yonaguni's "twin towers" similarly imply an original astronomical orientation of some kind, because they are not proper uprights. They both lean at the same angle, as though set in a deliberate alignment.

Perhaps most persuasive of all physical evidence on behalf of the sunken structure's man-made provenance are seventeen or so hieroglyphs carved into its sides, including at least one inscription. Four of the characters are repeated several times, but all were obviously incised by human hand, not through any natural agency. They are, as might be expected, inscrutable, although duplicated at only one other place on Earth, and most appropriately on the monumental structures described in our first chapter about the lost city of Nan Madol. The appearance of these otherwise unique glyphs at two of the world's most discernibly Lemurian sites goes far to underscore their common antediluvian origins and connection through the destroyed Motherland.

A single ideogram found at both Nan Madol and the Iseki Point structure could be exceptionally revealing. It is a *T*, the tau emblem of Mu. It does not seem coincidental, therefore, that a persistent Ryukyu myth describes the prehistoric builders of ancient megalithic structures found throughout the islands as giants, whose name—the Mujinto—was apparently derived from the lost Motherland. As Professor Kimura wrote, "The Yonaguni Monument may be considered as evidence signifying that Mu existed."

A few scuba-diver "kicks" away from Iseki Point's main subsurface structure stands a colossal formation referred to as "the stage." A perfect square of solid rock standing alone some eighteen feet above the sea floor, it is exactly seventy feet long on each side, and therefore extremely artificial in appearance. This impression is intensified by a particularly dramatic feature. While Thomas Holden was diving at Yonaguni for cable television's History Channel in 2000, his video camera captured the image of a gigantic human face on the stage. It had been discovered shortly before by another professional underwater photographer, Cecile Hagland. She was able to discern the faint outlines carved into the rock of a helmet or wings (a winged headdress?) streaming back from the head.

Alerted to this new find, the Japanese survey team took measurements of the effigy. Although severely eroded by unknown years of currents, it still bore traces left by its sculptor. Observers could make out the configuration of a nose, and the eyes were proportionate. As Professor Kimura stated, "The pupil [in the right eye of the face on the stage] is extended longitudinally." He referred to the stone head as a moai, the native Rapa Nui term used to identify the great statues of Easter Island—not an inappropriate characterization, because resemblances between the two widely separated sites may be more than circumstantially physical. The underwater stone heads (two have been found at the stage) face in the direction of Easter Island. And remarkably, the word for any prehistoric sacred structure in the local Okinawa dialect is *moai*. Although approximately 2,500 miles and unknown centuries lie between them, a relationship of some kind appears to link Rapa Nui and Yonaguni.

For all his doubts about the artificiality of Iseki Point's sunken attraction, Dr. Schoch could not avoid its comparison with similar buildings found on Okinawa, particularly near Noro, the prefecture capital. Another similar structure is Nakugusuku Castle. More of a ceremonial edifice and royal burial center than an actual military installation, built about 500 years ago and since subjected to numerous renovations, the castle foundations date to the late centuries of the first millennium B.C., although the vicinity was almost certainly revered as a sacred area long before. These are otherwise unique structures hewn from the naked rock featuring the same gigantic steps and broad plazas found at the underwater Yonaguni Monument. The tombs have not received much attention from archaeologists, who have been able to determine neither the age nor the identity of the culture responsible for their creation. They nonetheless represent a continuous architectural style unique to this part of the world, from under the sea to the land.

Dr. Schoch speculates that the prehistoric natives of Yonaguni modeled their burial vaults on an impressive natural formation just offshore, before it was engulfed by the waves. But the Iseki Point structure attained its subsurface condition 10,000 or 12,000 years ago, making the Okinawa tombs—if they were modeled on the monument—the oldest man-made structures on Earth, something few investigators would be willing to accept. More likely, we are following the progression of a building style beginning at a location presently under water—and, hence, anterior to more recent burial vaults on the Ryukyus.

These tombs are not the only parallels with the sunken monument. Mu-tubu-udundi is a secret martial art known only to masters directly descended from the first king of Japan's Ryukyu Islands. He brought the regimen with him from his island kingdom in the east, which had been overwhelmed by the sea. Adepts avoid physical confrontation, seeking rather to exhaust their opponents through an intricate series of controlled postures and dancelike movements, striking a blow only after all other options have been exhausted. Like China's t'ai chi, its Japanese precursor is also a form of mediation aimed at putting human biorhythms in accord with so-called "Earth energies." The practice's name, Mu-tubu-udundi, or "the self-disciplined way of Mu," derives from the lost Pacific civilization, similarly known for the spiritual disciplines and peaceful worldview of its inhabitants.

Another "castle," Okinawa's Shuri Citadel, like Nakugusuku, was built during the fifteenth century upon the ruins of a much older foundation. Curiously, its ground plan matches almost exactly the layout of Yonaguni's sunken monument and is surrounded by a similar "loop road." Professor Kimura additionally pointed out that the twin dragon statues guarding Shuri Citadel's sanctuary parallel the twin turtle effigies facing each other atop the Iseki Point structure. One Shuri Citadel dragon is portrayed with an open mouth, he said, while the jaws of the other are closed. On the underwater monument, the opposing turtles are identical, except that one extends its head and the other's is retracted.

The choice of beasts appropriately symbolizes their respective structures. In Asia, dragons traditionally represent telluric energies and the Earth itself, upon which Shuri Citadel was built. The turtle is a metaphorical image for abundance from under and on the sea and on land—an apt symbol for Yonaguni's sunken "castle." In Japanese folklore, Urashima Taro had compassion for a suffering turtle stranded on the beach and saved its life. In gratitude, the creature took him to the ocean bottom, where he was the guest of friendly spirits in a magnificent palace, the center of a once powerful kingdom, before its tragic demise beneath the waves. As a parting gift, the young boy was given the Peach of Immortality. This same fruit that granted eternal life to mortal human beings was carried by Xi Wang Mu, the Chinese goddess of mercy, from her palace before it sank beneath the Sunrise Sea.

Ho-ho-demi-no-Mikoto is cited in the *Nihongi*, a Japanese collection of pre-Buddhist myths, histories, and traditions, as a divine hero who descended to the ocean floor in an overturned basket. On his arrival, he visited a sunken citadel belonging to the sea-god. The Yonaguni Monument's existence was common knowledge among the islanders forty years before Kihachiro Aratake's official discovery, according to Celine Shinbutsu, although the structure was undoubtedly much older. The myths of Urashima Taro and Ho-ho-demi-no-Mikoto indicate that local awareness of the Yonaguni Monument goes back many generations.

The immortality-bestowing peaches or herbs described in these perennial stories are often associated in Southeast Asian myth with some formerly magnificent kingdom drowned during the ancient past by a terrific deluge. Several Chinese emperors were convinced that at least some specimens had survived the Great Flood and dispatched expeditions to find them in the southernmost islands of Japan—specifically Yonaguni, which is outstanding not only for its undersea ruins, but also for something known as "the long-life plant," or *cho-mei-gusa*. It grows only in the lower Ryukyus and is farmed in abundance on Yonaguni, where human longevity is the greatest on Earth.

In local myth, Nirai-Kanai was said to have landed in the Ryukyu Islands very long ago, after his enlightened kingdom far over the sea had been swallowed in a tempest of fire and storm. He taught the natives how to cultivate cho-mei-gusa, the plant of immortality, and built the first stone castles in the islands. Nirai-Kanai is also "the homeland very far away in the sea," regarded as a kingdom from which the ancestors of the Japanese Ama arrived after it was engulfed in the western Pacific Ocean.

Was cho-mei-gusa the long-sought-after "herb of immortality"? If so, are its present crops descended from the high agricultural practices for which the Lemurians were renowned? Does the existence of this unique plant on Yonaguni identify the island with Mu, or, at any rate, as one of its outposts? As Professor Kimura wondered, "It is a great mystery that such a huge object [the sunken monument] should exist next to so insignificant an island."

Dr. Kurt Lambeck, a world-class geologist at Canberra's Australian National University, has been studying fluctuating sea levels since 1980, and points out that Yonaguni sits at the margin of the Pacific and Asian plates, where tectonic stress may have generated the seismic violence necessary to bring about the inundation of Lemuria. He too was impressed with the obviously artificial appearance of the Iseki Point structure, which he characterized as a quarry that had been engulfed about 12,000 years ago. This is the time frame generally agreed upon by investigators for the monument's inundation. Before then, according to Celine Shinbutsu, "Okinawa was high and dry, firmly attached to the Asian continent. The Ryukyu chain was a bridge; it was open to animal and human traffic. Some of the oldest relics of Jomon culture are found in Okinawa. . . . Eventually, the ice melted, and the seas filled up again. What was once dry land became the ocean bed; what were once towering mountain peaks became dots of land in the crystal sea."

Carbon-14 tests carried out by Professor Kimura on coral algae removed from the monument yielded a date of 6,000 Y.B.P. However, these tests only show when the coral began to grow, not when the structure was flooded or when it was built. Backdating algae growth rates, Kimura postulated that it was inundated approximately 12,000 years ago, when sea levels were 100 to 120 feet lower than now. Until the end of Pleistocene times, the bottom of the monument stood on dry land. How old it may have been previous to the deluge no one can guess. It nonetheless represented a sophisticated degree of terraforming that may be associated only with the civilization of Mu, a conclusion compelled by the first of the great Lemurian floods that closed the last ice age.

While Yonaguni's underwater site is not unlike similar rock-hewn castles and tombs of Okinawa, it also bears a striking resemblance to ceremonial centers on the opposite side of the Pacific Ocean, along the shores of South America. Just south of Lima stand the gaunt ruins of Pachacamac, the religious capital of preconquest Peru and the seat of its most revered oracle. Built centuries before the rise of the Inca, it looms in broad tiers and gigantic steps leading to spacious plazas. At first glance, it seems as though the Yonaguni Monument had been transported from the bottom of the sea near Iseki Point to dry land on the Peruvian coast. Another South American look-alike towers 100 feet near the coast outside the city of Trujillo. Aptly named the "Temple of the Sun," its east–west solar alignment is identical to the sunken monument's orientation. The pre-Inca pyramid is an irregularly stepped platform of unfired adobe bricks built by a people remembered as the Moche. In addition to the physical appearance and alignment it shares with the Yonaguni Monument, the Temple of the Sun is 756 feet long. This measurement is extremely revealing because it is virtually the same length as the Yonaguni Monument. Its base dimensions are 758 feet east to west and 481 feet north to south.

Remarkably, these are the same original measurements of Egypt's Great Pyramid—758 feet across at the base and 481 feet tall. Seven hundred fifty-eight feet is also the diameter in Egyptian *aroura,* or "sides," of the innermost sacred citadel of Atlantis, as described by Plato in his dialogue *Critias.* Most pertinent to comparisons with the Yonaguni Monument, a crystalline granite rock sitting in the Nile River just above the

First Cataract is 481 feet wide. On it was built the "Remote Place," the Temple of P-aaleq, better known by its Greek name, Philae. Although its earliest-known buildings only go back to the fourth century B.C., they were erected upon much older structures of undetermined age, which gave rise to the site's characterization by local residents as the "Island in the Time of Ra," indicating its deep antiquity. But Philae shares more with Yonaguni's Monument than the 481-foot base length. Twelve thousand years ago, before the postglacial floods that ravaged much of the world, both places were located on the Tropic of Cancer. This is a circle defining the apparent journey of the sun around the Earth at about 23.5 degrees north of the equator. Yonaguni's position was particularly interesting, because it stood at the most northerly point reached by the sun's progress at the end of the last ice age. Every June 21 at high noon of the summer solstice, the sun stood directly overhead.

However, the small Ryukyu Islands and Philae were not alone in occupying the Tropic of Cancer. Following it around the globe, I noticed it strung together several other very ancient, fundamentally similar sites, all of them surrounded by water. Going westward from Yonaguni in postglacial times, the Tropic of Cancer intersected with the modern Chinese city of Amoy, known more than 1,000 years ago during the Sung dynasty as Chia-shu Island. In the late 1970s, archaeologists unearthed some of China's oldest Paleolithic artifacts along its east coast, surprising because the maritime objects—harpoon points, net weights, and so forth—proved that Chia-shu Island's early inhabitants were able sailors at a time when seafaring was thought to have been restricted to rivers and shorelines. No less significantly, these finds are beginning to persuade scholars that the Amoy area was the birthplace of Chinese civilization.

Traveling farther westward during late Pleistocene times to India, the Tropic of Cancer ran through the Bay of Cambay and what many archaeologists consider the subcontinent's first metropolis. Lothal was the port city for Mohenjo Daro, Harappa, and other Indus Valley urban centers that flourished in the early third millennium B.C. Lothal's harbor facilities were enormous for their time, featuring long stone jetties together with sheltered quaysides for large oceangoing vessels. Remarkably, Lothal's advanced city planning was without predecessor in India and appears to have been imported from some outside civilization where such sophisticated concepts had already enjoyed a long period of development.

From Lothal, the Tropic of Cancer continued in its westerly course in the late ice age through Egypt's Philae, across North Africa and the vastness of the Atlantic Ocean until it passed over what is now the obscure island of Andros, largest in the Bahamas, 150 miles southeast of Miami, Florida. It was here that Dr. Gregory Little found a sunken site in Nicolls Town Bay, near the extreme northeast end of Andros. In March 2003 he discovered a 1,375-foot-long, 150-foot-wide arrangement of cyclopean blocks in three well-ordered sloping tiers interspersed by two bands of smaller stones. Although standing fifteen feet beneath the surface, its top section is ten feet deep. The large stones composing the tiers average twenty-five by thirty feet and two feet thick. Each of the three tiers is fifty feet wide. Some suggestion of a ramp was discerned leading from the floor of the harbor lagoon to the top of the platform.

The structure's regular appearance and almost uniformly square-cut blocks argue persuasively for its man-made nature, which, given its location at a natural harbor in the North Atlantic current, may have been a quay, breakwater, or port facility of some kind. Underscoring this characterization, together with the ramp, are a number of five-inch-wide, five-inch-deep rectangles resembling postholes cut into some of the cyclopean stones just below the uppermost tier. These holes may have held mooring pylons used to tie up docked ships; they are very much like the rectangular holes divers point out on the Yonaguni Monument. Most if not all of the Andros blocks appear to have been quarried from local beach-rock and deliberately set in place. Dr. Little believes the formation could only have been built 12,000 or 10,000 years ago. In early 2005, his supposition seemed borne out when divers located what appeared to be the structure's base at some six fathoms. Postglacial sea levels that would have allowed for its construction were more than fifty feet lower than today.

Photo by William Donato

Massive square-cut blocks in the Andros platform.

From Andros, the Tropic of Cancer returned across the Pacific Ocean to Yonaguni. It seems more than ironic that two controversial underwater structures on either side of the world, discovered only eighteen years apart, were contemporaries in deep antiquity and located on the same global line. For at least four other sites of primary cultural significance (two of which own a common measurement), separated from one another by many hundreds or thousands of miles, to have additionally shared a connection is beyond coincidence. They point instead to a worldwide civilization of ice-age seafarers, who were also sun worshippers, as indicated by the Tropic of Cancer connecting them all, the solar orientations incorporated in the Yonaguni Monument, and Philae's association with Ra, the Egyptian sun-god.

Remarkably, the five ancient sites riding the northernmost passage of the sun around our planet connected the Pacific with Southeast Asia, India, Africa, and the Atlantic, suggesting a worldwide culture that flourished more than 12,000 years ago. This conclusion must be regarded by mainstream scholars as the incredible fantasy of lunatic-fringe investigators. It is not a theory, however, but a deduction arrived at from all available information, which goes on to show that the structure under some one hundred feet of water off Iseki Point is not alone on the sea floor.

After its discovery, divers widened their search throughout the Ryukyus in the hope of finding more evidence of a sunken civilization. They were not disappointed. About twenty-five miles west of the Okinawa capital at Naha, Mitsutoshi Taniguchi found a number of stone circles and nearby rectilinear features resembling building foundations under approximately ninety feet of water six miles southwest of Aka Island. At sixty feet across, a ringed formation of standing stones, each over six feet tall, could pass for an outstanding specimen of Neolithic construction from western Europe. To its northeast rears a similar, somewhat smaller version. The largest concentric feature, composed of small, roughly rounded stones, has a diameter of 481 feet. This is the same figure encountered at the Yonaguni Monument, its Nile counterpart on the island of Philae, and Egypt's Great Pyramid. Clearly, we are beginning to glimpse the reemergence of an architectural canon incorporated in sacred structures on both sides of the world in the deep past.

Other, less-well-defined features have been observed near neighboring islands. About 30 miles north of Aka, 19 miles west of Okinawa, and 220 miles northeast of Yonaguni are what appears to be a series of

stone wells off the southwestern coast of Aguni. Divers reported seeing stone walls and paved streets from thirty to more than ninety feet
beneath the surface of the sea hardly more than a half-mile off the shores
of Okinawa itself, some eighteen miles north of Noro, at the resort area
of Chatan.

Similar ruins have been observed among the Pescadores Islands, near
the Pen-hu Archipelago, between the islets of Don-Jyu and Shi-Hyi-Yu,
40 miles west of Taiwan, some 350 miles southwest of Yonaguni. In
August 2002, Professor We Miin Tian, from the department of marine
engineering at National Sun Yat Sen University in Kaohsiung City, Taiwan, located a thirty-foot-long stone wall standing about four feet high,
perpendicular to the sea floor, sixty feet beneath the surface of the ocean.
Twenty years before Professor Tian's discovery, a scuba diver from Taiwan, Steven Shieh, surveyed a pair of fifteen-foot-high stone walls under
water near Hu-ching, or Tiger Well Island. About 2,000 feet long, they
run at right angles to each other, one oriented north–south, the other
east–west, terminating in a large, circular feature.

These structures are only the merest fragments of a drowned kingdom celebrated in Taiwanese myth. It tells of Sura and Nakao, brother
and sister members of the Ami tribe, who dwelled in central Taiwan.
The catastrophe from which they escaped was said to have begun during
a full moon, accompanied by the sound of loud explosions coming from
the sea. It had been brought about by the gods to destroy human beings
for their impiety. "They say at that time [in the remote past] the mountains crumbled down," recounts the legend, "the Earth gaped, and from
the fissure a hot spring gushed forth, which flooded the whole face of
the Earth. Few living things survived the inundation." Another version
(the *Tsuwo*) describes birds dropping many thousands of stones into the
cataclysm, suggesting a meteor bombardment.

Sura and Nakao alone survived in a wooden vessel, which landed
them safely atop Mount Ragasan, where they began to repopulate the
Earth. However, their first offspring were living abortions that became
fish and crabs, because the pair committed the sin of incest without asking dispensation from the sun-god. Having angered him, they applied

to the moon-goddess. She forgave them, and the woman gave birth to a stone, from which sprang new generations of humankind. In this final detail of the Ami deluge myth is the lithic rebirth of humanity, the same theme encountered in Greek myth and numerous other flood accounts around the world. Another local flood story tells of a magnificent kingdom long ago overwhelmed by an angry Pacific Ocean. Its former seat of power was a splendid palace ringed with great walls of red stone. More provocative was the name by which it is still remembered in Taiwanese myth—Mu-Da-Lu—the Motherland itself.

A find at least as spectacular as Yonaguni's underwater monument, but not as well known or as thoroughly investigated, was made in the Korean Sea, about thirty miles west of the Japanese mainland, by Shun-Ichiroh Moriyama, a resident fisherman and diver. In early 1998, he claimed to have observed gigantic "pillars" near the small, uninhabited island of Okinoshima. The sighting inspired Toshiharu Arizumi, director of Cross Television, West Japan, to organize a team of scuba photographers in the hope of obtaining images of the allegedly sunken structures.

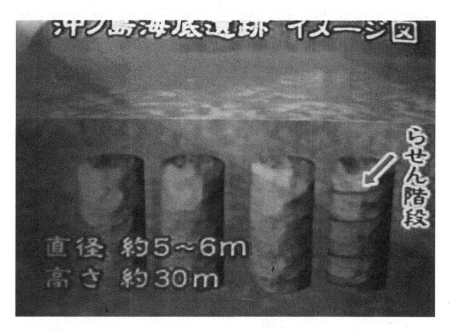

Illustration of the four stone towers under the Korean Sea near the Japanese island of Okinoshima.

Battling murderous currents and poor underwater visibility, the photographers were guided by Moriyama to the site of his discovery and were surprised to find eight erect towers, not "pillars," at a depth of 110 feet. The structures are uniformly gargantuan, standing ninety feet tall, their tops just twenty feet beneath the surface of the sea; their diameter range from thirty-one to thirty-six feet. A spiral staircase winds around the exterior of just one of the towers. Over the course of several hazardous expeditions, Arizumi's divers painstakingly measured the steps, which vary from twelve to fifteen inches wide, with a length of three to four feet. The function and age of these huge structures, to say nothing of their builders, is unknown, and likely to remain so given the murky, even treacherous diving conditions surrounding them.

Nonetheless, thanks to the daredevil persistence of his divers, Mr. Arizumi got the video footage he hoped for, and it was televised in April to an amazed viewing audience. Sadly, conventional scholars showed no such enthusiasm for a discovery that threatened to demolish their preconceived notions of prehistory. Had they inquired about its implications, however, they might have begun to piece together an archaeological puzzle spread over more than 900 miles of the ocean floor in a slightly curved line from the Korean Sea to Taiwan. Certainly, more pieces like Okinoshima, Yonaguni, and all the rest will be found, filling in and completing the picture of a sunken realm long lost to history but rediscovered by intrepid investigators using modern technology and faithfully preserved in the folk memory of native peoples around the Pacific World it once dominated.

SUMMARY

Two Hundred Thousand Years in One Thousand Words

Colonel James Churchward learned from monastery records in India that humanity first appeared on islands in the Pacific Ocean about 200,000 years ago. He was also told that humankind's first civilization gradually arose in the Pacific around 50,000 Y.B.P. This period coincided with the Upper Paleolithic, or Late Stone Age, famous for its cave art in southwestern France and for its lowered sea levels, allowing for occupation of Australia.

For the next 38,000 years of relative peace and isolation, the Pacific islanders developed the scientific and spiritual arts to a high degree of sophistication through close observance of natural law. They were ruled by a god-king, not unlike today's Dalai Lama, who presided over a gentle theocracy of priests. Their country was known as Mu, the "Motherland," less a specific geographical territory than a people and culture spread out over many lands from what is now western coastal America, throughout Oceania, to Japan. The inhabitants were Lemurians, or the residents of sea-girt Mu. Although they venerated numerous deities, the sun personified the Compassionate Intelligence that ordered the universe and attached the eternity of the human soul to recurring patterns evidenced in the cycles of nature. Spreading the

321

gospel of their mysticism around the world, they created the first global
civilization.

The Motherland itself was mostly a low-lying, tropical country,
much of it close to the equator and therefore beset by a hot climate.
The population lived in small fishing villages or on farms. Cities were
not unknown, but they were more ceremonial than urban centers. Step-
pyramids, temples, plazas, and other examples of sacred architecture
were rectilinear and oriented to various positions of the sun.

This prolonged civilized idyll lasted until 12,000 years ago, when the
last ice age came to an end, causing dynamic increases in sea level. Much,
but not all, of Mu was inundated, and large numbers of its inhabitants
fled to the Americas and Asia. Washington state's Kennewick Man and
his fellow Lemurians were killed by resident Mongoloids as the Jomon
culture arose in Japan.

In 3100 B.C., however, Comet Encke passed near the Earth, pro-
voking a global catastrophe. The lands of Mu were severely affected,
and some slipped beneath the sea. Many immigrants escaped to South
America, superseding a previous Lemurian colonization of Pacific coastal
Peru modern archaeologists know as the Norte Chico culture. Another
outpost that suffered greatly from the cataclysm occupied a large, fertile island in the mid-Atlantic Ocean settled by missionaries from Mu
millennia earlier. The destruction wrought by Comet Encke provoked a
fundamental change in the inhabitants, who felt themselves betrayed by
the Compassionate Intelligence they had been taught to revere, and they
broke away from the Motherland, going so far as to rename themselves
after their new capital—Atlantis.

The troublesome comet returned less than 1,000 years later to
unloose a bombardment of meteoritic material. Mu suffered, but
endured, then revived yet again. Its agricultural engineers transformed
the high hills of the Philippines into mountainous rice terraces, making Luzon the breadbasket of the Pacific. In 1917 B.C., the missionary
Miwoche brought Lemurian spiritual teachings to the Himalayas, where
they became the fundamental principles of Tibetan Buddhism. Then, in
1628 B.C., major volcanism and violent seismicity spawned by a return

of Comet Encke afflicted the south-central Pacific. Most of the lands of Mu dropped beneath the sea or were depopulated by 100-foot-high tsunamis. With its ceremonial centers toppled and infrastructure shattered beyond repair, the survivors abandoned what was left of their broken Motherland. Their arrival in other parts of the world acted as a powerful stimulus for the beginning of new societies, forming the basis of civilizations in Asia and America.

During the eighth century B.C., early or proto-Romans (Etruscans?) began celebrating the annual Lemuria festival to mollify the restless spirits (lemures) of their ancestors. Four hundred years later, the Lemurian domination of Japan ended with the collapse of the Jomon culture and the arrival of a Mongoloid people from Korea. They found the islands already inhabited by Caucasian indigenes, the descendants of once civilized Lemurians. As recently as the early nineteenth century, the last Lemurians were exterminated by Polynesians in the Poike Ditch Massacre at Easter Island. Later that same century, English scientist Philip Lutley Sclater postulated the existence of Lemuria to explain the occurrence of early primates on either side of the Indian Ocean. A contemporary, the German biologist Ernst Haeckel, concluded that humankind had first evolved in Lemuria.

But the first popular discussion of the Pacific Motherland was not published until 1926, by Colonel Churchward. His *Lost Continent of Mu,* based on a translation of ancient tablets purporting to describe the drowned civilization, ignited a controversy that persists to this day. Dismissed by most readers as a fantasy at best or a fabrication at worst, it found credibility sixty years later, when Kihachiro Aratake found a monumental building under water near Yonaguni, southernmost of the Japanese Ryukyu Islands. Its discovery was followed by that of at least a dozen other sunken structures off the shores of Japan, Taiwan, Pohnpei, Fiji, Peru, and North America. As more of these remnants are found, the image of lost Lemuria comes into clearer focus.

AFTERWORD

The Real Meaning of Lemuria

Perhaps after the catastrophe, popular anarchy super-
vened, and, in the sequel, a maddened democracy, leader-
less and without tradition, plumbed the depths of license
and degradation, as is invariably the way with an ignorant
and unorganized proletariat, until at last its wild career
ended in almost utter barbarism.

LEWIS SPENCE

A great body of evidence in the oral traditions of literally dozens of native peoples throughout the Pacific realm—from Southeast Asia, across Oceania, to the Americas—is consistent in its portrayal of Lemuria as the home of a technologically progressive, socially harmonious people. The success of their civilization had been generated by the so-called Perennial Philosophy when it became their national ethic, a moral standard of individual and civic behavior that later served as the basis of Tibet's Boen mysticism and Japan's Shinto religion after those lands were visited by missionaries from the Motherland.

Their worldview was not a "mystery-cult" in the sense that its tenets were available only to initiates, although it did have its esoteric Thirteenth School. All followers recognized a Compassionate Intelligence that revealed itself in the infinite complexity of the universe and expressed its will in natural laws. They further believed that the identity of this Compassionate Intelligence was found in the sum total of existence; hence, everything and everyone was considered a part of God. That accepted, their duty and fulfillment lay in cooperating with nature and their fellow humans. As such, Lemurians were not focused on self-indulgent materialism, economic competition, social standing, power politics, military strength, or even cultural wealth. They resembled no other population group in the world, save today's Tibetans, whose chief interest in life, individually and as a people, is their spiritual well-being.

For tens of thousands of years, the inhabitants of Mu matured in the isolation of their archipelagic realm. Then, around 40,000 years ago, widespread natural upheavals forced many of them from the shores of their ravaged Motherland. Their impact may still be traced in the archaeological ruins and folk memories of a dozen or more native peoples throughout Oceania and beyond, as presented in the preceding chapters. The ancient Pacific Islanders were far more than refugees, however. The global civilization they created was not driven by political, economic, or military agendas. It arose instead from a desire to transmute geologic violence from destructive to productive energies—to harness potentially cataclysmic forces for cultural and spiritual development. Antediluvian technology was born from this imperative, resulting in an *oikumene*, an ecumenical power operating in accord with nature.

By contrast, insatiable demands feeding on an ever-expanding consumption of finite planet resources today characterizes the industrialized world. No two human societies could have been more different from each other. That difference is clear in their opposing relationships with the Earth: Where one lived in harmony with it, the other was interested only in its exploitation. The Lemurians lacked our nuclear bombs and our fossil-fuel pollutants; we are hooked on an oil habit they would have condemned as psychotically suicidal, as are all self-indulgent addictions.

Among the distant places the Lemurians explored was a large, fertile, temperate island some 250 miles due west from the Straits of Gibraltar in the mid-Atlantic Ocean. Over the next thirty-four centuries, they were little more than colonists from the far-off Pacific Motherland. But around 4000 B.C., their Atlantic outpost was peacefully taken over by outsiders referred to by archaeologists as the seafaring megalith-builders of western Europe.

This meeting of peoples was mythically described by Plato in his dialogues *Timaeus* and *Critias,* which report that Poseidon arrived at the island to find it already inhabited by a race of mortals. He married a native woman, Kleito; she gave him five sets of twin boys who grew up to become the first kings of his New Order. The twins created a concentric arrangement of alternating moats and artificial islets as the basis for a great city unlike any other. The sea-god's first semi-divine son was Atlas, after whom the entire island was now known. His name, which means the Upholder, derived from his allegorical image as a mountain supporting the heavens, while signifying his invention of astronomy and astrology. In his mountainous shadow was built a splendid capital, the Daughter of Atlas, Atlantis. The megalith builders raised great standing stones oriented to various celestial phenomena as part of their Sky Father worship, which melded with the Mother Earth mysticism of the Lemurian residents.

Throughout the fifth millennium B.C., a hybrid civilization of Lemurian spirituality and Neolithic technology developed on the Atlantic island. In 3100 B.C., however, the first in a series of cometary catastrophes ravaged much of the rest of the world. Although Atlantis survived, it was devastated, and its shaken survivors, who lived in accord with natural law as divine will, felt themselves betrayed by the gods. They began to turn away from the spiritual principles that had guided them and their ancestors for countless generations. They were no longer Lemurians or megalith builders, but a new people, the Atlanteans, a name that reflected the change that had come over them. Applying their redoubtable skills to mining, they rapidly became brokers of precious metals for Bronze Age kingdoms demanding high-grade copper, which gave them an edge over their neighbors in weapons technology.

With the wealth of the civilized world pouring into their coffers, the Atlanteans rose to command the first superstate and world empire.

To protect their global investments, they raised fleets and armies, which grew into the instruments less of protection than of expansion. The Atlanteans set in motion an inevitable pattern that future imperialists—by whatever names they were and are known—would be forced to repeat over the next several thousand years. Ambition burgeoned into greed, requiring security, which descended into fear, resulting in military aggression. Successful at first in their virtual conquest of the Mediterranean World, the Atlanteans eventually suffered the unthinkable—military humiliation at the hands of a less sophisticated enemy, the numerically inferior Greeks.

Lemurian mystics had taught that moral law was not only inextricable from cosmic law, but that both were the same thing. Since all energy is interrelated—or, rather, nothing more than different inflections of a single energy—the good or evil humans do generates repercussions throughout society and the natural world. This was the fundamental principle discarded by the Atlanteans for their empire. But the truth of its metaphysics came crashing down on them with a final cataclysm that demolished their transnational enterprise and sank their capital into the sea. The Bronze Age they dominated for eighteen centuries ended, as Plato related, "in a day and a night."

By then, the Pacific Motherland had already been gone for 430 years. When the time came, as it inevitably does for all civilizations, to quit the world stage, some Lemurians sought refuge in central Asia and Japan, where their spiritual principles formed the basis, respectively, for two of humankind's great religions, Tibetan Buddhism and Japanese Shinto. Other survivors made genetic contributions to numerous population groups throughout Oceania and Pacific coastal North America. The Lemurian experience enriched the oral literature of Polynesians, Micronesians, Melanesians, Australians, Indonesians, Southeast Asians, and Southwest Native Americans. From the shores of South America to the islands of Japan, material evidence of the sunken kingdom is emerging from the sea bottom, but physical proof for the existence of Atlantis is as elusive as it has been since the Dark Ages that followed its annihilation.

The Atlanteans, who once controlled the richest, mightiest empire on Earth, would be deeply galled to know that today they are largely dismissed as nothing more than legendary, the fantasy of utopian dreamers. Their destruction was eerily similar to a hydrogen bomb blast that incinerated the city and knocked out the geologic props that supported the entire island. Its inundation was of a magnitude beyond all worst-case scenarios, engulfing upward of a million human beings. The event seared itself into the genetic memory of humankind, which accounts for our perennial fascination with Atlantis. Having been subjected to the equivalent of a nuclear strike, then thrust to the bottom of the ocean, Atlantis may be forever beyond the reach of researchers, except perhaps in dreams and nightmares.

The same may not be said of Lemuria. Many native traditions recount that its inhabitants were sufficiently forewarned, either by natural indications or psychic premonitions, and evacuated the Motherland in time to avoid its fate. Other sources, like the Hawaiian Kumulipo, contend that large numbers of victims were claimed by the final catastrophe. But not even these versions, except for Churchward's dubious "Lhasa Record," suggest anything comparable to the Atlantean holocaust. Much as our time dismisses the very notion of a moral–cosmic connection, could that prolonged Atlantean ethical imbalance resonating in nature have caused a more horrific cataclysm?

Interestingly, sunspots virtually disappeared between 1645 and 1715, an unusually prolonged period of relative world peace. Beginning in late 1945, however, from the first nuclear detonation continuing through the rest of the twentieth century's atomic testing, sunspot activity surged as never before in the history of solar observation. Sunspots are cooler regions on the surface that seriously disrupt electronic communications and, some investigators believe, interfere with normal human thought processes. From the mid-1950s, parapsychologists have traced a correlation between sunspot activity and upsurges of emotional disturbances in human behavior. Other mammals, and even fish, appear to be affected. Researchers speculate that the bioelectric field of many creatures is directly influenced by the sun's relative complexion. If so, modern science and ancient mysticism begin to complement each other.

None of this would have been news to the Lemurians. They tried to apply natural law to human society, seeking a harmony between themselves and the universe, an accord in which humankind would find its real identity. They understood the principle of the ego-as-adversary—that spiritual energy, the greatest power in the universe, could never be commanded, but only allowed to work its way on behalf of mere mortals pure-hearted enough to serve as its conduit. Here was the basis for their ideal role as co-creators with the Creator. But for that, purification was required. To achieve it, the Lemurians knew only one commandment, from which all their metaphysical musings flowed: "Be kind!" And only one sin that spawned all others: cruelty.

Their cousins on the other side of the globe chose more commonplace gods, the same idols of vain luxury, self-indulgence, and self-justifying theology worshipped today, all in the pursuit of ephemeral happiness. Edgar Cayce characterized the final phase of Atlantis as a struggle between the materialistic Sons of Belial and the monotheistic Followers of the Law of One. Their struggle of unbridled greed versus religious intolerance is now replayed in America between the likes of Enron capitalists and evangelical fundamentalists, although distinctions blur, as they did when Poseidon's empire entered its last days. The Atlanteans are us. The Atlanteans *were* Lemurians. The dilemma that separated them, not only at opposite ends of the world, but ethically poles apart, demonstrates how a single people can so divide itself into light and darkness. This moral dichotomy and its contrasting consequences for both vanished cultures is at the subconscious core of popular fascination for Atlantis and Mu. Resemblances between our time and theirs are numerous enough to invite comparison. One envisioned spiritual growth as the purpose of human evolution; the other adored progressive technology as the solution of all obstacles to physical happiness.

What would the world be like if Lemuria had not been destroyed so long ago? Had its development continued unbroken over the millennia into our time, the means to avoid all natural disasters might have been known and applied for many centuries already. Events like 2004's Indian Ocean tsunami might have been avoided, a consideration that alone justifies inquiry into the lost Motherland.

Cayce stated that more Atlantean souls than ever before reincarnated during the twentieth century—some to prevent the suicidal catastrophe that ended their world, others to replay it on an even more devastating scale. If so, the twenty-first century may be experiencing an unprecedented reincarnation of Lemurian souls as a natural counterbalance. Equilibrium was, after all, their watchword. Perhaps they might offset the darker tendencies of human nature with a perennial form of enlightenment signified by their ceremonial veneration of the sun. Humankind may yet swerve from a repetition of the global calamity that pushed it to the brink of extinction by seeking out the Motherland, where we were born with all the high hopes of a new and potentially godlike species.

Although her broken remains have lain at the bottom of the sea for the last thirty-three centuries, the Motherland's spirit is alive in the folk memories and high spirituality of more than a dozen different peoples around the Pacific Rim. And it appears to be growing in our collective consciousness the closer we approach the Great Crisis looming in the uncertain future. In this age where the unnatural is normal, nothing is too good for self-indulgence, and the Earth is pushed to the brink of ecological revolt, we need a different role model from our own past. The time has come for us to return to Lemuria.

Bibliography

INTRODUCTION: TERRA INCOGNITA

Diodorus of Sicily. *The Geography*. Vol. 1, no. 1. Translated by C. H. Oldfather. London: W. Heinemann, 1968.

Joseph, Frank. *The Temple of Mu*. TV documentary produced by AUS-TV International, Sydney, Australia, 2000.

Stoddy, Frederick. *Pioneers of Progress: Selected Biographies of Outstanding Nobel Prize Winners*. New York: Feathermount Press, Inc., 1925.

CHAPTER 1: A LOST SUPER SCIENCE

Alip, Eufonio M. *The Philippines of Yesteryears: The Dawn of History in the Philippines*. Manila, 1964.

Ashby, Gene. *A Guide to Ponape*. Eugene, Ore.: Rainy Day Press, 1987.

———. *Some Things of Value: Micronesian Customs and Beliefs*. Eugene, Ore.: Rainy Day Press, 1985.

Ballinger, Bill S. *Lost City of Stone: The Story of Nan Madol*. New York: Simon and Schuster, 1978.

Bator, Vamos-Toth. "Supreme Tamana Witness-Data." *Midwest Epigraphic Journal* 16, no. 2 (2002): 75–78.

Beardsley, Felicia. *Kosrae Historical Research Preservation Office (KHRPO) Report* 9(1) (2003).

Berkshire, Henry. "Can the Philippines 8th Wonder of the World Survive?" *UNESCO Bulletin* 24, no. 9 (2005).

Brown, John MacMillan. *The Riddle of the Pacific*. 1924. Reprint, Kempton, Ill.: Adventures Unlimited Press, 2003.

Cerve, W. S. *Lemuria: The Lost Continent of the Pacific*. 3rd ed. San Jose, Calif.: Supreme Grand Lodge of AMORC, 1942.

Childress, David Hatcher. *Ancient Micronesia and the Lost City of Nan Madol*. Kempton, Ill.: Adventures Unlimited Press, 1998.

331

———. *Lost Cities of Ancient Lemuria and the Pacific.* Kempton, Ill.: Adventures Unlimited Press, 1998.

Churchward, James. *The Lost Continent of Mu.* 1924. Reprint, Albuquerque: Brotherhood of Life, 1987.

Clarke, Arthur C. "The Other Side of Tomorrow." *Science Reader Magazine* 12, no. 5 (1996).

Corliss, William R. *Ancient Structures.* Glenbrook, Md: The Sourcebook Project, 2001.

Davis, Maria. "Weather Manipulation: Fact or Fantasy?" *OMNI* 11, no. 7 (1988).

Devereaux, Paul. *Earth Lights.* London: Royal Oak Press, 1993.

Eastlund, Bernard J. *Can We Control the Weather?* Washington, D.C.: National Public Radio, 6 September 1987.

Edmonds, I. G. *Micronesia.* New York: Bobbs-Merrill Co., 1974.

Hesse, Georgia. "Micronesian Paradise Not." The *San Francisco Examiner,* 12 December 1998, p. 8.

Hanlon, David. *Upon a Stone Altar.* Honolulu: University of Hawaii Press, 1988.

Imel, Martha Ann, and Dorothy Myers Imel. *Goddesses in World Mythology.* Oxford: Oxford University Press, 1993.

Knappert, Jan. *Pacific Mythology: An Encyclopedia of Myth and Legend.* London: Diamond Books, 1995.

Merritt, Abraham. *The Moon Pool.* New York: Collier Books, 1961.

Newman, Joseph. *The Energy Machine of Joseph Newman.* Press release. www.josephnewman.com.

Peattie, Mark R. *Nan'Yo: The Rise and Fall of the Japanese in Micronesia 1885 to 1945.* Honolulu: University of Hawaii Press, 1988.

Ramsay, Cynthia Russ. "On the Reef of Heaven" in *Mysteries of Mankind.* Washington, D.C.: National Geographic Society, 1992.

Rittlinger, Herbert. *Das mesenlose Ozean (The Measureless Ocean).* Munich: Franz Eher Verlag, 1939.

Saxe, Arthur. "The Nan Madol Area of Ponape." *Institute of Electrical Electronics and Engineers* 12, no. 5 (1969).

Tompsen, Edward. "More Than Half-a-Million Feared Dead in China Earthquake." The *New York Times,* 5 June 1976, p. 1.

von Daniken, Erich. *Odyssey of the Gods.* London: Hammer House, Ltd., 1990.

Zimmerer, Neil. *The Chronology of Genesis.* Kempton, Ill.: Adventures Unlimited Press, 2003.

CHAPTER 2: NAVEL OF THE WORLD

Andersen, Johannes C. *Myths and Legends of the Polynesians.* London: Harrap, 1928.

Billimoria, Dr. Rashnu. *The Rongo-Rongo and Mohenjo Daro Scripts.* Vol. 35. London: *Anthropos,* 1938.

Brown, *The Riddle of the Pacific.*

Casey, Robert. *Easter Island.* Indianapolis: Bobbs-Merrill, 1931.

Chance, Jack. "The Faces of Rapa Nui." *Atlantis Rising* 46 (2004).

Cremo, Michael, and Richard Thompson. *Forbidden Archaeology*. San Francisco: Bhaktivedanta Institute, 1993.

De Hevesy, Guillaume. *The Easter Island and Indus Valley Scripts*. Vol. 35. London: Anthropos, 1938.

Handy, E. S. *Polynesian Religion*. Honolulu: Bishop Museum, 1927.

Heine-Geldern, Richard. *Easter Island Script Controversy*. Vol. 35. London: Anthropos, 1938.

Heyerdahl, Thor. *Reports of the Norwegian Archaeological Expedition to Easter Island and the East Pacific*. Vol. 1 and 2. Chicago: Rand McNally, 1965.

Hunter, Dr. G. R. *Easter Island's Written Language*. Vol. 35. London: Anthropos, 1938.

Joyce, T. A. "The Mystery of the Easter Island Images." in *Wonders of the Past*, New York: Wise and Company, 1952.

Macintosh, Jane R. *The Peaceful Realm*. New York: McBurty Press, 2003.

Metraux, Alfred. *Easter Island*. London: Andre Deutsch, 1957.

Routledge, Katherine. *The Mystery of Easter Island*. 1919. Reprint, Kempton, Ill.: Adventures Unlimited Press, 1998.

Spence, Lewis. *The Problem of Lemuria*. London: Rider and Company, 1933.

Thompson, Dr. Gunnar. *American Discovery, the Real Story*. Seattle: Argonauts Misty Isles Press, 1994.

Wyse, Elizabeth, ed. *Past Worlds: The Times Atlas of Archaeology*. New York: Crescent Books, 1995.

CHAPTER 3: THE GIANTS SPEAK

Andersen, *Myths and Legends of the Polynesians*.

Barbara Ann Karamenos Institute. 15 April 2004. www.tbakaramenos.org, info@karamenos.org.

Brown, *The Riddle of the Pacific*.

Cerve, *Lemuria*.

Childress, David Hatcher. *Lost Cities of Ancient Lemuria and the Pacific*. Kempton, Ill.: Adventures Unlimited Press, 1989.

Churchward, *The Lost Continent of Mu*.

Daniel, Professor Glyn, ed. *The Illustrated Encyclopedia of Archaeology*. New York: Thomas Y. Crowell Company, 1977.

Fornander, Abraham. *An Account of the Polynesian Race*. Montpelier, Vt.: Charles E. Tuttle Company, 1885.

Hipskind, Gerald. "Easter Island." *Nature* 15, no. 3 (1892).

Huppertz, Dr. Josephine. "Ancestor Worship on Easter Island." *Epigraphic Journal* 16, no. 1 (2002): 71.

Imel, Martha Ann, and Dorothy Myers Imel. *Goddesses in World Mythology*. Oxford: Oxford University Press, 1993.

Jennings, Jesse D., ed. *The Prehistory of Polynesia*. Cambridge, Mass.: Harvard University Press, 1979.

Jordan, Michael, *Encyclopedia of the Gods*. New York: Facts On File, Inc., 1993.

MacKenzie, Donald A. *South Seas Myths and Legends*. London: Senate Books, 1930.

Margrave, Susan. *Stem-Cell Research Promising; Arguments Surrounding It Plentiful*. Henderson State University, http://www.hsu.edu/content.aspx?id=1705, 16 October 2004.

Maziere, Francis. *Mysteries of Easter Island*. New York: W. W. Norton, 1968.

McLaughlin, Shawn. "Lichenometry on Easter Island." Easter Island Foundation, letter to the author: ancient@compuserve.com, 27 September 2004.

Moerenhout, J. A. *Voyages aux Iles du Grand Ocean (Voyages to the Islands of the Great Ocean)*. Paris: Quintillion, 1837.

Routledge, Katherine. *The Mystery of Easter Island*. 1919. Reprint, Kempton, Ill.: Adventures Unlimited Press, 1998.

Scarboro, David. "Easter Island Possibilities." MadSci Network: webadmin@www. madsci.org

Spence, Lewis. *The Problem of Lemuria*.

Van Tilburg, Jo Anne. "Respect for Rapa Nu: Exhibition and Conservation of Easter Island Stone Statues" *Antiquity* 64 (1990): 249–58.

Yoshida, Professor Nobuhiro. "The Prehistoric Stone Towers of Japan and Easter Island." *Ancient American* 5, no. 31 (2000).

CHAPTER 4: ANCIENT OCEANIC TECHNOLOGY

Allen, M. R. *Male Cults and Secret Initiations in Melanesia*. Melbourne: Melbourne University Press, 1967.

Andersen, Johannes C. *Myths and Legends of the Polynesians*. London: Harrap, 1928.

Anell, Bengt. "Contributions to the History of Fishing in the Southern Seas." *Studia Ethnographica Upsaliensia* 9 (1955).

Best, Elston. *Maori Religion and Mythology*. Vol. 1 and 2. London: Wellington Press, 1924.

Bohr, Niels. *Hypo-Typograhica*. Translated by Helge Norcross. New York: Grosset and Dunlap, 1949.

Chevalier, Louis. *Revue de la Société d'Etudes Melanesiennes*. New Caldonia: University of New Caledonia Press, 1964.

Childress, David Hatcher. *Lost Cities of Ancient Lemuria and the Pacific*. Kempton, Ill.: Adventures Unlimited Press, 1989.

———. *Ancient Tonga and the Lost City of Mu'a*. Kempton, Ill.: Adventures Unlimited Press, 1996.

———. "The Kaimanawa Wall." *World Explorer* 1, no. 8 (1996) 19.

Corliss, William R. *Archaeological Anomalies: Small Artifacts*. Glenbrook, Md.: The Sourcebook Project, 2003.

———. *Ancient Man: A Handbook of Puzzling Artifacts*. Glenbrook, Md.: The Sourcebook Project, 1980.

Davis, Ester Payne. "The Strange Lat'te Stones of Guam." *World Explorer* 1, no. 2 (1992).

Duff, Roger. "The Prehistory of the Southern Cook Islands." *Canterbury Museum Bulletin* 6 (1974).

Etpison, Mandy T. *Palau: Portrait of Paradise*. Koror, Palau: NECO Marine Corp., 1995.

Heyerdahl, Thor. *Early Man and the Ocean*. New York: Doubleday, 1978.

Hodges, Henry. *Technology in the Ancient World*. London: Marboro Books, 1970.

"It's Still a Mystery." *World Explorer* 1, no. 4 (1994): 61.

Jennings, Jesse D., ed. *The Prehistory of Polynesia*. Cambridge, Mass.: Harvard University Press, 1979.

Knappert, Jan. *Indian Mythology, An Encyclopedia of Myth and Legend*. London: Diamond Books, 1995.

Mahler, Heinrich. "New Guinea's Strange Mummies." *Science Newsletter* 11, no. 4 (1936): 22.

Moss, Rosalind. *The Life After Death in Oceania and the Malay Archipelago*. London: Harrison House, Ltd., 1925.

O'Neill, Terry, ed. *Out of Time and Space*. St. Paul: Llewellyn Publications, 1999.

Reynolds, Philip K. *The Banana*. New York: Houghton Mifflin, 1927.

Rivers, W. H. R. "Pacific Monuments." *American Anthropologist*, 31, no. 9 (1915).

Roth, H. Ling. *The Natives of Sarawak and British North Borneo*. London: Harrison House, Ltd., 1896.

Rothovious, Andrew E. "Mysterious Cement Cylinders in New Caledonia." *Fate* 22, no. 7 (1973).

Sanders, Albert, "New Medical Research Breakthrough?" *The Detroit Free Press,* 15 April 2004, p. 8.

Smith, S. Percy. *Hawaiki: The Original Home of the Maori*. Wellington, New Zealand: Wellington Press, 1921.

Sorrenson, M. P. *Maori Origins and Migrations*. Auckland, New Zealand: Auckland University Press, 1979.

Spence, Lewis. *The Problem of Lemuria*.

Stern, William. "Stem-Cell Research Offers Bright Prospects for Future Cures." *London Daily Herald* 14 October 2004, p. 12.

Steubel, C., and B. Herman. *Tala o Vavao: The Myths, Legends and Customs of Old Samoa*. Auckland, New Zealand: Auckland Polynesian Press, 1987.

The Times of India, "Giant Skeleton Found on Fiji." July 14, 2002.

Yoshida, Nobuhiro. "Japan's Megalithic Links to Ancient America and Europe." *Ancient American* 3, no. 23 (1998).

CHAPTER 5: THE COLONEL OF MU

Caroli, Kenneth. Personal correspondence, November, 2004.

Churchward, James. *Cosmic Forces of Mu*. Vol. 2. 1935. Reprint, Santa Fe, N.Mex.: BE Books, 1998.

———. *Cosmic Forces of Mu*. Vol. 1. 1933. Reprint, Santa Fe: BE Books, 1998.

———. *The Children of Mu*. 1928. Reprint, Santa Fe: BE Books, 1988.

———. *Books of the Golden Age*. 1927. Reprint, Santa Fe: BE Books, 1997.

———. *The Sacred Symbols of Mu*. 1926. Reprint, Santa Fe: BE Books, 1988.

————. *The Lost Continent of Mu.*

Le Plongeon, Augustus. *Sacred Mysteries Among the Mayas and Quiches 11,500 Years Ago.* New York: Macoy, 1886.

————. *Queen Moo and the Egyptian Sphinx.* London: Kegan, Paul, Trench, Truebner, 1896.

Santesson, Hans. *Understanding Mu.* New York: Paperback Library, 1970.

CHAPTER 6: THE GARDEN OF EDEN?

Beckwith, Martha W. *The Kumulipo, A Hawaiian Creation Chant.* Chicago: University Press, 1951.

Cerve, W. S. *Lemuria: The Lost Continent of the Pacific.* 3rd ed. San Francisco, Calif.: Supreme Grand Lodge of AMORC, 1942.

Churchward, James. *The Lost Continent of Mu.* 1924. Reprint, Santa Fe, N.Mex.: BE Books, 1987.

Dodd, Edward. *Polynesia's Sacred Isle.* New York: Dodd, Mead and Company, 1976.

Etpison, Mandy T. *Palau: Portrait of Paradise.* Palau: Neco Marine, 1994.

Fornander, Abraham. *An Account of the Polynesian Race.* Montpelier, Vt.: Charles E. Tuttle Company, 1885.

Goodman, Dr. Jeffrey. *American Genesis.* New York: Doubleday, 1979.

Grundy, Martin A. "Native Americans: Really Out of Asia?" *Ancient American* 4, no. 3 (1999).

Haeckel, Ernst. "Human Origins." *The Hyklut Society Bulletin* 121 (1879).

Handy, E. S. *Polynesian Religion.* Honolulu, Hawaii: Bishop Museum, 1927.

Heyerdahl, Thor. *Reports of the Norwegian Archaeological Expedition to Easter Island and the East Pacific.* Vol. 2. Chicago: Rand McNally and Company, 1965.

Imel, Martha Ann, and Dorothy Myers Imel. *Goddesses in World Mythology.* Oxford: Oxford University Press, 1993.

Jordan, Michael. *Encyclopedia of the Gods.* New York: Facts On File, Inc., 1993.

Joseph, Frank. "Buhl Woman Sheds Light on Ancient Americans." *Ancient American* 4, no. 26 (1999).

————. "New Finds Demolish 'Bering Land-Bridge' Theory." *Ancient American* 20, no. 60 (2005): 27.

Knappert, Jan. *Pacific Mythology, An Encyclopedia of Myth and Legend.* London: Diamond Books, 1995.

Lever, Carol, and Peter Quinone. "Kennewick Man: May He Rest in Peace?" *Ancient American* 6, no. 37 (2001).

Le Plongeon, Augustus. *Sacred Mysteries Among the Mayas and Quiches.* London: kegan, Paul, Trench, Tuebner, 1898.

MacKenzie, Donald A. *Mythology of the Babylonian People.* London: The Gresham Publishing Company, Ltd., 1915.

Melville, Leinani. *Children of the Rainbow: The Religion, Legends and Gods of Pre-Christian Hawaii.* Wheaton, Ill.: Quest Books, Theosophical Publishing House, 1969.

Meyer, Priscilla S. "Rewriting America's History: Genetics and the South Pacific." *Ancient American* 2, no. 9 (1996).

Nugent, John. "Who Were the Original Native Americans?" *The Barnes Review* 5, no. 3 (1999).

Ogilvie-Herald, Chris. "Older Than Expected." *Quest* 1, no. 6 (1997).

Oppenheimer, Stephen. *Eden in the East, The Drowned Continent of Southeast Asia.* London: Weidenfeld and Nicolson, 1999.

Santesson, Hans. *Understanding Mu.* New York: Paperback Library, 1970.

Spence, Lewis. *The Problem of Lemuria.* London: Rider and Company, 1933.

Zimmerer, Neil. *The Chronology of Genesis.* Kempton, Ill.: Adventures Unlimited Press, 2003.

CHAPTER 7: HAWAIIAN MOTHERLAND

Alexander, W. D. *Polynesian Travels.* New York: McVey and Company, 1929.

Beckwith, Martha W. *Hawaiian Mythology.* Harmouth, Conn.: Yale University Press, 1940.

———. *The Kumulipo, A Hawaiian Creation Chant.* Chicago: University Press, 1951.

Bellwood, Peter. *Man's Conquest of the Pacific.* London: William Collins, 1978.

Cunningham, Scott. *Hawaiian Religion and Magic.* St. Paul: Llewellyn Publications, 1994.

Colum, Padraig. *Legends of Hawaii.* Harmouth, Conn.: Yale University Press, 1937.

Ellis, William. *Polynesian Researches.* Montpelier, Vt.: Charles E. Tuttle Company, 1833.

Emerson, Nathaniel B. *Unwritten Literature of Hawaii.* Washington, D.C.: Smithsonian Institute, 1909.

Hezel, Francis X. *The First Taint of Civilization.* Honolulu: University of Hawaii Press, 1983.

Imel, Martha Ann, and Dorothy Myers Imel. *Goddesses in World Mythology.* Oxford: Oxford University Press, 1993.

MacLaine, Shirley. *The Camino: A Journey of the Spirit.* New York: Pocket Books, 2000.

Malo, David. *Hawaiian Antiquities.* Honolulu: Bishop Museum, 1951.

Melville, Leinani. *Children of the Rainbow: The Religion, Legends and Gods of Pre-Christian Hawaii.* Wheaton, Ill.: Quest Books, Theosophical Publishing House, 1969.

Morwood, Mike, Thomas Sutikna, and Richard Roberts. "The People Time Forgot." *National Geographic* 207, no. 4 (2005): 6.

Olsen, Brad. *Sacred Places, North America.* San Francisco: Consortium of Collective Consciousness, 2003.

Puku'i, Mary Kawena. *The Water of Kane and Other Legends of the Hawaiian Islands.* Honolulu: Kamehameha Schools Press, 1994.

———. *New Pocket Hawaiian Dictionary.* Honolulu: University of Hawaii Press, 1992.

Rogers, Jim. *World Travels*. Wash.: Backpack Press, 1990.

Spence, Lewis. *The Problem of Lemuria*. London: Rider and Company, 1933.

Suggs, Robert. *The Hidden Worlds of Polynesia*. New York: Harcourt Brace, 1962.

———. *The Island Civilizations of Polynesia*. New York: Mentor Books, 1960.

The Bernice P. Bishop Museum Newsletter. Vol. 203. Honolulu: Bernice P. Bishop Museum, 1950.

Verrengia, Joseph B. *A Tiny Human, A Giant Find*. St. Paul: Pioneer Press, 28 October 2004.

Williams, Mark R. *In Search of Lemuria*. San Mateo, Calif.: Golden Era Books, 2001.

CHAPTER 8: LEMURIANS IN AMERICA

Alexander, William. *North American Mythology*. New York: Harcourt Brace, 1935.

Allen, Charles, "New Science in the Mountains." *Chicago Herald* 16 January 1999, p. 17.

Aveni, Michael. "Mystery Lines of the Desert." *Archaeology* 26, no. 64 (1998): 32.

Bierhorst, John. *The Mythology of South America*. New York: William Morrow and Company, Inc., 1982.

Childress, David Hatcher. *Lost Cities of North and Central America*. Kempton, Ill.: Adventures Unlimited Press, 1992.

———. *Lost Cities and Ancient Mysteries of South America*. Kempton, Ill.: Adventures Unlimited Press, 1986.

Churchward, James. *Cosmic Forces of Mu*. Vol. 1. 1933. Reprint, Santa Fe, N.Mex.: BE Books, 1998.

———. *The Lost Continent of Mu*. 1924. Reprint, Santa Fe, N.Mex.: BE Books, 1987.

Clark, Ella E. *Indian Legends of the Pacific Northwest*. Berkeley: University of California Press, 1953.

Davis, E. M., and S. Winslow. "Giant Ground Figures of the Prehistoric Deserts." *Proceedings of the American Philosophical Society* 109, no. 1 (1965).

Donato, William A. "What ever happened to the 'Western Whites'?" *Ancient American* 3, no. 17 (1997).

Dunbavin, Paul. *Atlantis of the West*. New York: Carrol and Graf, 2003.

Ellis, William. *Polynesian Researches*. Montpelier, Vt.: Charles E. Tuttle Company, 1833.

Flagmark, Knut R. *British Columbia Prehistory*. Ottawa: National Museums of Canada Press, 1986.

Glavin, Terry. *A Death Feast in Dimlahamid*. Vancouver: New Star Books, 1990.

Joseph, Frank. *Sacred Sites of the West*. Blaine, Wash.: Hancock House, 1997.

Keithahan, Edward S. *Monuments in Cedar*. Seattle: Superior Publishing Company, 1963.

Kirbus, Frederico. *Enigmas, Miserios y Secretos de America*. Rio de Janiero: Rio de Janiero Press, 1978.

Lee, Laura. "Super Technology of Ancient Egypt and Peru." *Ancient American* 3, no. 17 (1997).

McCall, Lynne, and Rosalind Pery. *California's Chumash Indians.* Santa Anna, Calif.: EZ Nature Books, 1990.

Marriott, Alice, and Carol K. Rachlin. eds. *American Indian Mythology.* New York: New American Library, 1968.

McNeary, Robert. "The Mystery of the Andes." *Reader's Digest* 68, no. 43 (1988): 52.

Moseley, Michael E. *The Incas and Their Ancestors.* London: Thames and Hudson, 1994.

Noorbergen, Rene. *Secrets of Lost Races.* New York: Barnes and Noble, 1977.

Posnansky, Arthur. *Tiahuanaco.* New York: Augustin Press, 1945.

Rainey, Froelich G. "Mystery of the Arctic." *Natural History* 46, no. 12 (1941): 148–155.

Reiche, Maria. *Mystery of the Desert.* Nazca, Peru: Self-published, 1968.

Scofield, Bruce. "Ecuador, America's Prehistoric Port of Call." *Ancient American* 3, no. 23 (1998).

Stoddy, Frederick. *Pioneers of Progress: Selected Biographies of Outstanding Nobel Prize Winners.* New York: Feathermount Press, Inc., 1925.

Spence, Lewis. *Mexico and Peru: Myths and Legends.* 1920. Reprint, London: Senate, 1994.

Steiner, Greg. "Mysterious Tiahuanaco." *World Explorer* 1, no. 6 (1995): 19.

Tompkins, Peter. *Secrets of the Mexican Pyramids.* New York: Harper and Row, 1970.

Waters, Frank. *Book of the Hopi.* New York: Viking Press, 1963.

Wherry, Joseph H. *Indian Masks and Myths of the West.* New York: Funk and Wagnells, 1969.

Wilkins, Harold T. *Mysteries of Ancient South America.* Kempton, Ill.: Adventures Unlimited Press, 2000.

Wyss, M. "Local Changes in Sea-Level Before Earthquakes in South America." *Seismological Society of America* 66 (1976): 903–914.

Zettl, Helmut. "Tiahuanaco and the Deluge." www.crystalinks.com/preinca2.html-27k.

CHAPTER 9: ASIA'S DEBT TO LEMURIA

Allen, Charles. *A Mountain in Tibet.* London: Futura Publications, 1983.

Bancroft, H. H. *New World Mythology.* Montpelier, Vt.: Charles E. Tuttle Company, 1889.

Blau, Tatjana, and Mirabai Blau. *Buddhist Symbols.* New York: Sterling Publishers, 2003.

Caroli, Kenneth. Personal correspondence, November, 2004.

Chamberlain, Basil Hall. "A Translation of the Kojiki" or "Records of Ancient Matters." *Translations of the Asiatic Society of Japan* 10, (1882).

Childress, David Hatcher. *Lost Cities of China, Central Asia and India.* Kempton, Ill.: Adventures Unlimited Press, 1985.

Christie, Anthony. *Chinese Mythology.* New York: Peter Bedrick Books, 1977.

Churchward, James. *The Sacred Symbols of Mu.* 1926. Reprint, Santa Fe, N.Mex.: BE Books, 1988.

Daniel, Glyn, Consultant Editor. *The Illustrated Encyclopedia of Archaeology.* New York: Thomas Y. Crowell Company, 1977.

Davis, Frederick H. *Myths and Legends of Japan.* Singapore: Graham Brash Publishing Company, 1989.

Dorson, Richard M. *Folk Legends of Japan.* Montpelier, Vt.: Charles E. Tuttle, 1962.

Jett, Stephen C., "The Jomon of Neolithic Japan: Early Ocean-Goers." *Pre-Columbiana* 1, no. 2 and 3 (1999).

Joe, Eugene B. *Navajo Sandpainting Art.* Phoenix: Treasurechest Publications, Inc., 1978.

Joseph, Frank. "Ancient Wonders of Japan." *Ancient American* 3, no. 17 (1997).

MacKenzie, Donald A. *Myths of China and Japan.* 1933. Reprint, New York: Gramercy Books, 1994.

Meggers, Betty J. "Jomon-Valdivia Similarities: Convergence or Contact." *Across Before Columbus?* Edgecomb, Maine: NEARA Publications, 1998.

Norbu, Namkhai. *Drung, Deu and Boen, Narrations, Symbolic Languages and the Boen Tradition in Ancient Tibet.* Translated by Adriano Clemente and Andrew Lukianowicz. New York: Library of Tibetan Works and Archives, 1988.

Schiller, Ronald. *Distant Secrets, Unravelling the Mysteries of Our Ancient Past.* New York: Carol Publishing Group, 1993.

Spence, Lewis. *The Problem of Lemuria.* London: Rider and Company, 1933.

Sykes, Edgerton. *Lemuria Reconsidered.* London: Markham House Press, Ltd., 1968.

Thompson, Dr. Gunnar. *American Discovery, the Real Story.* Seattle, Wash.: Argonauts Misty Isles Press, 1994.

Villasenor, David. *Tapestries in Sand: The Spirit of Indian Sand Painting.* San Francisco: Naturegraph Publishers, 1966.

Wyman, Leland C. *Navajo Sandpainting: Symbolism, Artistry, and Psychology.* Phoenix: Taylor Museum, 1960.

Yoshida, Nobuhiro. Japan's Megalithic Links to Ancient America and Europe." *Ancient American* 3, no. 23, (1998).

Yoshida, Professor Nobuhiro. "Stone Tablets of Mu." *Ancient American* 3, no. 21 (1997).

Zimmerer, Neil. *The Chronology of Genesis.* Kempton, Ill.: Adventures Unlimited Press, 2003.

CHAPTER 10: WHAT'S IN A NAME?

Ashby, Gene. *Micronesian Customs and Beliefs.* Eugene, Ore.: Rainy Day Press, 1985.

Codrington, R. H. *The Melanesians: Studies in Their Anthropology and Folklore.* Oxford: Clarendon Press, 1891.

Caroli, Kenneth. Personal correspondence. November, 1996.

Colebrook, H. T. *The Hindu Epics.* Chicago: William Regnery, 1900.

Cunningham, Scott. *Hawaiian Religion and Magic.* St. Paul, Minn.: Llewellyn Publications, 1994.

Edmonds, I. G. *Micronesia.* New York: Bobbs-Merrill Co., 1974.

Ellis, William. *Polynesian Researches.* Montpelier, Vt.: Charles E. Tuttle Company, 1833.

Fornander, Abraham. *An Account of the Polynesian Race.* Montpelier, Vt.: Charles E. Tuttle Company, 1885.

Heyerdahl, Dr. Thor. *The Maldive Mystery.* Annapolis, Md.: Adler-Adler, 1986.

Jacolliot, Louis. *Histoire de vierges: Les Peuples et les continents disparus.* Paris: Lacroix, 1879.

Joseph, Frank. *The Atlantis Encyclopedia.* Franklin Lakes, N.J.: Career Books, 2005.

Knappert, Jan. *Indian Mythology, An Encyclopedia of Myth and Legend.* London: Diamond Books, 1995.

MacKenzie, Donald A. *South Seas Myths and Legends.* London: Senate Books, 1930.

Melville, Leinani. *Children of the Rainbow: The Religion, Legends and Gods of Pre-Christian Hawaii.* Wheaton, Ill.: Quest Books, Theosophical Publishing House, 1969.

Mercatante, Anthony S. *Who's Who in Egyptian Mythology.* New York: Clarkson N. Potter, Inc., 1978.

Poignant, Rosslyn. *Oceanic Mythology.* London: Paul Hamlyn, 1967.

Smith, William Ramsay. *Aborigine: Myth and Legends.* London: George G. Harrap, 1930.

CHAPTER 11: THE SLEEPING PROPHET OF LEMURIA

Cayce, Edgar. *Atlantis, The Edgar Cayce Readings.* Vol. 22. Virginia Beach, Va.: A.R.E. Press, 1987.

———. *Mysteries of Atlantis Revisited.* Virginia Beach, Va.: A.R.E. Press, 1982.

Churchward, James. *The Lost Continent of Mu.* Santa Fe, N.Mex.: BE Books, 1987.

Evermann, Rudy. *The Gobi Desert.* London: Haversmill Press, Inc., 1955.

Joseph, Frank. *Edgar Cayce's Atlantis and Lemuria.* Virginia Beach, Va.: A.R.E. Press, 2001.

Marriott, Alice, and Carol K. Rachlin. eds. *American Indian Mythology.* New York: New American Library, 1968.

Oppenheimer, Stephen. *Eden in the East, The Drowned Continent of Southeast Asia.* London: Weidenfeld and Nicolson, 1999.

Plog, Stephen. *Ancient People of the American Southwest.* London: Thames and Hudson, 1997.

Smith, William Ramsay. *Aborigine: Myth and Legends.* London: George G. Harrap, 1930.

Spence, Lewis. *The Problem of Lemuria.* London: Rider and Company, 1933.

Steiger, Brad. *Atlantis Rising.* New York: Dell Publishing Co., Inc., 1973.

CHAPTER 12: THE DESTRUCTION OF LEMURIA

Alexander, William. *North American Mythology.* New York: Harcourt Brace, 1935.

Andersen, Johannes C. *Myths and Legends of the Polynesians.* London: Harrap, 1928.

Barberi, Franco, ed. *Volcanoes.* Kitchener, Ontario: Firefly Books, Ltd., 2003.

Caroli, Kenneth. Personal correspondence. 1989–2004.

———. "Catastrophe: An Investigation into the Origins of the Modern World." *Ancient American 5,* no 32, (2000).

Christy-Vitale, Joseph. *Watermark.* New York: Paraview Pocket Books, 2004.

Dobbs, Michael. "Terrible Ravages of the Indonesian Tsunami." *Washington Post,* 26 December 2004, p. 2.

Dunbavin, Paul. *Atlantis of the West.* New York: Carrol and Graf, 2003.

Eagle, Jonathan, and William Hutton. *Earth's Catastrophic Past and Future.* Virginia Beach, Va.: A.R.E. Press, 2004.

Ganguly, Dilip. "Devastating Waves Kill 11,000 after Quake." *Pioneer Press,* 27 December 2004.

Huggett, Richard. *Cataclysms and Earth History.* Oxford: Clarendon Press, 1989.

Imel, Martha Ann, and Dorothy Myers Imel. *Goddesses in World Mythology.* Oxford: Oxford University Press, 1993.

Jett, Stephen C. "The Jomon of Neolithic Japan: Early Ocean-Goers." *Pre-Columbiana 1,* no. 2 and 3 (1999).

Joseph, Frank. *Survivors of Atlantis.* Rochester, Vt.: Bear and Company, 2004.

Knappert, Jan. *Pacific Mythology, An Encyclopedia of Myth and Legend.* London: Diamond Books, 1995.

Le Plongeon, Dr. Augustus. *Sacred Mysteries Among the Mayas and Quiches 11,500 Years Ago.* New York: Macoy, 1886.

Ogilvie-Herald, Chris. "Older Than Expected." *Quest 1,* no. 6 (1997).

Oppenheimer, Stephen. *Eden in the East: The Drowned Continent of Southeast Asia.* London: Weidenfeld and Nicolson, 1999.

Palmer, Trevor, and Mark E. Bailey, eds. *Natural Catastrophes During Bronze Age Civilizations: Archaeological, Geological, Astronomical and Cultural Perspectives.* Oxford: Archaeo Press, 1998.

Poignant, Rosslyn. *Oceanic Mythology.* London: Paul Hamlyn, 1967.

Sandwell, David. *Floor Stratigraphy of the Mid-Pacific Ocean Basin.* Calif.: Scripps Oceanographic Institute, 1996.

Simkin, T., and L. Siebert. *Volcanoes of the World.* Phoenix: Geoscience Press, 1994.

Spence, Lewis. *The Problem of Lemuria.* London: Rider and Company, 1933.

CHAPTER 13: THE DISCOVERY OF LEMURIA

Abe, Hiroshi. "Sunken Structure at Yonaguni." *Tokyo: Mu Super Mystery Magazine 5,* no. 3 (1996).

Donato, William A. "Whatever Happened to the 'Western Whites'?" *Ancient American 3,* no. 17 (1997).

Jesmain, Marilyn. "Ancient Alaska and the Great Flood." *Ancient American* 6, no. 39 (2001).

Joseph, Frank. "Japan's Undersea Ruins." *Atlantis Rising* 13 (1997).

———. "Underwater City Discovered in Japanese Waters." *Ancient American* 3, no. 17 (1997).

———. "Topper Is Fifty Thousand Years Old." *Ancient American* 9, no. 60 (2004).

Kimura, Masaaki. *Diving Survey Report for Submarine Ruins off Yonaguni, Japan.* Okinawa: University of the Ryukyus Press, 2002.

Little, Dr. Gregory. *The Search for Atlantis.* Virginia Beach, Va.: A.R.E. Press, 2004.

Menzies, Robert J., and Edward Chin. "Cruise Report #2, Research Vessel Anton Bruun." *Cruise 11, OCLC333371904.* Galveston: Marine Laboratory, Texas A&M, 1966.

Pettyjohn, F. S. "The Caucasian 'Mummy People' of Alaska." *Ancient American* 6, no. 39 (2001).

Rainey, Froelich G. "Mystery of the Arctic." *Natural History* 46, no. 12 (1941): 148–155.

Sandwell, David T., and Walter H. F. Smith. *Exploring the Ocean Basins with Satellite Altimeter Data.* San Jose, Calif.: Scripps Institution of Oceanography, 1998.

Schoch, Robert M. "The Yonaguni Monument: An Enigmatic Underwater Feature off Japan." *Pre-Columbiana* 1, no. 2 and 3 (1999).

———. *Voices of the Rocks.* New York: Harmony Books, 1999.

Shinbutsu, Celine. *The Basic Facts of Submarine Ruins off Yonaguni, Japan.* Okinawa: University of the Ryukyus Press, 2002.

Spence, Lewis. *The Problem of Lemuria.* London: Rider and Company, 1933.

Vanderveer, Thomas, in a telephone interview with the author, 9 November 2004.

Yoshida, Professor Nobuhiro. "Huge 'Pillars', Staircase Found in Sea off Japan." Ancient American 4, no. 26 (1999).

Walton, Marsha, and Michael Coren. "The New Ancient Americans." *Scientist* 22, no. 63 (2004).

Wilkins, Harold T. *Mysteries of Ancient South America.* Kempton, Ill.: Adventures Unlimited Press, 1986.

Wood, W. W. "Tombs in the Islands of Rotuma." *Royal Anthropological Institute Journal.*

AFTERWORD: THE REAL MEANING OF LEMURIA

Spence, Lewis. *The Problem of Lemuria.* London: Rider and Company, 1933.

BOOKS OF RELATED INTEREST

Ancient High Tech
The Astonishing Scientific Achievements of Early Civilizations
by Frank Joseph

Military Encounters with Extraterrestrials
The Real War of the Worlds
by Frank Joseph

Power Places and the Master Builders of Antiquity
Unexplained Mysteries of the Past
by Frank Joseph

Atlantis and the Coming Ice Age
The Lost Civilization—A Mirror of Our World
by Frank Joseph

Before Atlantis
20 Million Years of Human and Pre-Human Cultures
by Frank Joseph

Advanced Civilizations of Prehistoric America
The Lost Kingdoms of the Adena, Hopewell, Mississippians, and Anasazi
by Frank Joseph

The Ancient Giants Who Ruled America
The Missing Skeletons and the Great Smithsonian Cover-Up
by Richard J. Dewhurst

The Suppressed History of America
The Murder of Meriwether Lewis and the Mysterious
Discoveries of the Lewis and Clark Expedition
by Paul Schrag and Xaviant Haze
Foreword by Michael Tsarion

Inner Traditions • Bear & Company
P.O. Box 388
Rochester, VT 05767
1-800-246-8648
www.InnerTraditions.com

Or contact your local bookseller